Microsoft® Official Academic Course

Microsoft Word 2010, Exam 77-881

WILEY

EDITOR	Bryan Gambrel
DIRECTOR OF SALES	Mitchell Beaton
EXECUTIVE MARKETING MANAGER	Chris Ruel
ASSISTANT MARKETING MANAGER	Debbie Martin
MICROSOFT STRATEGIC RELATIONSHIPS MANAGER	Merrick Van Dongen of Microsoft Learning
EDITORIAL PROGRAM ASSISTANT	Jennifer Lartz
CONTENT MANAGERS	Micheline Frederick, Kevin Holm
SENIOR PRODUCTION EDITOR	Kerry Weinstein
CREATIVE DIRECTOR	Harry Nolan
COVER DESIGNER	Jim O'Shea
INTERIOR DESIGNER	Amy Rosen
PHOTO EDITORS	Sheena Goldstein, Jennifer MacMillan
EXECUTIVE MEDIA EDITOR	Tom Kulesa
MEDIA EDITOR	Wendy Ashenberg

This book was set in Garamond by Aptara, Inc. and printed and bound by Courier Kendallville. The covers were printed by Lehigh Phoenix.

Founded in 1807, John Wiley & Sons, Inc. has been a valued source of knowledge and understanding for more than 200 years, helping people around the world meet their needs and fulfill their aspirations. Our company is built on a foundation of principles that include responsibility to the communities we serve and where we live and work. In 2008, we launched a Corporate Citizenship Initiative, a global effort to address the environmental, social, economic, and ethical challenges we face in our business. Among the issues we are addressing are carbon impact, paper specifications and procurement, ethical conduct within our business and among our vendors, and community and charitable support. For more information, please visit our website: www.wiley.com/go/citizenship.

ISBN 978-0-470-90766-5

Printed in the United States of America

10 9 8 7 6 5 4 3 2 1

Foreword From The Publisher

Wiley's publishing vision for the Microsoft Official Academic Course series is to provide students and instructors with the skills and knowledge they need to use Microsoft technology effectively in all aspects of their personal and professional lives. Quality instruction is required to help both educators and students get the most from Microsoft's software tools and to become more productive. Thus our mission is to make our instructional programs trusted educational companions for life.

To accomplish this mission, Wiley and Microsoft have partnered to develop the highest quality educational programs for information workers, IT professionals, and developers. Materials created by this partnership carry the brand name "Microsoft Official Academic Course," assuring instructors and students alike that the content of these textbooks is fully endorsed by Microsoft, and that they provide the highest quality information and instruction on Microsoft products. The Microsoft Official Academic Course textbooks are "Official" in still one more way—they are the officially sanctioned courseware for Microsoft IT Academy members.

The Microsoft Official Academic Course series focuses on *workforce development*. These programs are aimed at those students seeking to enter the workforce, change jobs, or embark on new careers as information workers, IT professionals, and developers. Microsoft Official Academic Course programs address their needs by emphasizing authentic workplace scenarios with an abundance of projects, exercises, cases, and assessments.

The Microsoft Official Academic Courses are mapped to Microsoft's extensive research and job-task analysis, the same research and analysis used to create the Microsoft Office Specialist (MOS) exams. The textbooks focus on real skills for real jobs. As students work through the projects and exercises in the textbooks, they enhance their level of knowledge and their ability to apply the latest Microsoft technology to everyday tasks. These students also gain resume-building credentials that can assist them in finding a job, in keeping their current job, or in furthering their education.

The concept of lifelong learning is today an utmost necessity. Job roles, and even whole job categories, are changing so quickly that none of us can stay competitive and productive without continuously updating our skills and capabilities. The Microsoft Official Academic Course offerings, and their focus on Microsoft certification exam preparation, provide a means for people to acquire and effectively update their skills and knowledge. Wiley supports students in this endeavor through the development and distribution of these courses as Microsoft's official academic publisher.

Today educational publishing requires attention to providing quality print and robust electronic content. By integrating Microsoft Official Academic Course products, WileyPLUS, and Microsoft certifications, we are better able to deliver efficient learning solutions for students and teachers alike.

Joseph Heider
General Manager and Senior Vice President

Preface

Welcome to the Microsoft Official Academic Course (MOAC) program for Microsoft Office 2010. MOAC is the collaboration between Microsoft Learning and John Wiley & Sons, Inc. publishing company. Microsoft and Wiley teamed up to produce a series of textbooks that deliver compelling and innovative teaching solutions to instructors and superior learning experiences for students. Infused and informed by in-depth knowledge from the creators of Microsoft Office and Windows, and crafted by a publisher known worldwide for the pedagogical quality of its products, these textbooks maximize skills transfer in minimum time. Students are challenged to reach their potential by using their new technical skills as highly productive members of the workforce.

Because this knowledge base comes directly from Microsoft, architect of the Office 2010 offering and creator of the Microsoft Office Specialist (MOS) exams (www.microsoft.com/learning/mcp/msbc), you are sure to receive the topical coverage that is most relevant to your personal and professional success. Microsoft's direct participation not only assures you that MOAC textbook content is accurate and current; it also means that students will receive the best instruction possible to enable their success on certification exams and in the workplace.

THE MICROSOFT OFFICIAL ACADEMIC COURSE PROGRAM

The Microsoft Official Academic Course series is a complete program for instructors and institutions to prepare and deliver great courses on Microsoft software technologies. With MOAC, we recognize that, because of the rapid pace of change in the technology and curriculum developed by Microsoft, there is an ongoing set of needs beyond classroom instruction tools for an instructor to be ready to teach the course. The MOAC program endeavors to provide solutions for all these needs in a systematic manner in order to ensure a successful and rewarding course experience for both instructor and student—technical and curriculum training for instructor readiness with new software releases; the software itself for student use at home for building hands-on skills, assessment, and validation of skill development; and a great set of tools for delivering instruction in the classroom and lab. All are important to the smooth delivery of an interesting course on Microsoft software, and all are provided with the MOAC program. We think about the model below as a gauge for ensuring that we completely support you in your goal of teaching a great course. As you evaluate your instructional materials options, you may wish to use the model for comparison purposes with available products.

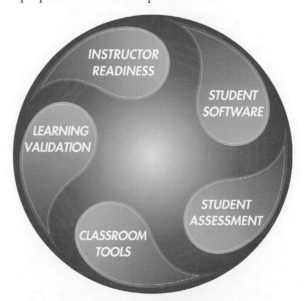

www.wiley.com/college/microsoft
or call the MOAC Toll-Free Number: 1+(888) 764-7001 (U.S. & Canada only)

PEDAGOGICAL FEATURES

The MOAC textbooks for Microsoft Office 2010 are designed to cover all the learning objectives for that MOS exam, which is referred to as its exam objective. The Microsoft Office Specialist (MOS) exam objectives are highlighted throughout the textbooks. Many pedagogical features have been developed specifically for Microsoft Official Academic Course programs. Unique features of our task-based approach include a Lesson Skill Matrix that correlates skills taught in each lesson to the MOS objectives; Certification, Workplace, and Internet Ready exercises; and three levels of increasingly rigorous lesson-ending activities, Competency, Proficiency, and Mastery Assessment.

Presenting the extensive procedural information and technical concepts woven throughout the textbook raises challenges for the student and instructor alike. The Illustrated Book Tour that follows provides a guide to the rich features contributing to Microsoft Official Academic Course program's pedagogical plan. Following is a list of key features in each lesson designed to prepare students for success on the certification exams and in the workplace:

- Each lesson begins with a **Lesson Skill Matrix**. More than a standard list of learning objectives, the skill matrix correlates each software skill covered in the lesson to the specific MOS exam objective domain.

- Each lesson features a real-world **Business case** scenario that places the software skills and knowledge to be acquired in a real-world setting.

- **Software Orientations** provide an overview of the software features students will be working with in the lesson. The orientation will detail the general properties of the software or specific features, such as a ribbon or dialog box; and it includes a large, labeled screen image.

- Concise and frequent **Step-by-Step** instructions teach students new features and provide an opportunity for hands-on practice. Numbered steps give detailed instructions to help students learn software skills. The steps also show results and screen images to match what students should see on their computer screens.

- **Illustrations** provide visual feedback as students work through the exercises. The images reinforce key concepts, provide visual clues about the steps, and allow students to check their progress.

- When the text instructs a student to click a particular button, **button images** are shown in the margin or in the text.

- Important technical vocabulary is listed in the **Key Terms** section at the beginning of the lesson. When these terms are used later in the lesson, they appear in bold italic type with yellow highlighter and are defined. The Glossary contains all of the key terms and their definitions.

- Engaging point-of-use **Reader Aids**, located throughout the lessons, tell students why this topic is relevant (*The Bottom Line*), provide students with helpful hints (*Take Note*), or show alternate ways to accomplish tasks (*Another Way*), or point out things to watch out for or avoid (*Troubleshooting*). Reader aids also provide additional relevant or background information that adds value to the lesson.

- **Certification Ready** features throughout the text signal students where a specific certification objective is covered. They provide students with a chance to check their understanding of that particular MOS exam objective and, if necessary, review the section of the lesson where it is covered. MOAC provides complete preparation for MOS certification.

- The **New Feature** icon appears near any software feature that is new to Office 2010.

- Each lesson ends with a **Skill Summary** recapping the MOS exam skills covered in the lesson.
- The **Knowledge Assessment** section provides a total of 20 questions from a mix of True/False, Fill in the Blank, Matching, or Multiple Choice, testing students on concepts learned in the lesson.
- **Competency, Proficiency, and Mastery Assessment** sections provide three progressively more challenging lesson-ending activities.
- **Internet Ready** projects combine the knowledge that students acquire in a lesson with web-based task research.
- Integrated **Circling Back** projects provide students with an opportunity to renew and practice skills learned in previous lessons.
- **Workplace Ready** features preview how the Microsoft Office 2010 system applications are used in real-world situations.
- The student companion website contains the **online files** needed for each lesson. These data files are indicated by the @ icon in the margin of the textbook.

The Bottom Line

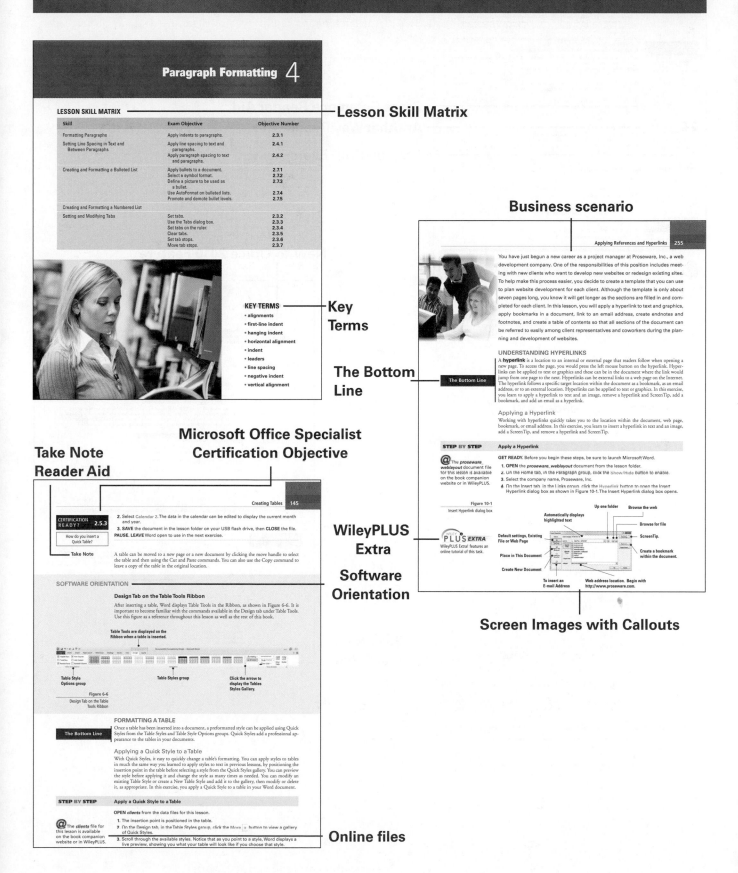

Paragraph Formatting 4

LESSON SKILL MATRIX ——————— Lesson Skill Matrix

Skill	Exam Objective	Objective Number
Formatting Paragraphs	Apply indents to paragraphs.	2.3.1
Setting Line Spacing in Text and Between Paragraphs	Apply line spacing to text and paragraphs.	2.4.1
	Apply paragraph spacing to text and paragraphs.	2.4.2
Creating and Formatting a Bulleted List	Apply bullets to a document.	2.7.1
	Select a symbol format.	2.7.2
	Define a picture to be used as a bullet.	2.7.3
	Use AutoFormat on bulleted lists.	2.7.4
	Promote and demote bullet levels.	2.7.5
Creating and Formatting a Numbered List		
Setting and Modifying Tabs	Set tabs.	2.3.2
	Use the Tabs dialog box.	2.3.3
	Set tabs on the ruler.	2.3.4
	Clear tabs.	2.3.5
	Set tab stops.	2.3.6
	Move tab stops.	2.3.7

KEY TERMS ——— Key Terms
- alignments
- first-line indent
- hanging indent
- horizontal alignment
- indent
- leaders
- line spacing
- negative indent
- vertical alignment

Business scenario

Applying References and Hyperlinks 255

You have just begun a new career as a project manager at Proseware, Inc., a web development company. One of the responsibilities of this position includes meeting with new clients who want to develop new websites or redesign existing sites. To help make this process easier, you decide to create a template that you can use to plan website development for each client. Although the template is only about seven pages long, you know it will get longer as the sections are filled in and completed for each client. In this lesson, you will apply a hyperlink to text and graphics, apply bookmarks in a document, link to an email address, create endnotes and footnotes, and create a table of contents so that all sections of the document can be referred to easily among client representatives and coworkers during the planning and development of websites.

UNDERSTANDING HYPERLINKS

The Bottom Line —— The Bottom Line

A **hyperlink** is a location to an internal or external page that readers follow when opening a new page. To access the page, you would press the left mouse button on the hyperlink. Hyperlinks can be applied to text or graphics and these can be in the document where the link would jump from one page to the next. Hyperlinks can be external links to a web page on the Internet. The hyperlink follows a specific target location within the document as a bookmark, as an email address, or to an external location. Hyperlinks can be applied to text or graphics. In this exercise, you learn to apply a hyperlink to text and an image, remove a hyperlink and ScreenTip, add a bookmark, and add an email as a hyperlink.

Applying a Hyperlink

Working with hyperlinks quickly takes you to the location within the document, web page, bookmark, or email address. In this exercise, you learn to insert a hyperlink in text and an image, add a ScreenTip, and remove a hyperlink and ScreenTip.

Microsoft Office Specialist Certification Objective

Take Note Reader Aid

Creating Tables 145

CERTIFICATION READY? 2.5.3
How do you insert a Quick Table?

2. Select **Calendar 2**. The data in the calendar can be edited to display the current month and year.
3. **SAVE** the document in the lesson folder on your USB flash drive, then **CLOSE** the file.
PAUSE. **LEAVE** Word open to use in the next exercise.

Take Note

A table can be moved to a new page or a new document by clicking the move handle to select the table and then using the Cut and Paste commands. You can also use the Copy command to leave a copy of the table in the original location.

SOFTWARE ORIENTATION ——————————

Design Tab on the Table Tools Ribbon

After inserting a table, Word displays Table Tools in the Ribbon, as shown in Figure 6-6. It is important to become familiar with the commands available in the Design tab under Table Tools. Use this figure as a reference throughout this lesson as well as the rest of this book.

Table Tools are displayed on the Ribbon when a table is inserted.

Table Style Options group

Table Styles group

Click the arrow to display the Tables Styles Gallery.

Figure 6-6
Design Tab on the Table Tools Ribbon

FORMATTING A TABLE

The Bottom Line

Once a table has been inserted into a document, a preformatted style can be applied using Quick Styles from the Table Styles and Table Style Options groups. Quick Styles add a professional appearance to the tables in your documents.

Applying a Quick Style to a Table

With Quick Styles, it easy to quickly change a table's formatting. You can apply styles to tables in much the same way you learned to apply styles to text in previous lessons, by positioning the insertion point in the table before selecting a style from the Quick Styles gallery. You can preview the style before applying it and change the style as many times as needed. You can modify an existing Table Style or create a New Table Style and add it to the gallery, then modify or delete it, as appropriate. In this exercise, you apply a Quick Style to a table in your Word document.

STEP BY STEP Apply a Quick Style to a Table

OPEN *clients* from the data files for this lesson.

The *clients* file for this lesson is available on the book companion website or in WileyPLUS.

1. The insertion point is positioned in the table.
2. On the Design tab, in the Table Styles group, click the More ▾ button to view a gallery of Quick Styles.
3. Scroll through the available styles. Notice that as you point to a style, Word displays a live preview, showing you what your table will look like if you choose that style.

—— Online files

STEP BY STEP Apply a Hyperlink

The *proseware_weblayout* document file for this lesson is available on the book companion website or in WileyPLUS.

GET READY. Before you begin these steps, be sure to launch Microsoft Word.

1. **OPEN** the *proseware_weblayout* document from the lesson folder.
2. On the Home tab, in the Paragraph group, click the Show/Hide button to enable.
3. Select the company name, Proseware, Inc.
4. On the Insert tab, in the Links group, click the Hyperlink button to open the Insert Hyperlink dialog box as shown in Figure 10-1. The Insert Hyperlink dialog box opens.

Figure 10-1
Insert Hyperlink dialog box

PLUS EXTRA
WileyPLUS Extra! features an online tutorial of this task.

— WileyPLUS Extra

— Software Orientation

Automatically displays highlighted text
Up one folder
Browse the web
Browse for file
Default settings, Existing File or Web Page
ScreenTip.
Place in This Document
Create a bookmark within the document.
Create New Document
To insert an E-mail Address
Web address location. Begin with http://www.proseware.com.

Screen Images with Callouts

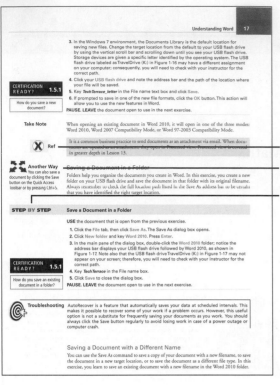

Cross Reference Reader Aid

Another Way Reader Aid

Step-by-Step Exercises

New to Office 2010 Feature

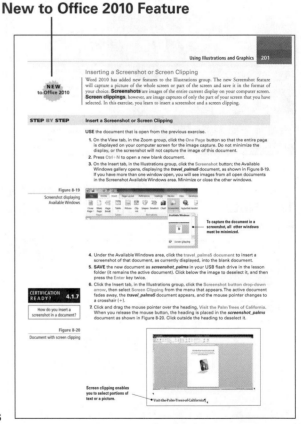

Troubleshooting Reader Aid

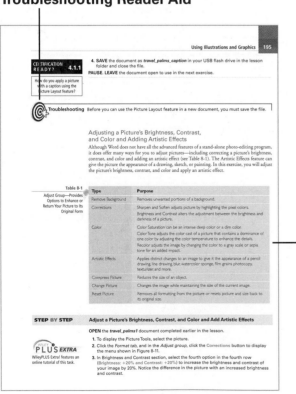

Easy-to-read Tables

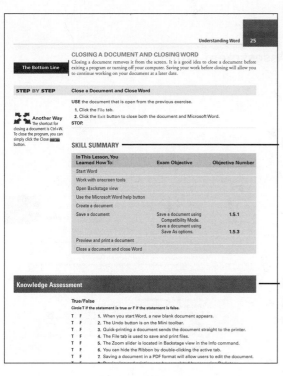

CLOSING A DOCUMENT AND CLOSING WORD

The Bottom Line

Closing a document removes it from the screen. It is a good idea to close a document before exiting a program or turning off your computer. Saving your work before closing will allow you to continue working on your document at a later date.

STEP BY STEP | Close a Document and Close Word

USE the document that is open from the previous exercise.

1. Click the File tab.
2. Click the Exit button to close both the document and Microsoft Word.

STOP.

Another Way
The shortcut for closing a document is Ctrl+W. To close the program, you can simply click the Close button.

SKILL SUMMARY ——————————————— **Skill Summary**

In This Lesson, You Learned How To:	Exam Objective	Objective Number
Start Word		
Work with onscreen tools		
Open Backstage view		
Use the Microsoft Word help button		
Create a document		
Save a document	Save a document using Compatibility Mode.	1.5.1
	Save a document using Save As options.	1.5.3
Preview and print a document		
Close a document and close Word		

Knowledge Assessment ———————— **Knowledge Assessment Questions**

True/False

Circle T if the statement is true or F if the statement is false.

T F 1. When you start Word, a new blank document appears.
T F 2. The Undo button is on the Mini toolbar.
T F 3. Quick-printing a document sends the document straight to the printer.
T F 4. The File tab is used to save and print files.
T F 5. The Zoom slider is located in Backstage view in the Info command.
T F 6. You can hide the Ribbon by double-clicking the active tab.
T F 7. Saving a document in a PDF format will allow users to edit the document.

Proficiency Assessment Projects

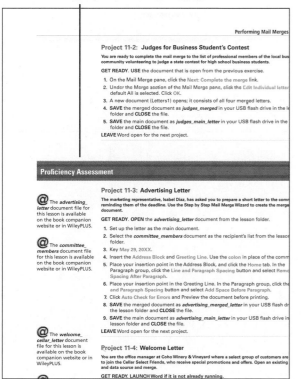

Performing Mail Merges

Project 11-2: Judges for Business Student's Contest

You are ready to complete the mail merge to the list of professional members of the local business community volunteering to judge a state contest for high school business students.

GET READY. USE the document that is open from the previous exercise.

1. On the Mail Merge pane, click the Next: Complete the merge link.
2. Under the Merge section of the Mail Merge pane, click the Edit Individual letter; default All is selected. Click OK.
3. A new document (Letters1) opens; it consists of all four merged letters.
4. SAVE the merged document as *judges_merged* in your USB flash drive in the le folder and CLOSE the file.
5. SAVE the main document as *judges_main_letter* in your USB flash drive in the folder and CLOSE the file.

LEAVE Word open for the next project.

Proficiency Assessment

@ The *advertising_letter* document file for this lesson is available on the book companion website or in WileyPLUS.

@ The *committee_members* document file for this lesson is available on the book companion website or in WileyPLUS.

Project 11-3: Advertising Letter

The marketing representative, Isabel Diaz, has asked you to prepare a short letter to the comm reminding them of the deadline. Use the Step by Step Mail Merge Wizard to create the merge document.

GET READY. OPEN the *advertising_letter* document from the lesson folder.

1. Set up the letter as the main document.
2. Select the *committee_members* document as the recipient's list from the lesso folder.
3. Key May 29, 20XX.
4. Insert the Address Block and Greeting Line. Use the colon in place of the comm
5. Place your insertion point in the Address Block, and click the Home tab. In the Paragraph group, click the Line and Paragraph Spacing button and select Remo Spacing After Paragraph.
6. Place your insertion point in the Greeting Line. In the Paragraph group, click the and Paragraph Spacing button and select Add Space Before Paragraph.
7. Click Auto Check for Errors and Preview the document before printing.
8. SAVE the merged document as *advertising_merged_letter* in your USB flash dr the lesson folder and CLOSE the file.
9. SAVE the main document as *advertising_main_letter* in your USB flash drive in lesson folder and CLOSE the file.

LEAVE Word open for the next project.

@ The *welcome_cellar_letter* document file for this lesson is available on the book companion website or in WileyPLUS.

Project 11-4: Welcome Letter

You are the office manager at Coho Winery & Vineyard where a select group of customers are to join the Cellar Select Friends, who receive special promotions and offers. Open an existing and data source and merge.

GET READY. LAUNCH Word if it is not already running.

Competency Assessment Projects

Creating Tables | 159

Competency Assessment

Project 6-1: Placements Table

Ms. Archer, the executive recruiter, asks you to start working on a placements table that will list the candidates that have been placed, the companies that hired them, and the date of hire.

GET READY. LAUNCH Word if it is not already running.

@ The *placements* file for this lesson is available on the book companion website or in WileyPLUS.

1. OPEN *placements* from the data files for this lesson.
2. Place the insertion point in the last column. Select the last column in the table. In the Layout tab, in the Table group, click the Select button and Select Columns.
3. On the Layout tab, in the Cell Size group, click the down arrow in the Width box until it reads .9".
4. Place the insertion point in the first column and select the first column in the table. In the Table group, click the Select button and Select Columns.
5. On the Layout tab, in the Cell Size group, click the down arrow in the Width box until it reads .9".
6. Select the Company column and change the width to 1.5".
7. Select the Date of Placement column and change the width to 1.3". Click in the table to deselect.
8. On the Design tab, in the Table Style Options group, click the Header Row check box and Banded Rows check box to turn on. Place your insertion point within the table.
9. On the Design tab, in the Table Styles group, select the Medium Shading 1 - Accent 1 style in the ninth column, second row in the Built-In gallery.
10. Select the Last column in the table.
11. On the Layout tab, in the Data group, click the Sort button. Under the My list has section, select Header Row. In the Sort dialog box, click OK. This will sort the column by date.
12. The table is selected. On the Layout tab, in the Table group, click the Properties button.
13. In the Table Properties dialog box, click Center alignment in the Table tab and click OK.
14. Select the header row.
15. On the Layout tab, in the Alignment group, click Align Center.
16. SAVE the document as *placements_table* in the lesson folder on your USB flash drive, then CLOSE the file.

LEAVE Word open for the next project.

Project 6-2: Quarterly Sales Data

Create a table showing the quarterly sales for Coho Vineyard.

GET READY. LAUNCH Word if it is not already running.

1. Create a new blank document.
2. On the Insert tab, in the Tables group, click the Table button. Drag to create a table that has 5 columns and 6 rows.
3. Enter the following data in the table as shown:

20XX	First Quarter	Second Quarter	Third Quarter	Fourth Quarter
Mark Hanson	19,098	25,890	39,088	28,789
Terry Adams	21,890	19,567	32,811	31,562
Max Benson	39,400	35,021	19,789	21,349
Cathan Cook	34,319	27,437	28,936	19,034

Mastery Assessment Projects

Circling Back exercises

Internet Ready

Workplace Ready

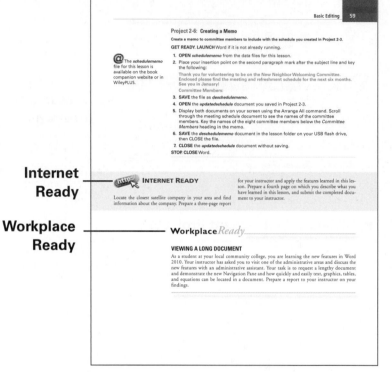

Conventions and Features Used in This Book

This book uses particular fonts, symbols, and heading conventions to highlight important information or to call your attention to special steps. For more information about the features in each lesson, refer to the Illustrated Book Tour section.

NEW to Office 2010

This icon indicates a new or greatly improved Windows feature in this version of the software.

The Bottom Line

This feature provides a brief summary of the material to be covered in the section that follows.

CLOSE

Words in all capital letters indicate instructions for opening, saving, or closing files or programs. They also point out items you should check or actions you should take.

CERTIFICATION READY?

This feature signals the point in the text where a specific certification objective is covered. It provides you with a chance to check your understanding of that particular MOS objective and, if necessary, review the section of the lesson where it is covered.

Take Note

Take Note reader aids, set in red text, provide helpful hints related to particular tasks or topics.

 Another Way

Another Way provides an alternative procedure for accomplishing a particular task.

 Ref

These notes, set in gray shaded boxes, provide pointers to information discussed elsewhere in the textbook or describe interesting features that are not directly addressed in the current topic or exercise.

ALT+Tab

A plus sign (+) between two key names means that you must press both keys at the same time. Keys that you are instructed to press in an exercise will appear in the font shown here.

Key Terms

Key terms appear in bold with highlighting.

Key My Name is

Any text you are asked to key appears in color.

Click OK

Any button on the screen you are supposed to click on or select will also appear in color.

BudgetWorksheet1

The names of data files will appear in bold, italic and red for easy identification.

Instructor Support Program

The *Microsoft Official Academic Course* programs are accompanied by a rich array of resources that incorporate the extensive textbook visuals to form a pedagogically cohesive package. These resources provide all the materials instructors need to deploy and deliver their courses. The following resources are available online for download.

- The **Instructor's Guide** contains solutions to all the textbook exercises as well as chapter summaries and lecture notes. The Instructor's Guide and Syllabi for various term lengths are available from the Instructor's Book Companion Site (www.wiley.com/college/microsoft).

- The **Solution Files** for all the projects in the book are available online from our Instructor's Book Companion Site (www.wiley.com/college/microsoft).

- The **Test Bank** contains hundreds of questions organized by lesson in multiple-choice, true/false, short answer, and essay formats and is available to download from the Instructor's Book Companion Site (www.wiley.com/college/microsoft). A complete answer key is provided.

  This title's test bank is available for use in Respondus' easy-to-use software. You can download the test bank for free using your Respondus, Respondus LE, or StudyMate Author software.

  Respondus is a powerful tool for creating and managing exams that can be printed to paper or published directly to Blackboard, WebCT, Desire2Learn, eCollege, ANGEL, and other eLearning systems.

- A complete set of **PowerPoint Presentations** is available on the Instructor's Book Companion site (www.wiley.com/college/microsoft) to enhance classroom presentations. Tailored to the text's topical coverage and Skills Matrix, these presentations are designed to convey key Microsoft Office 2010 concepts addressed in the text.

  All **images** from the text are on the Instructor's Book Companion site (www.wiley.com/college/microsoft). You can incorporate them into your PowerPoint presentations, or create your own overhead transparencies and handouts.

  By using these visuals in class discussions, you can help focus students' attention on key elements of Office 2010 and help them understand how to use it effectively in the workplace.

- The **MSDN Academic Alliance** is designed to provide the easiest and most inexpensive developer tools, products, and technologies available to faculty and students in labs, classrooms, and on student PCs. A free three-year membership is available to qualified MOAC adopters.

- **Office Grader** automated grading system allows you to easily grade student data files in Word, Excel, PowerPoint, or Access format, against solution files. Save tens or hundreds of hours each semester with automated grading. More information on Office Grader is available from the Instructor's Book Companion site (www.wiley.com/college/microsoft).

- The **Student Data Files** are available online on both the Instructor's Book Companion Site and for students on the Student Book Companion Site.

- Microsoft Official Academic Course books can be bundled with MOS exam vouchers from Certiport and MOS practice tests from GMetrix LLC or Certiport, available as a single bundle from Wiley, to create a **complete certification solution**. Instructors who use MOAC courseware in conjunction with a practice MOS exam find their students best-prepared for the MOS certification exam. Providing your students with the MOS exam voucher, is the ultimate workforce preparation.

- When it comes to improving the classroom experience, there is no better source of ideas and inspiration than your fellow colleagues. The **Wiley Faculty Network** connects teachers with technology, facilitates the exchange of best practices, and helps to enhance instructional efficiency and effectiveness. Faculty Network activities include technology training and tutorials, virtual seminars, peer-to-peer exchanges of experiences and ideas, personal consulting, and sharing of resources. For details, visit www.WhereFacultyConnect.com.

WILEYPLUS

Broad developments in education over the past decade have influenced the instructional approach taken in the Microsoft Official Academic Course programs. The way that students learn, especially about new technologies, has changed dramatically in the Internet era. Electronic learning materials and Internet-based instruction is now as much a part of classroom instruction as printed textbooks. WileyPLUS provides the technology to create an environment where students reach their full potential and experience academic success that will last a lifetime.

WileyPLUS is a powerful and highly integrated suite of teaching and learning resources designed to bridge the gap between what happens in the classroom and what happens at home and on the job. WileyPLUS provides instructors with the resources to teach their students new technologies and guide them to reach their goals of getting ahead in the job market by having the skills to become certified and advance in the workforce. For students, WileyPLUS provides the tools for study and practice that are available to them 24/7, wherever and whenever they want to study. WileyPLUS includes a complete online version of the student textbook; PowerPoint presentations; homework and practice assignments and quizzes; image galleries; test bank questions; grade book; and all the instructor resources in one easy-to-use website.

The following features are new to WileyPLUS for Office 2010:

- In addition to the hundreds of questions included in the WileyPLUS courses that are not included in the test bank or textbook, we've added over a dozen additional projects that can be assigned to students.
- Many more animated tutorials, videos, and audio clips to support students as they learn the latest Office 2010 features.

MSDN ACADEMIC ALLIANCE

Free Three-Year Membership Available to Qualified Adopters!

The Microsoft Developer Network Academic Alliance (MSDN AA) is designed to provide the easiest and most inexpensive way for universities to make the latest Microsoft developer tools, products, and technologies available in labs, classrooms, and on student PCs. MSDN AA is an annual membership program for departments teaching Science, Technology, Engineering, and Mathematics (STEM) courses. The membership provides a complete solution to keep academic labs, faculty, and students on the leading edge of technology.

Software available in the MSDN AA program is provided at no charge to adopting departments through the Wiley and Microsoft publishing partnership.

As a bonus to this free offer, faculty will be introduced to Microsoft's Faculty Connection and Academic Resource Center. It takes time and preparation to keep students engaged while giving them a fundamental understanding of theory, and the Microsoft Faculty Connection is designed to help STEM professors with this preparation by providing articles, curriculum, and tools that professors can use to engage and inspire today's technology students.

Contact your Wiley rep for details.

For more information about the MSDN Academic Alliance program, go to **msdn.microsoft.com/academic/**.

IMPORTANT WEB ADDRESSES AND PHONE NUMBERS

To locate the Wiley Higher Education Rep in your area, go to www.wiley.com/college, select Instructors under Resources, and click on the Who's My Rep link, or call the MOAC toll-free number: 1 + (888) 764-7001 (U.S. and Canada only).

To learn more about becoming a Microsoft Certified Professional and exam availability, visit www.microsoft.com/learning/mcp.

WHY MOS CERTIFICATION?

Microsoft Office Specialist (MOS) 2010 is a valuable credential that recognizes the desktop computing skills needed to use the full features and functionality of the Microsoft Office 2010 suite.

In the worldwide job market, Microsoft Office Specialist is the primary tool companies use to validate the proficiency of their employees in the latest productivity tools and technology, helping them select job candidates based on globally recognized standards for verifying skills. The results of an independent research study show that businesses with certified employees are more productive compared to non-certified employees and that certified employees bring immediate value to their jobs.

In academia, as in the business world, institutions upgrading to Office 2010 may seek ways to protect and maximize their technology investment. By offering certification, they validate that decision—because powerful Office 2010 applications such as Word, Excel, and Power-Point can be effectively used to demonstrate increases in academic preparedness and workforce readiness.

Individuals seek certification to increase their own personal sense of accomplishment and to create advancement opportunities by establishing a leadership position in their school or department, thereby differentiating their skill sets in a competitive college admissions and job market.

BOOK COMPANION WEBSITE

The students' book companion site for the MOAC series (www.wiley.com/college/microsoft), includes any resources, exercise files, and web links that will be used in conjunction with this course.

WILEY DESKTOP EDITIONS

Wiley MOAC Desktop Editions are innovative, electronic versions of printed textbooks. Students buy the desktop version for 50% off the U.S. price of the printed text and get the added value of permanence and portability. Wiley Desktop Editions provide students with numerous additional benefits that are not available with other e-text solutions.

Wiley Desktop Editions are NOT subscriptions; students download the Wiley Desktop Edition to their computer desktops. Students own the content they buy and keep it for as long as they want. Once a Wiley Desktop Edition is downloaded to the computer desktop, students have instant access to all of the content without being online. Students can also print the sections they prefer to read in hard copy. Students also have access to fully integrated resources within their Wiley Desktop Edition. From highlighting their e-text to taking and sharing notes, students can easily personalize their Wiley Desktop Edition as they are reading or following along in class.

COURSESMART

CourseSmart goes beyond traditional expectations providing instant, online access to the textbooks and course materials you need at a lower cost option. You can save time and hassle with a digital eTextbook that allows you to search for the most relevant content at the very moment you need it. To learn more go to: www.coursesmart.com.

PREPARING TO TAKE THE MICROSOFT OFFICE SPECIALIST (MOS) EXAM

The Microsoft Office Specialist credential has been upgraded to validate skills with the Microsoft Office 2010 system. The MOS certifications target information workers and cover the most popular business applications such as Word 2010, PowerPoint 2010, Excel 2010, Access 2010, and Outlook 2010.

By becoming certified, you demonstrate to employers that you have achieved a predictable level of skill in the use of a particular Office application. Employers often require certification either as a condition of employment or as a condition of advancement within the company or other organization. The certification examinations are sponsored by Microsoft but administered through exam delivery partners like Certiport.

To learn more about becoming a Microsoft Certified Application Specialist and exam availability, visit www.microsoft.com/learning/msbc.

Preparing to Take an Exam

Unless you are a very experienced user, you will need to use a test preparation course to prepare for the test to complete it correctly and within the time allowed. The Microsoft Official Academic Course series is designed to prepare you with a strong knowledge of all exam topics. With some additional review and practice on your own, you should feel confident in your ability to pass the appropriate exam.

After you decide which exam to take, review the list of objectives for the exam. This list can be found in Appendix A at the back of this book. You can also easily identify tasks that are included in the objective list by locating the Lesson Skill Matrix at the start of each lesson and the Certification Ready sidebars in the margin of the lessons in this book.

To take the MOS test, visit www.microsoft.com/learning/msbc to locate your nearest testing center. Then call the testing center directly to schedule your test. The amount of advance notice you should provide will vary for different testing centers, and it typically depends on the number of computers available at the testing center, the number of other testers who have already been scheduled for the day on which you want to take the test, and the number of times per week that the testing center offers MOS testing. In general, you should call to schedule your test at least two weeks prior to the date on which you want to take the test.

When you arrive at the testing center, you might be asked for proof of identity. A driver's license or passport is an acceptable form of identification. If you do not have either of these items of documentation, call your testing center and ask what alternative forms of identification will be accepted. If you are retaking a test, bring your MOS identification number, which will have been given to you when you previously took the test. If you have not prepaid or if your organization has not already arranged to make payment for you, you will need to pay the test-taking fee when you arrive.

Test Format

All MOS certification tests are live, performance-based tests. There are no multiple-choice, true/false, or short-answer questions. Instructions are general: you are told the basic tasks to perform on the computer, but you aren't given any help in figuring out how to perform them. You are not permitted to use reference material other than the application's Help system.

As you complete the tasks stated in a particular test question, the testing software monitors your actions. Following is an example question.

> Open the file named *Wiley Guests* and select the word *Welcome* in the first paragraph. Change the font to 12 point, and apply bold formatting. Select the words *at your convenience* in the second paragraph, move them to the end of the first paragraph using drag and drop, and then center the first paragraph.

When the test administrator seats you at a computer, you will see an online form that you use to enter information about yourself (name, address, and other information required to process your exam results). While you complete the form, the software will generate the test from a master test bank and then prompt you to continue. The first test question will appear in a window. Read the question carefully, and then perform all the tasks stated in the test question. When you have finished completing all tasks for a question, click the Next Question button.

You have 45 to 60 minutes to complete all questions, depending on the test that you are taking. The testing software assesses your results as soon as you complete the test, and the test administrator can print the results of the test so that you will have a record of any tasks that you performed incorrectly. A passing grade is 75 percent or higher. If you pass, you will receive a certificate in the mail within two to four weeks. If you do not pass, you can study and practice the skills that you missed and then schedule to retake the test at a later date.

Tips for Successfully Completing the Test

The following tips and suggestions are the result of feedback received from many individuals who have taken one or more MOS tests.

- **Make sure that you are thoroughly prepared.** If you have extensively used the application for which you are being tested, you might feel confident that you are prepared for the test. However, the test might include questions that involve tasks that you rarely or never perform when you use the application at your place of business, at school, or at home. You must be knowledgeable in all the MOS objectives for the test that you will take.

- **Read each exam question carefully.** An exam question might include several tasks that you are to perform. A partially correct response to a test question is counted as an incorrect response. In the example question on the previous page, you might apply bold formatting and move the words *at your convenience* to the correct location, but forget to center the first paragraph. This would count as an incorrect response and would result in a lower test score.

- **Use the Help system only when necessary.** You are allowed to use the application's Help system, but relying on the Help system too much will slow you down and possibly prevent you from completing the test within the allotted time. Use the Help system only when necessary.

- **Keep track of your time.** The test does not display the amount of time that you have left, so you need to keep track of the time yourself by monitoring your start time and the required end time on your watch or a clock in the testing center (if there is one). The test program displays the number of items that you have completed along with the total number of test items (for example, "35 of 40 items have been completed"). Use this information to gauge your pace.

- **You cannot return to a question once you've skipped it.** If you skip a question, you cannot return to it later. You should skip a question only if you are certain that you cannot complete the tasks correctly.

- **Make sure you understand the instructions for each question.** As soon as you are finished reading a question and you click in the application window, a condensed version of the instruction is displayed in a corner of the screen. If you are unsure whether you have completed all tasks stated in the test question, click the Instructions button on the test information bar at the bottom of the screen and then reread the question. Close the instruction window when you are finished. Do this as often as necessary to ensure you have read the question correctly and that you have completed all the tasks stated in the question.

If You Do Not Pass the Test

If you do not pass, you can use the assessment printout as a guide to practice the items that you missed. There is no limit to the number of times that you can retake a test; however, you must pay the fee each time that you take the test. When you retake the test, expect to see some of the same test items on the subsequent test; the test software randomly generates the test items from a master test bank before you begin the test. Also expect to see several questions that did not appear on the previous test.

Office 2010 Professional Six-Month Trial Software

Some editions of the textbooks in the MOAC Office 2010 series come with six-month trial editions of Office 2010 Professional. If your book includes a trial, there is a CD adhered to the inside cover of your book. This section pertains only to the editions that are packaged with an Office 2010 Professional trial.

STEP BY STEP	Installing the Microsoft Office System 2010 Six-Month Trial

1. Insert the trial software CD-ROM into the CD drive on your computer. The CD will be detected, and the Setup.exe file should automatically begin to run on your computer.
2. When prompted for the Office Product Key, enter the Product Key provided with the software, and then click Next.
3. Enter [your name] and [organization user name], and then click Next.
4. Read the End-User License Agreement, select the I Accept the Terms in the License Agreement check box, and then click Next.
5. Select the install option, verify the installation location or click Browse to change the installation location, and then click Next.
6. Verify the program installation preferences, and then click Next.

Click Finish to complete the setup.

UPGRADING MICROSOFT OFFICE PROFESSIONAL 2010 SIX-MONTH TRIAL SOFTWARE TO THE FULL PRODUCT

You can convert the software into full use without removing or reinstalling software on your computer. When you complete your trial, you can purchase a product license from any Microsoft reseller and enter a valid Product Key when prompted during setup.

UNINSTALLING THE TRIAL SOFTWARE AND RETURNING TO YOUR PREVIOUS OFFICE VERSION

If you want to return to your previous version of Office, you need to uninstall the trial software. This should be done through the Add or Remove Programs icon in Control Panel (or Uninstall a program in the Control Panel of Windows Vista).

STEP BY STEP	Uninstall Trial Software

1. Quit any programs that are running.
2. In Control Panel, click Programs and Features (Add or Remove Programs in Windows XP).
3. Click Microsoft Office Professional 2010, and then click Uninstall (Remove in Windows XP).

Take Note

If you selected the option to remove a previous version of Office during installation of the trial software, you need to reinstall your previous version of Office. If you did not remove your previous version of Office, you can start each of your Office programs either through the Start menu or by opening files for each program. In some cases, you may have to re-create some of your shortcuts and default settings.

www.wiley.com/college/microsoft
or call the MOAC Toll-Free Number: 1+(888) 764-7001 (U.S. & Canada only)

STUDENT DATA FILES

All of the practice files that you will use as you perform the exercises in the book are available for download on our student companion site. By using the practice files, you will not waste time creating the samples used in the lessons, and you can concentrate on learning how to use Microsoft Office 2010. With the files and the step-by-step instructions in the lessons, you will learn by doing, which is an easy and effective way to acquire and remember new skills.

Copying the Practice Files

Your instructor might already have copied the practice files before you arrive in class. However, your instructor might ask you to copy the practice files on your own at the start of class. Also, if you want to work through any of the exercises in this book on your own at home or at your place of business after class, you may want to copy the practice files.

STEP BY STEP	Copy the Practice Files

OPEN Internet Explorer.

1. In Internet Explorer, go to the student companion site: www.wiley.com
2. Search for your book title in the upper-right corner.
3. On the Search Results page, locate your book and click on the **Visit the Companion Sites** link.
4. Select **Student Companion Site** from the pop-up box.
5. In the left-hand column, under "Browse by Resource" select **Student Data Files**.
6. Now select **Student Data Files** from the center of the screen.
7. On the File Download dialog box, select **Save** to save the data files to your external drive (often called a ZIP drive or a USB drive or a thumb drive) or a local drive.
8. In the Save As dialog box, select a local drive in the left-hand panel that you'd like to save your files to; again, this should be an external drive or a local drive. Remember the drive name that you saved it to.

Acknowledgments

We'd like to thank the many reviewers who pored over the manuscript and provided invaluable feedback in the service of quality instructional materials.

Access 2010

Tammie Bolling, *Tennessee Technology Center—Jacksboro*

Mary Corcoran, *Bellevue College*

Trish Culp, *triOS College—Business Technology Healthcare*

Jana Hambruch, *Lee County School District*

Aditi Mukherjee, *University of Florida—Gainesville*

Excel 2010

Tammie Bolling, *Tennessee Technology Center—Jacksboro*

Mary Corcoran, *Bellevue College*

Trish Culp, *triOS College—Business Technology Healthcare*

Dee Hobson, *Richland College*

Christie Hovey, *Lincoln Land Community College*

Ralph Phillips, *Central Oregon Community College*

Rajeev Sachdev, *triOS College—Business Technology Healthcare*

Outlook 2010

Mary Harnishfeger, *Ivy Tech State College—Bloomington*

Sandra Miller, *Wenatchee Valley College*

Bob Reeves, *Vincennes University*

Lourdes Sevilla, *Southwestern College—Chula Vista*

Phyllis E. Traylor, *St. Philips College*

PowerPoint 2010

Natasha Carter, *SUNY—ATTAIN*

Dr. Susan Evans Jennings, *Stephen F. Austin State University*

Sue Van Lanen, *Gwinnett Technical College*

Carol J. McPeek, *SUNY—ATTAIN*

Michelle Poertner, *Northwestern Michigan College*

Tim Sylvester, *Glendale Community College (AZ)*

Project 2010

Tatyana Pashnyak, *Bainbridge College*

Debi Griggs, *Bellevue College*

Word 2010

Portia Hatfield, *Tennessee Technology Center—Jacksboro*

Terri Holly, *Indian River State College*

Pat McMahon, *South Suburban College*

Barb Purvis, *Centura College*

Janet Sebesy, *Cuyahoga Community College*

We would also like to thank Lutz Ziob, Jason Bunge, Ben Watson, David Bramble, Merrick Van Dongen, Don Field, Pablo Bernal, and Wendy Johnson at Microsoft for their encouragement and support in making the Microsoft Official Academic Course program the finest instructional materials for mastering the newest Microsoft technologies for both students and instructors. Finally, we would like to thank Lorna Gentry of Content LLC for developmental editing and Jeff Riley and his team at Box Twelve Communications for technical editing.

About the Author

Linda Silva

Linda has been teaching for seventeen years and has been working at El Paso Community College for more than thirty years. She is currently a full-time faculty member of the Administrative Assistant program—of which she was formerly the district-wide coordinator—and teaches part-time in the Business program. El Paso Community College has five campuses to serve the educational needs of the community population; it also has been recognized as the fastest-growing community college in Texas and the largest grantor of associate degrees to Hispanic students in the nation. Linda believes that EPCC is "the best place to start" and "the best place to continue."

The Administrative Assistant program has adopted textbooks from the MOAC series; the students enrolled in the program are required to take Microsoft application software courses (Word, Excel, PowerPoint, Access, and Outlook), which prepare them for the Microsoft Office Specialist exam. Linda's students have successfully passed the exams—one of them passed the MOS Excel 2007 exam with a perfect score of 1,000. Linda takes the exams ahead of her students and challenges them to beat her score.

Linda enjoys the art of innovative teaching, and when she is not teaching enjoys taking on new and exciting challenges.

Brief Contents

Contents

1 Understanding Word 1

2 Basic Editing 31

3 Character Formatting 60

4 Paragraph Formatting 79

5 Managing Text Flow 115

6 Creating Tables 140

7 Working with Themes, Quick Parts, Page Backgrounds, and Headers and Footers 163

8 Using Illustrations and Graphics 188

9 Proofing Documents 237

10 Applying References and Hyperlinks 254

11 Performing Mail Merges 274

12 Maintaining Documents and Working with Templates 296

13 Protecting and Sharing Documents 316

14   Using Advanced Options   352

LESSON SKILL MATRIX

Skill	Exam Objective	Objective Number
Starting Word		
Working with Onscreen Tools		
Opening Backstage View		
Using the Microsoft Word Help Button		
Creating a Document		
Saving a Document	Save a document using Compatibility Mode.	1.5.1
	Save a document using Save As options.	1.5.3
Previewing and Printing a Document		
Closing a Document and Closing Word		

KEY TERMS

- **AutoComplete**
- **Backstage view**
- **badges**
- **Block Style**
- **command**
- **Connection Status menu**
- **dialog box**
- **dialog box launcher**
- **groups**
- **I-beam**
- **insertion point**
- **KeyTips**
- **menu**
- **Mini toolbar**
- **mixed punctuation**

- nonprinting characters
- open punctuation
- Preview
- Print
- Quick Access Toolbar

- Redo
- Ribbon
- Save
- Save As
- ScreenTip

- settings
- shortcut menu
- tabs
- Undo
- Word Wrap

Tech Terrace Real Estate works with clients to buy, sell, and rent homes in a neighborhood that borders a local university. The company's agents regularly create letters, sales data, and other real estate information to be mailed to current and prospective clients. Microsoft Word is the perfect tool for this task. In this lesson, you learn how to navigate the Word window and use basic Word features to create and manage documents such as those used by Tech Terrace Real Estate.

SOFTWARE ORIENTATION

Microsoft Word's Opening Screen

Before you begin working in Microsoft Word, you need to acquaint yourself with the primary user interface (UI). When you first launch Microsoft Word, you will see a screen similar to that shown in Figure 1-1.

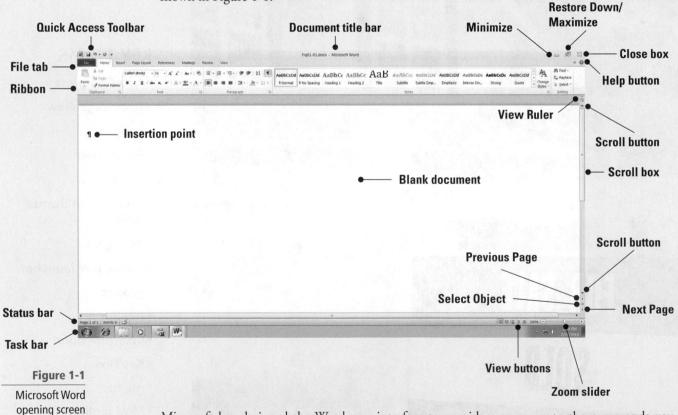

Figure 1-1

Microsoft Word opening screen

Microsoft has designed the Word user interface to provide easy access to the commands you need most often when creating and editing documents. (Note that your screen may vary somewhat from the one shown here, depending on your program's settings.) Use Figure 1-1 as a reference throughout this lesson as well as the rest of this book.

STARTING WORD

Microsoft Word is a word processing tool for creating different types of documents that are used in the work environment. When you first launch Word, a new blank document appears on your screen.

Starting Word

In this exercise, you learn how to start Word to produce a blank document.

When you start your computer, the screen you see is called the Windows desktop. From the desktop, you can launch Word by clicking the Word program icon or by choosing Microsoft Word from the Start menu. When Word is launched, the program opens with a blank document. The blinking **insertion point** in the upper-left corner of this document is where you will begin creating your text. When you place your cursor near it, the insertion point changes to a large "I," which is called the **I-beam**.

Take Note   If your computer is running an operating system other than Windows 7, such as Windows Vista or XP, you will be able to complete the lessons in this book, but some screenshots and steps might appear slightly different.

STEP BY STEP   **Start Word**

GET READY. Before you begin these steps, be sure to turn on and/or log on to your computer.

1. On the Windows task bar, click the Start 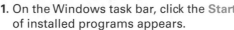 button, then click **All Programs**. A menu of installed programs appears.

2. Click the **Microsoft Office** folder.

3. Next click **Microsoft Word 2010** (see Figure 1-2). Word opens and a new blank document appears.

PAUSE. LEAVE the document open to use in the next exercise.

WileyPLUS Extra! features an online tutorial of this task.

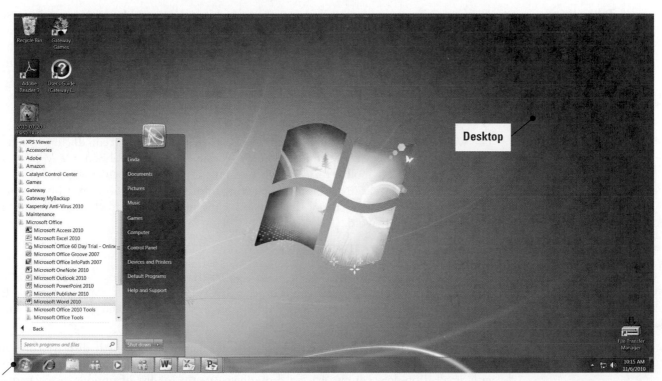

Figure 1-2

Starting Word

Another Way
To launch Word 2010 using Windows 7, click the Start button; then, in the Search Programs and Files box, key Microsoft Word 2010; and finally, click or press Enter. You can also search for a program or file by clicking the Start button and then keying the first two characters of the program or filename into the Search box; files and programs beginning with those letters will appear in the Start menu, as shown in Figure 1-3. You can also pin Word 2010 to the Start menu and task bar, so that it is always visible.

Another Way
When Office was installed on your computer, a shortcut icon may have been added to the Start menu or to your desktop. Double-click the shortcut icon on your desktop to start Word without having to go through the Start menu.

Figure 1-3

Launching Word using Windows 7

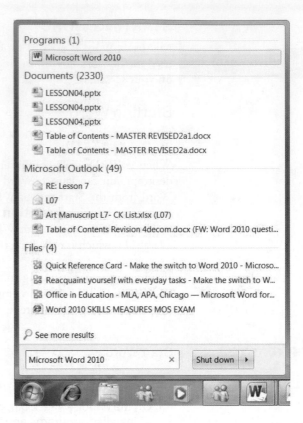

Take Note Windows 7 is a descendant of Windows Vista, and it is the latest Microsoft operating system. Windows 7 is for PC users at home, work, and school. It is a powerful tool that controls the user interface, storage devices, other software, peripheral devices, networks/security, system resources, and task scheduling. Microsoft has made Windows 7 quick to respond and customizable to accommodate your needs.

WORKING WITH ONSCREEN TOOLS

The Bottom Line The Word 2010 window has many onscreen tools to help you create and edit documents quickly and efficiently. In this section, you learn how to locate and use the Ribbon, the Mini toolbar, and the Quick Access Toolbar to access Word commands. A **command** is an instruction that you give to Word by clicking a button or entering information into a command box. You also learn how to use KeyTips, a tool that replaces some of the keyboard shortcuts from earlier versions of Microsoft Word.

Using the Ribbon

In Word 2010, the **Ribbon** is divided into eight **tabs**, or areas of activity. In turn, each tab contains several **groups**, or collections of related Word commands. In this exercise, you learn to use the Ribbon by making tabs active, hiding and displaying command groups, and using the dialog box launcher and drop-down arrows.

In all Office 2010 programs, the Ribbon is contextual, which means it displays commands related to the type of document or object that you have open and on screen. Command boxes with small drop-down arrows have a drop-down **menu**, or list of options, associated with them; you click the drop-down arrow to produce this menu. Most groups have a **dialog box launcher**—a small arrow in the lower-right corner of the group—that you click to launch a **dialog box** that displays additional options or information you can use to execute a command.

STEP BY STEP   **Use the Ribbon**

USE the document that is open from the previous exercise.

1. The Ribbon is located at the top of the Word screen. In your newly opened document, the Home tab is the active tab on the Ribbon, as shown in Figure 1-4. Note how the Ribbon is divided into groups.

Tabs   **Drop-down arrows**

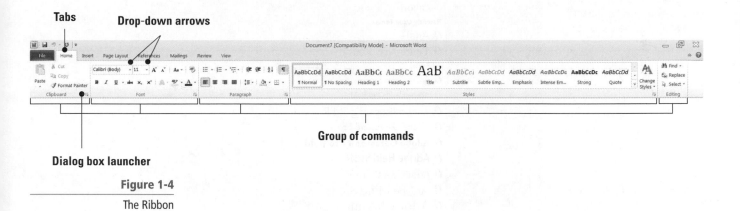

Dialog box launcher

Group of commands

Figure 1-4

The Ribbon

2. Review the other tabs on the Ribbon. Click the **Page Layout** tab to make it the active tab. Notice that the groups of commands change.
3. Click the **Home** tab.
4. Click the **dialog box launcher** in the lower-right corner of the Font group. The Font dialog box, as shown in Figure 1-5, appears. Click **Cancel** to close the dialog box.

Figure 1-5

Font dialog box

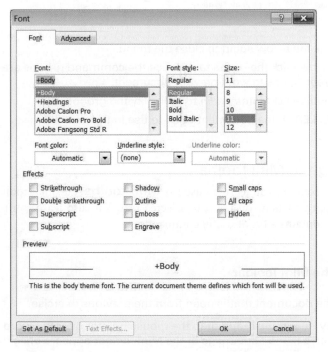

5. Click the drop-down arrow on the Font command box in the Font group to produce a menu of available fonts, as shown in Figure 1-6.

Figure 1-6

Font menu

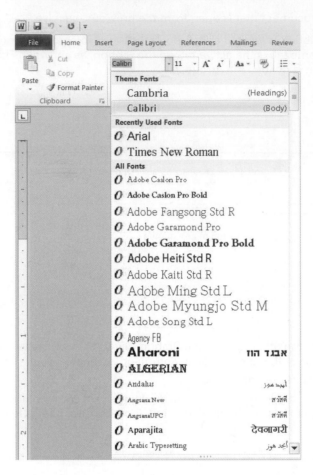

6. Click the arrow again to close the menu.

7. Double-click the Home tab. Notice the command groups are hidden to give you more screen space to work on your document.

8. Double-click Home again to redisplay the groups.

PAUSE. LEAVE the document open to use in the next exercise.

Using the Mini Toolbar

In this exercise, you learn to use the **Mini toolbar**, a small toolbar with popular commands that appears when you point to selected text. You also learn to display the **shortcut menu**, which contains a list of useful commands.

STEP BY STEP   **Use the Mini Toolbar**

USE the document that is open from the previous exercise.

1. Key mini toolbar and drag the mouse pointer over the word "toolbar" to select it. Notice that a faint image of the Mini toolbar appears once the word is selected, as shown Figure 1-7.

Figure 1-7

Faint version of the
Mini toolbar

2. Point to the Font command on the Mini toolbar. Notice the toolbar brightens.

3. Click the drop-down arrow on the Font command box. A font menu appears. Press Esc twice to exit the command box and close the Mini toolbar.

4. Now, position the insertion point on the selected text and right-click; the Mini toolbar appears, accompanied by a shortcut menu that displays a variety of commonly used commands (see Figure 1-8).

Figure 1-8

Mini toolbar and
shortcut menu

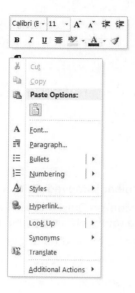

5. Click in a blank part of the document, then drag the mouse pointer over the text you typed at the beginning of the exercise. Finally, press the Delete key to remove the text.

PAUSE. LEAVE the document open to use in the next exercise.

Using the Quick Access Toolbar

The **Quick Access Toolbar** contains the commands that users access most often, such as Save, Undo, and Redo. You can customize the contents of the Quick Access Toolbar by clicking the drop-down arrow on the right side of the toolbar and choosing options from the menu that appears. In this exercise, you learn to use the commands on the Quick Access Toolbar. You also learn to customize the toolbar by changing its position in relation to the Ribbon.

STEP BY STEP   **Use the Quick Access Toolbar**

USE the document that is open from the previous exercise.

1. Click the Save 🖫 button on the Quick Access Toolbar.

2. The Save As dialog box appears. For now, you are reviewing the Save As dialog box. Later in the lesson, you will learn to save a document using this box.

3. Click Cancel.

4. Click the drop-down arrow at the Customize Quick Access Toolbar button. A menu appears, as shown in Figure 1-9.

Figure 1-9

Customizing the Quick
Access Toolbar

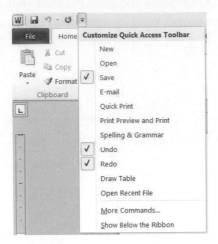

5. Click Show Below the Ribbon. The toolbar is moved.

6. Click the drop-down arrow at the Customize Quick Access Toolbar button again. Click Show Above the Ribbon to return the toolbar to its original position.

PAUSE. LEAVE the document open to use in the next exercise.

 Ref

In Lesson 14, you will learn to further customize the toolbar by adding buttons for other commands you use often.

Clicking the **Save** button in the Quick Access Toolbar quickly saves an existing document. When saving a document for the first time, you will need to specify the filename and target location, such as your USB flash drive. The **Save As** dialog box will save a document in a specific format. The **Undo** command lets you cancel or undo your last command or action. You can click the Undo command as many times as necessary to undo previously executed commands. Also, if you click the arrow beside the Undo command, a menu of actions you can undo appears. Clicking the **Redo** command repeats your last action. Note that commands on the Quick Access Toolbar are not available if their button is dimmed.

Using KeyTips

In Word 2010, **KeyTips** replace some keyboard shortcuts used in previous versions of Word. Every command on the Ribbon and the Quick Access Toolbar has a KeyTip. To display Key-Tips, press the Alt key; KeyTips then appear as small letters and numbers hovering over their associated commands. The small square labels that contain this information are called **badges**. In this exercise, you learn to display and use KeyTips.

STEP BY STEP   **Use KeyTips**

USE the document that is open from the previous exercise.

1. Press the Alt key. KeyTips appear on the Ribbon and Quick Access Toolbar to let you know which key to use to access specific commands or tabs. (See Figure 1-10.)

Figure 1-10

KeyTips

2. Press **H** to activate the Home tab.

3. Press **A** for alignment, then **C** to center the insertion point.

4. Press the **Alt** key again.

5. Press **H** to activate the Home tab.

6. Press **A** for alignment, then **L** to align the insertion point to the left.

PAUSE. LEAVE the document open to use in the next exercise.

Take Note   Shortcut keys are keys or combinations of keys pressed together to perform a command. Shortcut keys provide a quick way to give commands without having to take your hands from the keyboard. Keyboard shortcuts from previous versions of Word that began with Ctrl have remained the same. However, those that began with Alt are now different and require the use of KeyTips.

SOFTWARE ORIENTATION

Backstage Opening Screen

Before you begin working in Backstage view, you need to be familiar with Microsoft's Office new user interface (UI). When you first launch Microsoft Word and click the File tab, you should see a screen similar to that shown in Figure 1-11. This is what is known as Backstage view.

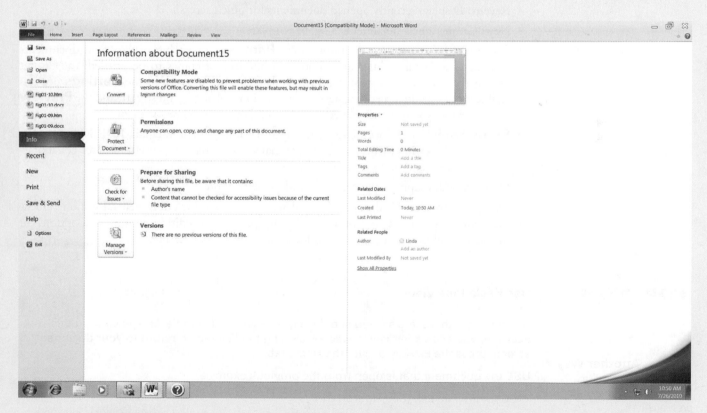

Figure 1-11

Backstage view

Use Figure 1-11 as a reference throughout this lesson as well as the rest of this book.

OPENING BACKSTAGE VIEW

Backstage view offers quick access to commands for performing many file management tasks—such as opening, closing, saving, printing, and sharing Word documents—all displayed in a single navigation pane that can be customized to meet your needs.

In Backstage view, commands enable you to work with document properties, grant permissions, save documents in PDF or other formats, share documents, and work with templates. Accessibility Checker can be used to check whether your document can be read by individuals with a disability. You can also print and preview a document in one action in Backstage view.

Here is a brief overview of the commands that appear in the Backstage view navigation pane:

- **Save:** Saves the current document using the new Word format.
- **Save As:** Saves a document in a specific format (Word 97-2003, PDF, TXT, RTF, HTM, and so on) and enables you to save documents in multiple locations, such as a USB flash drive, hard drive, network location, desktop, CD, or DVD.
- **Open:** Opens an existing document from any target location; if you open a document created in an earlier version of Word, Compatibility Mode automatically activates (the title bar indicates when Compatibility Mode is active).
- **Close:** Closes an open document (the program remains open).
- **Info:** The options in this group (shown open in Figure 1-11) prepare and mark documents as final so that no changes can be made to them; protect documents with a password or restricted permissions; add a digital signature; inspect the document for sensitive information; check document accessibility and compatibility; manage different versions of a document; and prepare documents for distribution.
- **Recent:** Displays recently opened documents for quick access.
- **New:** Creates a new document, blog, or template.
- **Print:** Offers several sets of options—the **Print** options enable you to send documents straight to a default printer and choose the number of copies to be printed; the Printer options enable you to choose a printer and set printer properties; the **Settings** options enable you to set document properties (orientation, collation, and so on); and the **Preview** screen enables you to visually check your document for errors before printing.
- **Save & Send:** Shares documents by saving and sending them in email, PDF, XPS, or other formats, or by saving them to a document management service (a useful tool for collaborating with others and publishing blog posts).
- **Help:** Provides support and tools for working with Word.
- **Options:** Provides Word document and setting options, including general options, document proofing options, save options, language preferences, editing options, and options for managing add-ins and templates and for keeping documents secure.

STEP BY STEP   **Use Backstage View**

As you begin this exercise, you should acquaint yourself with Backstage view. In this exercise, you access Backstage view by clicking the File tab. To return to your document screen, press the Esc key or click the Home tab.

Another Way
You can also activate Backstage view by pressing Alt+F.

USE the document that is open from the previous exercise.

1. Click the File tab. (See Figure 1-11.)
2. Notice that the Info command is the default command with available options.
3. Point to other commands with the arrow to view more options.
4. Press the Esc key or click the Home tab to exit Backstage view.

PAUSE. LEAVE the document open to use in the next exercise.

Take Note   You will learn more about the additional Backstage view options in Lesson 13.

USING THE MICROSOFT WORD HELP BUTTON

The Bottom Line

Microsoft Word has options for accessing the Help features installed and available on your computer. If you are connected to the Internet, you also can choose to use Microsoft's online Help features.

Take Note

When you hover over a command on the Ribbon, a **ScreenTip** will appear displaying the name of the command and additional information about the command. You also can click the Help button to get more information and advice.

Using the Help Button

Microsoft Word Help works much like an Internet browser and has many of the same buttons, such as Back, Forward, Stop, Refresh, Home, and Print. A quick way to find Help information is to key a word or words into the search box and then click the Search button. Word will display a list of related topics as links. In this exercise, you learn to open Word Help, to choose between online and offline Help content, and to use Help by keying in search words, browsing help topics, or choosing a topic from the Table of Contents.

The **Connection Status menu** in the lower-right corner of Word Help lets you determine whether the Help screen displays content available at Office Online (you must be connected to the Internet to access this content, which offers the most up-to-date help available) or only those topics currently installed on your computer. The Search drop-down menu enables you to specify the scope of topics you want to search, including All Word, Word Help, Word Templates, Word Training, or Developer References. You can print Help information within the Word Help main window by clicking the Print button.

STEP BY STEP   **Use the Help Button**

USE the document that is open from the previous exercise.

1. Make sure you are connected to the Internet.

2. Click the Microsoft Word Help ⑦ button in the upper-right corner of the screen. The Word Help window appears, as shown in Figure 1-12. In the upper-right corner, click the Maximize 🔲 button to expand the window. In Figure 1-12, the Connection Status command in the lower-right corner of the window indicates that Word is connected to Office.com. If your Connection status is set to Offline, your screen will look different.

Figure 1-12

Word Help window when online

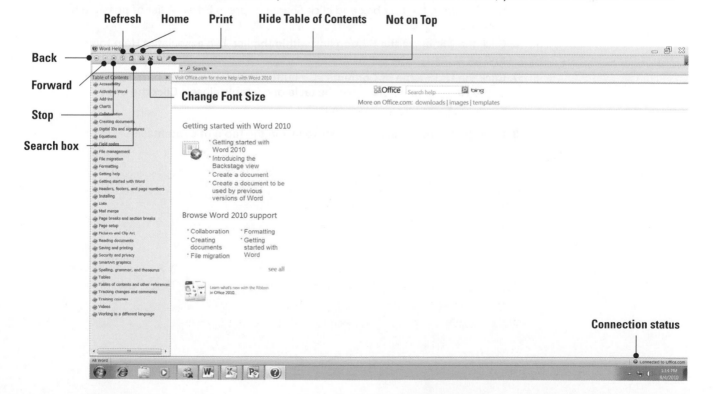

3. Click the **Connection Status** button to produce the Connection Status menu.

4. Click **Show content only from this computer**. Word Help appears, as shown in Figure 1-13.

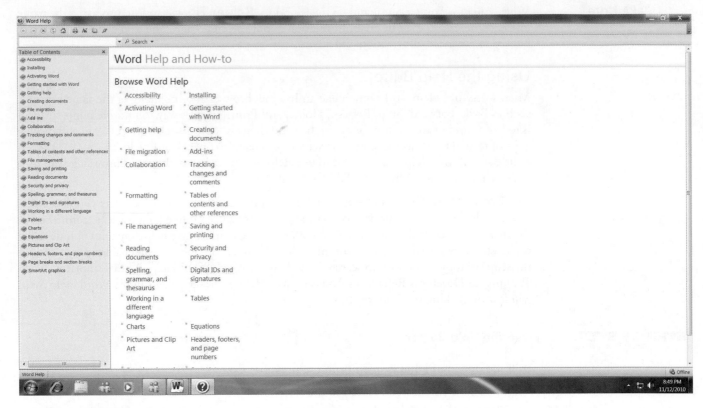

Figure 1-13

Word Help window when offline

5. Key **ribbon** in the text box and click **Search** or press **Enter**. A list of possible topics appears.

6. Click the **Minimize the Ribbon** link within the list. The associated Help topic appears.

7. Click the **Hide Table of Contents** button in the command bar at the top of the Help screen; notice that the table of contents closes. Click the **Show Table of Contents** button to reopen it.

8. Click the **Getting started with Word** link in the table of contents list.

9. Click the **What's new in Word 2010** link; the text for the topic appears in the window, as shown in Figure 1-14. Review the content.

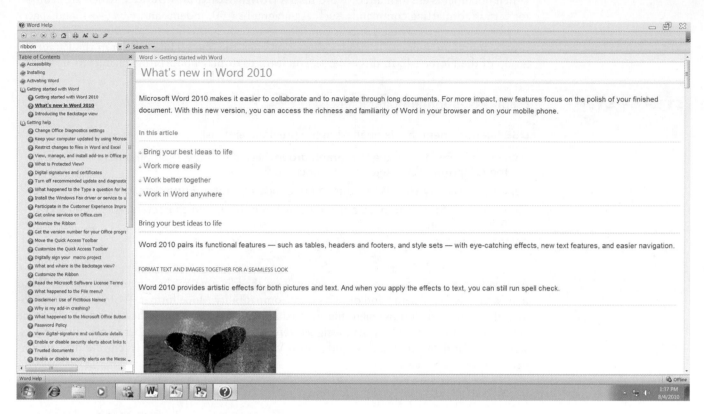

Figure 1-14

Word Help with table of contents and help topic displayed

10. Click the **Home** button.

11. Click the **Close** button to close Microsoft Word Help.

12. Press **F1** to activate Microsoft Word Help again.

13. Change the Connection Status from Offline to **Show Content from Office.com**, then click the **Introducing the Backstage view** link. Click the **Maximize** button and review the content.

14. Click the **Close** button to close Microsoft Word Help.

PAUSE. LEAVE the document open to use in the next exercise.

Another Way
The Word Help button also appears in some dialog boxes and ScreenTips for quick access to context-related help.

CREATING A DOCUMENT

The Bottom Line

When you start keying text at the insertion point in an open document, you have begun to create a Word document. As you type, Word inserts the text to the left of the insertion point and uses the program's defaults for margins and line spacing. Word also has a number of tools and automatic features to make creating a document easier, including nonprinting characters, AutoComplete, and Word Wrap.

When you key text into a new document, it will be inserted to the left of the insertion point and the document will be created using Word's defaults for margins and line spacing. The margin defaults are set to one-inch top, bottom, left, and right margins; the line spacing is set to 1.15; and the spacing after is set to 10 points.

Displaying Nonprinting Characters

When documents are formatted, Word inserts **nonprinting characters**, which are symbols for certain formatting commands, such as paragraphs (¶), indents and tabs (→), and spaces (•) between words. These symbols can help you create and edit your document. By default, these symbols are hidden. To display them, you click the Show/Hide button in the Paragraph group of the Home tab. In this exercise, you learn to display nonprinting characters in Word.

STEP BY STEP   **Display Nonprinting Characters**

USE the document that is open from the previous exercise.

1. On the Home tab, in the Paragraph group, click the Show/Hide (¶) button to display the nonprinting characters in the document.
2. Click the Show/Hide (¶) button again to hide the nonprinting characters.
3. Press Ctrl+Shift+* to once again display the nonprinting characters. This time, leave Show/Hide on.

PAUSE. LEAVE the document open to use in the next exercise.

After you create your first document, you will see the filename on the document title bar. Word names the file Document1 and displays it in Compatibility Mode format. Word assigns chronological numbers to all subsequent files that you open in that session. When you save and name your documents, the name you've assigned replaces the document number name originally assigned by Word. When you close and reopen Word, the program begins its chronological numbering at number 1 again.

Using AutoComplete

The **AutoComplete** command automatically completes the text of the current date, day of the week, and month. When you key the first four characters of the day of the week, a Screen-Tip appears with a suggestion for the completed text; press Enter to accept the suggestion. AutoComplete reduces the amount of time spent keying content or phrases in a document. In this exercise, you learn to use Word's AutoComplete feature.

STEP BY STEP   **Use AutoComplete**

USE the document open from the previous exercise.

1. Key August; as you key the first four characters, a ScreenTip appears. Press Enter to accept the suggested text.
2. Key Monday using the same process.
3. Click the Undo  button. Make sure the insertion point is positioned after August.

PAUSE. LEAVE the document open to use in the next exercise.

Another Way
To use Auto-Complete, you can also key the first four characters of the current date and then press Enter or F3.

Keying Document Text

Keying document text is easy in Word. Word sets default margins and line-spacing measurements for newly created documents, and **Word Wrap** automatically wraps text to the next line as it reaches the right margin. To separate paragraphs and create blank lines, all you need to do is press Enter. In this lesson, you create a letter using the Block Style format with mixed punctuation. Be sure to key the document exactly as shown in the steps that follow.

When sending professional correspondence to customers, it is good business practice to ensure the document is in an acceptable format and error free. The Block Style letter format has open or mixed punctuation and is common to many business documents. **Block Style** format aligns text along the left margin, including the date, inside address, salutation, body of the letter, closing, and signature. **Open punctuation** requires no punctuation after the salutation or the closing, whereas **mixed punctuation** requires a colon after the salutation and a comma after the closing.

STEP BY STEP   Create a Document

USE the document that is open from the previous exercise.

1. The insertion point should be positioned at the end of the word "August." Press the **spacebar** once and key **25, 20XX**. Press **Enter** twice.

2. Key the delivery address as shown:

   Ms. Miriam Lockhart (Press **Enter** once.)

   764 Crimson Avenue (Press **Enter** once.)

   Boston, MA 02136 (Press **Enter** twice.)

3. Key **Dear Ms. Lockhart**.

4. Press **Enter** once.

5. Key the following text and press **Enter** once after each paragraph.

   We are pleased that you have chosen to list your home with Tech Terrace Real Estate. Our office has bought, sold, renovated, appraised, leased, and managed more homes in the Tech Terrace neighborhood than anyone and now we will be putting that experience to work for you.

   Our goal is to sell your house quick for the best possible price.

   The enclosed packet contains a competitive market analysis, complete listing data, a copy of the contracts, and a customized house brochure. Your home has been input into the MLS listing and an Internet ad is on our website. We will be contacting you soon to determine the best time for an open house.

   We look forward to working with you to sell your home. Please do not hesitate to call if you have any questions.

6. Press **Enter** once.

7. Key **Sincerely,**.

8. Press **Enter** twice.

9. Key **Steve Buckley**. Your document should appear as shown in Figure 1-15.

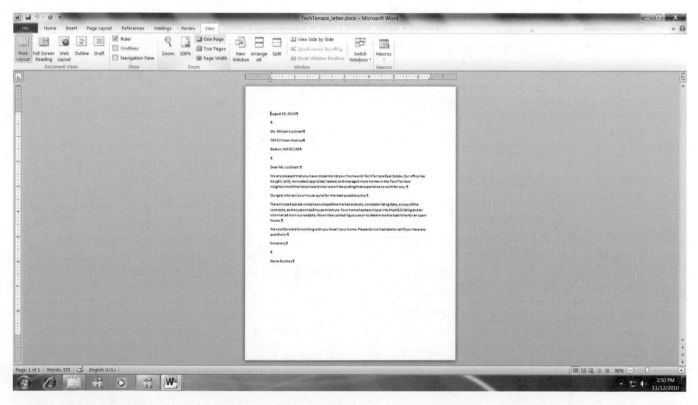

Figure 1-15

Block Style format with mixed punctuation

PAUSE. LEAVE the document open to use in the next exercise.

Take Note   To create a new blank document, click the File tab and then click the New command. "Blank document" will already be selected, so all you need to do is click Create. You can also open a new blank document using the keyboard shortcut Ctrl+N.

It is always important to save your document before closing the program. However, if you close the document or Word by accident, a prompt will appear, asking if you want to save your document. Choose Yes to save and close, No to close without saving, or Cancel to stop the Close command. The Spelling & Grammar commands will be discussed in Lesson 9.

SAVING A DOCUMENT

The Bottom Line

By default, newly created documents are saved with a specific filename closely related to the content of the document. After editing an existing document, you can choose to save that document with a new filename in a specific target location. In some cases, you may want to save the original and edited documents in the same target location but with different filenames. Keeping the original document will allow you to reference it at a future date.

Saving a Document for the First Time

When saving a document for the first time, you must specify a filename, the file type, and a target location where the document will be stored. The filename should help users find and identify the file, and the file location should be convenient for the file's future users. You can save files to portable storage devices such as CDs, DVDs, and USB flash drives, to your computer's desktop or hard drive, or to a network location. In this exercise, you learn to save a document with a specific filename to your USB flash drive.

STEP BY STEP   **Save a Document for the First Time**

USE the document that is open from the previous exercise.

1. If necessary, connect your USB flash drive to one of the USB ports on your computer.
2. Click the **File** tab, then click the **Save** command. The Save As dialog box opens, as shown in Figure 1-16.

Figure 1-16

Save As dialog box

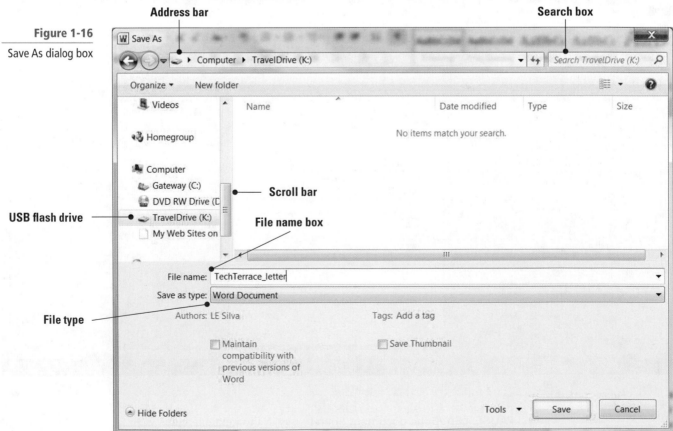

3. In the Windows 7 environment, the Documents Library is the default location for saving new files. Change the target location from the default to your USB flash drive by using the vertical scroll bar and scrolling down until you see your USB flash drive. Storage devices are given a specific letter identified by the operating system. The USB flash drive labeled as TravelDrive (K:) in Figure 1-16 may have a different assignment on your computer; consequently, you will need to check with your instructor for the correct path.

4. Click your **USB flash drive** and note the address bar and the path of the location where your file will be saved.

5. Key *TechTerrace_letter* in the File name text box and click **Save**.

6. If prompted to save in one of the new file formats, click the **OK** button. This action will allow you to use the new features in Word.

PAUSE. LEAVE the document open to use in the next exercise.

CERTIFICATION READY? **1.5.1**

How do you save a new document?

Take Note

When opening an existing document in Word 2010, it will open in one of the three modes: Word 2010, Word 2007 Compatibility Mode, or Word 97-2003 Compatibility Mode.

X **Ref**

It is a common business practice to send documents as an attachment via email. When documents are opened as an attachment, they open in Protected view. Protected view is covered in greater depth in Lesson 13.

Another Way
You can also save a document by clicking the Save button on the Quick Access Toolbar or by pressing Ctrl+S.

Saving a Document in a Folder

Folders help you organize the documents you create in Word. In this exercise, you create a new folder on your USB flash drive and save the document in that folder with its original filename. Always remember to check the full location path listed in the Save As address bar to be certain that you have identified the right target location.

STEP BY STEP **Save a Document in a Folder**

USE the document that is open from the previous exercise.

1. Click the **File** tab, then click **Save As**. The Save As dialog box opens.

2. Click **New folder** and key **Word 2010**. Press **Enter**.

3. In the main pane of the dialog box, double-click the **Word 2010** folder; notice the address bar displays your USB flash drive followed by Word 2010, as shown in Figure 1-17. Note also that the USB flash drive TravelDrive (K:) in Figure 1-17 may not appear on your screen; therefore, you will need to check with your instructor for the correct path.

4. Key *TechTerrace* in the File name box.

5. Click **Save** to close the dialog box.

PAUSE. LEAVE the document open to use in the next exercise.

CERTIFICATION READY? **1.5.1**

How do you save an existing document in a folder?

Troubleshooting AutoRecover is a feature that automatically saves your data at scheduled intervals. This makes it possible to recover some of your work if a problem occurs. However, this useful option is not a substitute for frequently saving your documents as you work. You should always click the Save button regularly to avoid losing work in case of a power outage or computer crash.

Saving a Document with a Different Name

You can use the Save As command to save a copy of your document with a new filename, to save the document in a new target location, or to save the document as a different file type. In this exercise, you learn to save an existing document with a new filename in the Word 2010 folder.

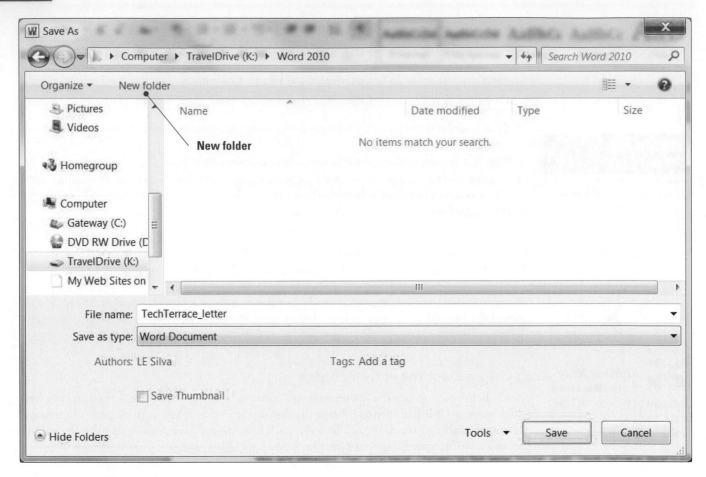

Figure 1-17

Save As dialog box in
a specific folder

Save Document in a Folder with a Different Name

USE the document that is open from the previous exercise.

1. Click the **File** tab and then click the **Save As** command to open the Save As dialog box.

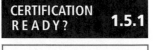

CERTIFICATION READY? **1.5.1**

How do you save an existing
document with a new filename
in a specific target location?

2. In the main pane of the dialog box, double-click the **Word 2010** folder.
3. Key *TechTerrace2* in the File name box.
4. Click **Save**.

PAUSE. LEAVE the document open to use in the next exercise.

Another Way
The Save As dialog
box can also be opened by
pressing F12. To locate your
USB flash drive, click the
drop-down arrow beside the
address bar at the top of the
dialog box, then scroll through
the listings and click the flash
drive.

Showing File Extensions

Word gives you the option of saving your document in a number of formats (see Figure 1-18), including as a Word template, as a Web page, in Rich Text Format, and as a PDF (Portable Document Format) file, which safeguards the document and preserves the intended formatting for viewing and printing. A document's file type is embedded in the filename as a file extension. File extensions are associated with certain programs. (The Save as type drop-down list shows the file type formats available in Windows 7, and Table 1-1 provides a description for some of the file extensions.) In this exercise, you learn how to display file extensions in Windows 7 and in Windows XP.

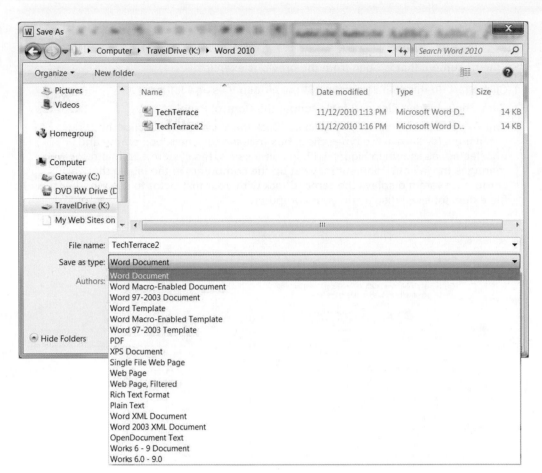

Figure 1-18

File type formats

Table 1-1

File Extensions

File Type	Description
Word Document (*.docx)	Used for Microsoft Word 2007 and 2010.
Word 97-2003 (*.doc)	Used for Microsoft Word 97-2003.
Word Template (*.dotx)	Template for Microsoft Word 2007 and 2010.
Word 97-2003 Template (*.dot)	Template for Microsoft Word 97-2003.
PDF (*.pdf)	Portable Document Format, which preserves the intended formatting of a file for later viewing and printing. PDF files open with Adobe Acrobat Viewer and can be edited using Adobe Acrobat.
XPS Document (*.xps)	XPS is a file format that preserves document formatting and enables file sharing.
Web Page (*.htm,*.html)	Both extensions denote HTML files, which stands for Hypertext Markup Language.
Rich Text Format (*.rtf)	RTF documents are opened with text editor programs such as Notepad, WordPad, and Microsoft Word. Only limited formatting is allowed.
Plain Text (*.txt)	Plain text documents are associated with Notepad, WordPad, and Microsoft Word. The .txt extension does not permit formatting other than spaces and line breaks.
OpenDocument Text (*.odt)	Used by some word processing applications such as OpenOffice.org and Google.docs. Some formatting may be lost when files are saved in this format.

STEP BY STEP   **Show File Extensions in Windows 7**

USE the document that is open from the previous exercise.

1. Click **Start**. In the Search box, key **Show hidden files and folders**.
2. Click **Show hidden files and folder** under the Control Panel.
3. The Folder Options dialog box appears. Click the **View** tab, then click the **Hide extensions for known file types** check box to leave the check box empty and unselected, as shown in Figure 1-19. In some cases, the system administrator who manages the lab environment may set up the computers in the lab so that each computer system displays the same. Check with your instructor to see whether the file extensions will display on your computer.

Figure 1-19

Folder Options dialog box

4. Click **OK** to close the Control Panel.

PAUSE. The Word program is still open from the previous exercise.

STEP BY STEP   **Show File Extensions in Windows XP**

1. Click **Start** on the Windows task bar.
2. Click **Control Panel**.
3. Double-click **Folder Options**.
4. Click the **View** tab, then click the **Hide extensions for known file types** check box to leave it unselected.
5. Click **OK** to close the Control Panel.

PAUSE. The Word program is still open from the previous exercise.

Another Way
By default, file extensions are off. If the file extensions on your computer are hidden, you can show them in Windows 7 using two different methods. Either choose Start > Control Panel > Appearance and Personalization > Folder Options or choose Start, key "folder options" in the Search box, and press Enter.

Choosing a Different File Format

The file format you choose can enable users working in an earlier version of Word to open and edit your document without losing its text formatting. In this exercise, you learn to save a document in a format compatible with an earlier version of Word.

Choose a Different File Format

USE the document that is open from the previous exercise.

1. Click the **File** tab, then click **Save As** to open the Save As dialog box.
2. In the Save As type box, click the drop-down arrow and choose **Word 97-2003 Document (*.doc)**. You should see the .doc extension in the File name box.

3. Key *TechTerrace2_97-2003* in the File name box. Select your USB flash drive and click **Save**.
4. Now you will save the document as another file type. Click the **File** tab and click **Save As**. In the Save As type box, click the drop-down arrow and choose **PDF (*.pdf)**, then click **Save**. The USB flash drive is already opened and the document will save with the same filename. If the Adobe Reader opens the document, click the **Close** ▭x▭ button.

PAUSE. LEAVE Word open for the next exercise.

Take Note PDF is a popular save-as format for documents. This file type preserves document formatting so users can view the document, but they can't change or copy it. In order to save in PDF format, you must download the appropriate add-in from microsoft.com.

Converting a Document

NEW to Office 2010

Compatibility Mode enables you to work in a document created in an earlier version of Word without saving the file in a different file format. In this exercise, you learn to use the Convert command to clear the compatibility options and convert a document to the Word 2010 file format.

Convert a Document

USE the document that is open from the previous exercise.

1. With the *TechTerrace2_97-2003.doc* document open, click the **File** tab.
2. In the main pane of the Info command, click **Convert**, then click **OK** to confirm the conversion, as shown in Figure 1-20. Converting the document clears the Compatibility Mode on the title bar and upgrades your document to Word 2010 format, which allows you to access Word's new features.

Figure 1-20

Convert prompt

The check box skips this step for future conversions.

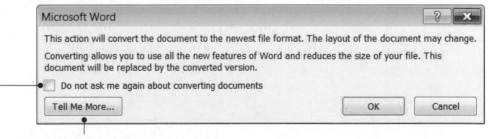

Opens the Word Help screen

3. To save the document in the Word 2010 file format, click the **File** tab.
4. Click **Save As**. Then in the File name box, key *TechTerrace_update*. The filename displays the .docx extension.

PAUSE. LEAVE the document open for the next exercise.

PREVIEWING AND PRINTING A DOCUMENT

The Bottom Line

The Print command is located on the File tab in Backstage view. There are three groups of printing options available, which enable you to print the document (either to a file or to a printer) and to choose a specific printer, the number of copies to be printed, the document's orientation, and other print settings. The Preview pane gives you an opportunity to see what your printed document will look like so you can correct errors before printing.

Previewing in Backstage

NEW to Office 2010

Before printing your document, you need to preview its contents so you can correct any text or layout errors. In this exercise, you learn to use Backstage view to preview your document.

The Print command feature includes three sets of options: Print, Printer, and Settings. Choosing the Print command automatically prints the document to the default printer. Use the selection arrow to change the number of copies to be printed. The Printer options enable you to select a printer, print to file, or change printer properties. Use the Settings options to print only specific pages or selections of the document, collate the document, and so on.

The Preview screen to the right of the Print options settings enables you to view your document as it will appear when it is printed, so you can make any necessary changes, such as changing the margins or orientation, before printing. The Preview screen lets you preview every page by clicking on the right and left arrows to page through multiple-page documents.

STEP BY STEP   **Use Print Preview**

USE the document that is open from the previous exercise.

1. Click the **File** tab, then click **Print** in the Backstage view navigation pane. The Print options and Print Preview screen appears, as shown in Figure 1-21.

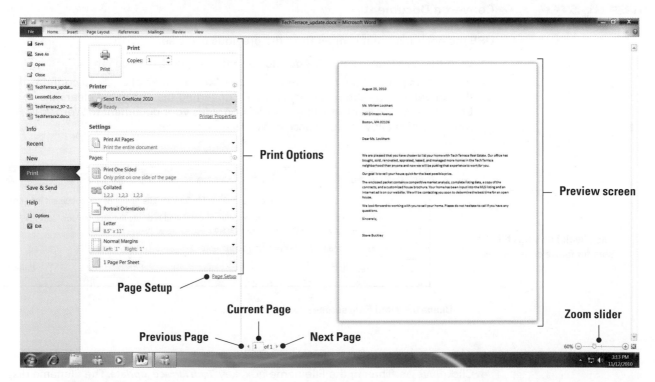

Figure 1-21

Print options and Print Preview screen

2. Click the **plus symbol (+)** on the **Zoom** slider located on the bottom-right of your screen until the zoom level changes to **100%**.

3. Press the **Esc** key or click the **Home** tab to close Backstage.

4. Click the **File** tab, then click **Save**. Your document will be saved with the same filename on your USB flash drive.

PAUSE. LEAVE the document open to use in the next exercise.

Ref   You will learn more about Page Setup in Lesson 5.

Choosing a Printer

If your computer is connected to multiple printers, you may need to choose a destination printer for your document. If your printer is already set up to print, as is the case in most classroom environments, you will not need to complete this exercise. Otherwise, follow this exercise to choose a printer.

Take Note   Before printing your document, check with your instructor.

STEP BY STEP   **Choose a Printer**

USE the document that is open from the previous exercise.

1. Click the **File** tab, then click **Print**.
2. In the Printer selection area, click the **drop-down arrow** to produce a list of all printers connected to your computer.
3. Select a printer, then click the **Printer** icon. (See Figure 1-22.)

Figure 1-22

Print options

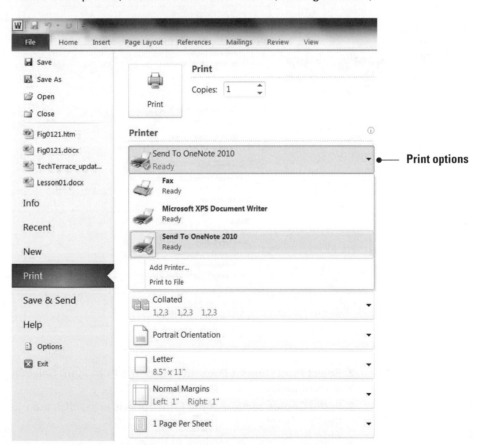

— **Print options**

PAUSE. LEAVE the document open to use in the next exercise.

Setting Print Options

Print Settings options enable you to select the number of copies to be printed; to print only selected content, the current page, or a custom range; and to select from a number of other options for printing properties, collation, and page layout. Changes to Settings options apply to the current document. In this lesson, you learn how to change the Settings options before printing.

STEP BY STEP **Print Settings**

USE the document that is open from the previous exercise.

1. Click the File tab, then click Print. Click the drop-down arrow on Print All Pages to produce the menu shown in Figure 1-23.

Figure 1-23

Print Settings

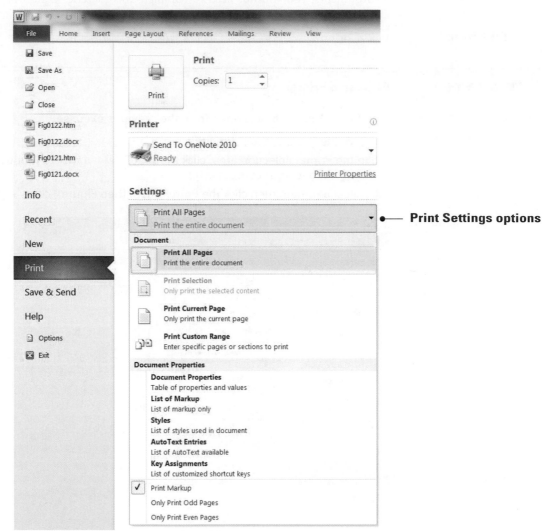

Print Settings options

2. Select Print Current Page, then click the Print icon. Selecting this option prints the current page.

3. In the Copies section of the Print options area, click the up arrow to select 2, then click the Print icon.

4. Click OK to print two copies of the letter.

5. Place your insertion point at the beginning of the third paragraph, then hold down the left mouse button and drag to the end of the paragraph to select it.

6. Click the File tab, then click Print. Click the Print All Pages drop-down arrow, then change the number of copies from 2 to 1 by clicking the down arrow. Next, click the Print icon.

PAUSE. LEAVE the document open to use in the next exercise.

 **Another Way**
You can also print a document by pressing Ctrl+P.

CLOSING A DOCUMENT AND CLOSING WORD

Closing a document removes it from the screen. It is a good idea to close a document before exiting a program or turning off your computer. Saving your work before closing will allow you to continue working on your document at a later date.

STEP BY STEP | **Close a Document and Close Word**

USE the document that is open from the previous exercise.

1. Click the **File** tab.
2. Click the **Exit** button to close both the document and Microsoft Word.

STOP.

Another Way
The shortcut for closing a document is Ctrl+W. To close the program, you can simply click the Close ▪x▪ button.

SKILL SUMMARY

In This Lesson, You Learned How To:	Exam Objective	Objective Number
Start Word		
Work with onscreen tools		
Open Backstage view		
Use the Microsoft Word help button		
Create a document		
Save a document	Save a document using Compatibility Mode.	1.5.1
	Save a document using Save As options.	1.5.3
Preview and print a document		
Close a document and close Word		

Knowledge Assessment

True/False

Circle T if the statement is true or F if the statement is false.

T   F   **1.** When you start Word, a new blank document appears.

T   F   **2.** The Undo button is on the Mini toolbar.

T   F   **3.** Quick-printing a document sends the document straight to the printer.

T   F   **4.** The File tab is used to save and print files.

T   F   **5.** The Zoom slider is located in Backstage view in the Info command.

T   F   **6.** You can hide the Ribbon by double-clicking the active tab.

T   F   **7.** Saving a document in a PDF format will allow users to edit the document.

T   F   **8.** Previewing and printing can be completed by accessing Backstage.

T   F   **9.** You can close a document using keyboard shortcuts and KeyTips.

T   F   **10.** The Help command cannot be accessed in dialog boxes.

Multiple Choice

Select the best response for the following statements.

1. The first screen you see when you start your computer is called the:
   a. Word screen.
   b. Windows 7 screen.
   c. desktop.
   d. screen saver.

2. When you select text, the faint image that appears is called a(n):
   a. I-beam.
   b. Mini toolbar.
   c. insertion point.
   d. All of the above

3. The _____ contains the commands you use most often, such as Save, Undo, and Redo.
   a. Quick Access Screen
   b. Quick toolbar
   c. Quick Access Toolbar
   d. Quick command

4. Letters and numbers that appear on the Ribbon when you press the Alt key are called:
   a. key trips.
   b. KeyTips.
   c. key pads.
   d. key shortcut tips.

5. The _____ lets you choose between the Help topics available online and the Help topics installed on your computer offline.
   a. Connection Status menu
   b. Connecting Status menu
   c. Connection Status Online menu
   d. Connection Status Offline menu

6. Which command would you use to save a document for the first time?
   a. Save
   b. Save As
   c. Save for the first time
   d. Either a or b

7. When you open new documents in Word, the program names them with a(n) _____ determined by the number of files opened during that session.
   a. chronological number
   b. odd number
   c. even number
   d. decimal number

8. Which of the following options would you use when saving a document with a new filename?
   a. Save
   b. Save As
   c. Ctrl+S
   d. Either a or b

9. Which of the following is an acceptable format for a business letter?

   a. Block style with mixed punctuation

   b. Semi-block style

   c. All text keyed to the left of the margin

   d. Block style with open punctuation

   e. Both a and d

10. Which of the following allows you to access the Help command?

   a. F1

   b.

   c. some dialog boxes

   d. All of the above

Competency Assessment

Project 1-1: Typing a Business Letter

You work for Proseware, Inc. and need to send a follow-up letter regarding price quotes. Key the letter in block style with mixed punctuation.

GET READY. LAUNCH Word if it is not already running.

1. Click the **File** tab, then click **Save As**. In the File name box, key *quotes*. Change the target location to the lesson folder on your USB flash drive and click **OK**.

2. At the insertion point, key **January 10, 20XX**.

3. Press **Enter** twice to create two blank lines.

4. Key the recipient's address as shown:

   Mr. David Pacheco (Press **Enter** once.)

   A. Datum Corporation (Press **Enter** once.)

   2133 Montana (Press **Enter** once.)

   El Paso, TX 79938 (Press **Enter** twice.)

5. Key the salutation **Dear Mr. Pacheco:**.

6. Press **Enter** once.

7. Key the body of the letter:

   It was our pleasure meeting with you last week to discuss quotes for the components you requested. As agreed upon, the specifications discussed will be provided to you once we receive final approval from you.

8. Press **Enter** once.

9. Key **At Proseware, Inc., we appreciate your business**.

10. Press **Enter** once.

11. Key the closing **Sincerely,**.

12. Press the **Enter** key twice.

13. Key **Joe Villanueva**.

14. Proof your document carefully.

15. Click the **File** tab, then click **Save**. The updated version of the letter will be saved with the same filename in the lesson folder on your USB flash drive.

PAUSE. LEAVE the document open for the next project.

Project 1-2: Printing a Document

After proofing the letter you just wrote, you are ready to print copies of the document.

GET READY. LAUNCH Word if it is not already running.

1. Use the *quotes* document you created in Project 1-1.
2. Click the File tab, then click Print. In the Copies section of the Print options area, click the up arrow to change the number of copies from 1 to 2.
3. Click the Print icon.
4. Click the File tab, then click Save.
5. Click the File tab, then click Close.

PAUSE. LEAVE Word open for the next project.

Proficiency Assessment

Project 1-3: Creating a Job Responsibilities Document

Your supervisor, Leonard Lachmann, has asked you to key your job duties and responsibilities into a new document.

GET READY. LAUNCH Word if it is not already running.

1. Click the File tab, then click the New command. Blank document is selected. Click Create to open a new blank document.
2. Click the File tab, then click Save As. In the File name box, key *jobresponsibilities*. Change the target location to the lesson folder on your USB flash drive and click OK.
3. Key October 4, 20XX. Press Enter twice.
4. Key Duties & Responsibilities: Press Enter once.
5. Key the following paragraphs and press Enter once after each paragraph:

    Manage a variety of user experience functions, including programming and promotions

    Manage the online customer experience by creating new site features and maintaining site usability

    Define the website's look and feel

    Partner with the Director of Technology on project planning

    Analyze site usage, feedback, and research

    Improve website experience and performance

    Manage a team of seven user-experience specialists, including graphic designers, information architects, copywriters, and developers

6. Proof your document carefully.
7. Click the File tab, then Save. The updated file will be saved with the same filename in the lesson folder on your USB flash drive.

PAUSE. LEAVE the document open for the next project.

Project 1-4: Saving in Different Formats

Now, you want to save your job responsibilities document in several different file formats.

GET READY. LAUNCH Word if it is not already running.

1. Use the *jobresponsibilities* document that is open from Project 1-3.
2. Click the File tab, then click Save As. In the Save As type box, click the drop-down arrow and choose Rich Text Format (*.rtf). Change the target location to the lesson folder on your USB flash drive and click Save.

3. Click the **File** tab, then **Save As**. In the Save As type box, click the drop-down arrow and choose **XPS Document (*.xps)**. Your USB flash drive is already identified as the target location. Click **Save**. The XPS Viewer will open by default; click the **Close** button.

4. Click the **File** tab and close the jobresponsibilities.XPS document.

5. Convert the jobresponsibilities.rtf document to the Word 2010 file format. To do so, click the **File** tab, then click **Convert**. Click **OK**.

6. Click the **File** tab, then **Save As**. In the File name box, key *jobresponsibilities_update*. Click **Save**. The document is saved on your USB flash drive with a new filename.

7. Click the **File** tab, then **CLOSE** the document.

PAUSE. LEAVE Word open for the next project.

Mastery Assessment

@ The *menu* file for this lesson is available on the book companion website or in WileyPLUS.

Project 1-5: Saving a Word Document as a Web Page

Your coworker at the Grand Coffee Shop has been working on a new menu for the shop. She asks you to review it before saving it as a Web page.

GET READY. LAUNCH Word if it is not already running.

1. Click the **File** tab, then **Open**. Change the target location from the default to your USB flash drive.

2. **OPEN** *menu* from the data files for this lesson.

3. **SAVE** the document *menu* as a Web Page (*.htm) file in the lesson folder on your USB flash drive. Then, **CLOSE** the file.

PAUSE. LEAVE Word open for the next project.

@ The *schedulememo* file for this lesson is available on the book companion website or in WileyPLUS.

Project 1-6: Completing a Memo

You need to open and complete a partially composed memo to the members of your neighborhood's welcoming committee.

GET READY. LAUNCH Word if it is not already running.

1. **OPEN** *schedulememo* from the data files for this lesson.

2. Leave two blank lines after the subject line and key the following:

Thank you for volunteering to be on the New Neighbor Welcoming Committee. Enclosed is the meeting and refreshment schedule for the next six months. See you in January!

Committee Members:

Mary Baker

Josie Camacho

Brian Clark

Dorothy Martinez

Hazel Loera

3. **SAVE** the document as *deschedulememo* in both **Word 2010 file format** and **PDF file format** in the lesson folder on your USB flash driver.

STOP. Close Word.

 **INTERNET READY**

Use Word Help to access online information about What's New in Word 2010. "Up to Speed with Word 2010" provides an online short course or a demo explaining the new features. Browse these or other topics in Word Help online.

Workplace *Ready*

SAVING A LETTER IN AN EARLIER VERSION OF WORD

You work for Tech Terrace Real Estate, where your job responsibilities include emailing home price listings to customers. You are aware that several customers have not upgraded from Office 2003; therefore, you would need to save the price documents as Word 97-2003 files or as PDF files so that these customers can open the documents.

Prepare a Block style letter to customers showing the price listing for five homes around town. Proof the letter carefully, then save it as a Word 97-2003 document and as a PDF.

LESSON SKILL MATRIX

Skill	Exam Objective	Objective Number
Changing and Organizing Document Views	Select zoom options.	1.1.1
	Split windows.	1.1.2
	Arrange windows.	1.1.3
	Arrange document views.	1.1.4
	Switch between windows.	1.1.5
	Open a document in a new window.	1.1.6
Navigating and Searching through a Document	Use the Navigation Pane.	2.2.1
	Use Go To.	2.2.2
	Use Browse by button.	2.2.3
	Use Highlight features.	2.2.4
	Set Find and Replace options.	2.2.5
Selecting, Replacing, and Deleting Text		
Cutting, Copying, and Pasting Text		

KEY TERMS

- copy
- cut
- Go To
- gridlines
- multi-selection
- Navigation Pane
- paste
- replace
- rulers
- scroll bar
- scroll box
- scroll buttons
- thumbnails
- wildcards

Star Bright Satellite Radio is the nation's leading satellite radio company. The company sells its subscription service to automobile owners, home listeners, and people on the go with portable satellite radios. The public relations department is responsible for promoting a favorable image of Star Bright Satellite Radio to the media, potential customers, and current customers. Microsoft Word 2010 is the perfect tool for viewing and searching through the department's many documents. In this lesson, you learn to navigate and view a document in Word.

SOFTWARE ORIENTATION

The View Tab

Word offers several different ways to view a document, locate text or objects quickly, and manipulate windows. After opening a document, you can access related commands on the View tab, shown in Figure 2-1. Use this figure as a reference throughout this lesson as well as the rest of the book.

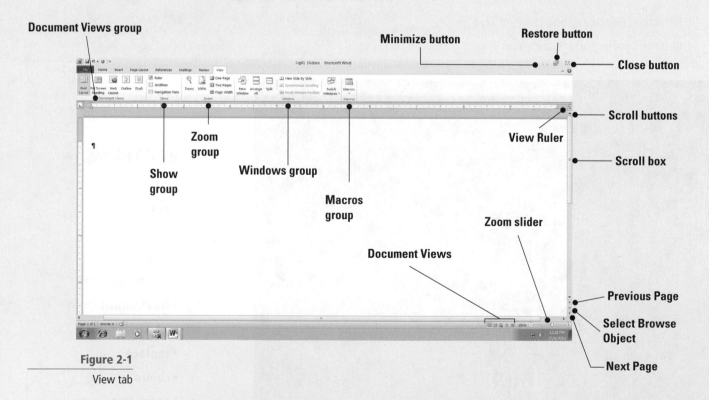

Figure 2-1

View tab

Word provides options to change a document's onscreen appearance by viewing the document in Full Screen, Web Layout, Outline, and Draft views. Adding horizontal rulers, vertical rulers, or gridlines; increasing or decreasing the document's page size; arranging the document windows; viewing the document side by side; or splitting the document can also change the view on the screen. In addition, the Navigation Pane provides options for browsing and conducting a search in a document.

CHANGING AND ORGANIZING DOCUMENT VIEWS

Word has a variety of options for opening an existing document and viewing a document. You can enable features to show gridlines, thumbnails, and rulers to help in navigating the document or you can zoom in or out. Word also allows you to open and arrange multiple document windows. You will learn about all of these features in this section.

Opening an Existing Document

Word enables you to open existing files in one of three forms: as an original document, as a copy of a document, or as a read-only document. In this exercise, you learn to open a document using the Open dialog box.

Clicking the Open command in the File tab produces the Open dialog box. You can use commands in the Open dialog box to open existing documents from target locations such as a USB flash drive, hard drive, network location, desktop, CD, DVD, or portable device. For the purpose of these exercises, the instructions assume that all data files are stored on your USB flash drive.

(X) Ref Opening and saving documents in Compatibility Mode was covered in Lesson 1.

STEP BY STEP **Open an Existing Document**

GET READY. Before you begin these steps, be sure to turn on and/or log on to your computer and start Word.

WileyPLUS Extra! features an online tutorial of this task.

1. Connect your USB flash drive to one of the USB ports on your computer.
2. Click the **File** tab.
3. Click **Open**. The Open dialog box appears. (See Figure 2-2, but note that your screen will not be identical to the figure.)

Figure 2-2

Open dialog box

Scroll bar – scroll down to locate your USB flash drive.

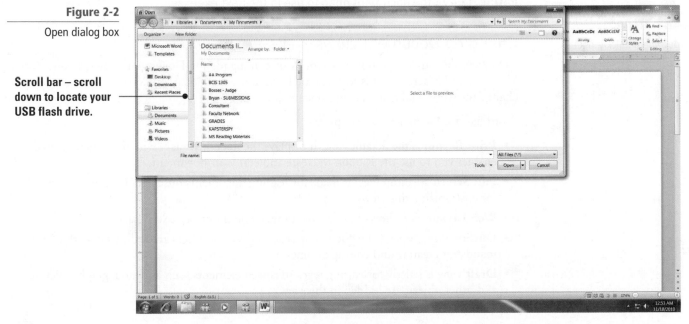

@ The *proposal* file for this lesson is available on the book companion website or in WileyPLUS.

4. Scroll down and locate the data files for this lesson on your USB flash drive. Double-click the **Lesson 2** folder to open it.
5. Locate and click *proposal* once.
6. Click the **Open** button. The document appears, as shown in Figure 2-3.

Figure 2-3

Open dialog box with subfolder

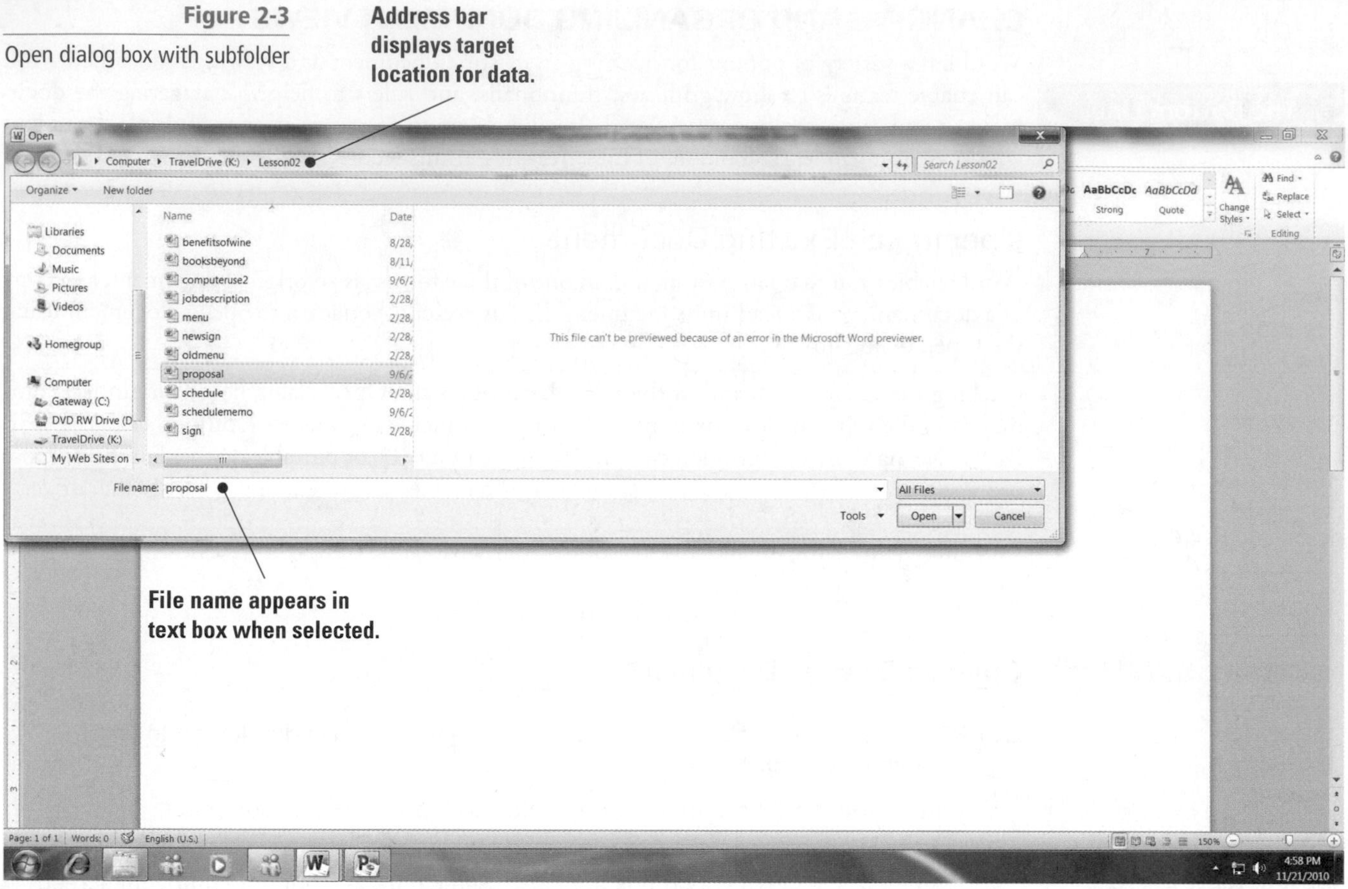

Address bar displays target location for data.

This file can't be previewed because of an error in the Microsoft Word previewer.

File name appears in text box when selected.

Another Way
To open a document quickly, double-click the filename.

PAUSE. LEAVE the document open to use in the next exercise.

Changing Document Views

The View tab on the Ribbon has groups of commands for Document Views, Show, Zoom, Window, and Macros. In this section, you learn to use the Document Views command group to change the way Word displays your document.

Word has five Document View options:

- **Print Layout** is the default view. It displays the document as it will look when printed and enables you to use the Ribbon to create and edit your document.
- **Full Screen Reading** view is made for reading documents onscreen. Options are available for customizing this view.
- **Web Layout** view shows how the document would look as a Web page.
- **Outline** view displays the document as an outline and offers an outline tab with commands for creating and editing outlines.
- **Draft** view is strictly for editing text. Advanced elements such as charts, graphs, pictures, and other objects are hidden in this view.

STEP BY STEP **Change Document Views**

USE the document that is open from the previous exercise.

1. Click the View tab to see the command groups that are available.

2. In the Document Views group, click the **Full Screen Reading** button to change to Full Screen Reading view, as shown in Figure 2-4.

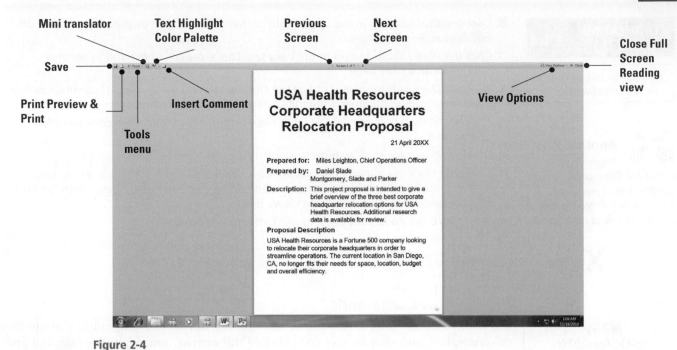

Figure 2-4

Full Screen Reading view

How do you change Word's view to Web Layout?

3. Click the **View Options** button in the upper-right corner of the screen to produce the View Options menu, as shown in Figure 2-5.

Figure 2-5

View Options menu

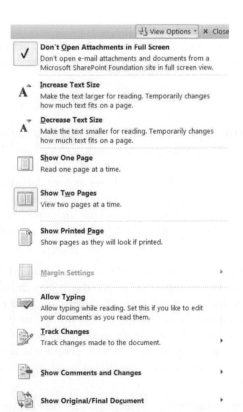

4. Choose **Increase Text Size**. The text size increases for better onscreen reading.

5. Click **View Options** again, then click **Show Two Pages**. Two pages of the document are displayed.

Another Way
The view com-
mands are also accessible in
the View button portion of
the status bar, located on the
lower-right side of the screen.

6. Click the Close button in the upper-right corner of the screen or press Esc to turn off Full Screen Reading view.

7. Click the Web Layout button in the View tab. This view will allow you to see the document as a Web page.

8. Click the Outline button, and notice the Outline tab and the groups of commands that appear for editing outlines. Click the Close Outline View button.

9. Click the View tab, then click the Draft view button. This view is typically used for editing text.

10. Click the Print Layout view button.

11. Note that the View options buttons are also available on the status bar at the bottom right of your screen. Click each button and compare the resulting views with the views you accessed from the Document Views tab.

PAUSE. LEAVE the document open to use in the next exercise.

(X) Ref

Lesson 12 covers using Outline View in master documents.

Using Show Commands

NEW
to Office 2010

The Show command group offers options for displaying various onscreen features that can help you create, edit, and navigate your document. In this exercise, you display the ruler and grid-lines. You also use the Navigation Pane to browse by headings and by page and to search for text.

Rulers are measuring tools to align text, graphics, and other elements used within a docu-ment. The top and bottom margins of a document can be easily adjusted manually using the vertical scroll bar. The horizontal ruler can be used to change a document's first-line indent,

hanging indent, and left and right indents. The markers display on the ruler as hanging

indent , left indent , and right indent . Manual tab settings can be set on the

horizontal ruler without launching the dialog box.

Gridlines provide a grid of vertical and horizontal lines that help you align graphics and other objects in your documents. Gridlines are displayed only in Print Layout view.

(X) Ref

Tabs are discussed in greater detail in Lesson 4.

NEW
to Office 2010

The **Navigation Pane** appears in the left side of the window when you select its com-mand in the Show group. The Navigation Pane has three tabs. The first tab, Browse Head-ings in your document, displays the structure of your document by levels based on the document's headings. The second tab, Browse Pages in your document, displays **thumbnails—** tiny images of your document pages. The third tab, Browse the results from the current search, displays a list of search results when you have used the Navigation Pane's search tool (marked by a search box and magnifying glass icon) to look for particular text or ob-jects in your document.

The search box lists the text or objects found in the document in the order those elements appear in the document. For example, the search boxes may indicate that the first instance of a word appears on page five, the next instance appears on page eight, and so on. The docu-ment appears highlighted in yellow and the text is bolded in the *Browse the results from the current search* tab. In the first tab, *Browse the headings in your document*, the section that has the found instance will appear highlighted. In the second tab, *Browse Pages in your document*, the thumbnail instances found will appear highlighted in yellow. To clear the search box, click the X in that box.

In this exercise, you learn to use show commands. The Navigation Pane will be discussed later in this lesson.

Use Show Commands

USE the document that is open from the previous exercise.

1. In the Show command group, click the **Ruler** check box to insert a check mark and activate the command. The horizontal and vertical rulers appear.
2. Click the **Gridlines** check box. A grid appears behind text on the page, as shown in Figure 2-6.

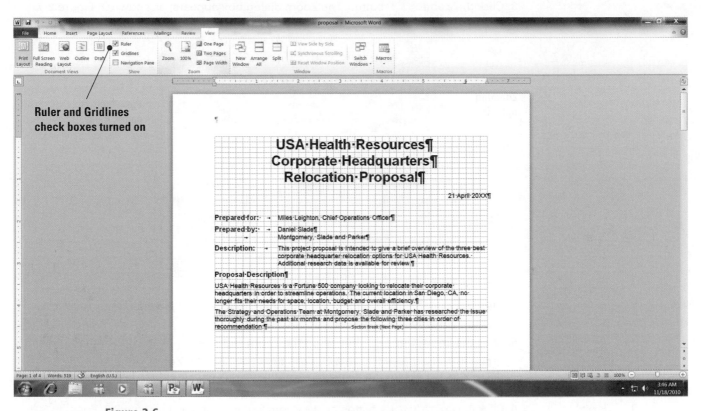

Figure 2-6

Gridlines and rulers

Another Way
You also can display the Ruler by clicking the View Ruler icon that is located on the right side of the screen above the vertical scroll bar.

3. Click the **Gridlines** check box to remove check marks.
4. Click the **Ruler** check box to remove the rulers from view.

PAUSE. LEAVE the document open to use in the next exercise.

Using Zoom

The Zoom group of commands lets you zoom in to get a closer view of a page or zoom out to see more of the document at a smaller size. These commands also enable you to determine how many document pages Word displays within a single screen. In this exercise, you use the Zoom commands to view one or two pages; you also use the Zoom slider in the status bar to increase or decrease the size of the displayed image.

Within the Zoom group, the Page Width button expands your document to fit the width of the window. The Zoom button launches the Zoom dialog box, where you have more options for zooming in and out. For instance, you can enter a specific number in the percent box to modify the view. Similarly, in the Zoom to section, you can expand the document by clicking a specific zoom amount up to 200%. The preview area shows how the document will appear on screen. The Zoom slider can also be used to zoom in and out; this slider is located in the bottom right of your screen on the status bar.

STEP BY STEP   **Use Zoom**

USE the document that is open from the previous exercise.

1. Click the One Page button in the Zoom command group to display one entire page on the screen.

2. Click the Two Pages button to switch to a display of two pages.

3. Click the Zoom button. The Zoom dialog box appears, as shown in Figure 2-7.

Figure 2-7

Zoom dialog box

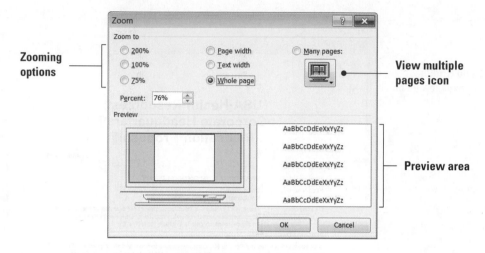

Zooming options

View multiple pages icon

Preview area

4. Click the radio button beside 200% in the Zoom to area of the dialog box, then click OK. The document image enlarges to twice its full size.

5. Click the Zoom Out ⊖ button on the Zoom slider, which is located at the right end of the status bar (see Figure 2-8). Each time you click the Zoom Out button, Word decreases the size of the displayed portion of your document by 10%. Click until the Zoom Out indicator displays 60%.

6. Click the Zoom In ⊕ button on the Zoom Slider, as shown in Figure 2-8. Zoom to 80%.

Figure 2-8

The Zoom In and Zoom Out buttons on the Zoom slider

Zoom slider

Zoom Out   **Zoom In**

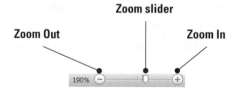

7. Drag the Zoom slider all the way to the left; Word reduces the document to thumbnail size.

8. Now, in the Zoom command group on the View tab, click the Page Width button. The document display expands to the width of the window.

9. Finally, in the Zoom command group, click the 100% button to return document to its normal size.

PAUSE. LEAVE the document open to use in the next exercise.

 Another Way
You can also click the percentage displayed to the left of the Zoom slider to open the Zoom dialog box.

Changing Window Views

The commands in the Window command group enable you to open and arrange multiple document windows. In this exercise, you learn to manipulate your screen by creating a second document in a new window, arranging multiple open documents on one screen, splitting a single document to view different parts, viewing multiple documents side by side, and switching between windows.

The commands in the Window command group are as follows:

- The **New Window** button opens a new window displaying the current document; this window shows the document name in the title bar followed by the number 2. Each new window you open in the same document receives a chronologically numbered name.

- The **Arrange All** button displays two or more windows on the screen at the same time. This is useful when comparing documents or when using information from multiple documents.

- The **Split** command divides one document window into two windows that scroll independently. This enables you to view two parts of a single document at the same time.

- The **View Side by Side** button allows you to view two documents next to each other. When you are viewing documents side by side, you can use the **Synchronous Scrolling** command to link the scrolling of the two documents so that you move through both at the same time. The **Reset Window Position** command repositions two side-by-side documents to appear equally sized on the screen.

- The **Switch Windows** button allows you to select which document will be the active document (the document that is ready for editing). The name of the active document appears on the title bar.

On occasion, you may need to move a window out of the way without exiting the associated application. This is where the three buttons in the upper-right corner of the Word screen come in handy. The Minimize button ▬ minimizes the window display—in other words, the window disappears and is replaced with an icon on the status bar. The Restore button 🗗 returns a document to its previous size by minimizing or maximizing its display. Finally, the Close button ✕ closes the window.

STEP BY STEP   **Change Window Views**

CERTIFICATION
READY?   **1.1.2**

How do you split a window?

USE the document that is open from the previous exercise.

1. In the Window command group, click the **New Window** button. A new window with **proposal:2** in the document title bar appears and becomes the active document.

2. In the Window command group, click the **Switch Windows** button. A menu of open windows appears, as shown in Figure 2-9.

Figure 2-9

Switch Windows button
and menu

CERTIFICATION
READY?   **1.1.3**

How do you arrange windows
to view two documents
side by side?

CERTIFICATION
READY?   **1.1.3**

How do you use
synchronous scrolling in the
side-by-side view?

CERTIFICATION
READY?   **1.1.4**

How do you arrange document
views?

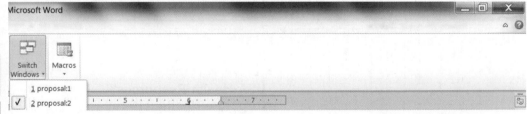

3. In the Switch Windows drop-down menu, click **proposal:1**. The original document becomes the active document.

4. Click the **Arrange All** button. Word displays the two windows, one above the other, on your screen, as shown in Figure 2-10.

5. Click the **View Side by Side** button to arrange the windows beside each other on the screen.

6. Note that **Synchronous Scrolling** is on by default. Place your insertion point on the slider in the vertical scroll bar and press the left mouse button as you move the slider up and down to scroll through the documents; notice that both scroll simultaneously.

7. On the document title bar, click the **proposal:2** document; this now becomes the active document.

8. Click the **Synchronous Scrolling** button to turn off that feature. Place your insertion point on the vertical scroll bar and scroll down; notice that the **proposal:2** document is now scrolling independently.

Document Title bar

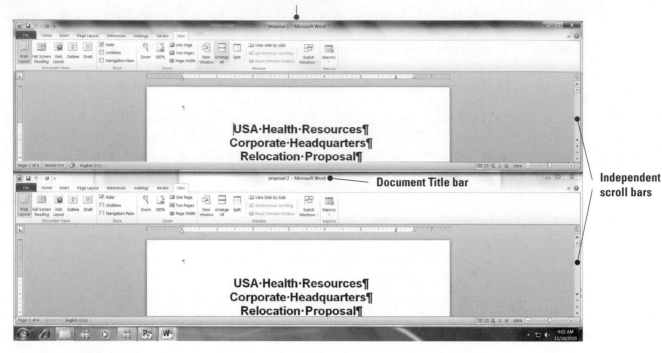

Figure 2-10

Two windows displayed using
the Arrange All command

Document Title bar

**Independent
scroll bars**

9. Click the **Close** button to close the ***proposal:2*** document.

10. Click the **Maximize** button on the ***proposal:1*** document to fill the screen.

11. Click the **Split** button. Notice you now have a horizontal split bar and a double-sided arrow. Position the split bar below Relocation Proposal and click the mouse button. The document window splits in two and the **Split** button changes to a **Remove Split** button (see Figure 2-11).

Figure 2-11

Split window and Remove
Split button

Split changes to Remove Split

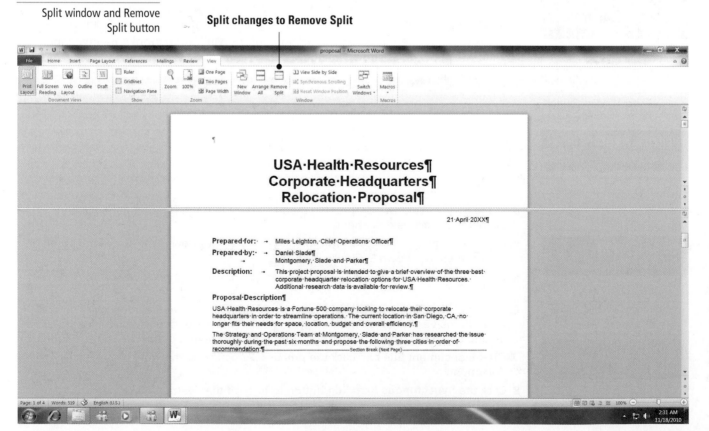

12. Click **Remove Split**.

13. Click the **Minimize** button, as shown in Figure 2-12. The document minimizes to become an icon in the Windows task bar at the bottom of the screen, and the desktop appears.

14. Click the *proposal* document's icon in the task bar to maximize the document back on the screen.

15. Click the **Restore** button to return the document to its minimized view.

16. Position the mouse pointer on the lower-right corner of the document window where you see the pattern of dots. Your mouse pointer becomes a double-sided arrow, or handle, as shown in Figure 2-13.

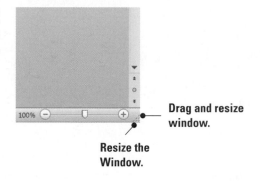

Drag and resize window.

Resize the Window.

17. Click and drag the handle toward the middle of the screen to decrease the size of the window.

18. Click the sizing corner again and drag it to the lower-right corner of the Word screen to increase the size of the window. Drag until the window fills the screen.

PAUSE. LEAVE the document open to use in the next exercise.

NAVIGATING AND SEARCHING THROUGH A DOCUMENT

As you already learned, the Navigation Pane contains commands for moving and searching through a document. You also can use Find command options, the mouse, scroll bars, and various keystroke and keyboard shortcut commands to navigate through Word documents. In this section, you practice using the mouse and scroll bar, keystroke commands, the Navigation Pane, and a number of command group commands to move quickly through a document; search for specific text, graphics, or other document elements; and remove or replace those elements.

Scroll bars allow a user to move up or down or side to side within a document. In Word, a vertical scroll bar appears on the right side of the document window, as shown in Figure 2-14; if the window view is larger than the viewing area, a horizontal scroll bar also appears at the bottom of the window to allow you to scroll left and right across the width of the document. You can click the **scroll buttons** to move up or down one line at a time, or you can click and hold a scroll button to scroll more quickly. You can also click and drag the **scroll box** to move through a document even faster or just click the scroll box to see a ScreenTip displaying your position in the document.

At the bottom of the vertical scroll bar, you can click the Previous Page button to move back to the previous page or click the Next Page button to move to the following page. Clicking the Select Browse Object button produces a pop-up menu displaying a number of different command buttons that enable you to jump to a new location within the document. In addition to Go To and Find, the commands in this box enable you to browse by field, endnote, footnote, comment, section, page, edits, headings, graphic, or tables.

Figure 2-14

Scroll bar, scroll box, and scroll buttons

- Scroll Up button
- Scroll box
- Scroll Up button
- Previous Page
- Select Browse Object
- Next Page

Using the Mouse and Scroll Bar to Navigate

Using the mouse in combination with the scroll bar is a simple way to scroll through a document.

STEP BY STEP   **Use the Mouse and Scroll Bar to Navigate**

USE the document that is open from the previous exercise.

1. Click the Scroll Down button to scroll down one line at a time.
2. Click and hold the Scroll Down button until you scroll all the way to the end of the document.
3. Position the mouse pointer on the scroll box. Click and hold to see a ScreenTip identifying your current location in the document (see Figure 2-15).
4. Drag the scroll box all the way to the top of the scroll bar; the view quickly scrolls to the beginning of the document.
5. Click the Select Browse Object button. A menu appears with various commands you can use to browse for specific text or elements within your document (see Figure 2-16).

Figure 2-15

Scroll box ScreenTip

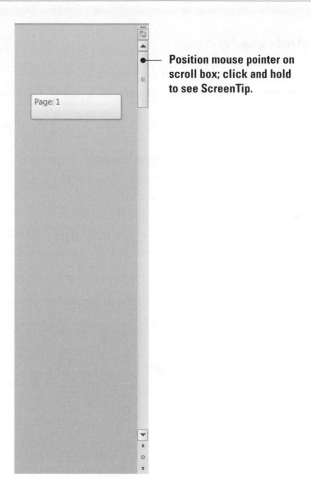

Position mouse pointer on
scroll box; click and hold
to see ScreenTip.

Page: 1

Figure 2-16

Select Browse Object menu

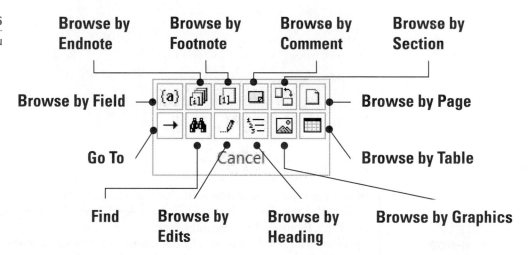

Browse by Endnote

Browse by Footnote

Browse by Comment

Browse by Section

Browse by Field

Browse by Page

Go To

Browse by Table

Find

Browse by Edits

Browse by Heading

Browse by Graphics

6. Move the mouse pointer over each button to see its name appear in the display box.

7. Click in a blank space in the document to remove the menu.

PAUSE. LEAVE the document open to use in the next exercise.

Using Keystrokes to Navigate

The arrow keys and other keyboard commands can also help you move through a document.

Use Keystrokes to Navigate

USE the document that is open from the previous exercise.

1. In the first line of the body of the document, position the insertion point before the U in USA.
2. On the keyboard, press the Right arrow key to move the insertion point one character to the right.
3. Press the Left arrow key to move one character to the left.
4. Press the Down arrow key to move down one line.
5. Press the End key to move to the end of the line.
6. Press the Page Down key to move down one screen.
7. Press the Ctrl+Home keys to move to the beginning of the document.

PAUSE. LEAVE the document open to use in the next exercise.

Table 2-1 lists these and other shortcut keys and keystroke commands you can use to navigate through a document.

Table 2-1

Keyboard shortcuts for navigating a document

Shortcut Key	Related Move
Left arrow	One character to the left
Right arrow	One character to the right
Up arrow	Up one line
Down arrow	Down one line
End	To the end of the line
Home	To the beginning of the line
Page up	Up one screen
Page down	Down one screen
Ctrl+Page down	Down one page
Ctrl+Page up	Up one page
Ctrl+Home	To beginning of the document
Ctrl+End	To end of the document

Searching within a Document

NEW
to Office 2010

Word's Find command is now located in the Navigation Pane in the Show group on the View tab, as well as on the Home tab in the Editing group. Either of these approaches will open the Navigation Pane. By using the Navigation Pane, you can easily locate specific text, graphics, objects, and equations within a document. The document will contain highlighted text, and the Navigation Pane will display the results in a yellow border. The third tab, Browse the results from your current search, will place the results in the order they appear in the document. In this exercise, you learn to use the Navigation Pane to search for every occurrence of a specific word within a document.

In the Home tab on the Editing group, the drop-down arrow by the Find button displays a menu that contains the Find, Advanced Find, Replace, and Go To commands. The Find command opens the Navigation Pane; the Advanced Find command opens the Find and Replace dialog box with Find as the active tab; the Replace command opens the Find and Replace dialog box with Replace as the active tab; and the Go To command opens the same dialog box with Go To as the active tab.

Figure 2-17

Navigation Pane displaying
additional options

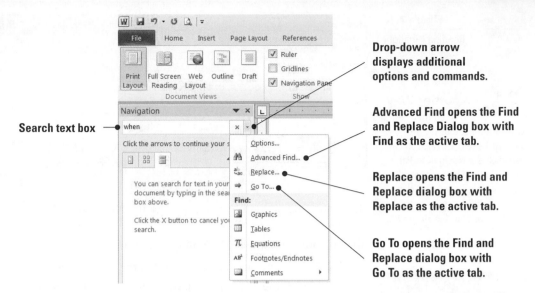

Search text box

Drop-down arrow
displays additional
options and commands.

Advanced Find opens the Find
and Replace Dialog box with
Find as the active tab.

Replace opens the Find and
Replace dialog box with
Replace as the active tab.

Go To opens the Find and
Replace dialog box with
Go To as the active tab.

To highlight every occurrence of a particular word or phrase in your document, you must activate Advanced Find. To do so, click the drop-down arrow by the Search text box, as shown in Figure 2-17, then click Advanced Find. The Find and Replace dialog box opens; within that box, key your desired word or phrase, then click the drop-down arrow on the Reading Highlight button and select Highlight All. When you close the Find and Replace dialog box, each instance of your desired word or phrase is highlighted in the document. To clear all occurrences of highlighted text, return to the Advanced Find options, click the Reading Highlight button, and then select Clear Highlighting.

STEP BY STEP   **Use the Navigation Pane to Search for Text in a Document**

USE the document that is open from the previous exercise.

1. Click the **View** tab; then, in the Show command group, click the **Navigation Pane** check box. The Navigation Pane opens.

2. Key **relocation** in the Search text box; the text is highlighted in the document and in the Browse Headings, Browse Pages, and Browse Results tabs of the Navigation Pane.

3. Click the third tab, **Browse the results from your current search**. Note that the found text is bolded, and it appears in the order of its occurrence in the document.

4. Click the first tab, **Browse the headings in your document**, and note highlighted headings. Then click the second tab, **Browse the pages in your document**, and note the highlighted found text in the thumbnails.

5. Click the **Browse the pages in your document** tab and click each **thumbnail**. Use the scroll bar to navigate to thumbnail four, then click that thumbnail.

6. Click the **X** in the Search text box to end your search. Press **Ctrl+Home** to move the insertion point to the beginning of the document.

7. Click the **magnifying glass** icon on the right side of the Navigation Pane box to produce a list of available options.

8. Click the **Advanced Find** button. The Find and Replace dialog box opens.

9. The word "relocation" should be in the Find what text box; click the **Find Next** button. Click the **Reading Highlight** button to **Highlight All** instances of this word. Then click **Close** (see Figure 2-18).

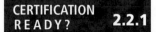

CERTIFICATION READY?   **2.2.1**

How do you browse by heading using the Navigation Pane?

CERTIFICATION READY?   **2.2.1**

How do you browse by page using the Navigation Pane?

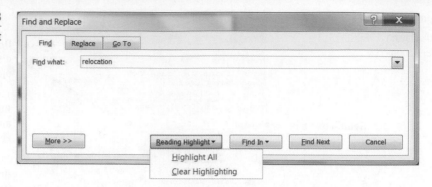

Figure 2-18
Reading Highlight

Another Way
To open the Navigation Pane using the keyboard, press Ctrl+F. You can also click the Navigation Pane button in the Show group of the View tab, or you can click the drop-down arrow in the Editing group on the Home tab.

Take Note

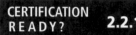

CERTIFICATION READY? **2.2.1**

How do you use the Navigation Pane to search and review your results?

CERTIFICATION READY? **2.2.4**

How do you highlight text in a document using the Navigation Pane?

10. In the Show command group, click the Navigation Pane check box to turn off this pane.

To end your search, click the X in the text box.

11. **SAVE** the document as *proposal_1* in the lesson folder of your USB flash drive. **PAUSE. LEAVE** the document open to use in the next exercise.

For more search options, click the More>> button in the Find and Replace dialog box. In the Search Options area that appears, you can choose additional criteria to refine the search process—for example, you can opt to match case or whole words only. You can also use **wildcard** characters to find words or phrases that contain specific letters or combinations of letters. Simply key a question mark (?) to represent a single character—for example, keying **b?t** will find *bat, bet, bit,* and *but*. Similarly, key an asterisk (*) to represent a string of characters—for example, **m*t** will find *mat, moment,* or even *medium format*.

Within the Find and Replace dialog box, you can click the Format button to find text with specific formatting, such as a particular font, paragraph setting, or style. You can also click the Special button to find special elements in a document, such as fields, footnote marks, or section breaks.

Replacing Text in a Document

Located on the Home tab in the Editing group, the Replace command opens the Find and Replace dialog box. You can use the Replace command to replace one word or phrase with another. You can also use the Find and Replace command to search for and **replace** formatting—such as a specific font color, bolding, or italics. It is also possible to search for and replace special characters and document elements such as page breaks and tabs. In this exercise, you learn to search for and replace a word with a particular type of formatting.

STEP BY STEP **Replace Text in a Document**

USE the document that is open from the previous exercise.

1. Place the insertion point at the beginning of the document by pressing **Ctrl+Home**.
2. Click the **Home** tab to make it active. In the Editing group, click the **Replace** button; the Find and Replace dialog box opens.
3. Click the **More>>** button to review the options, then click the **<<Less** button to hide them.
4. In the Find what box, key **Montgomery, Slade and Parker**. (If "relocation" appears in the Find what box, select it and press **Delete**, then key in the new search string.)
5. In the Replace with box, key **Becker, Steele and Castillo**.

Another Way
To open the Replace tab in the Find and Replace dialog box using the keyboard, press Ctrl+H.

6. Click **Find Next**. Word searches for the first occurrence of the phrase **Montgomery, Slade and Parker** and highlights it.
7. Click **Replace All**. Word searches for all occurrences of the phrase Montgomery, Slade and Parker and replaces them with Becker, Steele and Castillo. Word then displays a message revealing how many replacements were made, as shown in Figure 2-19.

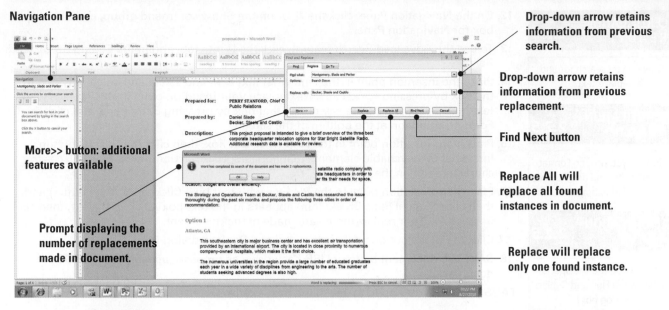

Navigation Pane

Drop-down arrow retains
information from previous
search.

Drop-down arrow retains
information from previous
replacement.

More>> button: additional
features available

Find Next button

Replace All will
replace all found
instances in document.

Prompt displaying the
number of replacements
made in document.

Replace will replace
only one found instance.

Figure 2-19

Find and Replace message

8. Click **OK**.

9. Position the insertion point at the beginning of the document. Click the **View** tab; then, in the Show command group, click the **Navigation Pane** check box. Click the drop-down arrow or magnifier so that the ScreenTip displays Find Options and additional search commands, then click **Replace**. In the Find what text box, key **Becker, Steele and Castillo**; then, in the Replace with text box, key **Montgomery, Slade and Parker**. Keep your insertion point in the Replace text box.

10. Click the **More>>** button to expand the dialog box to include additional search and replace options (see Figure 2-20).

11. Click the **Format** button and select **Font** from the drop-down list; the Find Font dialog box appears. In the Font area, use the scroll bar to scroll to Garamond, and then click to select it. In the Font Style area, select **Bold Italics**, size 14. Click the **Font Color** drop-down arrow, then select **dark red** in the Standard Colors chart and click **OK**. Below the Replace With text box, you will see the format selections. Click **Replace All**; two replacements will be completed. Click **OK**, then **Close**.

Figure 2-20

Find and Replace dialog box
with Search Options

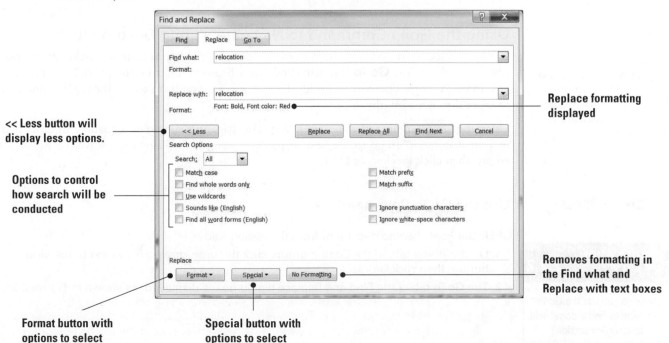

<< Less button will
display less options.

Replace formatting
displayed

Options to control
how search will be
conducted

Removes formatting in
the Find what and
Replace with text boxes

Format button with
options to select

Special button with
options to select

CERTIFICATION READY? 2.2.5

How do you search for and replace text?

12. On the Navigation Pane, click the **X**, or on the Show command group, click the check box for Navigation Pane.

13. To use the Advanced Search feature, click the **Home** tab, and in the Editing group, click **Replace**.

14. Place the insertion point in the Find what text box, and select and delete any text in the box by pressing **Backspace**. Next, place your insertion point in the Replace with text box, select and delete any text in that box by pressing **Backspace**, and click the **No Formatting** button at the bottom of the screen.

CERTIFICATION READY? 2.2.5

How do you use the Format button in the Find and Replace dialog box?

15. Place your insertion point in the Find what text box, then click the **Special** button. In the list of searchable elements that appears, click **Section Break**; Word places the characters **(^b)** in the text box.

16. Place your insertion point in the Replace with text box. Click the **Special** button and then click **Manual Page Break**; **(^m)** appears in the text box. Click **Find Next**, then click **Replace All**. Four replacements are made in the document.

CERTIFICATION READY? 2.2.5

How do you use the Special button in the Find and Replace dialog box?

17. Click the **Close** button to close the Find and Replace dialog box.

18. **SAVE** the document on your USB flash drive as *proposal_update*, then **CLOSE** the document.

PAUSE. LEAVE Word open to use in the next exercise.

Take Note

> Section breaks are covered in Lesson 5.

You can use the Find and Replace tool to replace specific punctuation within a document. For instance, say you pressed the spacebar twice at the end of each sentence and you would like to replace each set of two spaces with only one space. In the Find What text box, press the **spacebar** twice; then, in the Replace with text box, press the **spacebar** once and click the Replace All button. Upon doing this, Word replaces all instances of double spacing with single spaces.

When replacing text, you can confirm each replacement to make sure it is correct by clicking Replace instead of Replace All.

Troubleshooting If you experience problems when using the Replace command to replace formatting or one of the special elements, display the Find and Replace dialog box again. Review the Find what text box for correct spelling or correct element. Below the Replace with text box is the Formatting to replace text. For instance, if you are replacing search text with a color and bold as the style, below the Replace with text box, you will see *Font: Bold, Font color: Red* (see Figure 2-20).

Using the Go To Command to Navigate a Long Document

In a longer document, you may need to move through the document more quickly than is possible by scrolling. The **Go To** command and Select Browse Object button provide ways to navigate through longer documents quickly. In this exercise, you learn to use the Go To command to move through a lengthy document.

The ***booksbeyond*** file for this lesson is available on the book companion website or in WileyPLUS.

Using the Go To command will jump to a specific page, table, graphic, equation, or other item in your document. To go to the next or previous item of the same type, leave the Enter box empty, then click Previous or Next.

STEP BY STEP **Use the Go To Command**

OPEN the ***booksbeyond*** document from the lesson folder.

1. On the **Home** tab, in the Editing group, click the drop-down arrow next to the Find button, then click **Go To**.

2. The GoTo tab of the Find and Replace dialog box is displayed, as shown in Figure 2-21.

CERTIFICATION READY? 2.2.2

How do you use the Go To command to find a page, field, heading, or section?

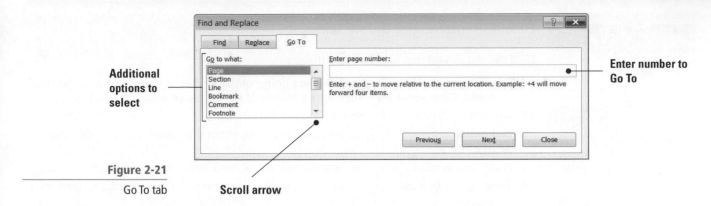

Additional options to select

Enter number to Go To

Figure 2-21

Go To tab

Scroll arrow

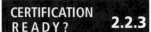

CERTIFICATION
READY?   2.2.3

How do you use the Select
Browse Object command?

Another Way
To open the Go
To tab in the Find and Replace
dialog box using the keyboard,
press Ctrl+G or use the Select
Browse Object command.

3. In the Go to what box, Page is selected by default. In the Enter page number box, key 6, then click Go To. The insertion point moves to page 6 of the document.

4. In the Go to what box, select **Line**. In the Enter line number box, key **23**, then click **Go To**. The insertion point moves to line 23 in the document.

5. In the Go to what box, scroll down and select **Field**. In the Enter field name box, Any Field displays. Click **Next**. The insertion point moves to the field. Click **Close**.

6. In the bottom-right corner of the vertical scroll bar, locate and click the **Select Browse Object** command, then click the **Go To** command. The Find and Replace dialog appears.

7. Click the **Select Browse Object** command, then click the Find command and key **books**. Click **Find Next** until all occurrences are found. A prompt will appear when Word has finished searching. Click **OK**.

8. Click the **Cancel** button to close the Find and Replace dialog box.

PAUSE. LEAVE the document open to use in the next exercise.

 Ref

Fields are described in Lesson 12.

Take Note   Word keeps track of the last three locations where you keyed or edited text. To go to a previous editing location in your document, press Shift+F5.

SELECTING, REPLACING, AND DELETING TEXT

The Bottom Line

Word offers a number of tools for selecting, deleting, and replacing text. You also can apply formatting to selected text. In this exercise, you use the mouse and keyboard to select text and delete it or replace it with new text.

Selecting, Replacing, and Deleting Text

You can delete text in Word documents by pressing the Backspace key to delete characters to the left of the insertion point, pressing the Delete key to delete characters to the right of the insertion point, or selecting text and pressing either the Delete key or Backspace key. In this exercise, you learn to select and delete text and to key in replacement text. You also practice using the Undo and Redo buttons in the Quick Access Toolbar.

The **multi-selection** feature of Word enables you to select multiple text items that are not adjacent. For example, to select every other line in a paragraph, select the first line, then press and hold the Ctrl key as you select the other lines by clicking the left mouse button. To replace text in a Word document, simply select the text, then key new text. To cancel a selection, click in any blank area of the document screen.

STEP BY STEP   Select, Replace, and Delete Text

USE the document that is open from the previous exercise.

1. Position your insertion point at the beginning of the first paragraph, to the left of the *B* in *Books*. Click and drag across until **Books and Beyond** is selected.

2. Key **B & B**. *Books and Beyond* is replaced with *B & B*.

3. In the first sentence of the second paragraph, position the insertion point after the word *understand*.

4. Press **Backspace** to delete the word *understand*, then key **realize**.

5. Scroll to the bottom of page one. Position the insertion point in any word in the last paragraph. Triple-click the mouse to select the entire paragraph.

6. Click in a blank part of the page, such as the margin, to deselect the paragraph. Then place your insertion point at the beginning of the last paragraph on the first page, beginning with *I understand if I have . . .* and click.

7. Move the pointer to the end of the sentence (*HR Department.*), press the **Ctrl** key, and click. The sentence is now selected.

8. Press **Backspace** to delete the sentence.

9. Click the **Undo** button in the Quick Access Toolbar to undo the action.

10. Click the **Redo** button in the Quick Access Toolbar to redo the action.

11. **SAVE** the document as ***booksbeyond_updates*** in the lesson folder on your USB flash drive.

PAUSE. LEAVE the document open to use in the next exercise.

Another Way
The Select button in the Editing command group of the Home tab lets you select all text in a document, select objects behind text, or select text with similar formatting.

As you've seen, when you position the mouse pointer to the left of the margin, it changes to a selection arrow that enables you to click to select the entire line to the right of the pointer. You then can drag down to continue selecting adjacent words, lines of text, or entire paragraphs. Table 2-2 lists this and other techniques for selecting text with the mouse.

Table 2-2

Selecting text with the mouse

To Select	Do This
Any amount of text	Click and drag across the text
A word	Double-click the word
A line	Click in the left margin with the mouse pointer
Multiple lines	Click and drag in the left margin
A sentence	Hold Ctrl and click anywhere in the sentence
A paragraph	Double-click in the left margin or triple-click in the paragraph
The entire document	Triple-click in the left margin

You also can use keyboard commands to select text. Table 2-3 shows various keyboard shortcuts you can press to select text.

Table 2-3	To Select	Key This
Selecting text with the keyboard	One character to the right	Shift+Right Arrow
	One character to the left	Shift+Left Arrow
	To the end of a word	Ctrl+Shift+Right Arrow
	To the beginning of a word	Ctrl+Shift+Left Arrow
	To the end of a line	Shift+End
	To the beginning of a line	Shift+Home
	To the end of a document	Ctrl+Shift+End
	To the beginning of a document	Ctrl+Shift+Home
	The entire document	Ctrl+A
	To the end of a paragraph	Ctrl+Shift+Down Arrow

CUTTING, COPYING, AND PASTING TEXT

The Bottom Line

It is often necessary to copy or remove text from one location in a document and place it in another. When you **cut** text, Word removes it from the original location and places the deleted text in the Clipboard collection. When you **copy** text, Word places a duplicate copy in the Clipboard. The **Paste** command then pastes text from the Clipboard to a new location in either the original document or a new document. In this exercise, you learn two different ways to copy and move text—using the Clipboard and using the mouse.

NEW to Office 2010

Entries placed in the Clipboard can be placed anywhere in a document by positioning the insertion point in the new location then selecting one of the three Paste options shown in Table 2-4 and Figure 2-22.

Table 2-4	Paste Option	Description	Sample Item Placed on Clipboard	How Item Displays When Pasted
Paste option descriptions	Keep source formatting	Keeps the selected text with the original format, including hyperlinks	**FORMATTING WILEYPLUS.COM**	**FORMATTING WILEYPLUS.COM**
	Merge formatting	If the text contains fonts of different sizes and colors, the paste will produce black text with Calibri (Body) 12-point formatting	Paste	Paste
	Keep text only	Regardless of its font, size, and formatting, when pasted, the text will appear in 10-point Calibri (Body).	**College**	College

Copying and Moving Text with Clipboard Commands

The Clipboard enables you to cut or copy multiple items and paste them into any Office document. In this exercise, you learn to use the Clipboard command group on the Home tab to copy and move text.

Figure 2-22

Paste options

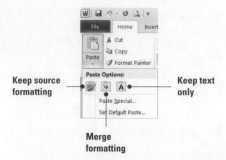

Keep source formatting

Merge formatting

Keep text only

Collected items stay on the Clipboard until all Office programs are closed or you click the Clear All button in the Clipboard task pane. The Clipboard holds up to 24 items; if another item is added, the first item is deleted from the Clipboard and the latest item is placed at the top of the list. Each entry in the Clipboard includes an icon representing the source Office program and a portion of copied text or a thumbnail of a copied graphic. By default, when text is selected, a message appears on the status bar showing how many words are selected and the total number of words in the document.

STEP BY STEP **Use the Clipboard to Copy and Move Text**

USE the document that is open from the previous exercise.

1. Select the **first paragraph** of the document.
2. On the Home tab, in the Clipboard group, click the **Cut** button.
3. Click to place the insertion point in front of the first character of the sentence that begins "*Only the president . . .*"
4. Click the **Clipboard** command group dialog box launcher to display the Clipboard task pane.
5. In the list of cut items, move your mouse pointer to the text you cut in step 2, and click the drop-down arrow to produce the menu shown in Figure 2-23.

Figure 2-23

Clipboard task pane options

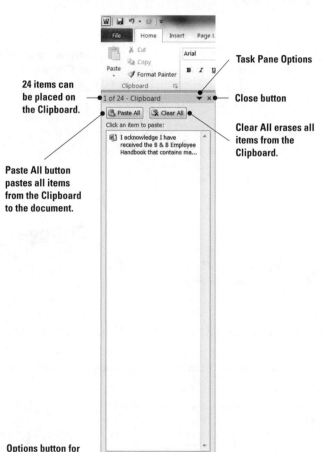

24 items can be placed on the Clipboard.

Task Pane Options

Close button

Clear All erases all items from the Clipboard.

Paste All button pastes all items from the Clipboard to the document.

Options button for displaying the Clipboard

 Another Way
To copy an item to the Clipboard using the keyboard, select the item, then press Ctrl+C. To cut a selected item using the keyboard, press Ctrl+X. To paste the item most recently collected on the Clipboard, click to locate the insertion point, then press Ctrl+V on the keyboard. To produce a pop-up menu containing Cut, Copy, and Paste commands, right-click in the document.

6. Click **Paste** to insert the text into the document in the new location.

7. Click the **Close** button on the Clipboard task pane.

PAUSE. LEAVE the document open to use in the next exercise.

Take Note   Your Clipboard task pane may look different depending on how many items have been collected.

The Options drop-down arrow at the bottom of the Clipboard task pane offers multiple options for displaying the Clipboard. Table 2-5 describes these options.

Table 2-5

Options for displaying the Clipboard

Option	Description
Show Office Clipboard Automatically	Automatically displays the Clipboard when copying.
Show Office Clipboard When Ctrl+C Pressed Twice	Automatically displays the Clipboard when you press Ctrl+C twice.
Collect Without Showing Office Clipboard	The Clipboard is not displayed when copying or cutting text.
Show Office Clipboard Icon on Taskbar	Displays the Clipboard icon in the status area of the system task bar when the Clipboard is active. Turned on by default.
Show Office Near Taskbar When Copying	Displays the "collected item" message when copying items to the Clipboard. Turned on by default.

Using the Mouse to Copy or Move Text

To move a selection of text, use your mouse to drag and drop the selection in a new location. Hold the Ctrl key while you drag to copy the text. When you are moving text by dragging, the pointer shows a box, and when you are copying text by dragging, the pointer shows a box with a plus sign (+). Text that you cut or copy using the mouse is not stored in the Clipboard collection.

STEP BY STEP   **Use the Mouse to Copy or Move Text**

USE the document that is open from the previous exercise.

1. Select the second paragraph on the first page, beginning with "*I acknowledge I have received . . .*"

2. Press the **Ctrl** key as you click, then drag the selected phrase and drop it above the last paragraph on the first page. The pointer shows a plus sign (+) as you drag, indicating that you are copying the selected text.

3. Click **Undo**.

4. Select the third paragraph, beginning with "*Only the president . . .*" Hold the left mouse button, and drag and drop the selected text to position it above the second paragraph on the first page. Notice the phrase is moved to the new location. Click **Undo**.

5. **SAVE** the document in the lesson folder on your USB flash drive.

CLOSE Microsoft Word.

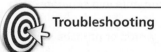 **Troubleshooting**   By default, drag-and-drop editing is turned on so that you can drag the pointer to move and copy text. This option can be turned on or off in Backstage view. To do so, click the File tab, then click Word Options. Click Advanced and, under Editing options, select or clear the Allow Text to Be Dragged and Dropped check box. (Advanced Word Options will be covered in depth in Lesson 14.)

SKILL SUMMARY

In This Lesson, You Learned How To:	Exam Objective	Objective Number
Change and organize document views	Select zoom options.	1.1.1
	Split windows.	1.1.2
	Arrange windows.	1.1.3
	Arrange document views.	1.1.4
	Switch between windows.	1.1.5
	Open a document in a new window.	1.1.5
Navigate and search through a document	Use the Navigation Pane.	2.2.1
	Use Go To.	2.2.2
	Use Browse by button.	2.2.3
	Use Highlight features.	2.2.4
	Set Find and Replace options.	2.2.5
Select, replace, and delete text		
Cut, copy, and paste text		

Knowledge Assessment

True/False

Circle T if the statement is true or F if the statement is false.

T F **1.** The New Window command launches a new window that contains the current document.

T F **2.** By selecting text, the user has the ability to change the font and font size, bolding, and deleting text.

T F **3.** Full Screen Reading view displays the document as it will look when printed.

T F **4.** The Zoom slider is located in the View menu.

T F **5.** The Synchronous Scrolling button is used when viewing documents side by side.

T F **6.** The Switch Windows command allows you to toggle between documents.

T F **7.** Double-clicking a word in a document will select the word.

T F **8.** When you key text in the search box while in the Navigation Pane, Word highlights this text by bolding the results in the document.

T F **9.** The Arrange All command places all open documents in a separate window on the screen.

T F **10.** You can use the Navigation Pane to search for words or phrases in a document.

Multiple Choice

Select the best response for the following statements.

1. Which Word feature enables you to select multiple pieces of text that are not next to each other?
   a. Multi-selection feature
   b. Multi-task feature
   c. Multi-select all text feature
   d. Ctrl+A feature

2. _____ are reduced-size versions of images.
   a. Thumbdrives
   b. Thumb documents
   c. Thumbnails
   d. Preview panes

3. The Split command will split a document:
   a. vertically.
   b. in a new window.
   c. side by side.
   d. horizontally.

4. In what view is Synchronous Scrolling active?
   a. Split
   b. Arrange All
   c. New Window
   d. View Side by Side

5. When Heading Styles have been applied to a document, the user has the option to navigate through the document using which tab on the Navigation Pane?
   a. Browse the headings
   b. Browse the pages
   c. Browse the results from your current search
   d. None of the above

6. Commands for replacing text with formatted text are located in the:
   a. Find and Replace dialog box.
   b. Advanced Options in the Navigation Pane.
   c. dialog box that opens when you press Ctrl+H.
   d. All of the above

7. The keyboard shortcut for finding text is:
   a. Ctrl+H.
   b. Ctrl+F.
   c. Ctrl+G.
   d. Ctrl+5.

8. The Replace command can be opened using:
   a. the Find and Replace dialog box.
   b. Ctrl+H.
   c. Advanced Options in the Navigation Pane.
   d. All of the above

9. Which wildcard would you use to find a single character?
   a. ?
   b. *
   c. **
   d. ??

10. The Go To command allows you to navigate by page, text, graphics, equations, or tables by initiating the:
   a. Select Browse Object command.
   b. F5 shortcut key.
   c. Find and Replace dialog box.
   d. All of the above.

Competency Assessment

Project 2-1: Updating a Sign

The Grand Street Coffee Shop places a sign on the door and near the order counter listing the featured coffees of the day. You need to update today's sign.

GET READY. LAUNCH Word if it is not already running.

1. Click the File tab and choose Open.
2. Click the location of the data files for this lesson.
3. Locate and open the *sign* document.
4. Click the File tab, then Save as. In the File name box, key *newsign.*
5. Click Save.
6. Position the I-beam before the *M* in *Morning Blend*. Drag over the words to select *Morning Blend*.
7. Key Grand Street Blend.
8. Click the Home tab. In the Editing group, click Replace.
9. Place the insertion point in the Find What text box and key Kona Blend.
10. Click in the Replace With text box and key Hawaiian Blend.
11. Click the More >> button.
12. Click the Format button and select Font. In the Font text box, click the scroll bar down arrow and select Comic Sans MS; for the Style, select Bold Italics; for the font size, select 26; and for the font color, select dark blue in the Standard Colors. Click OK, then click the << Less button.
13. Click Find Next, then the Replace button. Click OK, then Close.
14. Position the I-beam before the *T* in *Try Me* and click to place the insertion point.
15. Key $1 and press the spacebar.
16. In the next line, double-click the word Mocha to select it.
17. Key White Chocolate.
18. Click the View tab. In the Zoom group, click One Page.
19. Click Page Width.
20. Click the File tab and choose Save As from the menu.
21. Locate your USB flash drive.
22. **SAVE** the document in the lesson folder on your USB flash drive.
23. Click the File tab. Point to Print preview, then click Print.
24. Click the File tab and select Close.

PAUSE. LEAVE Word open for the next project.

Project 2-2:   Editing a Job Description

Star Bright Satellite Radio is hiring. Edit the job description so that it can be sent to the human resources department for processing and posting.

GET READY. LAUNCH Word if it is not already running.

1. Click the File tab and choose Open.
2. Click the location of the data files for this lesson. Locate and click *jobdescription* one time to select it. Click Open.
3. Click the File tab, then Save as. In the File name box, key *updatedjobdescription*.
4. In the second line of the document, position the I-beam before the *D* in *Date* and click to place the insertion point.
5. Beginning at the *D*, click and drag down and to the right until Date Posted and the line below it, *5/15/10*, is selected.
6. Press Backspace to delete both lines.
7. In the Duties & Responsibilities heading, position the insertion point before the &. Press Shift and then press the Right arrow key to select &.
8. Key and. The & is replaced with the word *and*.
9. Position the mouse pointer in the left margin beside the line in the first bulleted list that reads *Define the web site's look and feel*. Click to select the line.
10. Press the Delete key to delete the line.
11. In the *Education and/or Experience* heading, position the I-beam to the right of the letter r in *or*.
12. Press Backspace three times to delete the *r, o,* and */*.
13. In the first line of the bulleted list that begins *College degree required . . .*, click to position the insertion point after m*aster's degree*.
14. Press the spacebar and key preferred.
15. Click the View tab. In the Zoom command group, click Zoom, click 75%, and click OK. Click Page Wide, then click 100% on the Zoom command group.
16. Save the document in the lesson folder on your USB flash drive.
17. **CLOSE** the file.

PAUSE. LEAVE Word open for the next project.

@ The *jobdescription* file for this lesson is available on the book companion website or in WileyPLUS.

Proficiency Assessment

Project 2-3: Creating a Schedule

You are chair of the New Neighbor Welcoming Committee in your neighborhood. The group meets monthly at a committee member's house. A different committee member is responsible for bringing refreshments to each meeting. Use Word to create a schedule to share with members, then view the document in different views.

GET READY. LAUNCH Word if it is not already running.

1. **OPEN** *schedule* from the data files for this lesson. Save the file as *updatedschedule* in the lesson folder of your USB flash drive.
2. For the May 11 meeting details, key D. Lorenzo, 7501 Oak, 8 p.m. Beside *refreshments*, key S. Wilson.
3. The June 15 meeting details are R. Mason, 7620 Oak, 8 p.m., and J. Estes is bringing the refreshments.
4. View the document in a New Window. Then click Switch windows.
5. Click Web Layout, then click Draft view.

@ The *schedule* file for this lesson is available on the book companion website or in WileyPLUS.

6. Click the Split button, and position the split under the second title, *Meeting and Refreshment Schedule*. Click Remove Split.

7. Close *updatedschedule*.

8. **SAVE** the document in the lesson folder on your USB flash drive, then **CLOSE** the file.

PAUSE. LEAVE Word open for the next project.

Project 2-4: Finding and Replacing Text

In this exercise, you find and replace text using the Format and Special buttons.

GET READY. LAUNCH Word if it is not already running.

@ The *computeruse2* file for this lesson is available on the book companion website or in WileyPLUS.

1. **OPEN** *computeruse2* from the data files for this lesson.

2. **SAVE** the document as *computer_update* in the lesson folder on your USB flash drive.

3. Use the Advanced Find command to find all occurrences of the word attorney and highlight them.

4. Use the Find and Replace dialog box to replace all paragraph marks in the document with manual line breaks. Then place your insertion point at the beginning of the document.

6. Open the Navigation Pane and use the search box to find the word section in the document. Review the second and third tabs to see the found text.

7. Use the Select Browse Object button in the scroll bar, go to page 4, and then go to line 25.

8. **SAVE** the document in the lesson folder on your USB flash drive, then **CLOSE** the document.

PAUSE. LEAVE Word open for the next project.

Mastery Assessment

Project 2-5: Fixing the Coffee Shop Menu

A co-worker at the Grand Coffee Shop has been working on a new menu for the coffee shop. She asks you to take a look at it before she sends it to a graphic designer. You find the old menu file and decide to compare the two.

GET READY. LAUNCH Word if it is not already running.

@ The *menu* file for this lesson is available on the book companion website or in WileyPLUS.

@ The *oldmenu* file for this lesson is available on the book companion website or in WileyPLUS.

1. **OPEN** *menu* from the data files for this lesson.

2. **OPEN** *oldmenu* from the data files for this lesson.

3. View the two files side by side to compare them.

4. Find and insert the two items that are missing from the new menu.

5. Find and change five pricing errors on the new menu.

6. **SAVE** the corrected menu as *newmenu* in the lesson folder on your USB flash drive, then CLOSE the file.

7. **CLOSE** the *oldmenu* file.

PAUSE. LEAVE Word open for the next project.

Project 2-6: Creating a Memo

Create a memo to committee members to include with the schedule you created in Project 2-3.

GET READY. LAUNCH Word if it is not already running.

 The *schedulememo* file for this lesson is available on the book companion website or in WileyPLUS.

1. **OPEN** *schedulememo* from the data files for this lesson.

2. Place your insertion point on the second paragraph mark after the subject line and key the following:

   Thank you for volunteering to be on the New Neighbor Welcoming Committee. Enclosed please find the meeting and refreshment schedule for the next six months. See you in January!

   Committee Members:

3. **SAVE** the file as *deschedulememo*.

4. **OPEN** the *updatedschedule* document you saved in Project 2-3.

5. Display both documents on your screen using the Arrange All command. Scroll through the meeting schedule document to see the names of the committee members. Key the names of the eight committee members below the *Committee Members* heading in the memo.

6. **SAVE** the *deschedulememo* document in the lesson folder on your USB flash drive, then CLOSE the file.

7. **CLOSE** the *updatedschedule* document without saving.

STOP. CLOSE Word.

INTERNET READY

Locate the closest satellite company in your area and find information about the company. Prepare a three-page report for your instructor and apply the features learned in this lesson. Prepare a fourth page on which you describe what you have learned in this lesson, and submit the completed document to your instructor.

Workplace*Ready*

VIEWING A LONG DOCUMENT

As a student at your local community college, you are learning the new features in Word 2010. Your instructor has asked you to visit one of the administrative areas and discuss the new features with an administrative assistant. Your task is to request a lengthy document and demonstrate the new Navigation Pane and how quickly and easily text, graphics, tables, and equations can be located in a document. Prepare a report to your instructor on your findings.

3 Character Formatting

LESSON SKILL MATRIX

Skill	Exam Objective	Objective Number
Manually Formatting Characters	Apply character attributes.	2.1.1
Using the Format Painter	Use Format Painter.	2.1.3
Formatting Text with Styles	Apply styles.	2.1.2
Removing Text Formatting		

KEY TERMS

- character
- character styles
- font
- monospace
- paragraph styles
- point size
- proportional space
- sans serif
- serif
- Text Effects

With more than 20 million members and 2,600 facilities, the YMCA ("the Y") is the nation's largest community service organization. Health and fitness programs offered at the Y include group exercises for adults and youth, family time, sports and recreation, and group interests for senior citizens. The staff and volunteers at the Y need to create various types of documents for announcing and advertising programs throughout the year and for organizing and registering members for participation in these programs. Microsoft Word is a great tool for creating professional-looking documents that will capture attention. In this lesson, you learn how to use character formatting to create professional-looking documents.

SOFTWARE ORIENTATION

The Font Group

As you learn to format text, it is important to become familiar with the Font group of commands. The Font group, shown in Figure 3-1, is displayed in the Home tab of the Ribbon.

Figure 3-1

The Font group

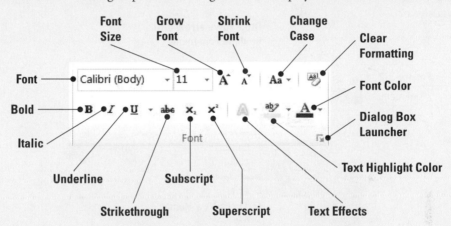

The Font group contains commands for changing the appearance of text. Refer to this figure throughout this lesson as well as the rest of the book.

FORMATTING CHARACTERS MANUALLY

The Bottom Line

Formatting characters makes your text more appealing and more readable.

Changing Fonts and Font Sizes

A **character** is any single letter, number, symbol, or punctuation mark. A **font** is a set of characters that have the same design. Each font has a unique name, such as Garamond or Arial. Microsoft Word has a variety of fonts and font sizes to help you communicate your intended message in a document. In this exercise, you use commands from the Font command group and the Mini toolbar to apply a specific font and font size to selected text.

Font sizes are measured in points. **Point size** refers to the height of characters, with one point equaling approximately 1/72 of an inch. Point sizes range from the very small 8-point size to 72 points or higher. Below are a few examples of fonts and sizes.

This is an example of Garamond 10 point.

This is an example of Arial 14 point.

This is an example of Juice ITC 18 point.

The Font group in the Home tab contains menus for changing both font type and font size. You can also access the same commands using the Mini toolbar or by right-clicking to access a shortcut menu. To change text font or size using any of these tools, you first must select the text.

Another way to change the size of text is to select the text and click the Grow Font $\text{A}^{\hat{}}$ button to increase the font size or the Shrink Font $\text{A}^{\check{}}$ button to decrease the size.

STEP BY STEP   **Change Fonts and Font Sizes**

GET READY. Before you begin these steps, be sure to LAUNCH Microsoft Word.

1. Connect your USB flash drive to one of the USB ports on your computer.
2. Click the File tab, then click Open. The Open dialog box appears.
3. Use the vertical scroll bar to scroll down and locate the data files for this lesson on your USB flash drive. Double-click the Lesson 3 folder to open it.
4. Locate and open the file named *class_descriptions*.
5. Within the document, select Preston Creek Family YMCA.
6. In the Font group of the Home tab, click the Font drop-down arrow to display the Font menu. The menu appears, as shown in Figure 3-2.

WileyPLUS Extra! features an online tutorial of this task.

@ The *class_descriptions* file is available on the book companion website or in WileyPLUS.

Drop-down arrow will produce Font menu.

Figure 3-2

Font menu

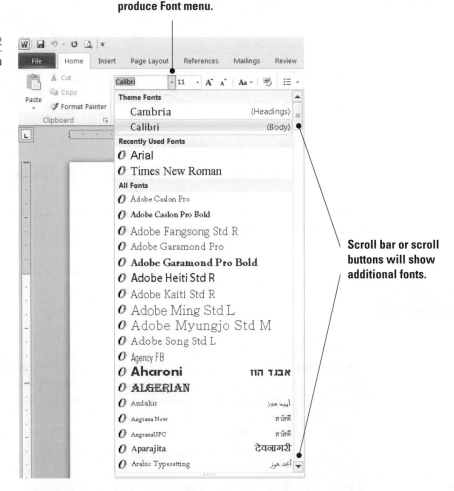

Scroll bar or scroll buttons will show additional fonts.

7. Scroll down the list and position the mouse pointer on Arial. Notice that as you point to each font in the list, the selected text changes with a live preview of what it would look like in that font.
8. Click Arial.

9. With the text still selected, click the **drop-down arrow** on the Font Size menu. The menu appears, as shown in Figure 3-3.

Figure 3-3

Font Size menu

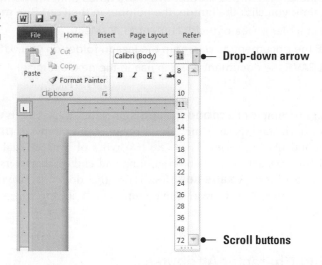

Drop-down arrow

Scroll buttons

10. Click **18**.

11. Select **Group Exercise Class Descriptions**.

12. Click the **drop-down arrow** to open the Font menu, then select **Arial**.

13. With the text still selected, open the Font Size menu and select **14**.

14. Select the remainder of text in the document. Point to the selected text to display the Mini toolbar. Click the **drop-down arrow** on the Font menu on the Mini toolbar and choose **Calibri** (see Figure 3-4).

Figure 3-4

Font menu on the Mini toolbar

The Font menu

Mini toolbar contains some commands from the Font and Paragraph groups.

15. With text still selected, click the **Font Size** menu on the Mini toolbar and choose **12**.

16. Click in a **blank area** of the document to deselect.

17. Select **Preston Creek Family YMCA**. In the Font group, click the **Grow Font** $\mathbf{A}^{\hat{}}$ button once to increase the size of the text.

18. Click the **Grow Font** $\mathbf{A}^{\hat{}}$ button two more times until the point size is **24**. Notice that each time you click the button, the number in the Font Size menu changes.

19. Click in a **blank area** of the document to deselect.

20. **SAVE** the document as *classes* in the lesson folder on your USB flash drive.

PAUSE. LEAVE the document open to use in the next exercise.

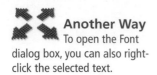

Another Way
To open the Font dialog box, you can also right-click the selected text.

Take Note   Courier is an example of a **monospaced** font, which means all its characters take up the same amount of horizontal space. Times New Roman is an example of **proportional** font, because the horizontal spacing varies. There are two types of proportional fonts: serif and sans serif. **Serif** fonts have small lines at the beginning and end of characters and are usually used with large amounts of text. A **sans serif** font is one that does not have the small line extensions on its characters. Times New Roman is an example of a serif font, whereas Arial and Calibri are sans serif fonts.

Applying Character Attributes

In addition to changing the font and font size of text, you can change the appearance of characters to apply emphasis to text. In this exercise, you learn how to apply character attributes such as bolding, italics, font colors, and outlines to selected text in Word documents.

The Font group in the Home tab includes the commands for applying bold, italic, and underline attributes to draw attention to words or phrases in your document. You can use these attributes one at a time, such as **Bold**, or together, such as **Bold Underline**. Select the text to apply one or more of the character attributes using the Font command group, the Mini toolbar, or keyboard shortcuts or by right-clicking to access a shortcut menu.

Click the Font command group dialog box launcher to open the Font dialog box with more options for formatting characters. In this dialog box, you can specify a font color, underline style, and a variety of other effects, such as small caps, strikethrough, superscript, and shadow.

NEW to Office 2010

New to the Font command group is **Text Effects**. Text Effects $\mathbf{A}$ ▾ add a distinctive appearance to selected text, such as outline, shadow, glow, and reflection. To add Text Effects to selected text, click the drop-down arrow on the Text Effects button, then select from the available options on the menu. To remove effects, select the affected text, then click the Clear Formatting button on the Font group.

STEP BY STEP   **Apply Character Attributes**

USE the document that is open from the previous exercise.

1. Select the title of the document, **Preston Creek Family YMCA**. In the Font command group, click the **Bold** $\mathbf{B}$ button.

2. Select the subtitle, **Group Exercise Class Descriptions**, and click the **Italic** I button.

3. Select **Active Older Adults** and click the **Bold** $\mathbf{B}$ button.

4. With the text still selected, click the **Underline** $\underline{\mathbf{U}}$ ▾ button.

Another Way
You also can select text and then press the keyboard shortcut Ctrl+B to apply bolding.

Another Way
You also can use the keyboard shortcut Ctrl+I to apply italics to selected text.

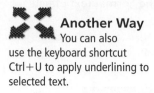

Another Way
You can also use the keyboard shortcut Ctrl+U to apply underlining to selected text.

5. With the text still selected, click the drop-down arrow beside the Underline button. A menu of underlining choices appears, as shown in Figure 3-5.

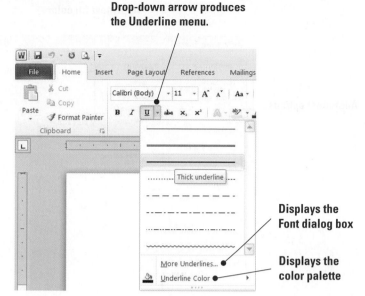

Drop-down arrow produces the Underline menu.

Displays the Font dialog box

Displays the color palette

Figure 3-5

Underline menu

6. Click Thick Underline, the third line down in the menu.

7. Select the title, Preston Creek Family YMCA. In the Font group, click the dialog box launcher. The Font dialog box appears, as shown in Figure 3-6.

8. In the Effects section, click the Small Caps check box to insert a check mark.

9. Click the drop-down arrow on the Font Color menu. A menu of colors appears. A ScreenTip will appear when you place your insertion point over the colors; click red from the Standard Colors section at the bottom.

Figure 3-6

Font dialog box

Font dialog box launcher

Font style   Font Size

Font

Effects

Preview

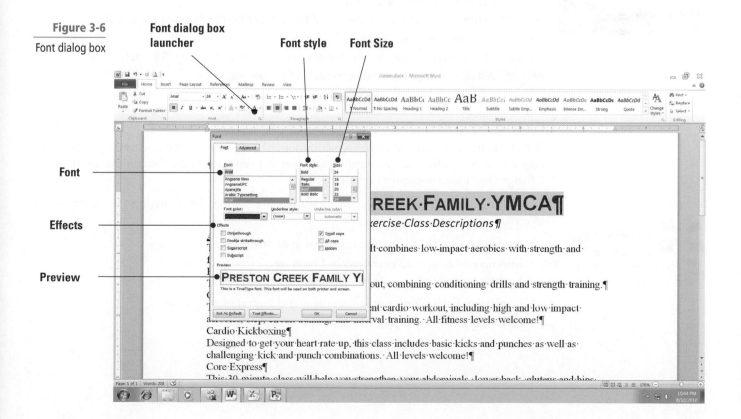

10. Click the Text Effects button at the bottom of the dialog box. The Format Text Effects dialog box opens, as shown in Figure 3-7.

Figure 3-7

Format Text Effects dialog box

Apply text fill color

Additional options

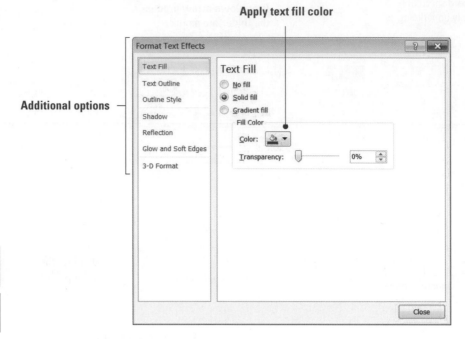

CERTIFICATION READY? **2.1.1**

How do you bold, italicize, and underline text?

11. In the Fill Color options area, click the Color drop-down arrow. From the Standard colors menu that appears, select dark blue.

12. In the directory in the left pane of the dialog box, click Text Outline, then select Solid line in the options that appear in the right pane.

CERTIFICATION READY? **2.1.1**

How do you change text color?

13. In the Outline Style category, change the width from .75 to 1.5 pt. Click Close to close the Format Text Effects dialog box. Each character in the selected text will now have a noticeable solid-colored outline.

14. In the Font dialog box, click the Small Caps check box to remove the check mark.

15. Click OK, then deselect the text.

CERTIFICATION READY? **2.1.1**

How do you apply Text Effects to selected text?

16. **SAVE** the document as *classes_1* in the lesson folder on your USB flash drive.

PAUSE. LEAVE the document open to use in the next exercise.

Changing Case

When you need to change the case (capitalization) of text, Word provides several options and an easy way to choose the one you want. In this exercise, you learn to use the commands in Word's Change Case menu to change capitalization.

The Change Case menu in the Font group has five options for changing the capitalization of text:

Another Way
Click the Font Color **A** button on the Ribbon to launch a menu of colors.

- **Sentence case:** Capitalizes the first word in each sentence
- **lowercase:** Changes all characters to lowercase
- **UPPERCASE:** Changes all characters to capital letters
- **Capitalize Each Word:** Capitalizes the first character of each word
- **tOGGLE cASE:** Changes each character to its opposite case

STEP BY STEP   **Change Case**

USE the document that is open from the previous exercise.

1. Select the title, Preston Creek Family YMCA. In the Font group, click the Change Case **Aa** button. A menu of case options appears, as shown in Figure 3-8.

Figure 3-8

Change Case menu

Click on the drop-down arrow to display the Change Case menu.

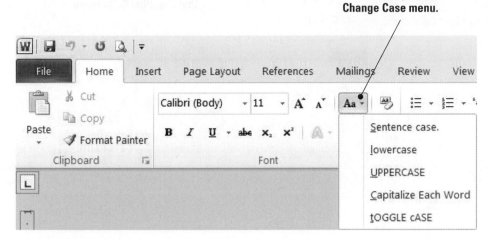

2. Click UPPERCASE. All letters are capitalized.
3. With the text still selected, click the Change Case **Aa** button again and select lowercase.
4. With the text still selected, click the Change Case **Aa** button again, then click Capitalize Each Word.
5. Select Ymca. Click the Change Case **Aa** button again and choose UPPERCASE.
6. Click in a blank area of the document to deselect the text.
7. SAVE the document as *classes_2* in the lesson folder on your USB flash drive.

PAUSE. LEAVE the document open to use in the next exercise.

Highlighting Text

The Highlighting tool in the Font group enables you to apply a highlighting color across text to stress the importance of that text and draw attention to it quickly. In this exercise, you learn to use Word's Text Highlighting feature to add highlighting color to selected text.

To highlight text, first select the text you want to emphasize, then click the Text Highlight Color button in the Font group and select the color of your choice. To remove highlighting, select the highlighted text and choose No Color from the Text Highlight Color menu.

STEP BY STEP   **Highlight Text**

USE the document that is open from the previous exercise.

1. In the Font group, click the Text Highlight Color ᵃᵇ⁄ button. Place your insertion point within the document, and notice that Highlighting is turned on and the pointer changes to a highlighter pen icon.
2. Under the Core Express heading in your document, select the last sentence, This new class is open to all fitness levels! When you release the mouse button, the text is highlighted in yellow.

3. Click the Text Highlight Color 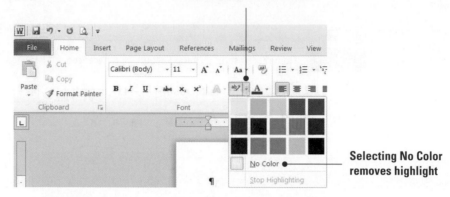 ▾ button again to turn off Highlighting.

4. Select the text you highlighted in step 2. Click the drop-down arrow beside the Text Highlight Color ▾ button. A menu of colors appears, as shown in Figure 3-9. Click turquoise (the third color from the left in the top row of the menu). Notice the highlight color in the text and the Text Highlight Color ▾ button in the Ribbon has changed to turquoise.

Figure 3-9

Text Highlight Color menu

Text Highlight Color menu

Selecting No Color removes highlight

5. Select the text again. Click the Text Highlight Color ▾ button again to remove the highlight color by selecting No Color.

6. **SAVE** the document with the same filename in the lesson folder on your USB flash drive.

PAUSE. LEAVE the document open to use in the next exercise.

USING THE FORMAT PAINTER

The Bottom Line

To format your text so that it has the look and feel you want, you may need to copy existing formatting. The Format Painter helps you copy formats to use in other areas of the document without having to repeat the same steps.

Using the Format Painter

The Format Painter command is located in the Clipboard group on the Home tab. It is used to copy attributes and other formatting from one block of text and apply them to other selected text within the document. When you activate Format Painter, the mouse pointer becomes a paintbrush. Clicking once on the Format Painter button enables you to copy and apply the format once; double-clicking allows you to apply the copied format to as many locations as you wish. In this exercise, you learn to use the Format Painter to copy and apply formatting to selected text.

STEP BY STEP   **Use the Format Painter**

USE the document that is open from the previous exercise.

1. Select the Active Older Adults heading.

CERTIFICATION READY?   **2.1.3**

How do you use the Format Painter to copy and apply formats to text?

2. On the Home tab, in the Clipboard group, click the Format Painter ✦ Format Painter button once; Format Painter copies the formatting from your selected text, and the pointer changes to a paintbrush icon when you point to text.

CERTIFICATION
READY?   2.1.3

How do you use the Format
Painter to apply copied
formats to multiple items?

Another Way
The Format Painter
button is also available on the
Mini toolbar. In addition, to
repeat the last Format Painter
action, you can press the F4
shortcut key.

3. Use the paintbrush pointer to select the next heading, Boot Camp. The copied format is applied, and the Format Painter is turned off.

4. With Boot Camp still selected, double-click the Format Painter *Format Painter* button. Notice the status bar message "Use the mouse to apply the previously copied paragraph formatting onto other text, or press Esc to cancel." Notice also that the mouse pointer becomes a paintbrush icon when you place it over text. You will now be able to apply the same formatting to several items in the document.

5. Select the next heading, Cardio Combo. The copied format is applied.

6. Select the next heading, Cardio Kickboxing. The copied format is applied again.

7. Select the remaining headings to apply the copied format. When you are finished with the last heading, click the Format Painter *Format Painter* button to turn it off.

8. **SAVE** the document as *classes_3* in the lesson folder on your USB flash drive.

PAUSE. LEAVE the document open to use in the next exercise.

FORMATTING TEXT WITH STYLES

The Bottom Line

Word provides predefined Quick Styles for formatting documents instantly with a number of character and paragraph attributes. Modifications can be made to existing styles, or new styles can be created and placed in the Quick Styles list, current document, or template. In this exercise, you learn to apply a style and to modify an existing style.

The Styles window lists the same Quick Styles displayed in the Styles Gallery. When you point to a style in the list, a ScreenTip displays the style's properties.

When you choose **paragraph styles**, the formats are applied instantly to all text in the paragraph where the insertion point is located, whether or not that text is selected. Styles created for paragraphs are marked in the Styles window by a paragraph mark to the right of the style name.

Character styles are applied to individual characters or words that you select. Character styles have a lowercase letter *a* beside them.

Sometimes, a style can be used for either paragraphs or characters. These linked styles have a paragraph symbol as well as a lowercase *a* beside them. Select the text to which you want to apply a linked style.

Applying Styles

In this exercise, you learn to use Word's Quick Styles to apply paragraph styles and character styles to selected text and paragraphs within your document.

STEP BY STEP   **Apply a Style**

USE the document that is open from the previous exercise.

1. Select the Active Older Adults heading. In the Styles command group on the Home tab, click Heading 1. The style is applied to the heading.

2. Use multi-selection to select all the headings, then click Heading 1. The Heading 1 style is applied to all the remaining headings.

3. In the second sentence of the Active Older Adults description, select low-impact. In the Styles group, click the dialog box launcher. The Styles window appears, as shown in Figure 3-10.

Figure 3-10

Styles window

Clicking the More down arrow displays a menu.

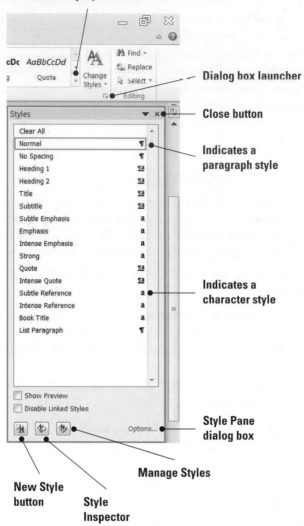

Dialog box launcher

Close button

Indicates a paragraph style

Indicates a character style

Style Pane dialog box

Manage Styles

New Style button

Style Inspector

4. Point to Subtle Emphasis in the Styles list. Notice a ScreenTip appears and the lowercase *a* to the right of the style name becomes an arrow. Click Subtle Emphasis. The style is applied to the selected text.

5. In the Boot Camp description, select challenging and click Subtle Emphasis in the Styles window.

6. In the Core Express description, select strengthen and click Subtle Emphasis in the Styles window.

7. In the Indoor Cycling description, select high-energy and click Subtle Emphasis in the Styles window.

8. In the Yoga description, select breathing and relaxation and click Subtle Emphasis in the Styles window. Deselect the text. Click the X to close the Styles window.

9. **SAVE** the document as *classes_4* in the lesson folder on your USB flash drive.

PAUSE. LEAVE the document open to use in the next exercise.

CERTIFICATION READY?   **2.1.2**

How do you apply a style to text?

Modifying Styles

You can make modifications to an existing style using the Modify Style dialog box. Word also gives you the option of where to place changes made to styles, such as adding them to the Quick List, current document, or applying them to new documents based on a template. In this exercise, you learn to use the Modify Style options to modify styles in Word.

To change an existing style, right-click the style's name in the Style window, then click Modify, as shown in Figure 3-11. Character attributes can be applied to a style by clicking on the Bold **B** button, Italics *I* button and/or the Underline **U** ▾ button. Similarly, clicking the drop-down arrow for Font and Font Size allows you to adjust both of these settings.

The Modify Styles dialog box has options for where to place the new modified style. The modified style can be placed on the Quick Style list so you can access it quickly. Selecting the option to *save the style only in this document* will affect only the current document. Selecting the option for *new documents based on a template* ensures that the same style is applied. For instance, say you are writing a group research paper and would like uniformity for the paper. Providing everyone within the group with a copy of the template would ensure consistency in the formatting of the paper. All styles within the document update automatically.

STEP BY STEP   **Modify Styles**

USE the document that is open from the previous exercise.

1. Under Change Styles in the Style group, click the drop-down arrow to display the Styles window. Select Subtle Emphasis, then right-click to display the Subtle Emphasis menu, as shown in Figure 3-11.

Figure 3-11

Subtle Emphasis menu

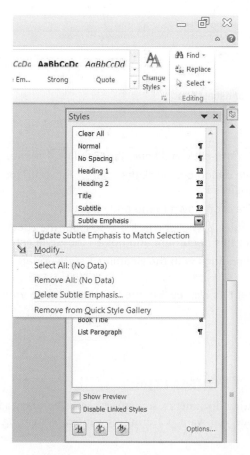

2. Click **Modify**. The Modify Style dialog box appears, as shown in Figure 3-12.

3. Click the **Bold** **B** button.

4. Click the **Font Color drop-down arrow**, then select **red** in the Standard Colors section. Notice the preview in the dialog box changes.

5. Click the **Add to Quick Style List** check box to clear it. The modifications you just made will apply to this document and not on the Style list, as shown in Figure 3-12.

Figure 3-12

Modify Style dialog box displaying Subtle Emphasis

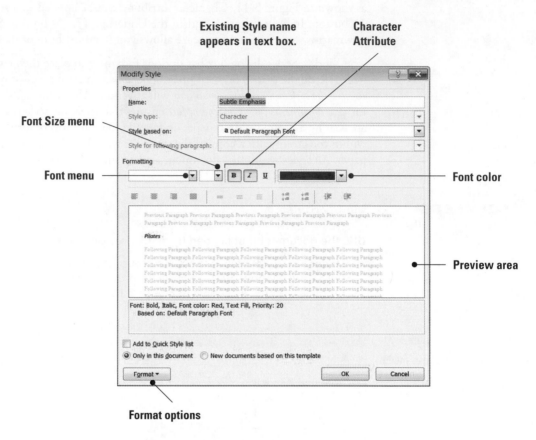

Existing Style name appears in text box.

Character Attribute

Font Size menu

Font menu

Font color

Preview area

Format options

6. Click **OK**.

7. Select **Heading 1**, right-click to display the Heading 1 menu, then click **Modify**.

8. In the Modify Style dialog box, click the **Font Color drop-down arrow**. From the drop-down menu, choose **red**.

9. Open the Font Size drop-down menu and select **14**.

10. Click the **Add to Quick Style list** check box to clear the check mark. The modifications made will apply to this document and not on the Style list.

11. Click **OK**. All the headings with the Heading 1 style update automatically to the new color and size.

12. **SAVE** the document as *classes_5* in the lesson folder on your USB flash drive. CLOSE the file.

STOP. CLOSE Word.

REMOVING TEXT FORMATTING

The Bottom Line

When you are formatting documents, sometimes you need to try a few different options before you get the appearance you want. Clearing unwanted formatting is easy using Word's Clear Formatting button.

Using the Clear Formatting Button

The Clear Formatting button is located in the More area of the Styles group. Click the drop-down arrow to display a menu that lets you clear formatting from selected text. In this exercise, you learn to use the Clear Formatting button.

STEP BY STEP	Use the Clear Formatting Button

USE the document that is open from the previous exercise.

1. Select **Active Older Adults**. In the Styles group, click the **More drop-down arrow**, then click **Clear Formatting**. The formatting is removed and only plain text remains.

2. Press and hold **Ctrl** and select **Boot Camp**; continue to hold the **Ctrl** key to select the remaining headings, then click the **Clear Formatting** button in the Styles group. (By holding the **Ctrl** key, you can use multi-selection to select nonadjacent text.) Deselect all text and click the **X** to close the Style window.

Another Way
To remove formatting you can also click Clear Formatting on the Font group.

3. **SAVE** the document as *classes_6* in the lesson folder on your USB flash drive.

CLOSE Word.

X Ref   Refer to Lesson 2 for more information about multi-selection.

SKILL SUMMARY

In This Lesson, You Learned How To:	Exam Objective	Objective Number
Manually format characters	Apply character attributes.	**2.1.1**
Using the format painter	Use Format Painter.	**2.1.3**
Formatting text with styles	Apply styles.	**2.1.2**
Removing text formatting		

Knowledge Assessment

True/False

Circle T if the statement is true or F if the statement is false.

T F **1.** Toggle Case changes each character to its opposite case.

T F **2.** Applying bolding to text gives it special emphasis.

T F **3.** The Format Painter is found on the Mini toolbar.

T F **4.** The default color for Text Highlighting is pink.

T F **5.** The Shrink Font button increases point size.

T F **6.** The Clear Formatting button clears text from one location and lets you apply it in another location.

T F **7.** You can only highlight text with the colors yellow or turquoise.

T F **8.** The Font dialog box has an option to display the underline menu.

T F **9.** To apply a Quick Style, select the text, then select the style from the Style group.

T F **10.** Quick Styles cannot be modified.

Multiple Choice

Select the best response for the following statements.

1. When measuring point size, one point is equal to a character height of:
   a. 1/10 of an inch.
   b. 1/12 of an inch.
   c. 1/72 of an inch.
   d. 1/18 of an inch.

2. The Underline button in the Font group contains options to underline selected text with a(n):
   a. thick underline.
   b. double underline.
   c. dotted underline.
   d. All of the above

3. A _____ is a set of characters that have the same design.
   a. point size
   b. Font
   c. paragraph style
   d. a and b

4. If you key a paragraph in uppercase and need to change it to sentence case without having to rekey the paragraph, which option would you would use?
   a. Change Case
   b. Change Size of Case
   c. Sentence Case
   d. Toggle Case

5. The _____ makes text look like it was marked with a fluorescent-colored pen.
   a. Highlighter tool
   b. Highlighting Text tool
   c. Highlighting Color tool
   d. Shading Text tool

6. The _____ lets you copy the format of text and apply those attributes to different text.
   a. Formatter
   b. Copy Special
   c. Format Painter
   d. Both a and b

7. The _____ feature removes all formatting from the selected text.
   a. Formatting Cleared
   b. Erase Formatting
   c. Remove Formatting
   d. Clear Formatting

8. Tiny lines at the ends of characters are known as:
   a. serifs.
   b. sans serifs.
   c. monospaces.
   d. proportional lines.

9. To increase the point size of selected text, click the:
   a. Increase font button.
   b. Grow font button.
   c. Enlarge font button.
   d. Enhance font button.

10. Changing the font and font size of selected text can be completed using:

    a. the Font dialog box.

    b. the Mini toolbar.

    c. the Font group of the Home tab.

    d. All of the above

Competency Assessment

Project 3-1: Formatting a Sales Letter

Star Bright Satellite Radio will be sending sales letters to people who have just purchased new vehicles equipped with their radios. Add some finishing formatting touches to this letter.

GET READY. LAUNCH Word if it is not already running.

1. **OPEN** the *letter* document from the data files for this lesson.

2. **SAVE** the document as *sales_letter* in the lesson folder on your USB flash drive.

3. In the second paragraph, select the first sentence, Star Bright Satellite. . . .

4. In the Font group on the Home tab, click the Bold button.

5. In the second paragraph, select the fifth sentence, Star Bright also broadcasts. . . .

6. In the Font group, click the Italic button.

7. In the fourth paragraph, select the first sentence, Star Bright is only $10.95 a month.

8. In the Font group, click the Bold button.

9. In the second sentence of the fourth paragraph, select Subscribe.

10. In the Font group, click the Change Case drop-down arrow, then click UPPERCASE.

11. With the word still selected, click Bold, then deselect the text.

12. **SAVE** the document in the lesson folder on your USB flash drive, then **CLOSE** the document.

PAUSE. LEAVE Word open for the next project.

@ The *letter* file for this lesson is available on the book companion website or in WileyPLUS.

Project 3-2: Formatting a Flyer

GET READY. LAUNCH Word if it is not already running.

1. **OPEN** *volunteercoaches* from the data files for this lesson.

2. **SAVE** the document as *volunteers* in the lesson folder on your USB flash drive.

3. Select We Need You! Click the drop-down arrow in the Font menu, then click Arial Black.

4. Click the drop-down arrow in the Font Size menu, then click 48.

5. Select Volunteer Coaches Needed For Youth Sports. Click the drop-down arrow in the Font menu, then click Arial Black.

6. Click the drop-down arrow in the Font Size menu, then click 18.

7. Select Sports include and the four lines below it. Click the drop-down arrow in the Font menu, then click Calibri. Click the drop-down arrow in the Font Size menu, then click 18.

8. Select the four sports listed, then click the Italic button.

@ The *volunteercoaches* file for this lesson is available on the book companion website or in WileyPLUS.

9. Select the three lines of contact information, beginning with *Contact Patrick Edelstein . . .* Click the drop-down arrow in the Font menu, then click Arial Black. Click the drop-down arrow in the Font Size menu, then click 11.

10. Select YMCA. Click the drop-down arrow in the Font Color button, then choose red from the Standard Colors section.

11. With the text still selected, click the Bold button. Click the drop-down arrow in the Font menu, then click Arial Black. Click the drop-down menu in the Font Size menu, then click 36. Deselect the text.

12. **SAVE** the document in the lesson folder on your USB flash drive, then **CLOSE** the file.

LEAVE Word open for the next project.

Proficiency Assessment

Project 3-3: Creating a Flyer

The Grand Street Coffee Shop has decided to install a wireless Internet service for customers. To announce the news, create a flyer for distribution in the coffee shop.

GET READY. LAUNCH Word if it is not already running.

1. **OPEN** *wireless* from the data files for this lesson.

@ The *wireless* file for this lesson is available on the book companion website or in WileyPLUS.

2. **SAVE** the document as *WiFi* in the lesson folder on your USB flash drive.

3. Follow the instructions in Figure 3-13 to format the document.

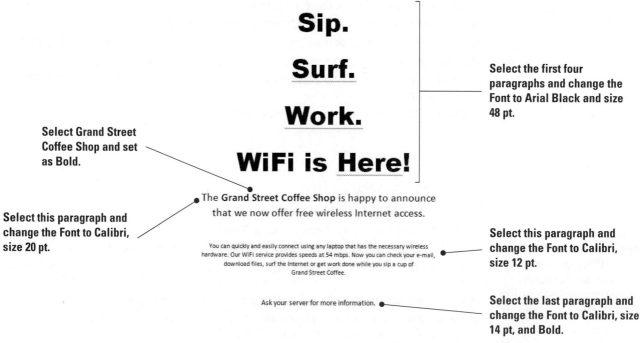

Select the first four paragraphs and change the Font to Arial Black and size 48 pt.

Select Grand Street Coffee Shop and set as Bold.

Select this paragraph and change the Font to Calibri, size 20 pt.

Select this paragraph and change the Font to Calibri, size 12 pt.

Select the last paragraph and change the Font to Calibri, size 14 pt, and Bold.

Sip.

Surf.

Work.

WiFi is Here!

The **Grand Street Coffee Shop** is happy to announce that we now offer free wireless Internet access.

You can quickly and easily connect using any laptop that has the necessary wireless hardware. Our WiFi service provides speeds at 54 mbps. Now you can check your e-mail, download files, surf the Internet or get work done while you sip a cup of Grand Street Coffee.

Ask your server for more information.

4. **SAVE** the document in the lesson folder on your USB flash drive, then **CLOSE** the file.

LEAVE Word open for the next project.

Project 3-4: Formatting Nutritional Information

Customers of the Grand Street Coffee Shop have asked about the nutritional makeup of some of the blended coffee items on the menu. Format a document you can post or make available for customers to take with them.

GET READY. LAUNCH Word if it is not already running.

@ The *nutritioninfo* file for this lesson is available on the book companion website or in WileyPLUS.

1. **OPEN** *nutritioninfo* from the data files for this lesson.
2. SAVE the document as *nutrition* in the lesson folder on your USB flash drive.
3. Select Grand Street Coffee Shop. On the Font menu, click Juice ITC.
4. With the text still selected, change the font size to 28.
5. Click the Font Color menu and select dark blue in the Standard Colors section.
6. Select Nutritional Information.
7. In the Font group, click the dialog box launcher. In the Effects section, click the Small Caps box and change the font size to 12 and the font color to dark blue. Click OK.
8. Select Brewed Coffee, Caffé Latte, Caffé Mocha, Cappuccino, and White Chocolate Mocha, then click the Font dialog box launcher. Click the All Caps box, change the font size to 12, make the text both Bold and Italic, and change the font color to dark blue. Click OK.
9. Select the three lines of text under the *Brewed Coffee* heading. Click Italic on the Font group. Use the Format Painter to copy the format to the text under each heading.
10. **SAVE** the document in the lesson folder on your USB flash drive, then CLOSE the file.

LEAVE Word open for the next project.

Mastery Assessment

Project 3-5: Formatting a Resume

Your friend Mike asks you to help him with his resume. Format the resume so that it looks professional.

GET READY. LAUNCH Word if it is not already running.

@ The *resume* file for this lesson is available on the book companion website or in WileyPLUS.

1. **OPEN** *resume* from the data files for this lesson.
2. **SAVE** the document as *mzresume* in the lesson folder on your USB flash drive.
3. Format the resume to the following specifications:
   - Format Mike's name with Cambria, 24 pt., bold.
   - Change his address, phone, and email information to Times New Roman 9 pt.
   - Change the main headings by bolding and italicizing; change the font to Cambria and the font size to 16.
   - For job titles, apply Times New Roman, 12 pt., small caps, and bold.
   - Italicize the sentence or sentences before the bulleted lists.
   - For places and years of employment, as well as the college name, apply Times New Roman, 12 pt., and small caps.
4. **SAVE** the document in the lesson folder on your USB flash drive, then **CLOSE** the file.

LEAVE Word open for the next project.

Project 3-6: Formatting References

Your friend Mike liked your work on his resume so much that he asks you to format his reference list with the same design as his resume.

GET READY. LAUNCH Word if it is not already running.

 The *references* file for this lesson is available on the book companion website or in WileyPLUS.

1. **OPEN** *references* from the data files for this lesson.
2. **SAVE** the document as *mzreferences* in the lesson folder on your USB flash drive.
3. **OPEN** *mzresume* from the data files for this lesson.
4. View the documents side by side and compare the fonts, styles, sizes, and attributes of both. Update the *mzreferences* document by changing the font, styles, size, and attributes to match those in the *mzresume* document.
5. **SAVE** the document and **CLOSE** the file.

CLOSE Word.

INTERNET READY

Search the Internet for information on the national YMCA or your local YMCA. Create a flyer listing some of the programs available that are available in the summer. Prepare a letter for the newsletter in which you solicit volunteers to assist with the upcoming scheduled events for the summer. All members of the YMCA will receive a copy of this flyer and letter. For the letter, use Times New Roman font with a size of 12 points. For the flyer, apply whatever text effects, font colors, text highlight colors, and font styles you think make your document interesting and attractive.

Workplace *Ready*

APPLYING CHARACTER FORMATTING

At your college, visit the department that posts job opportunities for college students seeking part-time employment. Determine how you can improve the posting document's appearance by applying different character attributes and by using the Styles available in Word.

Write a letter to the director indicating the research you completed and recommending specific changes to the advertisement's text formatting and layout that you believe will better attract potential students. Submit your letter to your instructor.

LESSON SKILL MATRIX

Skill	Exam Objective	Objective Number
Formatting Paragraphs	Apply indents to paragraphs.	2.3.1
Setting Line Spacing in Text and Between Paragraphs	Apply line spacing to text and paragraphs.	2.4.1
	Apply paragraph spacing to text and paragraphs.	2.4.2
Creating and Formatting a Bulleted List	Apply bullets to a document.	2.7.1
	Select a symbol format.	2.7.2
	Define a picture to be used as a bullet.	2.7.3
	Use AutoFormat on bulleted lists.	2.7.4
	Promote and demote bullet levels.	2.7.5
Creating and Formatting a Numbered List		
Setting and Modifying Tabs	Set tabs.	2.3.2
	Use the Tabs dialog box.	2.3.3
	Set tabs on the ruler.	2.3.4
	Clear tabs.	2.3.5
	Set tab stops.	2.3.6
	Move tab stops.	2.3.7

KEY TERMS

- alignments
- first-line indent
- hanging indent
- horizontal alignment
- indent
- leaders
- line spacing
- negative indent
- vertical alignment

You are employed at Books and Beyond, an independent used bookstore. Your job responsibilities include receiving and assessing used books, issuing trade credit, stocking the bookshelves, and placing special orders. Because you have good computer skills, you are also responsible for creating and modifying documents as needed. Currently, you are working on the store's employee handbook. In this lesson, you learn how to use Word's formatting features to change the appearance of paragraphs. In particular, you learn to set indents, change alignment and line spacing, create numbered and bulleted lists, set tabs, and use shading and borders.

SOFTWARE ORIENTATION

The Indents and Spacing Tab in the Paragraph Dialog Box

The Paragraph dialog box contains Word's commands for changing paragraph alignment, indentation, and spacing. The Indents and Spacing tab of the Paragraph dialog box is shown in Figure 4-1. Use this figure as a reference throughout this lesson as well as the rest of this book.

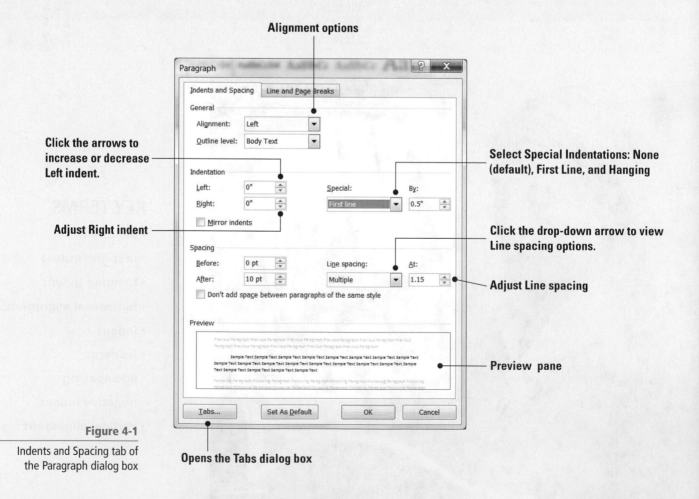

Figure 4-1

Indents and Spacing tab of the Paragraph dialog box

FORMATTING PARAGRAPHS

The Bottom Line

Paragraph formatting is an essential part of creating effective, professional-looking documents in Word. Word's paragraph formatting feature enables you to determine paragraph alignment, indentation, and spacing between paragraphs. Word's formatting features also enable you to add shading and borders to further enhance paragraph text and to remove paragraph formatting altogether.

Setting Indents

Indents can be used to set paragraphs off from other text in your documents. Word documents can include first-line indents, hanging indents, and negative indents. The commands for indenting paragraphs are available in the Paragraph command group on the Home tab, as well as in the Paragraph command group of the Page Layout tab. Both command groups have dialog box launchers that give you access to additional commands. In this exercise, you learn to set indents using the dialog box and the ruler.

An **indent** is a blank space inserted between text and the left or right margin. A **first-line indent** inserts blank space between the left margin and the first line of the paragraph (one-half inch is the default setting for this indent). A **hanging indent**, common in legal documents, begins the first full line of text in a paragraph at the left margin; all of the remaining lines in the paragraph are then indented from the left margin. A **negative indent** extends paragraph text into the left margin. You can indent paragraphs from the left margin, the right margin, or both, and you can set the sizes of indents using Word's paragraph-formatting tools. You can also drag the markers on the ruler to set indents. Table 4-1 shows the various indent markers as they appear on the ruler.

Table 4-1

Types of Indents on the Ruler

Indent Option	Associated Marker on the Ruler
First-line indent	
Hanging indent	
Left indent	
Right indent	
Negative indent	

STEP BY STEP   **Set Indents**

WileyPLUS Extra! features an online tutorial of this task.

@ The *acknowledgement* file for this lesson is available on the book companion website or in WileyPLUS.

GET READY. Before you begin these steps, be sure to launch Microsoft Word.

1. Connect your USB flash drive to one of the USB ports on your computer.
2. Click the File tab, then click Open. The Open dialog box appears.
3. Use the vertical scroll bar to scroll down and locate the data files for this lesson on your USB flash drive. Double-click the data files folder for this lesson to open it.
4. Locate and **OPEN** the file named *acknowledgement*.
5. Click the View tab. Then, in the Show group, click the check box that displays the Ruler.
6. Click to place the insertion point at the beginning of the first paragraph.
7. On the Home tab, in the Paragraph group, click the drop-down arrow to display the Paragraph dialog box. The Indents and Spacing tab is the active tab.

8. In the Indentation section of this tab, change the Special selection by clicking the drop-down arrow and selecting **First line**. The By box lists 0.5 inches by default, as shown in Figure 4-2. Click OK.

Figure 4-2

Paragraph dialog box

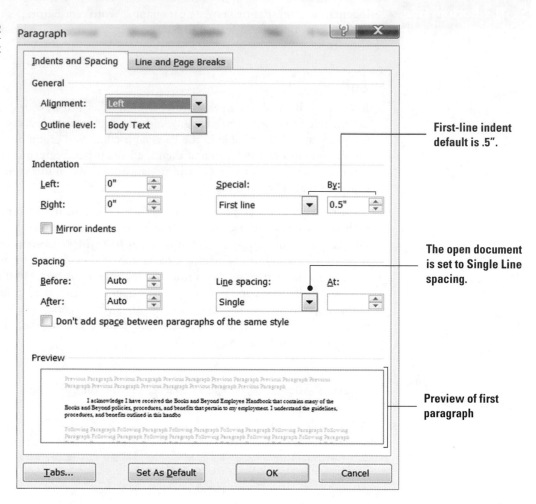

First-line indent
default is .5".

The open document
is set to Single Line
spacing.

Preview of first
paragraph

9. Figure 4-3 displays the paragraph with the first-line indent you just set.

Figure 4-3

Ruler with first-line indent
marker on first paragraph

First-line indent at .5"
marker on ruler

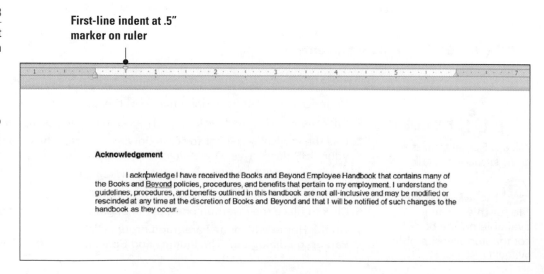

Another Way
You can also click to place the insertion point before the first line in the paragraph, then drag the first-line indent marker on the ruler (see Figure 4-3) to the place where you want the text to be indented. The insertion point can also be placed anywhere within the paragraph to set the indent.

10. Click to place the insertion point in the second paragraph.

11. On the horizontal ruler, press and hold the left mouse button and drag the hanging indent ⌂ marker to **0.5** inches. Your screen should match Figure 4-4.

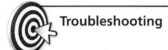

First-line indent at left margin

Acknowledgement

    I acknowledge I have received the Books and Beyond Employee Handbook that contains many of the Books and Beyond policies, procedures, and benefits that pertain to my employment. I understand the guidelines, procedures, and benefits outlined in this handbook are not all-inclusive and may be modified or rescinded at any time at the discretion of Books and Beyond and that I will be notified of such changes to the handbook as they occur.

I also understand the Employee Handbook does not constitute a contract, expressed or implied, nor is it to be interpreted to be a contract between Books and Beyond and myself. I understand the company is an at-will employer, and I am an employee-at-will, which means the employment relationship may be terminated at anytime by either myself or Books and Beyond (unless I am under an employee contract and following the terms and conditions therein).

Troubleshooting If the horizontal ruler is not visible along the top of the document, click the View Ruler button at the top of the vertical scroll bar to display it, or click the View tab and choose Ruler from the Show command group.

Another Way
You can also click to place the insertion point on the hanging indent marker on the ruler (see Figure 4-4), then drag the marker to set the hanging indent.

12. Place the insertion point in the third paragraph.

13. On the Page Layout tab, in the Paragraph group, click the up arrow next to Indent Left ten times to indent the left side of the paragraph to **1 inch** on the ruler.

14. Click the up arrow next to Indent Right ten times to indent the right side of the paragraph to **1 inch** on the ruler (see Figure 4-5). Notice the paragraph has moved in 1 inch from both the left and the right margin and the paragraph is indented on both sides.

**Indent Left is 1"
from the left
margin.**

**Indent Right is 1"
from the right
margin.**

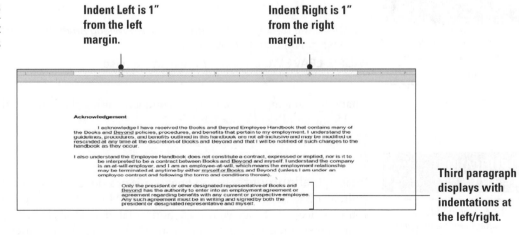

Acknowledgement

    I acknowledge I have received the Books and Beyond Employee Handbook that contains many of the Books and Beyond policies, procedures, and benefits that pertain to my employment. I understand the guidelines, procedures, and benefits outlined in this handbook are not all-inclusive and may be modified or rescinded at any time at the discretion of Books and Beyond and that I will be notified of such changes to the handbook as they occur.

I also understand the Employee Handbook does not constitute a contract, expressed or implied, nor is it to be interpreted to be a contract between Books and Beyond and myself. I understand the company is an at-will employer, and I am an employee-at-will, which means the employment relationship may be terminated at anytime by either myself or Books and Beyond (unless I am under an employee contract and following the terms and conditions therein).

Only the president or other designated representative of Books and Beyond has the authority to enter into an employment agreement or agreement regarding benefits with any current or prospective employee. Any such agreement must be in writing and signed by both the president or designated representative and myself.

**Third paragraph
displays with
indentations at
the left/right.**

Another Way
To indent the first line of a paragraph, click in front of the line and press Tab. To indent an entire paragraph, select the whole paragraph and press Tab.

15. Place the insertion point in the last paragraph.

Figure 4-6

Ruler with negative indent

16. On the ruler, press and hold the left mouse button and drag the left indent marker into the left margin at –0.5 inches, as shown in Figure 4-6.

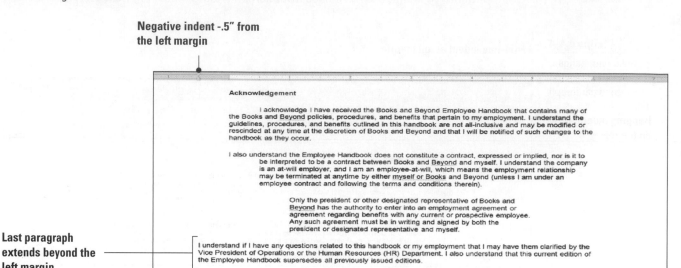

Negative indent -.5" from the left margin

Last paragraph extends beyond the left margin.

Figure 4-7

Sample document displaying several indentations

17. Your document should look similar to the one shown in Figure 4-7.

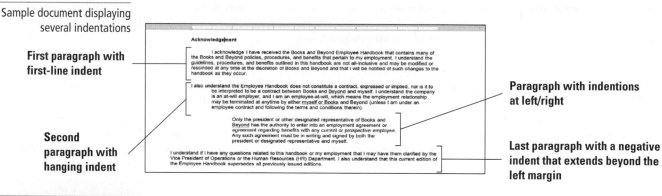

First paragraph with first-line indent

Second paragraph with hanging indent

Paragraph with indentions at left/right

Last paragraph with a negative indent that extends beyond the left margin

CERTIFICATION READY? 2.3.1

How do you format a paragraph with a first-line indent?

18. SAVE the document as *handbook_acknowledgement* in the lesson folder on your USB flash drive, then **CLOSE** the file.

PAUSE. LEAVE Word open for the next exercise.

Take Note Changing paragraph indents can be completed using the Ruler or the Paragraph dialog box on the Home and Page Layout tabs.

CERTIFICATION READY? 2.3.1

How do you format a paragraph with a hanging indent?

Changing Alignment

Paragraph **alignment** refers to how text is positioned between a document's margins. By default, text is left-aligned at the top of the page. However, as you continue to format a document, you may need to change your text's horizontal or vertical alignment. In this exercise, you learn to align text left, center, right, and justified and to vertically center text in the document.

CERTIFICATION READY? 2.3.7

How do you move a marker on the ruler?

Horizontal alignment refers to how text is positioned between the left and right margins. There are four types of horizontal alignments: left align, center, right align, or justify. Horizontal alignment can be changed in the Paragraph group, which can be accessed on both the Home tab and the Page Layout tab. Also, when the Paragraph dialog box is open and the Indents and Spacing tab is active, you can change alignment in the General section of the tab. Alternatively, you can use various shortcut keys, as shown in Table 4-2.

Table 4-2

Horizontal Alignment Options

Another Way
To access the Paragraph dialog box using the shortcut method, place the insertion point in the paragraph, then right-click and select Paragraph from the menu that appears.

Option	Button	Shortcut Keys	Description
Align left	▤	Ctrl+L	Lines up text flush with the left margin, leaving a ragged right edge
Center	▤	Ctrl+E	Centers text between the left and right margins, leaving ragged edges on both sides
Align right	▤	Ctrl+R	Lines up text flush with the right margin, leaving a ragged left edge
Justify	▤	Ctrl+J	Lines up text flush on both the left and right margins, adding extra space between words as necessary for a clean look

Vertical alignment refers to how text is positioned between the top and bottom margins of the page. Text can be aligned vertically at the top margin, at the center of the page, or at the bottom of the page, or it can be justified. Top-of-the-page vertical alignment is the default when launching Word. Centered vertical alignment places the text evenly between the top and bottom margins. Bottom vertical alignment places text next to the bottom margin of the document. Finally, justified vertical alignment aligns text evenly between the top, bottom, left, and right margins. (See Table 4-3.)

There are two ways to set vertical alignment.

- From the Page Layout tab, in the Page Setup group, launch the Page Setup dialog box. From the Layout tab, under the Page group, you will find the Vertical Alignment pull-down menu.
- From the File tab, select Print and then Page Setup. This launches the Page Setup dialog box also. From the Layout tab, under the Page group, you will find the Vertical Alignment pull-down menu.

Table 4-3

Vertical Alignment Options

Option	Description
Top vertical alignment	Aligns text at the top margin
Centered vertical alignment	Aligns text between the top and bottom margins
Bottom vertical alignment	Aligns text at the bottom margin
Justified vertical alignment	Aligns text equally between the top, bottom, left, and right margins

STEP BY STEP | **Change Alignment**

OPEN *introduction* from the data files from this lesson.

@ The *introduction* file for this lesson is available on the book companion website or in WileyPLUS.

1. Click to place the insertion point in the first paragraph.
2. On the Home tab, in the Paragraph group, click the Justify 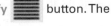 button. The paragraph is justified between the left and right margins.
3. Place the insertion point in the second paragraph.
4. On the Home tab, in the Paragraph group, click the drop-down arrow to launch the Paragraph dialog box. The Indents and Spacing tab should be selected.
5. In the Alignment list under General, click the drop-down arrow, then click Centered. Click OK. The paragraph is centered between the left and right margins.
6. Place the insertion point in the third paragraph.

7. Press **Ctrl+R** to align the text on the right. The right side of the paragraph is now even, while the left is uneven.

8. On the Page Layout tab, in the Page Setup group, click the drop-down arrow to open the Page Setup dialog box. Then, click the **Layout** tab.

9. In the Vertical alignment list under Page, click the drop-down arrow and select **Center**.

10. In the Apply To list under Preview, Whole document is selected, as shown in Figure 4-8.

Figure 4-8

Page Setup dialog box

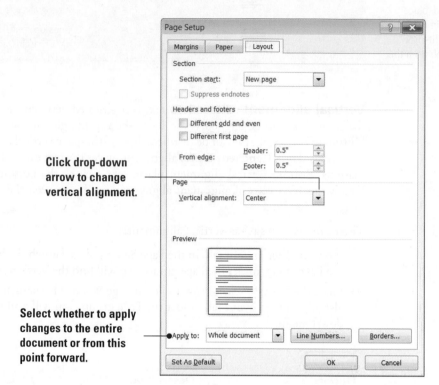

Click drop-down arrow to change vertical alignment.

Select whether to apply changes to the entire document or from this point forward.

11. Click **OK**. The text is centered between the top and bottom margins, as shown in Figure 4-9.

Figure 4-9

Horizontal and vertical alignments

Paragraph Justified

Text Centered

Text Align Right

Text Align Left

Vertical alignment centers text between top and bottom.

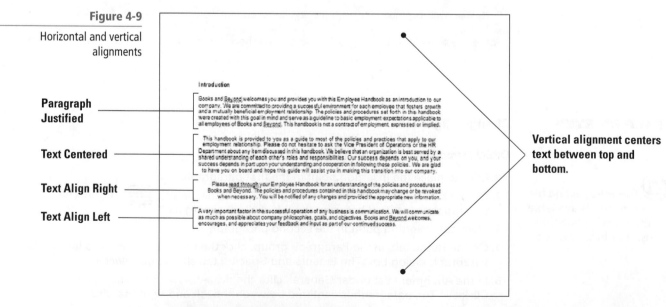

12. **SAVE** the document as *handbook_introduction* in the lesson folder on your USB flash drive, then **CLOSE** the file.

PAUSE. LEAVE Word open for the next exercise.

Shading a Paragraph

In this exercise, you learn to use Word's Shading feature to color the background behind selected text or paragraphs.

To apply shading to a paragraph, click the Shading button in the Paragraph group. To choose another color, click the drop-down arrow next to the Shading button, and choose a color in the current theme or a standard color from the Shading menu (place your insertion point over a color to see a ScreenTip with the color's precise name). To remove shading, click No Color.

Click More Colors to open the Colors dialog box, where additional options are available. You can choose standard colors in the Standard tab, or you can create a custom color from the Custom tab.

STEP BY STEP   **Shade a Paragraph**

OPEN the *diversity* file from the data files for this lesson.

@ The *diversity* file for this lesson is available on the book companion website or in WileyPLUS.

1. Place the insertion point in the first paragraph.
2. On the Home tab, in the Paragraph group, click the **drop-down arrow** next to the Shading ⬧ ⌄ button to display the menu shown in Figure 4-10.

Figure 4-10

Shading menu

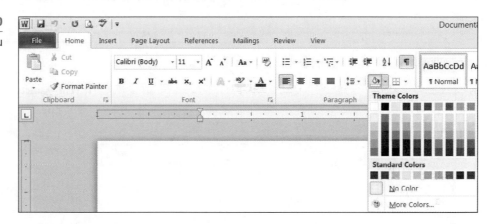

3. In the Theme Colors palette, click the color in the third row of the last column (**Orange, Accent 6, Lighter 40%**), as shown in Figure 4-11.

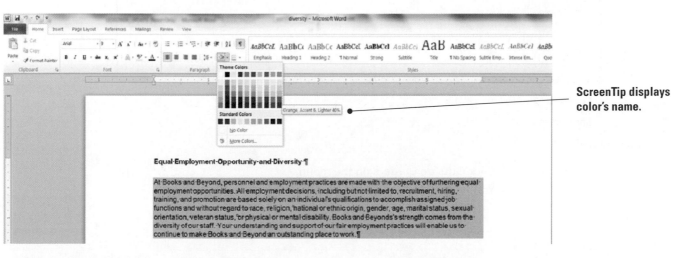

ScreenTip displays color's name.

Figure 4-11

Shaded paragraph

4. **SAVE** the document as *handbook_diversity* in the lesson folder on your USB flash drive.

PAUSE. LEAVE the document open to use in the next exercise.

Placing a Border around a Paragraph

Like shading, borders can add interest and emphasis to paragraphs. Borders can be formatted with a variety of styles, colors, and widths. In this exercise, you use Word's Border options to apply a border to a paragraph in your document.

You can apply a border to a paragraph by clicking the Border button in the Paragraph group on the Home tab. To change the border style, click the drop-down arrow next to the Border button.

For additional options, click the Borders and Shading option on the Border menu to display the Borders tab of the Borders and Shading dialog box. You can choose a number of border colors and styles in this dialog box, or you can remove a border completely. This dialog box also contains tabs for page border options and shading.

STEP BY STEP   **Place a Border around a Paragraph**

USE the document that is open from the previous exercise.

1. Place the insertion point in the second paragraph.
2. On the Home tab, in the Paragraph group, click the **drop-down arrow** next to the Border ⊞ ▾ button to display the menu shown in Figure 4-12.

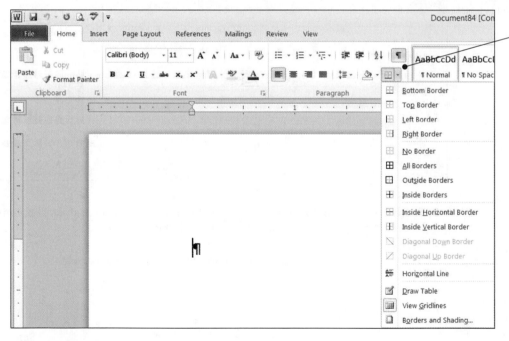

Click drop-down arrow to display Border menu.

Figure 4-12

Border menu

3. Click **Outside Borders** on the menu.
4. Your document should look similar to Figure 4-13.

Figure 4-13

Shading and border

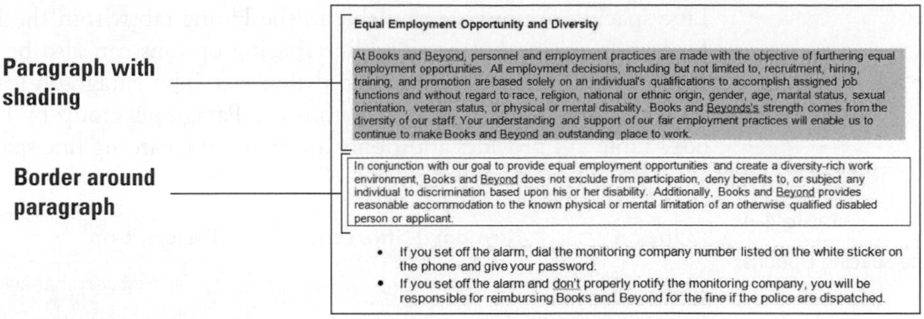

Paragraph with shading

Border around paragraph

Another Way
The Borders and Shading dialog box can be accessed by clicking the drop-down arrow next to the Border button, then clicking Borders and Shading.

> Equal Employment Opportunity and Diversity
>
> At Books and Beyond, personnel and employment practices are made with the objective of furthering equal employment opportunities. All employment decisions, including but not limited to, recruitment, hiring, training, and promotion are based solely on an individual's qualifications to accomplish assigned job functions and without regard to race, religion, national or ethnic origin, gender, age, marital status, sexual orientation, veteran status, or physical or mental disability. Books and Beyonds's strength comes from the diversity of our staff. Your understanding and support of our fair employment practices will enable us to continue to make Books and Beyond an outstanding place to work.
>
> In conjunction with our goal to provide equal employment opportunities and create a diversity-rich work environment, Books and Beyond does not exclude from participation, deny benefits to, or subject any individual to discrimination based upon his or her disability. Additionally, Books and Beyond provides reasonable accommodation to the known physical or mental limitation of an otherwise qualified disabled person or applicant.
>
> • If you set off the alarm, dial the monitoring company number listed on the white sticker on the phone and give your password.
> • If you set off the alarm and don't properly notify the monitoring company, you will be responsible for reimbursing Books and Beyond for the fine if the police are dispatched.

5. **SAVE** the document with the same filename in the lesson folder on your USB flash drive.

PAUSE. LEAVE Word open for the next exercise.

Take Note   Borders can also be added to pages, sections, tables, cells, graphic objects, and pictures.

Clearing the Formats from a Paragraph

After formatting your document, you may decide that you no longer want any formatting in a paragraph or that you want to begin again. The Clear Formatting command provides an easy way to change a paragraph back to plain text. When you execute this command, all formatting is removed, and the font and font size revert to the original document settings. In this exercise, you use the Clear Formatting command to clear all formats from selected paragraphs in Word.

STEP BY STEP   **Clear Paragraph Formats**

USE the document that is open from the previous exercise.

1. Select the first two paragraphs.
2. On the Home tab, in the Font group, click the Clear Formatting button.

X   **Ref**

You can also clear formatting in the Styles group by clicking the More button. For more information, see Lesson 3.

3. **SAVE** the document as *handbook_eeo* in the lesson folder on your USB flash drive, then **CLOSE** the file.

PAUSE. LEAVE Word open for the next exercise.

SETTING LINE SPACING IN TEXT AND BETWEEN PARAGRAPHS

The Bottom Line

In Word, you can determine how much space separates lines of text, and you also can set the spacing between paragraphs. By default, Word sets line spacing (the space between each line of text) to 1.15. Line spacing is paragraph based and can be customized by specifying a point size. Paragraph spacing, which affects the space above and below paragraphs, is set to 10 points after each paragraph by default. The higher the point size is, the greater the space between paragraphs is. In this exercise, you learn to set both line and paragraph spacing.

Setting Line Spacing

Line spacing is the amount of space between the lines of text in a paragraph. In this exercise, you learn to set line spacing using a number of Word paragraph formatting tools.

Line spacing options are available in the Home tab within the Paragraph group by using the Line and Spacing button. The line spacing options can also be accessed through the Indents and Spacing tab of the Paragraph dialog box. The Paragraph formatting tools can also be accessed in the Page Layout tab within the Paragraph group by launchingthe Paragraph dialog box. Table 4-4 provides additional information regarding line spacing options and descriptions.

Table 4-4

Line Spacing Options

Option	Keyboard Shortcut	Description
Single	Ctrl+1	Default option that accommodates the largest font in a line, plus a small amount of extra space.
1.5	Ctrl+5	One-and-one-half times the amount of space used in single spacing.
Double	Ctrl+2	Twice the amount of space used in single spacing.
At least		Sets the spacing at the minimum amount needed to fit the largest font on the line.
Exactly		Sets the spacing at a fixed amount that Word does not adjust.
Multiple		Sets the spacing at an amount that is increased or decreased from single spacing by a percentage that you specify. Setting the line spacing to 1.3, for example, increases the space by 30%.

STEP BY STEP   **Set Line Spacing in a Paragraph**

OPEN the *handbook_introduction* document you completed earlier in this lesson.

1. Place the insertion point in the first paragraph.

2. On the Home tab, in the Paragraph group, click the **Line and Paragraph Spacing** button to display the Line Spacing menu, as shown in Figure 4-14.

Figure 4-14

Line Spacing menu

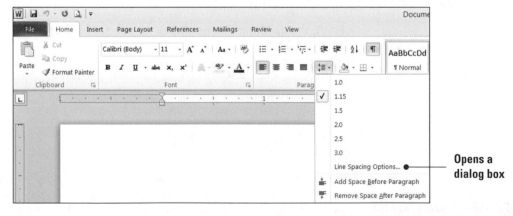

Opens a dialog box

3. Select **2.0** to double-space the selected text.

4. Place the insertion point in the second paragraph.

5. On the Home tab, in the Paragraph group, click the **drop-down arrow** next to the Line and Paragraph Spacing button to display the menu.

6. To set more precise spacing measurements, click **Line Spacing Options** to display the Indents and Spacing tab of the Paragraph dialog box.

CERTIFICATION READY?   **2.4.1**

How do you change the line spacing in a paragraph?

7. In the Line Spacing section, click the **drop-down arrow** and select **Exactly** in the Line Spacing list. In the At list, click the **up** arrow until it reads **14 pt**. The line spacing is increased.

8. Click **OK**.

9. **SAVE** the document as **handbook_introduction_1** in the lesson folder on your USB flash drive.

PAUSE. LEAVE the document open to use in the next exercise.

Setting Paragraph Spacing

Paragraphs are usually separated by a blank line in Word documents. When you press the Enter key at the end of a paragraph, Word adds the designated space above or below the paragraph. By default, the spacing after a paragraph is set to 10 points and the spacing before paragraphs is set to zero, but you can change these settings for a single paragraph or for an entire document. In this exercise, you learn to set paragraph spacing.

To increase or decrease paragraph spacing, click the Before and After up or down arrows in the Indents and Spacing tab of the Paragraph dialog box. The Paragraph dialog box can be accessed using the dialog box launcher in the Paragraph group of the Home tab, the dialog box launcher in the Paragraph group of the Page Layout tab, or by right-clicking and selecting Paragraph from the menu that appears.

Paragraph spacing can also be changed in the Paragraph group on the Home tab by clicking the Line Spacing button to Add Space Before or After Paragraph or Remove Space Before or After Paragraph.

STEP BY STEP	**Set Spacing around a Paragraph**

USE the document that is open from the previous exercise.

1. Place the insertion point in the third paragraph.

CERTIFICATION READY?   **2.4.2**

How do you set spacing before and after paragraphs?

2. On the Home tab, in the Paragraph group, click the **drop-down arrow** to display the Paragraph dialog box. The Indents and Spacing tab is the active tab.

3. In the Spacing section, click the **up arrow** next to Before until it reads **24 pt**.

4. Click the **up arrow** next to After until it reads **24 pt**.

5. Click **OK**. Notice the spacing between the paragraphs.

6. With the insertion point still in the third paragraph, click the **drop-down arrow** next to the Line and Paragraph Spacing ⬍☰ button in the Paragraph group to display the Line Spacing menu.

Another Way
You also can use the Paragraph command group on the Page Layout tab to change paragraph spacing.

7. Click **Remove Space Before Paragraph**.

8. **SAVE** the document as **handbook_introduction_2** in the lesson folder on your USB flash drive, then CLOSE the file.

PAUSE. LEAVE Word open for the next exercise.

CREATING AND FORMATTING A BULLETED LIST

The Bottom Line

Bulleted lists are an effective way to format lists of items that don't have to appear in any specific order. (Use numbered lists for items that fall in a set order.) Items in a bulleted list are marked by small icons—dots, diamonds, and so on. In Word, you can create bulleted lists from scratch, change existing lines of text into a bulleted list, choose from a number of bullet styles, create levels within a bulleted list, and insert a symbol or picture as a bullet.

Creating a Bulleted List

By creating and formatting a bulleted list, you can draw attention to major points in a document. In this exercise, you learn to create and format such a list.

STEP BY STEP   **Create a Bulleted List**

OPEN *alarm* from the data files for this lesson.

@ The *alarm* file for this lesson is available on the book companion website or in WileyPLUS.

WILEY PLUS EXTRA

WileyPLUS Extra! features an online tutorial of this task.

1. Select the two sentences below the phrase Please keep in mind:.
2. On the Home tab, in the Paragraph group, click the Bullets ▤ ▾ button. Notice that a solid circle appears before the selected paragraph.
3. Click to place the insertion point at the end of the second bulleted sentence.
4. Press Enter. Word automatically continues the bulleted list by supplying the next bulleted line.
5. Beside the new bullet, key If you do not know your four-digit code and password, please get it from the HR department.
6. Select the entire bulleted list.
7. To change the format of the bulleted list, click the drop-down arrow next to the Bullets ▤ ▾ button to display the menu shown in Figure 4-15. The bulleted items may not match your screen.

Figure 4-15

Bullet formatting options

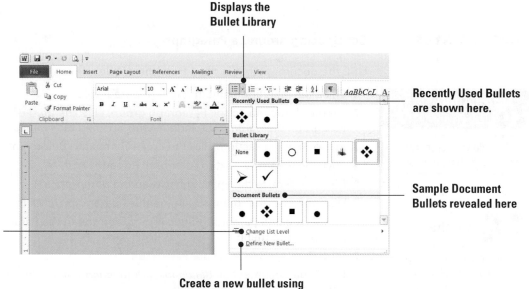

Displays the Bullet Library

Recently Used Bullets are shown here.

Sample Document Bullets revealed here

Change List Level displays different bullet levels.

Create a new bullet using a symbol or picture.

Take Note   To change a bulleted list to a numbered list (or vice versa), select the list and then click either the Bullets button or the Numbering button. If you wish to remove one of the bullets from the Library, complete this process in the Bullet Library section of the Bullet drop-down menu by selecting the bullet and right-clicking to remove it.

8. Click the hollow circle in the Bullet Library.
9. Place the insertion point in the second bulleted item.

10. Click the **drop-down arrow** next to the **Bullets** [icon] ▾ button, point to Change List Level, and note the levels that appear (see Figure 4-16). When you point to the Level List, a ScreenTip will appear displaying the level.

Figure 4-16

Change List Level

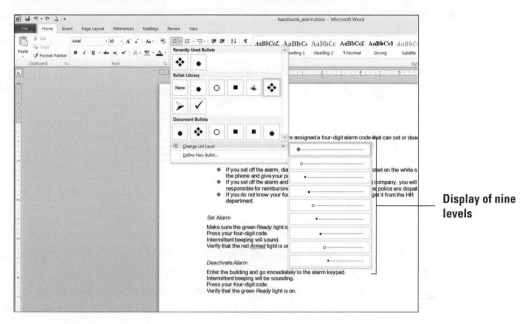

Display of nine levels

11. Click to select **Level 2**. The Bullet item is demoted from Level 1 to Level 2.

12. Place the insertion point in the third bulleted item.

13. Click the **drop-down arrow** next to the **Bullets** [icon] ▾ button, then point to Change List Level to produce a menu of list-level options.

14. Click to select **Level 3**. Your document should look similar to the one shown in Figure 4-17.

Figure 4-17

Bullet levels

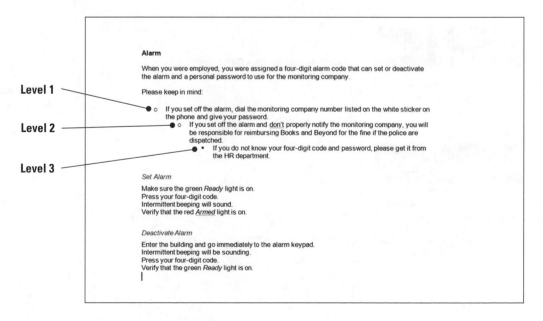

Level 1

Level 2

Level 3

15. **SAVE** the document as **handbook_alarm** in the lesson folder on your USB flash drive.

16. Select the second and third bulleted items and click the **drop-down arrow** next to the **Bullets** [icon] ▾ button. Point to Change List Level and promote the selected bullets to **Level 1**. The two selected items now match the first bulleted item.

17. Select the three **Level 1 bulleted items**.

18. Click the **drop-down arrow** next to the **Bullets** [icon] ▾ button, then click **Define New Bullet**.

19. Click the **Symbol** button in the Define New Bullet dialog box. The Symbol dialog box opens, as shown in Figure 4-18.

Figure 4-18

Symbol dialog box

Opens the Picture Bullet dialog box.

Opens the Font dialog box

The drop-down arrow lists additional fonts.

Opens the Symbol dialog box

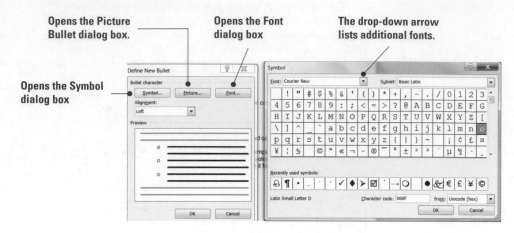

20. Change the Font by clicking the **drop-down arrow**. Scroll down and select **Wingdings**.
21. Select the **bell** in the first row, sixth column. Click **OK** to close the Symbols dialog box.
22. Click **OK** to close the Define New Bullet dialog box.
23. **SAVE** the document as *handbook_alarm1* in the lesson folder on your USB flash drive.
24. The three bulleted items are still selected. Click the **drop-down arrow** next to the Bullets ▮≡ ▾ button, then click **Define New Bullet**.
25. Click the **Picture** button in the Define New Bullet dialog box. The Picture Bullet dialog box opens, as shown in Figure 4-19.

Figure 4-19

Picture Bullet dialog box

Search for a picture by name or by scrolling through.

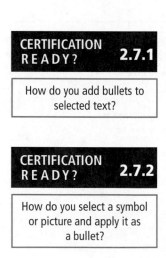

CERTIFICATION READY? 2.7.1

How do you add bullets to selected text?

CERTIFICATION READY? 2.7.2

How do you select a symbol or picture and apply it as a bullet?

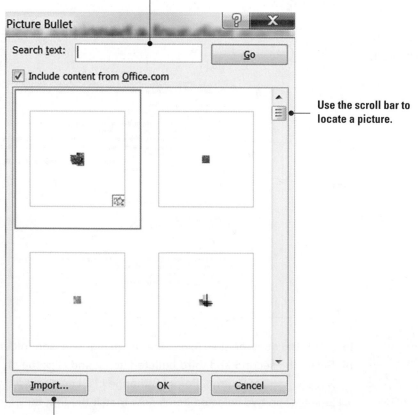

Use the scroll bar to locate a picture.

Import picture from another target location.

CERTIFICATION READY? **2.7.3**

How do you define a new bullet?

26. Select the fifth picture in the first column. Click OK to close the Picture Bullet dialog box, then click OK to close the Define New Bullet dialog box. The new picture bullet appears in the selected text. Deselect the bulleted items.

27. **SAVE** the document as *handbook_alarm_update* in the lesson folder on your USB flash drive.

PAUSE. LEAVE Word open for the next exercise.

CERTIFICATION READY? **2.7.5**

How do you promote and demote bullet levels?

Turning Automatic Bulleting On and Off with AutoFormat

After you have clicked the Bullet button to create a bulleted list, Word's AutoFormat feature automatically continues the bulleted format. In this exercise, you learn how to turn off this automatic bulleting feature in Word.

STEP BY STEP **Turn Automatic Bulleting On or Off with AutoFormat**

USE the document that is open from the previous exercise.

1. Click the File tab to open Backstage view, then click Options.

2. Click Proofing.

3. Click AutoCorrect Options, then click the AutoFormat As You Type tab.

4. Under the section Apply As You Type, select the Automatic Bulleted Lists check box to clear its check mark (an empty check mark indicates the feature is off). To turn Automatic Bulleted Lists back on, click again to place a check mark in the box (see Figure 4-20).

Figure 4-20

AutoCorrect dialog box displaying the AutoFormat As You Type tab

Check mark indicates feature is on.

AutoFormat As You Type tab

Empty check box indicates feature is off.

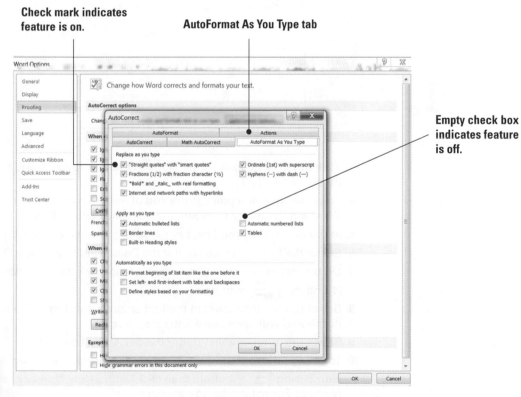

CERTIFICATION READY? **2.7.4**

How do you use AutoFormat to turn on or off the automatic bulleted list feature?

5. Click OK to close the AutoCorrect dialog box, then click OK to close the Word Options dialog box.

PAUSE. LEAVE the document open to use in the next exercise.

Ref   You will learn more about working with lists and multilevel lists in Lesson 12.

CREATING AND FORMATTING A NUMBERED LIST

The Bottom Line   You can quickly add numbers to existing lines of text to create a list, or Word can automatically create a numbered list as you key.

Creating a Numbered List

In this exercise, you learn how to create and format a numbered list in Word.

STEP BY STEP   **Create a Numbered List**

USE the *handbook_alarm_update* document from the previous exercise.

1. Select the four sentences under the Set Alarm heading.
2. On the Home tab, in the Paragraph group, click the **drop-down arrow** next to the Numbering ⅀☰ ▾ button to display the Numbering Library shown in Figure 4-21.

Figure 4-21

Numbering formatting options appear in the Numbering Library

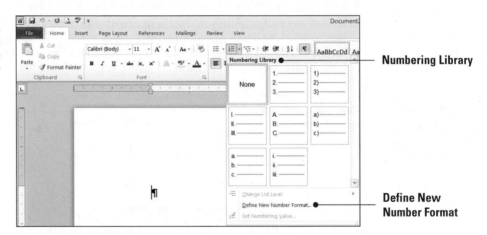

3. Click the **second option** after None in the first row, second column. The rows are numbered 1., 2., 3., . . .
4. Place the insertion point at the end of item number 4 and press **Enter**. Notice that Word automatically numbers the next line sequentially.
5. In the new numbered line, key **Leave the premises immediately**.
6. Select the four sentences under the Deactivate Alarm heading.
7. On the Home tab, in the Paragraph group, click the **drop-down arrow** next to the Numbering ⅀☰ ▾ button.
8. Select the **numbered list** in the first column, third row. The four sentences are numbered with lowercase letters: a., b., c., d.
9. Select the **numbered list** under the *Set Alarm* heading.
10. To change the format of the numbered list, click the **drop-down arrow** next to the Numbering ⅀☰ ▾ button, then click **Define New Number Format**. The Define New Number Format dialog box appears.

11. Click the **drop-down arrow** under the Number style section and select **uppercase roman numerals** (see Figure 4-22). The format for the selected text changed to uppercase roman numerals.

Figure 4-22

Define New Number
Format dialog box

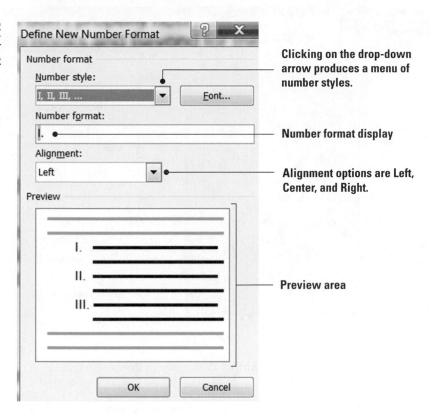

Clicking on the drop-down
arrow produces a menu of
number styles.

Number format display

Alignment options are Left,
Center, and Right.

Preview area

12. Click **OK**.

Take Note   To change the formatting of list numbers, click any number to select the entire list. If you select the text as well, the formatting of both the text and the numbering will change.

13. SAVE the document as *alarm_update* in the lesson folder on your USB flash drive, then **CLOSE** the file.

PAUSE. LEAVE the document open to use in the next exercise.

Take Note   The same process used in Backstage for turning automatic bulleting on and off in Word's AutoFormat feature is applied the same way for the Automatic Numbering List.

Creating an Outline-Style List

Bulleted lists, numbered lists, and multilevel lists are used in documents to provide small, quick, user-friendly pieces of information. In comparison, outline-style lists are typically used to create items such as meeting agendas and legal documents.

STEP BY STEP   **Create an Outline-Style List**

OPEN *outline* from the data files for this lesson.

1. Position the insertion point on the blank line after the Discussion Outline heading.

@ The *outline* file for this lesson is available on the book companion website or in WileyPLUS.

2. On the Home tab, in the Paragraph group, click the **Multilevel List** button. A menu of list formats appears. Notice that when you position the mouse pointer over the formats, they enlarge and expand.

3. Click the format style in the Current List section, as shown in Figure 4-23. The number 1. is inserted for you.

Figure 4-23

Multilevel List menu

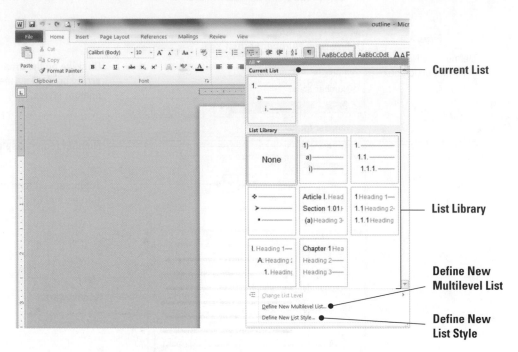

Current List

List Library

Define New Multilevel List

Define New List Style

Take Note   Use the Tab key or Shift+Tab to move to different levels.

4. Key Experience, then press the Enter key.

5. Key Communication with Client and press the Enter key.

6. Press the Tab key and key Initial Meeting. Press the Enter key.

7. Press the Tab key and key Identify Position. Press the Enter key.

8. Press the Tab key and key Qualifications. Press the Enter key.

9. Key Compensation Package and press the Enter key.

10. Key Time Frame and press the Enter key.

11. Press Shift+Tab once to move back one level. Key Progress Reporting and press the Enter key.

12. Press Shift+Tab to move back one more level. Key Methods for Finding Candidates and press the Enter key.

13. Press the Tab key. Key Database and press the Enter key.

14. Key Contacts and press the Enter key.

15. Key Networking.

16. **SAVE** the document as *discussion_outline* in the lesson folder on your USB flash drive.

PAUSE. LEAVE the document open for use in the next exercise.

Sorting a List's Contents

You can sort a single-level list in much the same way that you sort a column in a table.

STEP BY STEP   **Sort a List's Contents**

USE the document that is open from the previous exercise.

1. Select the bulleted list under the Philosophy section.

2. On the Home tab, in the Paragraph group, click the Sort ⚲↓ button. The Sort Text dialog box appears. Click **OK**. Notice the Sort by field is listed by Paragraphs, the Type is listed by Text, and the Ascending order option is selected.

3. **SAVE** the document in the lesson folder on your USB flash drive.

PAUSE. LEAVE the document open to use in the next exercise.

Changing a List's Formatting

Word provides several options for changing the look of a list. You can change a list's formatting by changing the type of bullet or numbering that is displayed. Some formats, such as round bullets, work well for most documents.

STEP BY STEP   **Change a List's Formatting**

USE the document that is open from the previous exercise.

1. Select the bulleted list.

2. On the Home tab, in the Paragraph group, click the drop-down arrow on the Bullets button. A menu appears, as shown in Figure 4-24.

Figure 4-24

Bullet Library

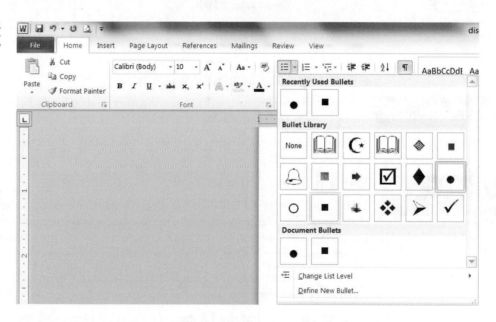

3. Click the square bullet format in the Bullet Library.

4. Select the multilevel list you keyed earlier.

5. On the Home tab, in the Paragraph group, click the drop-down arrow on the Multilevel List button. A menu appears.

6. Under List Library, click the third format in the top row.

7. **SAVE** the document in the lesson folder on your USB flash drive.

PAUSE. LEAVE Word open for the next exercise.

SOFTWARE ORIENTATION

Tab Dialog Box

Tabs in Word insert blank spaces before or within text and paragraphs. You will use the Tabs dialog box, shown in Figure 4-25, to set and clear tabs in Word. Use this figure as a reference throughout the remainder of this lesson as well as the rest of the book.

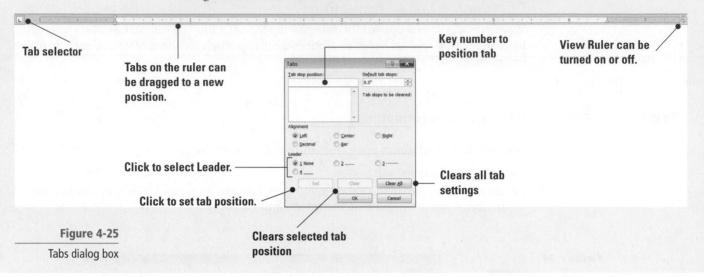

Tab selector

Tabs on the ruler can be dragged to a new position.

Key number to position tab

View Ruler can be turned on or off.

Click to select Leader.

Clears all tab settings

Click to set tab position.

Clears selected tab position

Figure 4-25

Tabs dialog box

SETTING AND MODIFYING TABS

The Bottom Line

As you previously learned, you can use the ruler to set tabs. To be more precise, you can also use the options available in the Tabs dialog box.

Take Note

To view Tabs as they are being set, display nonprinting characters, as discussed in Lesson 1.

CERTIFICATION READY?   **2.3.2**

What are the two ways that you can set tabs?

Setting Tabs on the Ruler

By default, left-aligned tab stops are set every half-inch on the ruler. To set a tab at a different position on the ruler, you can click the tab selector at the left end of the ruler, then position the insertion point on the ruler and click. A ScreenTip will appear showing the type of tabs at the tab selector. In this exercise, you learn to set tabs on Word's ruler.

Table 4-5 lists the types of tabs available in Word and their descriptions. To view tabs on the ruler, place your insertion point over the text.

After tabs are set, press the Tab key; the insertion point will stop at the position set. To move a tab stop to a different position on the ruler, click and drag it left or right to a new position.

Table 4-5

Tab Stops on the Ruler

Name	Button	Description
Left tab	**L**	Left-aligns text at the tab place indicated on the horizontal ruler
Center tab	**⊥**	Centers text at the place indicated on the horizontal ruler
Right tab	**⌐**	Right-aligns text at the place indicated on the horizontal ruler
Decimal tab	**⊥·**	Aligns numbers around a decimal point at the place indicated on the horizontal ruler
Bar tab	**|**	Inserts a vertical bar line at the place indicated on the horizontal ruler

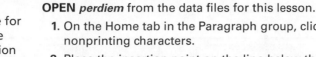

Set Tabs on the Ruler

 The *perdiem* file for this lesson is available on the book companion website or in WileyPLUS.

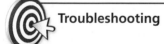

WileyPLUS Extra! features an online tutorial of this task.

OPEN *perdiem* from the data files for this lesson.

1. On the Home tab in the Paragraph group, click the Show/Hide (¶) button to show nonprinting characters.
2. Place the insertion point on the line below the Meals & Incidentals Breakdown heading.
3. Click the tab selector at the left of the ruler until the Center ⊥ tab appears.

   A ScreenTip will appear when you place your pointer over the tab selector. The tab selector and horizontal ruler are shown in Figure 4-26, displaying the different types of tabs.

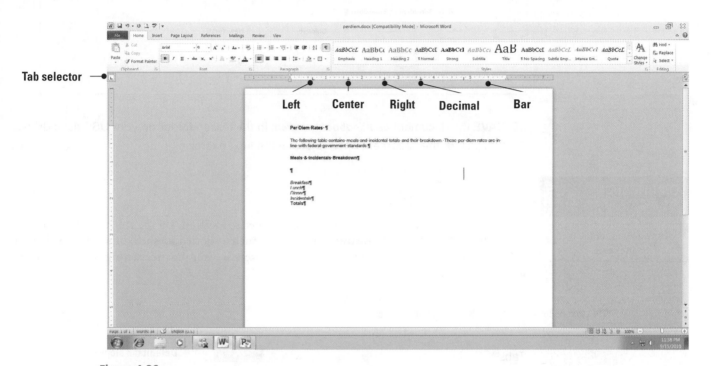

Figure 4-26

Tab selector and horizontal ruler with tab sets

Troubleshooting If the horizontal ruler is not visible, click the View Ruler button at the top of the vertical scroll bar.

4. Click the ruler at the 2.5-inch mark to set a Center ⊥ tab.

5. Click the ruler at the 4-inch mark to set a Center ⊥ tab.
6. Press Tab and key Chicago.
7. Press Tab and key New York.
8. Select the list of words starting with *Breakfast* and ending with *Totals*.
9. Click the tab selector until the Right ⊐ tab appears.
10. Click the ruler at the 1-inch mark to set a Right ⊐ tab.

11. Deselect and place the insertion point in front of each word and press **Tab** to align it at the Right tab. Your document should look similar to the one shown in Figure 4-27.

Figure 4-27

Right tab formatting

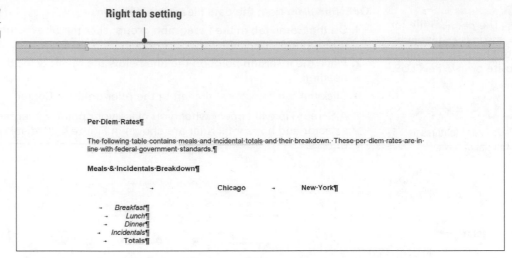

12. **SAVE** the document as *handbook_perdiem* in the lesson folder on your USB flash drive.

PAUSE. LEAVE the document open to use in the next exercise.

CERTIFICATION READY? 2.3.4

How do you set tabs on the ruler?

Using the Tabs Dialog Box

The Tabs dialog box is useful for setting tabs at precise locations on the ruler, clearing all tabs, and setting tab leaders. Tab **leaders** are symbols such as dotted, dashed, or solid lines that fill the space before a tab (see Figure 4-28). In this exercise, you practice setting tabs and leaders using the Tabs dialog box.

Figure 4-28

Tabs dialog box

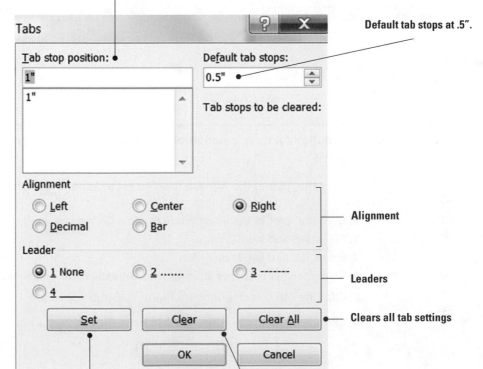

USE the document that is open from the previous exercise.

1. Select the list of words starting with Breakfast and continuing to the end of the document.

2. On the Home tab, in the Paragraph group, click the drop-down arrow to launch the Paragraph dialog box.

3. Click the Tabs button on the bottom left of the Paragraph dialog box to display the Tabs dialog box (see Figure 4-28).

Another Way
To open the Tabs dialog box, double-click any tab stop on the ruler.

4. In the Tab stop position box, key 2.6. In the Alignment section, Right is already selected. In the Leader section, select 2, then click Set. After setting individuals tabs, you must click Set to position the tab setting.

5. In the Tab stop position box, key 4.1. In the Alignment section, Right is already selected. In the Leader section, select 2, then click Set. Setting a leader provides a guide to the next tab setting.

CERTIFICATION READY?   2.3.3

How do you set tabs using the dialog box?

6. Click OK.

7. Place the insertion point after the word Breakfast and press Tab.

8. Key $10 and press Tab.

9. Key $12. Repeat this process for each line, keying the numbers shown in Figure 4-29.

Figure 4-29

Tabs and tab leaders formatting

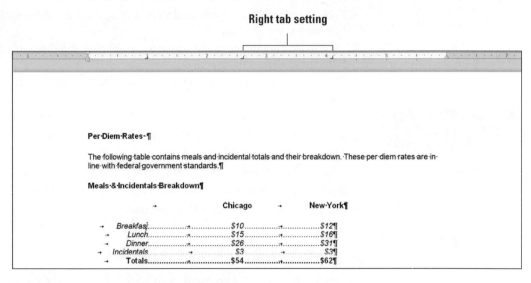

10. SAVE the document as *handbook_perdieum_1* in the lesson folder on your USB flash drive.

PAUSE. LEAVE the document open to use in the next exercise.

Moving Tabs

Tabs can be placed in a new position on the ruler by dragging with the mouse pointer.

STEP BY STEP   Move Tabs

USE the document that is open from the previous exercise.

1. Select the block of text beginning with Breakfast . . . and ending with . . . $62. Include the nonprinting character (¶).

2. Position the mouse pointer at 4.1" on the ruler until you see the Right Tab ScreenTip.

3. Press and hold the left mouse button and drag on the ruler to 5.1". Release the left mouse button. Notice the Right tab setting for the five lines is positioned at 5.1" on the ruler.

CERTIFICATION READY? 2.3.7

How do you reposition tabs on the ruler?

4. Select **New York**. Drag the **Center tab** setting and position it at **5"** on the ruler.

5. **SAVE** the document as *handbook_perdiem_2* in the lesson folder on your USB flash drive.

PAUSE. LEAVE the document open to use in the next exercise.

Clearing Tabs

Tabs can be removed by dragging, or you can use the Tabs dialog box to clear one or all tabs. To remove a tab stop from the ruler, click and drag it off the ruler. When you release the mouse button, the tab stop disappears. Or, open the Tabs dialog box, where you can choose to clear one tab or all tabs. In this exercise, you practice clearing tabs from your Word document.

STEP BY STEP   **Clear Tabs**

USE the document that is open from the previous exercise.

1. Place the insertion point on the last line (**Totals**).

2. Move your mouse pointer to the tab stop at **5.1"** on the ruler.

3. Press and hold the mouse button and drag it off the ruler. Release the mouse button to remove the tab stop.

4. On the Home tab, in the Paragraph group, click the **drop-down arrow** to launch the Paragraph dialog box.

5. Click the **Tabs** button on the bottom left of the dialog box to display the Tabs dialog box.

6. In the Tab stop position list, click **2.6"**, then click **Clear** to clear that tab.

7. Click the **Clear All** button to clear all tabs on that line.

8. Click **OK** to close the Tabs dialog box.

9. Select all the text on the **Totals** line and press the **Delete** button to delete it.

10. **SAVE** the document with the same filename, then **CLOSE** the file.

PAUSE. LEAVE Word open for the next exercise.

CERTIFICATION READY? 2.3.5

How do you clear tabs using the ruler and the Tabs dialog box?

Setting Tab Stops

Tab stops can be reset from the default of 0.5 inch. Each time you press the Tab key, the tab moves half an inch on the ruler. Thus, by pressing the Tab key twice, for example, the insertion point moves to one inch on the ruler. In this exercise, you practice setting tab stops.

STEP BY STEP   **Set Tab Stops**

1. **OPEN** a new blank document. Click the **File** tab, and select **New**. Choose **Blank Document**, and then **Create** to open a new blank document.

2. Press the **Tab** key once.

3. Press the **Tab** key two more times; the insertion point is now positioned at 1½ inches on the ruler.

4. Press the **Tab** key three times; the insertion point moves to the 3-inch mark on the ruler. Press **Enter**.

5. On the Home tab, in the Paragraph group, click the **dialog box launcher**.

6. In the Paragraph dialog box, click the **Tabs** button to open the Tabs dialog box.

7. Click the **up arrow** below Default Tab Stops until it stops at 1 inch. Click **OK**.

8. Press the **Tab** key three times and notice the insertion point on the ruler now stops at every 1 inch.

STOP. CLOSE Word without saving the changes.

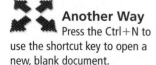

Another Way
Press the Ctrl+N to use the shortcut key to open a new, blank document.

CERTIFICATION READY? 2.3.6

How do you change tab stops from the default setting?

Take Note   Many of the predesigned document layout options in Word 2010 make it possible to create documents such as an index or table of contents without having to set any tabs manually.

SKILL SUMMARY

In This Lesson, You Learned How To:	Exam Objective	Objective Number
Format paragraphs	Apply indents to paragraphs.	2.3.1
Set line spacing in text and between paragraphs	Apply line spacing to text and paragraphs.	2.4.1
	Apply paragraph spacing to text and paragraphs.	2.4.2
Create and format a bulleted list	Apply bullets to a document.	2.7.1
	Select a symbol format.	2.7.2
	Define a picture to be used as a bullet.	2.7.3
	Use AutoFormat on bulleted lists.	2.7.4
	Promote and demote bullet levels.	2.7.5
Create and format a numbered list		
Set and modifying tabs	Set tabs.	2.3.2
	Use the Tabs dialog box.	2.3.3
	Set tabs on the ruler.	2.3.4
	Clear tabs.	2.3.5
	Set tab stops.	2.3.6
	Move tab stops.	2.3.7

Knowledge Assessment

True/False

Circle T if the statement is true or F if the statement is false.

T F   1. Pressing the Enter key will indent the first line of a paragraph.

T F   2. An indent is the space between a paragraph and the document's left and/or right margin.

T F   3. You can use the ruler to set tabs.

T F   4. A bar tab inserts a vertical bar line at the place indicated on the vertical ruler.

T F   5. Tab leaders are dotted, dashed, or solid lines that fill the space before a tab.

T F   6. The Clear Formatting command will only clear the fonts applied to the selected text.

T F   7. Horizontal alignment refers the position of text with regard to the top and bottom margins of a document.

T F   8. Centered vertical alignment aligns text between the top and bottom margin.

T F   9. Indents can be changed using the markers on the ruler.

T F   10. The shortcut to double-space a paragraph is Ctrl+2.

Multiple Choice

Select the best response for the following statements.

1. Which of the following is not a type of indent?
   a. Hanging
   b. Negative
   c. Positive
   d. First-line

2. Which word(s) refers to how text is positioned between the top and bottom margins of the page?
   a. Horizontal alignment
   b. Vertical alignment
   c. Justified
   d. Line spacing

3. Which line spacing command sets the spacing at a fixed amount that Word does not adjust?
   a. Exactly
   b. Double
   c. Multiple
   d. At least

4. Where is the View Ruler button located?
   a. In the Tabs dialog box
   b. At the top of the vertical scroll bar
   c. In the Paragraph group
   d. All of the above

5. What does dragging a tab off the ruler do?
   a. Moves it to another position
   b. Turns it into a left-aligned tab
   c. Clears it
   d. Hides it from view

6. Bullets can be defined by adding a:
   a. symbol.
   b. box.
   c. picture.
   d. Both a and c

7. Which property of borders can be changed in the Borders tab of the Borders and Shading dialog box?
   a. Color
   b. Width
   c. Style
   d. All of the above

8. The inverted L ⌐ sets which tab on the ruler?
   a. Left
   b. Right
   c. Center
   d. Decimal

9. Which tab setting would you use to align a list of currency values?
   a. Decimal
   b. Center
   c. Right
   d. Decimal with leaders
10. Defining a New Number format applies to which of the following styles?
   a. I, II, III
   b. 1), 2), 3)
   c. 1., 2., 3.
   d. All of the above

Competency Assessment

Project 4-1: Lost Art Photos

You are employed in the marketing department at Lost Art Photos and have been asked to format a promotional document.

GET READY. LAUNCH Word if it is not already running.

1. **OPEN** *photos* from the data files for this lesson.
2. **SAVE** the document as *lost_art_photos* in the lesson folder on your USB flash drive.
3. **SELECT** the document's title.
4. On the Home tab, in the Paragraph group, click **drop-down arrow** on the Border ⊞ ▾ button.
5. Scroll down and click **Borders and Shading** to open the Borders and Shading dialog box.
6. In the Setting list, click **Shadow**. On the Width list, click **3 pt**.
7. Click **OK** to close the Borders and Shading dialog box.
8. On the Home tab, in the Paragraph group, click the **drop-down arrow** next to the Shading ⌕ ▾ button.
9. Under Theme Colors, click the color that is labeled **Olive Green, Accent 3, Lighter 60%**.
10. Select the first paragraph.
11. On the Home tab, in the Paragraph group, click the **Line Spacing** ⇕☰ button.
12. Click **1.0** on the menu.
13. Select **Affordable Prints**.
14. Click the **down arrow** next to the Border ⊞ ▾ button.
15. Click **Outside Borders** from the selection.
16. Click the **drop-down arrow** next to the Shading ⌕ ▾ button.
17. Click the color that is labeled **Olive Green, Accent 3, Lighter 40%**.
18. Double-click the **Format Painter** ✣ Format Painter to copy the formatting of *Affordable Prints* to each of the other headings: *Quality Product, Options, Options, Options,* and *Satisfaction Guaranteed.* Click the Format Painter to turn it off.
19. **SAVE** the document in the lesson folder on your USB flash drive, then **CLOSE** the file.

LEAVE Word open for the next project.

@ The *photos* file for this lesson is available on the book companion website or in WileyPLUS.

Project 4-2: General Performance Expectation Guidelines

In your job at Books and Beyond, you continue to work on documents that will be part of the employee handbook.

GET READY. LAUNCH Word if it is not already running.

@ The *guidelines* file for this lesson is available on the book companion website or in WileyPLUS.

1. **OPEN** *guidelines* from the data files for this lesson.
2. **SAVE** the document as *handbook_guidelines* in the lesson folder on your USB flash drive.
3. Select the two lines that begin Verbal discussion . . . and Written warning . . ..
4. On the Home tab, in the Paragraph group, click the drop-down arrow next to the Bullets ⫶☰ ▾ button and select the solid circle.
5. Place the insertion point after the second sentence in the list and press Enter.
6. Key Termination as the third bulleted item.
7. Select the double-spaced lines beginning with abuse, misuse . . . and ending with falsification, misinterpretation . . . .
8. Click the drop-down arrow next to the Bullets ⫶☰ ▾ button and click Define New Bullet.
9. Click the Symbol button, then click the drop-down arrow in the Font box and select Wingdings. In the fifth row, fifth column, select the solid diamonds. Click OK to close the Symbol dialog box, then click OK to close the Define New Bullet dialog box.
10. Select the remaining paragraphs beginning with insubordination, willful disregard . . . and ending with engaging in conduct . . . .
11. Click the drop-down arrow next to the Bullets ⫶☰ ▾ button and click Define New Bullet.
12. Click the Picture button and in the search text box, key diamond and click GO. Select the second diamond and click OK to close the Picture Bullet dialog box; then click OK to close the Define New Bullet dialog box.
13. Select the first, second, third, and last paragraph in the document.
14. On the Home tab, in the Paragraph group, and click the Justify ☰ button.
15. With the paragraphs still selected, apply the first-line indent by launching the Paragraph dialog box. On the Home tab, in the Paragraph group, click the drop-down arrow to launch the *Paragraph* dialog box. Under Special, select the drop-down arrow and select First Line Indent ▽. Click OK to close the Paragraph dialog box.
16. **SAVE** the document in the lesson folder on your USB flash drive, then **CLOSE** the file.

LEAVE Word open for the next project.

Proficiency Assessment

Project 4-3: PTA Officers

You are a volunteer at the local elementary school and have been asked to format a PTA document that lists the officers for the upcoming school year.

@ The *pta* file for this lesson is available on the book companion website or in WileyPLUS.

GET READY. LAUNCH Word if it is not already running.

1. **OPEN** *pta* from the data files for this lesson.
2. **SAVE** the document as *pta_officers* in the lesson folder on your USB flash drive.

3. Use the Tabs dialog box to format the document as shown in Figure 4-30.

Figure 4-30

Formatted PTA document tabs

Set a Right tab at 1.38".

Set a Left tab at 2".

Set a Right tab at 5.5" with a leader.

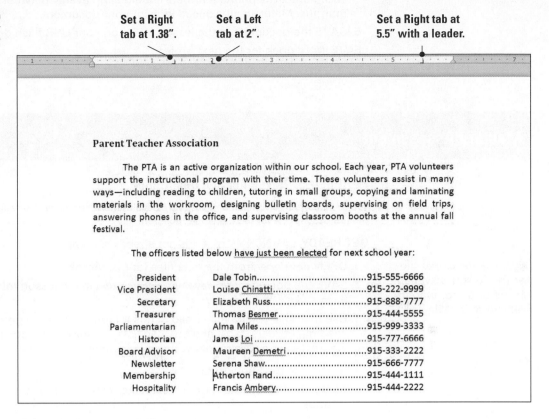

Parent Teacher Association

The PTA is an active organization within our school. Each year, PTA volunteers support the instructional program with their time. These volunteers assist in many ways—including reading to children, tutoring in small groups, copying and laminating materials in the workroom, designing bulletin boards, supervising on field trips, answering phones in the office, and supervising classroom booths at the annual fall festival.

The officers listed below have just been elected for next school year:

President	Dale Tobin	915-555-6666
Vice President	Louise Chinatti	915-222-9999
Secretary	Elizabeth Russ	915-888-7777
Treasurer	Thomas Besmer	915-444-5555
Parliamentarian	Alma Miles	915-999-3333
Historian	James Loi	915-777-6666
Board Advisor	Maureen Demetri	915-333-2222
Newsletter	Serena Shaw	915-666-7777
Membership	Atherton Rand	915-444-1111
Hospitality	Francis Ambery	915-444-2222

4. SAVE the document in the lesson folder on your USB flash drive, then **CLOSE** the file. **LEAVE** Word open for the next project.

Project 4-4: Phone List

Create a list of numbers that you call frequently to keep beside your phone.

GET READY. LAUNCH Word if it is not already running.

1. CREATE a new Word document.

2. SAVE the document as *phone_list* in the lesson folder on your USB flash drive.

3. Create a list of phone numbers and title it Numbers To Post. Create a numbered list and apply tab settings as shown in Figure 4-31.

Figure 4-31

Phone list

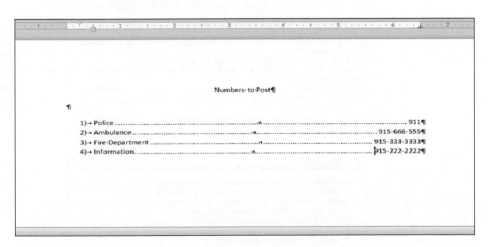

Numbers to Post¶

¶

1)→ Police..A... 911¶
2)→ Ambulance...A.. 915-666-5555¶
3)→ Fire Department...A.. 915-333-3333¶
4)→ Information..A.. 915-222-2222¶

4. Create a **Right** tab setting at **6.5"** with **dot leaders**, then key the phone number beside each name. The phone numbers should align evenly between the left and right margins. Maintain a balanced look for your document.

5. **SAVE** the document in the lesson folder on your USB flash drive, then **CLOSE** the file.

LEAVE Word open for the next project.

Mastery Assessment

Project 4-5: Developer Job Description

You are a content specialist at a software development company. Your supervisor asks you to format the job description for the developer position.

GET READY. LAUNCH Word if it is not already running.

@ The *developer* file for this lesson is available on the book companion website or in WileyPLUS.

1. **OPEN** *developer* from the data files for this lesson.

2. **SAVE** the document as *developer_description* in the lesson folder on your USB flash drive.

3. Use the skills you have learned in this lesson—such as alignment, line spacing, shading, borders, tabs, and bulleted lists—to format the document as shown in Figure 4-32. Be sure to follow these guidelines:

   a. Display the Show/Hide.

   b. Delete all of the nonprinting character marks (¶) in the document where a blank line appears.

   c. For the title, apply the shading **Orange, Accent 6, Lighter 40%** and set the paragraph Spacing After to 24 pts.

   d. Select the headings Position Title, Position Objective, and Reports To and apply the shading to **Orange, Accent 6, Lighter 80%**.

Figure 4-32

Developer job description

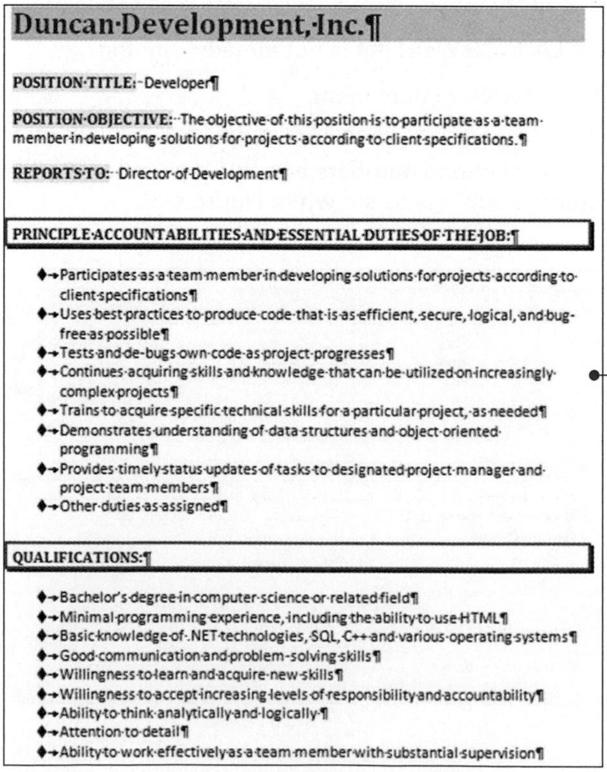

Duncan·Development,·Inc.¶

POSITION·TITLE:··Developer¶

POSITION·OBJECTIVE:··The·objective·of·this·position·is·to·participate·as·a·team·member·in·developing·solutions·for·projects·according·to·client·specifications.¶

REPORTS·TO:··Director·of·Development¶

PRINCIPLE·ACCOUNTABILITIES·AND·ESSENTIAL·DUTIES·OF·THE·JOB:¶

◆→Participates·as·a·team·member·in·developing·solutions·for·projects·according·to·client·specifications¶
◆→Uses·best·practices·to·produce·code·that·is·as·efficient,·secure,·logical,·and·bug-free·as·possible¶
◆→Tests·and·de-bugs·own·code·as·project·progresses¶
◆→Continues·acquiring·skills·and·knowledge·that·can·be·utilized·on·increasingly·complex·projects¶
◆→Trains·to·acquire·specific·technical·skills·for·a·particular·project,·as·needed¶
◆→Demonstrates·understanding·of·data·structures·and·object·oriented·programming¶
◆→Provides·timely·status·updates·of·tasks·to·designated·project·manager·and·project·team·members¶
◆→Other·duties·as·assigned¶

QUALIFICATIONS:¶

◆→Bachelor's·degree·in·computer·science·or·related·field¶
◆→Minimal·programming·experience,·including·the·ability·to·use·HTML¶
◆→Basic·knowledge·of·.NET·technologies,·SQL,·C++·and·various·operating·systems¶
◆→Good·communication·and·problem-solving·skills¶
◆→Willingness·to·learn·and·acquire·new·skills¶
◆→Willingness·to·accept·increasing·levels·of·responsibility·and·accountability¶
◆→Ability·to·think·analytically·and·logically¶
◆→Attention·to·detail¶
◆→Ability·to·work·effectively·as·a·team·member·with·substantial·supervision¶

Follow the steps in Project 4-5 to create a matching document.

e. Select the headings, Principle Accountabilities and Essential Duties of the Job and Qualifications and apply a border with the Shadow setting; Width: 2¼″; Color: Orange, Accent 6, Darker 50%.

f. Set the paragraph Spacing After to 12 pts. after each paragraph headings: Position Title and Position Objective.

g. For the Reports To heading, set the paragraph Spacing After to 24 pts. after Director of Development.

h. Under the heading, Principle Accountabilities and Essential Duties of the Job apply the solid diamond bullets to the paragraphs.

i. At the beginning of the first bulleted item under Principle Accountabilities and Essential Duties of the Job and Qualifications set the paragraph Spacing Before to 12 pts.

j. After the last bulleted item under *Principle Accountabilities* and *Essential Duties of the Job,* set the Spacing After to 18 pts.

4. **SAVE** the document in the lesson folder on your USB flash drive, then **CLOSE** the file.

LEAVE Word open for the next project.

Project 4-6: Rabbit Show

You are a volunteer at the annual Falls Village Fair, and you have been assigned to work on a document about one of the exhibits. The person who created the document was not as familiar with line spacing, tabs, and lists as you are, so you need to format the document as shown in Figure 4-33.

GET READY. LAUNCH Word if it is not already running.

1. **OPEN** *rabbit* from the data files for this lesson.

2. **SAVE** the document as *rabbit_show* in the lesson folder on your USB flash drive.

3. Make any adjustments necessary to format the tabs, line spacing, and lists as shown in Figure 4-33, following these guidelines:

   a. On the title, remove the first-line indent and make sure the alignment is set to Center.

   b. Select the first six lines under the heading, remove the first-line indent, then remove all existing tab settings and reset the tab settings to a Right tab at **2″** and **6″** with leaders.

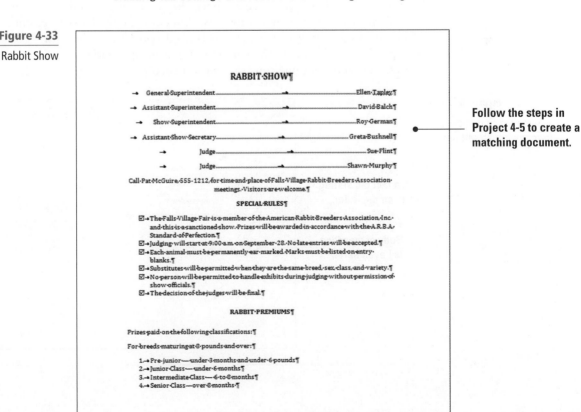

The *rabbit* file for this lesson is available on the book companion website or in WileyPLUS.

Figure 4-33

Rabbit Show

Follow the steps in Project 4-5 to create a matching document.

    c. Remove extra paragraph mark before and after **Call Pat** . . . and center.

    d. Remove all formatting, tabs, and indents. Apply a bullet using a check mark within a box under the heading Special Rules.

    e. Remove the nonprinting character mark before the heading **RABBIT PREMIUMS**. Change the paragraph spacing by setting the Spacing Before/After to 18 pts.

    f. Select the items under RABBIT PREMIUMS and clear formatting. Beginning with **Pre-Junior** and ending with **Senior Class** . . . , apply the numbering list **1., 2., 3., 4.**

4. Adjust the text so that it all fits on one page.

5. SAVE the document in the lesson folder on your USB flash drive, then **CLOSE** the file. **CLOSE** Word.

INTERNET READY

Many online resources can provide you with solutions to challenges that you might face during a typical workday. Search the Microsoft website for Work Essentials—a place where you can find information on how to use Microsoft Word efficiently to perform typical business tasks and activities. Explore the resources and content that Work Essentials offers and write a short paragraph about one particular tool or solution that could be useful on the job and how you could use it to be more productive.

Workplace *Ready*

SALES REPORT

Your manager has asked you to assist in preparing a memorandum to the regional director in reference to the third-quarter sales report. Prepare a memorandum demonstrating skills you learned from this lesson in setting tabs. A memorandum is an interoffice communication within an organization (see Figure 4-34). Add two paragraphs with three sentences within both paragraphs explaining the sales report. Create appropriate headings and tab settings for figures. Save and print one copy for your instructor.

Figure 4-34

Sample memorandum format with tab settings

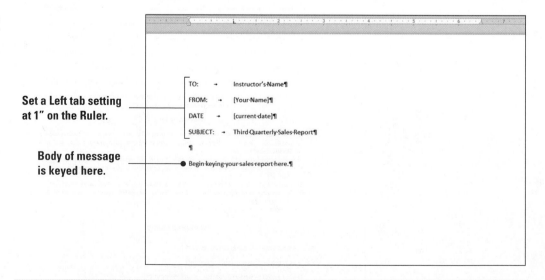

Set a Left tab setting at 1″ on the Ruler.

Body of message is keyed here.

Circling Back 1

The National Association of Professional Consultants is a professional organization that serves a varied membership of consultants. Each year, the association has a three-day professional development conference. The association is now planning the upcoming conference. As the association's membership manager, your job includes a wide variety of tasks related to organizing and communicating information about membership. In addition, you are working with the conference planning committee to help secure speakers for the conference and market the conference to members.

Project 1: Letter

@ The *conf_speaker* file for this Circling Back is available on the book companion website or in WileyPLUS.

GET READY. LAUNCH Word if it is not already running.

1. **OPEN** the *conf_speaker* letter from the Circling Back data files folder. Modify and customize the letter.
2. Replace the fields in the document by keying the following information:

    [Your Name]: Susan Pasha

    [Street Address]: 5678 Circle St.

    [City, ST ZIP Code]: Kansas City, MO 64163

    [Recipient Name]: Daniel Slade

    [Title]: President, Strategies and Operations

    [Company Name]: Montgomery, Slade and Parker

    [Street Address]: 3333 Lakeside Way

    [City, ST ZIP Code]: Chicago, IL 60611

    [Recipient Name]: Mr. Slade

    [Your Name]: Susan Pasha

    [Title]: President
3. Save the document as *conference_speaker* in your USB flash drive in the lesson folder.
4. Change the date of the letter to June 15, 20XX.
5. In the first sentence of the body of the letter, select travel agents' and key consultants'.
6. In the second sentence, select Alpine Ski House in Breckenridge, Colorado and key Lakeview Towers in South Lake Tahoe, California.
7. Select the text you just keyed and apply the bold font style.
8. Change the date of the evening to September 16 and apply the bold font style.
9. In the last sentence of the letter, select convention and key conference.
10. SAVE the document with the same filename.
11. Below the Susan Pasha title, President, press the Enter key and key National Association of Professional Consultants.
12. Customize the margins by changing the top to 2″, left and right to 1″.
13. On the View tab, in the Zoom group, click the One Page button to view the document on the screen.
14. Click Page Width.
15. SAVE the changes and **CLOSE** the document.

PAUSE. LEAVE Word open for the next project.

Project 2: Attachment

Create a document that will be sent to the staff and volunteers who are assisting with the National Association of Professional Consultants Conference. Update them on the upcoming events fees.

GET READY. LAUNCH Word if it is not already running.

1. **OPEN** a blank document.
2. Key Update on Fees, and press Enter.

3. Set Center tabs on the first line at 3.88" and 4.88".

4. Key the following titles:

   Early Bird, and press Tab.

   Regular, and press Enter.

5. Set a Right tab at 4" with dot leaders and set a Right tab at 5".

6. Key the following:

   Conference Registration, and press Tab.

   $500, and press Tab.

   $600, and press Enter.

   Hotel, and press Tab.

   $195, and press Tab.

   $250, and press Enter.

   Exhibitor's Fee, and press Tab.

   $250, and press Tab.

   $350, and press Enter.

7. SAVE the document as *update_for_conference* in your USB flash drive in the lesson folder.

8. Adjust the tab stops and move them as follows:

   Move the Center tab from 3.88" to 4.88" and 4.88" to 6.38".

   Move the Right tab settings from 4" to 5" and 5" to 6.5".

9. Select the title and apply a Heading 1 style and center.

10. Add a paragraph border with a 3-D setting, Dark Blue, Text 2 Theme Color, with a width of 3 pts.

11. SAVE the changes and CLOSE the file.

PAUSE. LEAVE Word open for the next project.

Project 3: Finding and Replacing Text

You will be working on a document and removing all formatting from the whole document using the Find and Replace commands. You will apply styles to specific text and apply the paragraph spacing after to the heading.

GET READY. LAUNCH Word if it is not already running.

1. **OPEN** the *group_info* document from the lesson folder.

2. Remove all formatting in the document.

3. **SAVE** the document as *group_update* in your USB flash drive in the lesson folder.

4. Select Lakeville.NET User's Group and paste in both the Find what and Replace with boxes of the Find and Replace dialog box.

5. In the Replace with box, replace the formatting with the following changes.

6. Under the Format button select Font and select bold, size 14, change the font color to Dark Red, and select All caps under Effects.

7. Three occurrences are replaced.

8. Apply the Heading 2 style to FAQ.

9. Apply the Intense Emphasis style to How do I join your group?, When is the next meeting?, How do I sponsor a meeting?, How do I receive the newsletter?, and Locations and Directions.

10. Set a Paragraph spacing after on the first line heading.

11. **SAVE** the document with the updated changes and close the file.

PAUSE. CLOSE Word.

@ The *group_info* file for this Circling Back is available on the book companion website or in WileyPLUS.

Managing Text Flow 5

LESSON SKILL MATRIX

Skill	Exam Objective	Objective Number
Setting Page Layout	Set margins.	**3.1.1**
Working with Breaks	Insert nonbreaking spaces. Add hyphenation. Remove a break. Insert a section break.	**3.1.2** **3.1.3** **3.1.5** **3.1.7**
Controlling Pagination	Force a page break.	**3.1.6**
Setting Up Columns	Add columns.	**3.1.4**
Inserting a Blank Page into a Document	Insert a blank page into a document.	**3.1.8**

KEY TERMS

- **columns**
- **hyphenation**
- **landscape orientation**
- **margins**
- **nonbreaking spaces**
- **page break**
- **portrait orientation**
- **orphan**
- **section break**
- **widow**

As a marketing associate for First Bank, you are involved in a wide variety of marketing and communications projects. In particular, you are responsible for creating and maintaining marketing collateral—brochures, posters, and other printed product information—that supports the sale of a product. It is time to update the personal Checking Choices document that your bank provides to people interested in opening new accounts. Word is a great tool for producing documents such as this. In this lesson, you will learn to work with page layout, control paragraph behavior, work with section and page breaks, create and format columns, and insert a blank page.

SOFTWARE ORIENTATION

Page Layout Tab

The Page Layout tab contains groups of commands that will produce a formatted document's layout for the entire document or sections of the document. Commands in the Page Setup group allow you to set margins, change the document's orientation, and adjust the paper size for the entire document or sections in the document. Inserting section breaks into the document enables you to change the page setup for an existing section in the document without affecting the other pages in the document. The hyphenation command provides options to hyphenate words in a document automatically or manually, and the nonbreaking space wraps text to the next to avoid breaks at the right margin to create a uniform look.

Figure 5-1

Page Layout tab

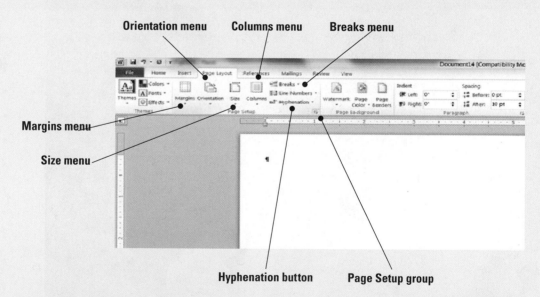

In the Paragraph group, Word contains features that control how a paragraphs breaks within the document and pages. You control the pagination in the document by preventing widows and orphans to break in the document, or keeping text together, lines together, and determining where page breaks will occur in the document.

You can manage the text flow in the document by creating multiple columns in a document, customize the column settings, and insert column breaks in the Page Setup group.

In the Insert tab, you can insert a blank page in the document to begin a new page.

SETTING PAGE LAYOUT

The layout of a page helps communicate your message. Although the content of your document is obviously very important, having appropriate margins, page orientation, and paper size all contribute to the document's readability and appearance.

Setting Margins

Margins are the blank borders that occupy the top, bottom, and sides of a document. You can change margins from Word's default size of one inch using commands in the Page Setup group in the Page Layout tab. You can choose from a gallery or set Customize Margins in the Page Setup dialog box. In the Page Setup group, click the Margins menu, and a set of predefined margin settings are available for selection. Click the setting of your choice and the whole document will reflect the changes. Click the Custom Margins command to display the Page Setup dialog box, where you can specify custom margin sizes. In this exercise, you customize a document's margins.

STEP BY STEP　　　**Set Margins**

GET READY. Before you begin these steps, be sure to launch Microsoft Word.

1. **OPEN** the **proposal** file for this lesson.
2. Delete the extra blank lines above *USA Health Resources*.
3. On the Page Layout tab, in the Page Setup group, click the **drop-down arrow** to display the Margins menu; then choose **Narrow**, as shown in Figure 5-2. The margins are set to 0.5″ from top, bottom, left, and right.

 The *proposal* file for this lesson is available on the book companion website or in WileyPLUS.

Figure 5-2

Margins menu

WILEY PLUS EXTRA

WileyPLUS Extra! features an online tutorial of this task.

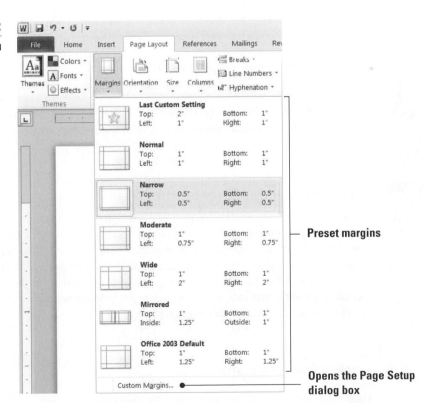

4. In the Page Setup group, click the drop-down arrow to display the Margins menu; then click Custom Margins to open the Page Setup dialog box shown in Figure 5-3. Change the bottom, left, and right margins to 1" and the top margin to 2". Changing the margins affects all pages within the document. Click OK.

Figure 5-3

Page Setup dialog box

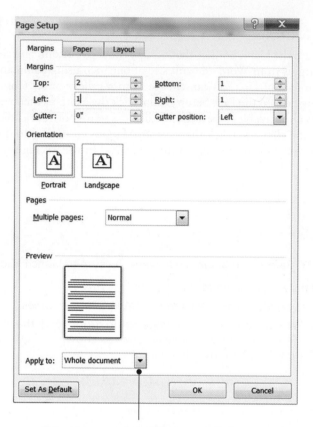

Select how margin settings are applied.

5. **SAVE** the document in the lesson folder of your USB flash drive as *draft_proposal*. **PAUSE. LEAVE** the document open to use in the next exercise.

Selecting a Page Orientation

A document's orientation determines what direction the text extends across the page. A document in portrait orientation is 8 ½" × 11", whereas a document in landscape orientation is 11" × 8½". As you plan and format a document, you must choose its page orientation. In this exercise, you change a document's orientation from portrait (the default) to landscape In **Portrait orientation**, a format commonly used for business documents, text extends across the shorter length of the document. **Landscape orientation**, commonly used for brochures, graphics, tables, and so on, orients text across the longer dimension of the page.

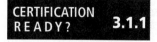 **Select a Page Orientation**

USE the document that is open from the previous exercise.

1. In the Page Setup group of the Page Layout tab, click the drop-down arrow to display the Orientation menu, then select Landscape, as shown in Figure 5-4. The page orientation changes to Landscape.

2. Click the File tab, then Print, to preview the document in Backstage view. On the right side of the pane, the document displays in landscape.

Figure 5-4

Orientation menu

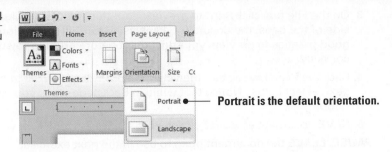

Portrait is the default orientation.

3. **SAVE** document as **_draft1_proposal_** in the lesson folder on your USB flash drive.

PAUSE. LEAVE the document open to use in the next exercise.

Choosing a Paper Size

While the standard paper size of 8½″ × 11″ is the default setting, Word provides several options for formatting documents for a variety of paper sizes. For instance, invitations, postcards, legal documents, or reports all require a different paper size. Many printers provide options for printing on different sizes of paper, and in some cases, you may need to change or customize the paper size in Word as you format your document. Legal documents, for example, must be formatted for 8½″ × 14″ paper. In this exercise, you will change the size of paper from the default.

STEP BY STEP   **Choose a Paper Size**

USE the document that is open from the previous exercise.

1. In the Page Setup group of the Page Layout tab, click the **drop-down arrow** to display the Orientation menu, then select **Portrait**. The orientation is changed back to portrait from the previous exercise.

2. From the Page Setup group of the Page Layout tab, click the **drop-down arrow** to display the Size menu, then select **Legal**, as shown in Figure 5-5. Word provides preset document sizes, or you can customize the paper size by clicking the **More Paper Sizes** button.

Figure 5-5

Size menu

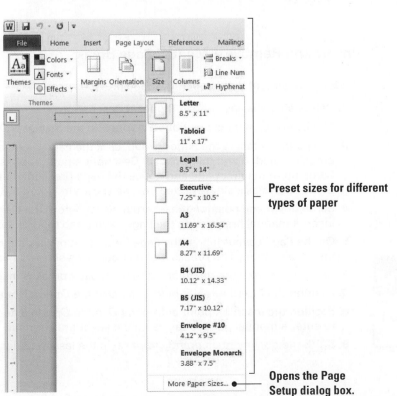

Preset sizes for different types of paper

Opens the Page Setup dialog box.

3. On the File tab, click **Print** to preview your document in Backstage view. On the right side of the pane, the document displays in portrait orientation and legal size. It is good practice to preview your document before printing to ensure the text will print correctly.

4. Click the **Page Layout** tab, then click the **drop-down arrow** to display the Size menu; next, select **Letter**. Notice that while in Backstage view, you can access the tabs on the ribbon.

5. **SAVE** document as *draft2_proposal* in the lesson folder on your USB flash drive.

PAUSE. LEAVE the document open to use in the next exercise.

WORKING WITH BREAKS

The Bottom Line

Word automatically inserts page breaks in multipage documents. There may be times, however, when you will be working with documents that contain various objects or special layouts that require you to control where a page or section breaks. You can insert and remove these manual page breaks and section breaks, and you can control word hyphenation or set nonbreaking spaces in Word.

Inserting and Removing a Manual Page Break

A **page break** is the location in a document where one page ends and a new page begins. You may also decide where to insert the manual page break or set specific options for those page breaks. Page breaks display as a single dotted line with the words Page Break in the center in the Print Layout view (as shown in Figure 5-6). In Print Layout view, Word displays a document page by page, one after the other, on a blue background. In this exercise, you learn to insert and remove a manual page break.

The Breaks menu contains options for inserting three types of breaks:

- **Page:** Inserts a manual page break where one page ends and a new page begins
- **Column:** Inserts a manual column break where text will begin in the next column after the column break
- **Text Wrapping:** Separates the text around objects on a web page, such as caption text from body text

STEP BY STEP   **Insert and Remove a Manual Page Break**

USE the document that is open from the previous exercise.

1. Delete all blank lines above Proposal Description.

2. The insertion point is positioned before *P* in the *Proposal Description* heading.

3. On the Insert tab, in the Pages group, click the **Page Break** button. A manual page break is inserted and the Proposal Description paragraph is forced to the next page. Scroll up to the first page and notice the page break marker that has been inserted and that displays as a single dotted line, as shown in Figure 5-6.

4. Scroll down and position the insertion point before the *O* in the *Option 1* heading to insert a manual break using the Page Layout tab to force text to the next page.

5. On the Page Layout tab, in the Page Setup group, click the **drop-down arrow** to display the **Breaks** menu. The Breaks menu appears, as shown in Figure 5-7.

6. Select **Page** from the menu and a manual page break is inserted.

7. Position the insertion point before the *O* in the *Option 2* heading and repeat step 5.

8. Position the insertion point before the *O* in the *Option 3* heading and press **Ctrl+Enter** to enter a manual page break using the keyboard shortcut.

9. **SAVE** the document as *draft3_proposal* in the lesson folder on your USB flash drive.

CERTIFICATION READY?   3.1.6

How do you force a manual page break?

Figure 5-6

Page Break in Print Layout View

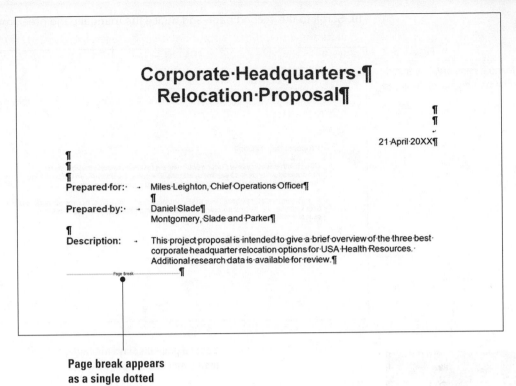

Page break appears
as a single dotted

Figure 5-7

Breaks menu

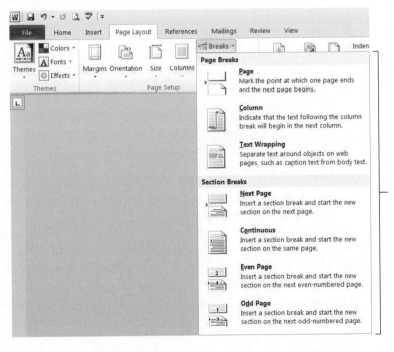

The two types of break
are Page breaks and
Section Breaks.

10. Scroll to the second page and notice the manual page break marker, shown in Figure 5-8.

Figure 5-8

Manual page break with hidden formatting marks displayed

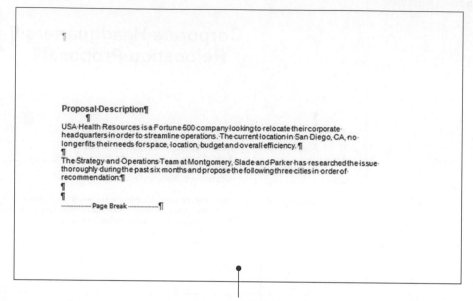

Proposal·Description¶
¶
USA·Health·Resources·is·a·Fortune·500·company·looking·to·relocate·their·corporate·
headquarters·in·order·to·streamline·operations.·The·current·location·in·San·Diego,·CA,·no·
longer·fits·their·needs·for·space,·location,·budget·and·overall·efficiency.·¶
¶
The·Strategy·and·Operations·Team·at·Montgomery,·Slade·and·Parker·has·researched·the·issue·
thoroughly·during·the·past·six·months·and·propose·the·following·three·cities·in·order·of·
recommendation:¶
¶
¶
------------ Page·Break ------------¶

**Second page displays hidden
marks and manual page break.**

11. On page 2, select the Page Break marker and press the Backspace key. The page break is deleted, and text from the previous page is moved to page 2.

12. Scroll up to page 1, select the Page Break marker below the last paragraph in the Description, and press the Backspace key. The Proposal Description heading is moved to page 1.

13. Select the remaining Page Break markers and press Delete.

14. Keep the document open without saving the changes made in the last three steps.

PAUSE. LEAVE the document open to use in the next exercise.

CERTIFICATION
READY? **3.1.6**

How do you delete a manual page break?

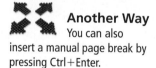 **Another Way**
You can also insert a manual page break by pressing Ctrl+Enter.

Take Note Click the Show/Hide **¶** button to view page breaks and section breaks for editing purposes.

Inserting Section Breaks

A **section break** is used to create a layout or formatting changes in a portion of a document. It appears with a dotted double line, labeled *Section Break*. You can use section breaks to create a section in your document that contains a page with margins and orientation that is different from the remainder of the document. You can select and delete section breaks just as you can remove page breaks. In this exercise, you will insert a continuous section break and then change the margins for that section.

There are four available options for creating section breaks in Word, as shown in Table 5-1.

Table 5-1

Types of Section Breaks

Type	Description
Next Page	Inserts a section break and starts the new section on the next page.
Continuous	Inserts a section break and starts the new section on the same page
Even Page	Inserts a section break and starts the new section on the next even-numbered page
Odd Page	Inserts a section break and starts the new section on the next odd-numbered page

STEP BY STEP   **Insert a Section Break**

USE the document that is open from the previous exercise.

1. Scroll up to page 1 and position the insertion point after *Relocation Proposal.*

2. On the Page Layout tab, in the Page Setup group, click the Breaks menu. Then, under Section Breaks, select Continuous.

3. Position the insertion point on the blank line before *P* in *Prepared for...*

4. On the Page Layout tab, in the Page Setup group, click the drop-down arrow to display the Breaks menu.

5. In the Section Breaks section of the menu, select Next Page. A section break is inserted in your document, as shown in Figure 5-9. Inserting a section break allows you format the document without affecting the other pages in the document.

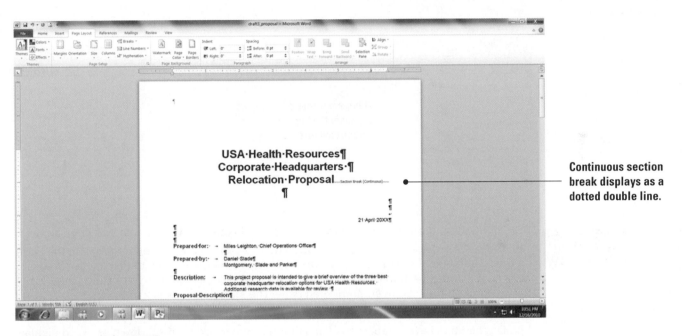

Continuous section break displays as a dotted double line.

Figure 5-9

Section break

6. Position the insertion point before the *O* in the Option 1 heading.

7. On the Page Layout tab, in the Page Setup group, click the drop-down arrow to display the Breaks menu.

8. Under Section Breaks, select Next Page. The Next Page break begins a new section on the following page.

9. Place the insertion point on page 1 and select the three line headings to include the blank line below. Click the drop-down arrow to display the Page Setup dialog box.

10. In the Margins tab, change the top margin from 2″ to 1″. In the lower-left corner of the dialog box, notice the Apply to section displays as This section.

11. Click the Layout tab and under the Page section, Vertical alignment, select Center, then click OK. The changes made in the Layout tab will be applied to this section.

12. Click the File tab, then click Print to preview your document in Backstage view. The first page is vertically centered, as shown in Figure 5-10, while the remaining pages are vertically aligned at the top with a 2″ margin. Use the directional arrows in Backstage to go to the next page. Press the Esc key.

13. Position the insertion point anywhere on page 3. In the Page Setup group, click the drop-down arrow to display the Page Setup dialog box. In the Margins tab, change the top margin from 2″ to 1″. The margins for pages 3 and 4 are set to 1″.

14. **SAVE** the document as ***draft4_proposal*** in the lesson folder on your USB flash drive.

Figure 5-10

Document with section break
and vertical centering

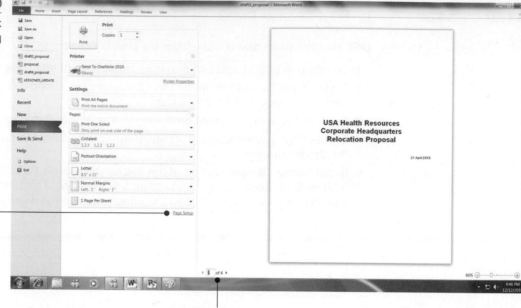

Page Setup dialog box
can be accessed through
Backstage view.

Navigate through
document using the
directional arrow.

CERTIFICATION READY? 3.1.7

How do you insert an odd
page section break?

CERTIFICATION READY? 3.1.7

How do you insert an even
page section break?

15. Highlight and press **Delete** to remove each of the section breaks that you have applied.

16. On the first page, position the insertion point before the *P* in *Prepared for*. On the Page Layout tab, in the Page Setup group, click the **drop-down arrow** to display the Breaks menu. Under Section Breaks in the Breaks menu, select **Even Page** to start a new section on the next even-numbered page. The status bar reads 2 of 3.

17. Position the insertion point before *O* in *Option 1* heading.

18. On the Page Layout tab, in the Page Setup group, click the **drop-down arrow** to display the Breaks menu, then select **Odd Page** to start a new section on the next odd-numbered page. The status bar reads 3 of 4. Section breaks have been inserted for both Even and Odd Pages.

19. **SAVE** the document as *draft5_proposal* in the lesson folder on your USB flash drive, then **CLOSE** the file.

PAUSE. LEAVE Word open to use in the next exercise.

Section breaks can be used to change types of formatting for:

- Columns
- Footnotes and endnotes
- Headers and footers
- Line numbering
- Margins
- Page borders
- Page numbering
- Paper size or orientation
- Paper source for a printer
- Vertical alignment of text on a page

Take Note   Remember that when you delete a section break, you remove the section formatting as well.

Using Hyphenation

Hyphens, shown as the punctuation mark -, are used to join words and separate syllables of a single word. By default, **hyphenation** is off in Word; all words appear on a single line, rather than hyphenated. As you format a document, however, you might need to determine when to apply a hyphen. In this exercise, you practice using Word's hyphenation feature.

Note the differences here between a document with hyphenation and one without hyphenation.

Without hyphenation:

As a marketing associate for First Bank, you are involved in a wide variety of marketing and communications projects.

With hyphenation:

As a marketing associate for First Bank, you are involved in a wide variety of marketing and communications projects.

STEP BY STEP	Insert Hyphens in a Document

OPEN *relocation_proposal* from the data files for this lesson.

 The *relocation_proposal* file for this lesson is available on the book companion website or in WileyPLUS.

1. On the Page Layout tab, in the Page Setup group, click the Hyphenation drop-down arrow and select Automatic; review your document.
2. Click the drop-down arrow to display the Hyphenation menu and select None, as shown in Figure 5-11.

Figure 5-11

Hyphenation menu

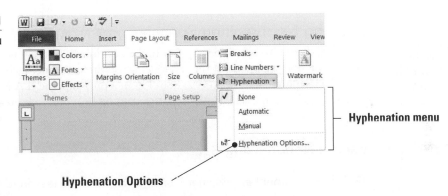

Hyphenation Options

WILEY PLUS EXTRA

WileyPLUS Extra! features an online tutorial of this task.

CERTIFICATION READY?   3.1.3

How do you apply manual hyphenation in a document?

3. Click the Hyphenation drop-down arrow again, and select Manual. The Manual Hyphenation dialog box stops at the first suggested text for hyphenation (*headquarter*), as shown in Figure 5-12. Click Yes. Manual Hyphenation will allow you to determine where to hyphenate the word by clicking Yes, No, or Cancel, and you can decide where to position the insertion point.

Figure 5-12

Manual Hyphenation dialog box

4. Click Yes to *headquarters*. Click No to *issue* and *ample*. Click Yes to *technology* and *location*. When Word stops at *transportation,* move the insertion point to the third hyphen (after "*ta*") and click Yes. Click No to *proximity* and Yes to *business*. The Hyphenation prompt will appear when Word has completed the process of searching for words to hyphenate within the document. Click OK.
5. **SAVE** the document as *relocation1_proposal* in the lesson folder on your USB flash drive.

CERTIFICATION READY?   3.1.3

How do you apply hyphenation in a document automatically?

6. Click the Hyphenation drop-down arrow and select Hyphenation Options to open the Hyphenation dialog box, as shown in Figure 5-13. Click the Automatically hyphenate document check box. Click OK.

Figure 5-13

Hyphenation dialog box

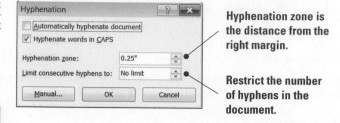

Hyphenation zone is the distance from the right margin.

Restrict the number of hyphens in the document.

Take Note

7. Click the Hyphenation drop-down arrow and select Hyphenation Options. Then, in the Hyphenation dialog box, key *.75"* in the Hyphenation zone. The Hyphenation zone is the distance from the right margin in which Word is allowed to hyphenate words. The default is set at 0.25". As the zone is increased, fewer words will require hyphenation.

To reduce the number of hyphens in your document, make the hyphenation zone wider. To reduce the raggedness of the right margin, make the hyphenation zone narrower.

8. Click the up arrow to set the Limit Consecutive Hyphens to 2. Click OK. The number of hyphens in the document is restricted once the default is changed from No Limit.

9. **SAVE** the document as *relocation2_proposal* in the lesson folder on your USB flash drive, then **CLOSE** the file.

PAUSE. LEAVE Word open to use in the next exercise.

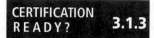 The *employment_ offer_letter* file for this lesson is available on the book companion website or in WileyPLUS.

Inserting Nonbreaking Spaces

Word will determine when to wrap text to the next line as it reaches the right margin. In some instances, you may want to keep the text together on the same line, such as for a date (November 19, 20XX), a telephone number ((999) 888-5555), a proper name (LA Martinez), and so on. In this exercise, you learn to insert **nonbreaking spaces** in Word, to keep selected text on a single line.

STEP BY STEP   **Insert a Nonbreaking Space**

OPEN the document *employment_offer_letter* from the lesson folder.

1. On the Home tab, in the Paragraph group, click the Show/Hide ¶ button to display hidden marks on the page.

2. In the first paragraph of the document at the end of the second line, the month and day are in two separate lines.

3. Place your insertion point after the *r* in *November*. Select the nonprinting space mark between *"November"* and *"3".*

4. Click the Insert tab, and in the Symbols group, click drop-down arrow on Symbols, then More Symbols to open the Symbols dialog box.

5. Click the Special Characters tab, then select the Nonbreaking Space option in the *Character* list. Click Insert, then click Close. Inserting a nonbreaking space prevents the month and date from separating.

6. **SAVE** the document as *employment_confirmed* in the lesson folder on your USB flash drive, then **CLOSE** the file.

PAUSE. LEAVE Word open to use in the next exercise.

Another Way

Using the shortcut keys Ctrl+Shift+Space is a quick way to insert a nonbreaking space.

Troubleshooting To keep text together, you must select all spaces between words and insert the nonbreaking space option in the Symbol dialog box.

CONTROLLING PAGINATION

The Bottom Line A well-organized and formatted document will capture and maintain the reader's attention.

Controlling Widows and Orphans

To maintain an appealing appearance and readable content, you may need to keep the first or last line of a paragraph from appearing alone on the page. Word provides options for keeping text lines together and avoiding single lines of text at the top or bottom of a page. In this exercise, you will manage Word's Widow/Orphan Control.

A **widow** is the last line of a paragraph that appears at the top of a page, as shown in Figure 5-14.

Figure 5-14

A widow at the top of a page

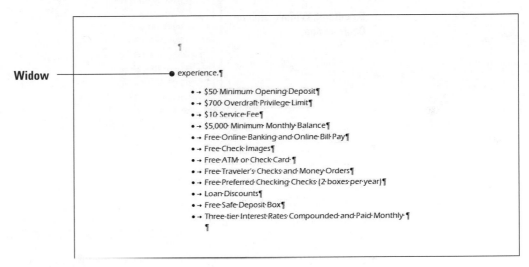

An **orphan** is the first line of a paragraph that appears alone at the bottom of a page, as shown in Figure 5-15.

Figure 5-15

An orphan at the bottom of a page

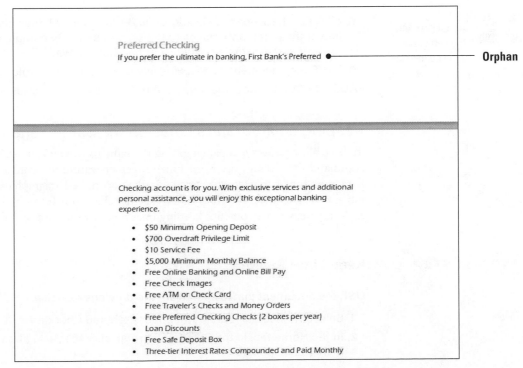

Turn on Widow/Orphan Control

OPEN the *checking* document from the data files for this lesson.

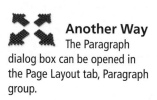 The *checking* file for this lesson is available on the book companion website or in WileyPLUS.

1. Scroll to the top of page 2 and notice the widow *experience. . .* at the top of the page.
2. On page 1 of the document, select the **three-line paragraph** under Preferred Checking, including the widow.
3. On the Home tab, in the Paragraph group, click the **dialog box launcher**. The Paragraph dialog box appears.
4. Click the **Line and Page Breaks** tab, as shown in Figure 5-16.

Figure 5-16

Paragraph dialog box

By default, Widow/Orphan Control is on.

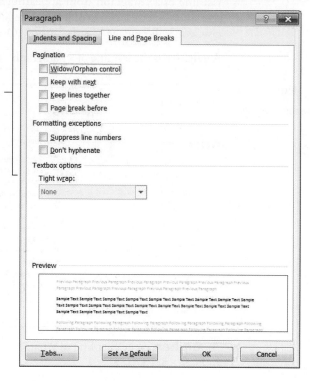

Another Way
The Paragraph dialog box can be opened in the Page Layout tab, Paragraph group.

5. Click the check box to select **Widow/Orphan Control**, then click **OK**. Notice that another line of the paragraph moves to the second page. By default, Widow/Orphan Control is on, and in this exercise, Widow/Orphan Control was off.
6. **SAVE** the document as *checking_choices* in the lesson folder on your USB flash drive.

PAUSE. LEAVE the document open to use in the next exercise.

Keeping a Paragraph's Lines on the Same Page

To keep all sentences of a paragraph on the same page, you can use Word's Keep Lines Together command. By default, the Keep Lines Together feature in Word is off. To keep the lines of a paragraph together, select the paragraph, then open the Paragraph dialog box in the Page Layout tab and click to select the Keep Lines Together check box from the Line and Page Breaks tab. In this exercise, you will practice keeping lines together on the selected paragraph.

Keep Lines Together

USE the document that is open from the previous exercise.

1. Select the **two-line paragraph** under Preferred Checking.
2. In the Home tab, in the Paragraph group, click the **dialog box launcher**. The Paragraph dialog box appears.

3. On the Line and Page Breaks tab, click to select the **Keep Lines Together** box, then click **OK**. Notice that the two lines that were at the bottom of page 1 moved to page 2.

4. SAVE the document as *checking_choices2* in the lesson folder on your USB flash drive.

PAUSE. LEAVE the document open to use in the next exercise.

Keeping Two Paragraphs on the Same Page

Word considers any line of text followed by an Enter to be a paragraph. For instance, when you press Enter after keying a heading, the heading becomes a paragraph. To keep two paragraphs on the same page, you will select both paragraphs, then, in the Lines and Page Break tab of the Paragraph dialog box, click to select the Keep with Next check box. In this exercise, you will practice keeping two paragraphs together on the same page, such as a heading and the text below it, using Word's Keep with Next command.

| STEP BY STEP | **Keep Two Paragraphs on the Same Page** |

USE the document that is open from the previous exercise.

1. Select the Preferred Checking heading and the four-line paragraph below it.

2. On the Home tab, in the Paragraph group, click the **dialog box launcher**. The Paragraph dialog box appears.

3. On the Line and Page Breaks tab, click to select the **Keep with Next** box, then click **OK**. Notice that the two paragraphs (the heading and paragraph that follows) are together and have moved to page 2.

4. SAVE the document as *checking_choices3* in the lesson folder on your USB flash drive.

PAUSE. LEAVE the document open to use in the next exercise.

Forcing a Paragraph to the Top of a Page

Automatic page breaks usually occur at acceptable places in a Word document, but there may be times when you need to force a paragraph to the top of a page. In this exercise, you practice inserting a page break before a paragraph, to force the paragraph to the top of the next page.

| STEP BY STEP | **Force a Paragraph to the Top of a Page** |

USE the document that is open from the previous exercise.

1. Position the insertion point before the *S* in the Senior Preferred Checking heading.

2. On the Home tab, in the Paragraph group, click the **dialog box launcher**. The Paragraph dialog box appears.

3. On the Line and Page Breaks tab, click to select the **Page Break Before** box, then click **OK**. Using this command will force text to the top of a new page.

4. SAVE the document as *checking_choices4* in the lesson folder on your USB flash drive.

PAUSE. LEAVE the document open to use in the next exercise.

CERTIFICATION
READY?   **3.1.6**

How do you force a page
break in a document?

SETTING UP COLUMNS

The Bottom Line

Columns are vertical blocks of text in which text flows from the bottom of one column to the top of the next. Newspapers, magazines, and newsletters are formatted in columns because of the large amounts of text. Text formatted into columns will produce shorter lines and a white space between columns. By default, Word documents are formatted as single column, but you can change that formatting to display multiple columns or columns of varying widths.

Creating Columns

In this exercise, you will practice creating columns within an existing Word document.

STEP BY STEP   **Create Columns**

USE the document that is open from the previous exercise.

1. Place the insertion point in front of *F* in Free Checking on page 1.
2. On the Page Layout tab, in the Page Setup group, click the **drop-down arrow** to display the Columns menu. The Columns menu appears, as shown in Figure 5-17.

Figure 5-17

Columns menu

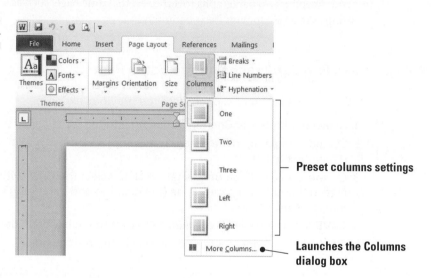

Preset columns settings

Launches the Columns dialog box

CERTIFICATION READY?   **3.1.4**

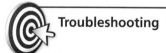

How do you create columns?

3. Select **Two**. The text in the document following the Personal Checking Choices heading is formatted into two columns.
4. **SAVE** the document as *checking_draft* in the lesson folder on your USB flash drive.

PAUSE. LEAVE the document open to use in the next exercise.

Troubleshooting When formatting existing text into columns, avoid selecting the document's title heading if you wish to keep it as a single column.

Formatting Columns

In addition to Word's common column formats, you can customize column formats to fit the text and the purpose of your document. By default, when you click the Columns button and select from the Column menu options, the whole document is formatted as columns. Using the Columns dialog box, you can apply column formatting to the whole document or a selected part of the document, only. You also can change a document formatted in multiple columns back to a single-column document. In this exercise, you learn to format columns in Word.

On the Page Layout tab, in the Page Setup group, the Columns menu lists these options for creating common column formats:

- **One:** Formats the text into a single column
- **Two:** Formats the text into two even columns
- **Three:** Formats the text into three even columns
- **Left:** Formats the text into two unequal columns—a narrow one on the left and a wide one on the right

• **Right:** Formats the text into two uneven columns—a narrow one on the right and a wide one on the left

• **More Columns:** Contains options for customizing columns

Click the Line Between box to insert a vertical line between columns.

STEP BY STEP   **Format Columns**

USE the document that is open from the previous exercise.

1. On the Page Layout tab, in the Page Setup group, click the **drop-down arrow** to display the Columns menu. The insertion point should be position in front of *Free Checking*.

2. Select **More Columns**. The Columns dialog box appears, as shown in Figure 5-18.

Figure 5-18

Columns dialog box

Change the number of columns.

Column width can be automatically set or adjusted manually.

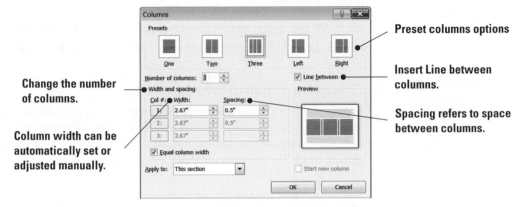

Preset columns options

Insert Line between columns.

Spacing refers to space between columns.

3. In the Number of columns box, key **3** or click the up arrow once.

4. Click the **Line between** check box.

5. Click **OK**.

6. Position the insertion point before the *S* in the Senior Preferred heading. The Page Break Before that was added earlier in this lesson will be removed in the next step.

7. In the Page Layout tab, within the Paragraph group, click the **dialog box launcher**. In the Line and Page Breaks tab of the dialog box, click to deselect the **Page Break Before** box and click **OK**. The Page Break Before command is removed from the document and the text moves to the previous page. Click **OK**.

8. In the Page Layout tab, change the Orientation option to **Landscape** and click **Margins**, then **Custom Margins** to open the Page Setup dialog box. Change the **Top** and **Bottom** margin settings to **0.5"**, and in the Apply To selection box at the bottom of the Margins tab, notice that this will affect the Whole Document. Click **OK**.

9. Place the insertion point in front of the *V* in *Value Checking*. Click the **drop-down arrow** to display the Breaks menu, then select **Columns** to insert a column break. Value Checking and the text below move to the second column.

10. Place the insertion point in front of the *P* in Preferred Checking and click the **drop-down arrow** to display the Breaks menu, then select **Column** break. Preferred Checking and the text below move to the third column.

11. Place the insertion point in front of the *S* in Senior Preferred Checking and click the **drop-down arrow** to display the Breaks menu, then select **Column**. The text is moved to the top of the next page.

12. Select the two headings beginning with First Bank . . . Personal Checking Choices.

13. Click the **drop-down arrow** in Columns and select **One**. The first two headings are now single columns.

14. Press the **Enter** key after the *s* in Choices. Notice the Continuous Section Break separating the heading and the columns.

15. Select the two headings and on the Home tab, in the Paragraph group, click the **Center** button. Applying the Center feature does not affect the text in the columns as shown in Figure 5-19.

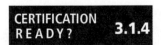

CERTIFICATION READY? **3.1.4**

How do you format columns?

CERTIFICATION READY? **3.1.4**

How do you change a multiple column to a single column?

CERTIFICATION READY? **3.1.4**

How do you insert a column break?

Figure 5-19

Formatted with columns

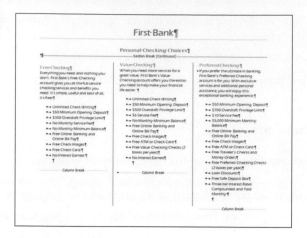

16. **SAVE** the document as *checking_draft1* in the lesson folder on your USB flash drive.

PAUSE. LEAVE the document open to use in the next exercise.

Changing Column Widths

Column widths can be even or you can specify varying column widths. Word provides an option to keep the columns with the same width by selecting the Equal Column Width option. Column width and spacing settings are displayed for the first column only and can be set to a specific width. In this exercise, you learn to change column widths in Word documents.

STEP BY STEP   **Change Column Widths**

USE the document that is open from the previous exercise.

1. Place your insertion point anywhere in the first column.
2. On the Page Layout tab, in the Page Setup group, click the drop-down arrow to display the Columns menu.
3. Select **More Columns**. The Columns dialog box appears.
4. Key **2** in the **Number of Columns** box or click the down arrow.
5. Select the text in the **Width** box and key **3.25**. Press the Tab key to move to the Spacing box. Notice that the spacing adjusted automatically to **2.5**. Click **OK**. The Apply to section will only affect the columns.
6. On the Page Layout tab, in the Page Setup group, click the drop-down arrow to display the Columns menu and select **More Columns**.
7. Click the **Three** columns button. Select the text in the **Width** box and key **2.3**. Press the Tab key to move to the Spacing box. Notice that the spacing adjusted automatically to 1.05. Click **OK**.
8. **SAVE** the document as *checking_draft2* in the lesson folder on your USB flash drive.

PAUSE. LEAVE the document open to use in the next exercise.

CERTIFICATION READY? 3.1.4

How do you change column widths?

INSERTING A BLANK PAGE INTO A DOCUMENT

The Bottom Line

When creating or editing a document, you may need to insert a blank page to add more text, graphics, or a table. Rather than pressing the Enter key enough times to insert a blank page, Word provides a Blank Page command.

Inserting a Blank Page

You can insert a blank page at any point within a document—the beginning, middle, or end. To insert a blank page, position the insertion point and click the Blank Page command in the Pages group on the Insert tab. To delete a blank page, use the Show/Hide (¶) button to display hidden characters, then select and delete the page break. In this exercise, you will practice inserting a blank page in the middle of the document.

STEP BY STEP   **Insert a Blank Page**

USE the document that is open from the previous exercise.

1. Position the insertion point before the *F* in Free Checking.
2. On the Insert tab, in the Pages group, click Blank Page (see Figure 5-20). Page 2 is a blank page.

Figure 5-20

Blank page

Blank Page command inserts a blank page at the insertion point.

<table>
<tr><td>CERTIFICATION READY?</td><td>3.1.8</td></tr>
</table>

How do you insert a blank page?

3. Click the Undo [icon] button on the Quick Access Toolbar.
4. **SAVE** the document with the same filename in the lesson folder on your USB flash drive, then **CLOSE** the file.

STOP. CLOSE Word.

SKILL SUMMARY

In This Lesson, You Learned How To:	Exam Objective	Objective Number
Set page layout	Set margins.	**3.1.1**
Work with breaks	Insert nonbreaking spaces.	**3.1.2**
	Add hyphenation.	**3.1.3**
	Remove a break.	**3.1.5**
	Insert a section break.	**3.1.7**
Control pagination	Force a page break.	**3.1.6**
Set up columns	Add columns.	**3.1.4**
Insert a blank page into a document	Insert a blank page into a document.	**3.1.8**

Knowledge Assessment

True/False

Circle T if the statement is true or F if the statement is false.

T   F   **1.** A page height that is larger than the page width is characteristic of portrait orientation.

T   F   **2.** In Word, the default margin size is 1.5 inches for the top, bottom, left, and right margins.

T   F   **3.** Columns are blank spaces on the sides, top, and bottom of a document.

T   F   **4.** Paper size refers to landscape or portrait orientation.

T   F   **5.** Widow/Orphan Control is on by default.

T   F   **6.** A column break moves text from one column to the next.

T   F   **7.** Use Widow/Orphan Control to keep all lines of a paragraph together on the same page.

T   F   **8.** Word considers a heading a paragraph.

T   F   **9.** A continuous section break starts the new section on the next page.

T   F   **10.** A page break is the location in a document where one page ends and a new page begins.

Multiple Choice

Select the best response for the following statements.

1. What is the term for the last line of a paragraph when it is left alone at the top of a page?

   a. Orphan

   b. Widow

   c. Widow/Orphan Control

   d. Keep Lines Together

2. What is the first line of a paragraph that is left alone at the bottom of a page called?

   a. Widow

   b. Orphan

   c. Widow/Orphan Control

   d. Keep Paragraphs Together

3. Pressing **Ctrl+Enter** produces what?

   a. A section break

   b. A next page break

   c. A page break

   d. A continuous break

4. Which of the following is used to create layout or formatting changes in a portion of a document?

   a. Section break

   b. Page break

   c. Next Page break

   d. Text wrapping

5. Which would be used to move vertical blocks of text from the bottom of one block of text to the top of the next block of text (on the same page)?

   a. Column breaks

   b. Section breaks

   c. Two columns

   d. Three columns

6. Which of the following inserts an empty page at the insertion point?

   a. Shift+Enter

   b. Alt+Enter

   c. Blank Page command

   d. Page Break command

7. Which of the following displays the Columns dialog box?

   a. Columns button

   b. More Columns command

   c. Right-click

   d. All of the above

8. Which of the following is used to keep two adjacent words on the same line?
   a. Keep lines together
   b. Keep paragraphs together
   c. Nonbreaking space
   d. Nonbreaking hyphen

9. Hyphens are used to:
   a. join words.
   b. separate syllables.
   c. break single words into one word.
   d. All of the above

10. Which of the following is true of the Manual Hyphenation command?
    a. It automatically stops at a word and asks you to decide where to hyphenate.
    b. It hyphenates words automatically.
    c. It does not allow hyphenating on any words.
    d. None of the above.

Competency Assessment

Project 5-1: YMCA Newsletter

Format some data for the YMCA into a two-column newsletter.

GET READY. LAUNCH Word if it is not already running.

@ The *ynews* file for this lesson is available on the book companion website or in WileyPLUS.

1. **OPEN** *ynews* from the data files for this lesson.
2. Click the Show/Hide ¶ [¶] button.
3. Position the insertion point before the *M* in the heading, Mother's Day Out. . . .
4. On the Page Layout tab, in the Page Setup group, click the Breaks button and select Continuous from the menu.
5. On the Page Layout tab, in the Page Setup group, click the Columns button and select Two.
6. Position the insertion point before the *F* in the Fall Soccer. . . heading.
7. On the Page Layout tab, in the Page Setup group, click the Breaks button and select Column.
8. On the Page Layout tab, in the Page Setup group, click the Columns button and click More Columns.
9. In the Columns dialog box, click the up arrow on the Width box to change to 2.8. The number in the Spacing box should adjust to .9".
10. Click the Line Between box and click OK.
11. Click the Show/Hide ¶ [¶] button.
12. **SAVE** the document as *ymca_newsletter* in the lesson folder on your USB flash drive, then **CLOSE** the file.

PAUSE. LEAVE Word open for the next project.

Project 5-2: Computer Use Policy

You are updating First Bank's computer use policy and you need to adjust the flow of text on the page.

GET READY. LAUNCH Word if it is not already running.

@ The *computer-usepolicy* file for this lesson is available on the book companion website or in WileyPLUS.

1. **OPEN** *computerusepolicy* from the data files for this lesson.

2. Scroll to the top of page 3. Position the insertion point before the *e* in engaging in illegal activity.

3. On the Home tab, in the Paragraph group, click the **dialog box launcher**. On the Line and Page Breaks tab, click to select the **Widow/Orphan Control** box and click **OK**.

4. Position the insertion point in the last line of page 3 that begins *D. Anyone obtaining. . . .*

5. On the Home tab, in the Paragraph group, click the **dialog box launcher**. On the Line and Page Breaks tab, click the **Keep Lines Together** box, then click **OK**.

6. Position the insertion point before the *S* in the Section Ten heading.

7. On the Home tab, in the Paragraph group, click the **dialog box launcher**. On the Line and Page Breaks tab, click the **Page Break Before** box and click **OK**.

8. Place the insertion point at the beginning of the document. Click the **Page Layout** tab and in the Page Setup group, click the **Hyphenation** button, then click **Hyphenation Options**. Click to select the **Automatically hyphenate the document** check box, and change the Hyphenation zone setting to **.50**, with a consecutive hyphens limit of **3**.

9. In the first page, beginning with Sample Computer Use Policy, select the hidden space mark after March.

10. On the Insert tab on the Symbols group, click the **Symbols** button, then choose **More Symbols**. Click the **Special Characters** tab then select **Nonbreaking Spaces**. Click **Insert**, then **Close**. Select the nonprinting space mark before *2* in the year and press **Ctrl+Shift+Spacebar**.

11. **SAVE** the document as *new_computeruse_policy* in the lesson folder on your USB flash drive, then **CLOSE** the file.

PAUSE. LEAVE Word open for the next project.

Proficiency Assessment

Project 5-3: Coffee Shop Brochure

Your supervisor at the Grand Street Coffee Shop asks you to format the information in their coffee menu as a brochure.

GET READY. LAUNCH Word if it is not already running.

@ The *coffeemenu* file for this lesson is available on the book companion website or in WileyPLUS.

1. **OPEN** *coffeemenu* from the data files for this lesson.

2. Change the page orientation to **Landscape**.

3. Position the insertion point before the *M* in the Menu heading and insert a **Continuous** section break.

4. Create an uneven, two-column format using the **Left** column setting. Position the insertion point in front of Coffee and select text to the end of the document.

5. Position the insertion point before the *N* in the *Nutritional* heading and insert a **Column** break.

6. Increase the amount of space between columns to **.7"**. The document should fit to one page.

7. **SAVE** the document as *coffee_shop_brochure* in the lesson folder on your USB flash drive, then **CLOSE** the file.

PAUSE. LEAVE Word open for the next project.

Project 5-4: Mom's Favorite Recipes

Your mom asks you to help her create a small cookbook filled with her favorite recipes that she can share with family and friends. She has emailed you a Word document containing a few recipes to help you get started with creating a format.

GET READY. LAUNCH Word if it is not already running.

@ The *recipes* file for this lesson is available on the book companion website or in WileyPLUS.

1. **OPEN** *recipes* from the data files for this lesson.
2. Position the insertion point before the *C* in the Chicken Pot Pie heading and insert a Continuous section break.
3. Position the insertion point before the *B* in the Breads heading and insert a Next Page section break.
4. Position the insertion point before the *B* in the Banana Nut Bread/Chocolate Chip Muffins headings and insert a Continuous section break.
5. Position the insertion point anywhere within the Chicken Pot Pie recipe.
6. Format this and the remaining recipes in the Main Dishes section into two even columns with .9" spacing between columns and a line between.
7. Position the insertion point anywhere within the *Banana Nut Bread* recipe.
8. Format this and the remaining recipes in the *Breads* section into two even columns with .9" spacing between columns and a line between.
9. Position the insertion point before the *R* in the Ranch Chicken heading and insert a column break.
10. Position the insertion point before the *E* in the *Easy Pumpkin Bread/Muffins* heading and insert a column break.
11. Position the insertion point before the *C* in the *Chocolate Zucchini Bread* heading and insert a column break.
12. Position the insertion point under *Very Blueberry Coffee Cake/Muffins,* and select the hidden space mark between *cream cheese* for the second ingredient *1/2 (8 oz) package of . . .* and add a nonbreaking space. Click the Insert tab, in the Symbols groups, click More Symbols, then click the Special Character tab and select the Nonbreaking space option. In the ninth ingredient, select the hidden space mark between the words *or* and *huckleberries,* and add a nonbreaking space.
13. Click the Show/Hide ¶ ⟨ ¶ ⟩ button to hide formatting marks.
14. **SAVE** and the document as *favorite_recipes* in the lesson folder on your USB flash drive, then **CLOSE** the file.

PAUSE. LEAVE Word open for the next project.

Mastery Assessment

Project 5-5: Threefold Bank Brochure

The Checking Choices document needs to be formatted to accommodate the whole document on one page. Your task is to use the features learned in this lesson and apply them to this document as shown in Figure 5-21.

GET READY. LAUNCH Word if it is not already running.

@ The *checking-acctchoices* file for this lesson is available on the book companion website or in WileyPLUS.

1. **OPEN** *checkingacctchoices* from the data files for this lesson.
2. Reformat the document using a page size of 8½ × 14 with Landscape orientation. Create the brochure to look like the one shown in Figure 5-21.
3. Remove the Next Page section break after the heading, *Personal Checking Choice.* Delete the blank line above *Free Checking.* Change the columns to four columns, and add column breaks before each column heading. After *Personal Checking Choices* apply a Spacing After to 18 pt.

Figure 5-21

Checking brochure

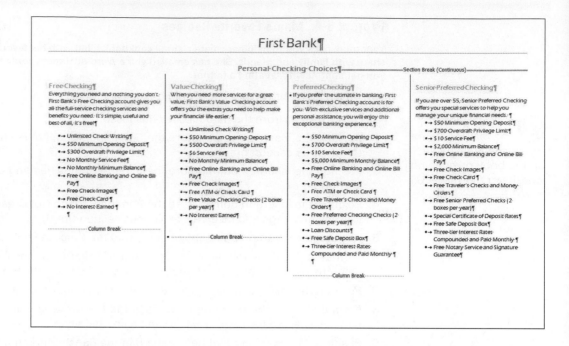

4. **SAVE** the document as *checking_brochure* in the lesson folder on your USB flash drive, then **CLOSE** the file.

PAUSE. LEAVE Word open for the next project.

Project 5-6: Reformat the YMCA Newsletter

As an alternative to the layout you created earlier, reformat the YMCA newsletter with two uneven columns.

GET READY. LAUNCH Word if it is not already running.

1. **OPEN** *ynewsletter* from the data files for this lesson.
2. Reformat the newsletter with two uneven columns using the Right column setting.
3. Format the document on one page. (Hint: Delete the column break in the first column and add a column break in front of *Volunteer Coaches. . . .*)
4. **SAVE** the document as *right_ymca_newsletter* in the lesson folder on your USB flash drive, then **CLOSE** the file.

STOP. CLOSE Word.

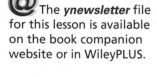 The *ynewsletter* file for this lesson is available on the book companion website or in WileyPLUS.

 INTERNET READY

Have you considered starting your own business someday? Use the Internet to research small business checking accounts from three different banks. What are the fees? What services are offered? What are the restrictions? Create a three-column document comparing the account features of each bank side by side.

Workplace *Ready*

CREATING COLUMNS

Visit the Student Government Association on your campus and review their marketing materials. Determine how you can improve the appearance of any form on file and incorporate the skills you learned in this lesson. Select a form that is a single column and apply three columns, letter size, landscape orientation, and other features to improve the document.

6 Creating Tables

LESSON SKILL MATRIX

Skill	Exam Objective	Objective Number
Creating a Table	Use the Insert Table dialog box.	2.5.1
	Use Draw Table.	2.5.2
	Insert a Quick Table.	2.5.3
	Convert text to a table.	2.5.4
Formatting a Table	Use a table to control page layout.	2.5.5
Managing Tables	Sort content.	2.6.1
	Add a row to a table.	2.6.2
	Add a column to a table.	2.6.3
	Manipulate rows.	2.6.4
	Manipulate columns.	2.6.5
	Define the header row.	2.6.6
	Convert tables to text.	2.6.7
	View gridlines.	2.6.8

KEY TERMS

- ascending
- cells
- descending
- header row
- merge cells
- Quick Tables
- sort
- split cells
- tables

Karen Archer is an executive recruiter. Many large companies hire her to find professional talent to fill communications and marketing executive positions within their firms. You were recently hired as her assistant, and although the business is small, you are expected to display a high degree of professionalism, confidentiality, and integrity. Because it is a small business, you are asked to perform many different duties. One of your main duties is to assist Ms. Archer with the constant updating of tables that contain data related to current clients, potential clients, and potential candidates for placement. Microsoft Word's table tools can help you successfully manage this information. In this lesson, you will learn to format lists as well as create, format, and manage tables.

CREATING A TABLE

A **table**, such as the one shown in Figure 6-1, is an arrangement of data made up of horizontal rows and vertical columns. **Cells** are the rectangles that are formed when rows and columns intersect. Tables are ideal for organizing information in an orderly manner. Calendars, invoices, and contact lists are all examples of tables that you see and use every day. Word provides several options for creating tables, including the dragging method, the Insert Table dialog box, table drawing tools, and the Quick Table method.

Figure 6-1

A table created in Word

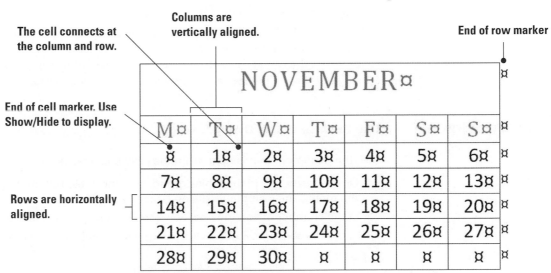

Inserting a Table by Dragging

In this exercise, you learn how easily and quickly you can create a table from the Table menu by dragging the mouse pointer to specify the number of rows and columns. Using this method, you can create a new empty table with up to eight rows and ten columns.

STEP BY STEP	**Insert a Table by Dragging**

GET READY. Before you begin these steps, **LAUNCH** Microsoft Word and **OPEN** a new blank Word document.

1. On the Insert tab, in the Tables group, click the Table button. The Insert Table menu appears.
2. Point to the cell in the fifth column, second row. The menu title should read *5×2 Table*, as shown in Figure 6-2. Click the mouse button to create the table.

WileyPLUS Extra! features an online tutorial of this task.

Figure 6-2

Insert Table menu

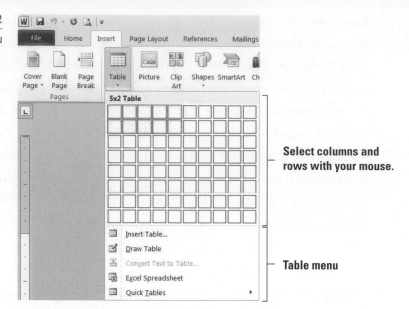

Select columns and rows with your mouse.

Table menu

3. Click below the table and press **Enter** twice to insert a blank line.

4. SAVE the document as *tables* in the lesson folder on your USB flash drive.

PAUSE. LEAVE the document open to use in the next exercise.

Using the Insert Table Dialog Box

The Insert Table dialog box lets you create large tables by specifying up to 63 columns and thousands of rows. In this exercise, you use the Insert Table dialog box to insert a table with nine columns and three rows. Note that in the Insert Table dialog box, you can click the up and down arrows or key in the number of columns and rows needed in a table.

STEP BY STEP   **Use the Insert Table Dialog Box**

USE the document that is open from the previous exercise.

1. On the Insert tab, in the Tables group, click the **Table** button. Select **Insert Table** from the menu. The Insert Table dialog box appears.

2. In the Number of columns box, click the **up arrow** until **9** is displayed.

3. In the Number of rows box, click the **up arrow** until **3** is displayed, as shown in Figure 6-3.

Figure 6-3

Insert Table dialog box

AutoFit options

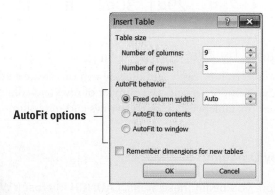

4. Click **OK** to insert the table. You inserted a new table with 9 columns and 3 rows.

5. Click below the table and press **Enter** twice to insert a blank line.

6. SAVE the document in the lesson folder on your USB flash drive.

PAUSE. LEAVE the document open to use in the next exercise.

Drawing a Table

Word provides the option to draw complex tables using the Draw Table command, which lets you draw a table as you would with a pencil and piece of paper. The Draw Table command transforms the mouse pointer into a pencil tool, which you can use to draw the outline of the table, then draw rows and columns exactly where you need them. In this exercise, you use the Draw Table command from the Table menu.

STEP BY STEP   **Draw a Table**

USE the document that is open from the previous exercise.

1. On the View tab, in the Show group, click the **check box** to display the Ruler.
2. On the Insert tab, in the Tables group, click the **Table** button. Select **Draw Table** from the menu. The pointer becomes a pencil tool.
3. To begin drawing the table shown in Figure 6-4, click at the blinking insertion point and drag down and to the right until you draw a rectangle that is approximately **3 inches high** and **6 inches wide**.

Figure 6-4

Drawing a table

Use the horizontal and vertical rulers as a guide to draw a table.

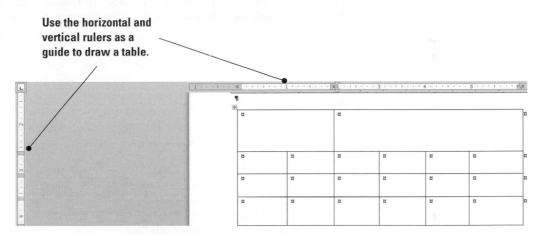

4. Starting at about 0.5 inch down from the top, click and drag the pencil from the left border to the right border to draw a horizontal line.
5. Draw two more horizontal lines about 0.5 apart.
6. Starting at about 1 inch from the left side, click and drag the pencil from the first line you drew to the bottom to create a column.
7. Move over about 1 inch and draw a line from the top of the table to the bottom. If you drew a line in the wrong position, click the Eraser on the Draw Borders group and begin again.
8. Draw three more vertical lines about 1 inch apart from the first horizontal line to the bottom of the table to create a total of six columns. Your table should look similar to Figure 6-4. Click the **Draw Table** button on Draw Borders to turn the pencil tool off.
9. Click below the table and press **Enter** twice to create a blank line. If necessary, place your insertion point outside of the last cell, and then press **Enter**.
10. **SAVE** the document in the lesson folder on your USB flash drive.

PAUSE. **LEAVE** the document open to use in the next exercise.

CERTIFICATION READY?   **2.5.2**

How do you draw a table?

Take Note

You have now seen three ways to insert a blank table. Text separated by commas, tabs, paragraphs, or another character can also be converted to a table with the Convert Text to Table command on the Table menu.

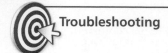 **Troubleshooting** When drawing tables with the pencil tool, note that this tool will draw squares and rectangles as well as lines. If you are trying to draw a straight line and you move the pencil off your straight path, Word may think you are trying to draw a rectangle and insert one for you. If this happens, just click the Undo button on the Quick Access Toolbar and try again. It might take a bit of practice to master the difference between drawing straight lines and drawing rectangles.

Inserting a Quick Table

Quick Tables are built-in preformatted tables, such as calendars and tabular lists to insert and use in your documents. Word provides a variety of Quick Tables that you can insert into your documents. In this exercise, you will insert a Quick Table calendar into a document. The Quick Table calendar can be edited to reflect the current month and year.

STEP BY STEP **Insert a Quick Table**

USE the document that is open from the previous exercise.

1. On the Insert tab, in the Tables group, click the **Table** button. Select **Quick Tables** from the menu. A gallery of built-in Quick Tables appears, as shown in Figure 6-5.

Figure 6-5

Built-In Quick Table gallery

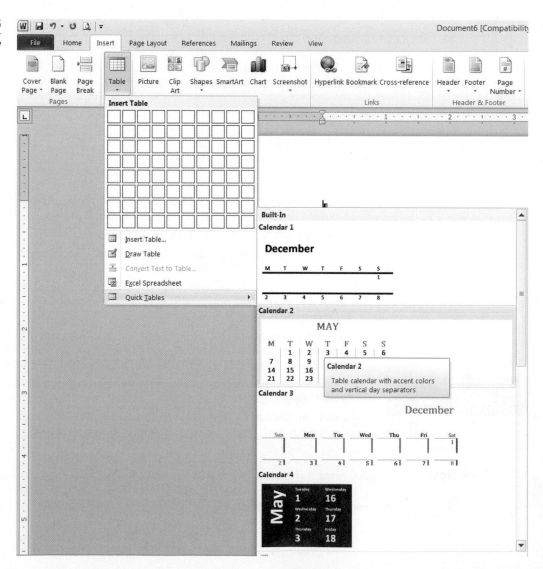

CERTIFICATION
R E A D Y ?   **2.5.3**

How do you insert a
Quick Table?

2. Select **Calendar 2**. The data in the calendar can be edited to display the current month
   and year.
3. **SAVE** the document in the lesson folder on your USB flash drive, then **CLOSE** the file.

PAUSE. LEAVE Word open to use in the next exercise.

Take Note   A table can be moved to a new page or a new document by clicking the move handle to select
the table and then using the Cut and Paste commands. You can also use the Copy command to
leave a copy of the table in the original location.

SOFTWARE ORIENTATION

Design Tab on the Table Tools Ribbon

After inserting a table, Word displays Table Tools in the Ribbon, as shown in Figure 6-6. It is
important to become familiar with the commands available in the Design tab under Table Tools.
Use this figure as a reference throughout this lesson as well as the rest of this book.

**Table Tools are displayed on the
Ribbon when a table is inserted.**

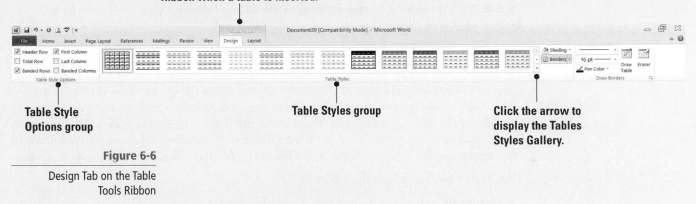

**Table Style
Options group**

Table Styles group

**Click the arrow to
display the Tables
Styles Gallery.**

Figure 6-6

Design Tab on the Table
Tools Ribbon

FORMATTING A TABLE

The Bottom Line   Once a table has been inserted into a document, a preformatted style can be applied using Quick
Styles from the Table Styles and Table Style Options groups. Quick Styles add a professional appearance to the tables in your documents.

Applying a Quick Style to a Table

With Quick Styles, it easy to quickly change a table's formatting. You can apply styles to tables
in much the same way you learned to apply styles to text in previous lessons, by positioning the
insertion point in the table before selecting a style from the Quick Styles gallery. You can preview
the style before applying it and change the style as many times as needed. You can modify an
existing Table Style or create a New Table Style and add it to the gallery, then modify or delete
it, as appropriate. In this exercise, you apply a Quick Style to a table in your Word document.

STEP BY STEP   **Apply a Quick Style to a Table**

OPEN *clients* from the data files for this lesson.

1. The insertion point is positioned in the table.

@ The *clients* file for
this lesson is available
on the book companion
website or in WileyPLUS.

2. On the Design tab, in the Table Styles group, click the **More** ⤓ button to view a gallery
   of Quick Styles.
3. Scroll through the available styles. Notice that as you point to a style, Word displays a
   live preview, showing you what your table will look like if you choose that style.

4. Scroll down to the fourth row under the Built-in section and select the fourth style over in the row, the Medium List 2 – Accent 3 style, as shown in Figure 6-7.

Figure 6-7

Quick Style gallery

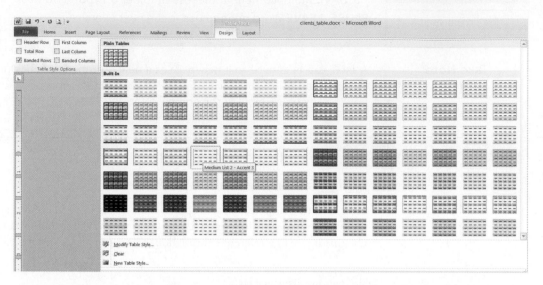

5. SAVE the document as *clients_table* in the lesson folder on your USB flash drive.

PAUSE. LEAVE the document open to use in the next exercise.

Turning Table Style Options On or Off

Table Style Options enable you to change the appearance of the Quick Styles you apply to your tables. Table Style Options, which are linked to the Table Style you have selected, apply globally throughout the table. For example, if you select the Banded Columns option, all even-numbered columns in the table will be formatted differently than the odd-numbered columns. In this exercise, you learn to turn Table Style Options on or off by clicking each option's check box.

Table Style Options include the following:

- **Header Row:** Formats the top row of the table
- **Total Row:** Formats the last row, which usually contains column totals
- **Banded Rows:** Formats even rows differently than odd rows
- **First Column:** Formats the first column of the table
- **Last Column:** Formats the last column of the table
- **Banded Columns:** Formats even columns differently than odd columns

STEP BY STEP **Turn Table Style Options On or Off**

USE the document that is open from the previous exercise.

1. The insertion point should still be in the table. If you click outside the table, the Design and Layout tabs will not be available.

2. On the Design tab, in the Table Style Options group, click the First Column check box. Notice that the format of the first column of the table changes, as do the Table Styles in the Quick Style gallery.

3. Click the Banded Rows check box to turn the option off. Color is removed from the rows.

4. Click the Banded Rows check box to turn it on again. Color is reapplied to every other row.

5. SAVE the document in the lesson folder on your USB flash drive.

PAUSE. LEAVE the document open to use in the next exercise.

SOFTWARE ORIENTATION

Layout Tab on the Table Tools Ribbon

When you are working with tables, Word displays a new contextual Table Tools ribbon that is only visible when a table is in use. The Table Tools Ribbon has two tabs: the Design tab and the Layout tab. The Layout tab, as shown in Figure 6-8, includes commands for changing the entire format of a table as well as commands for changing the appearance of individual table components, such as cells, columns, and rows. Use this figure as a reference throughout this lesson as well as the rest of this book.

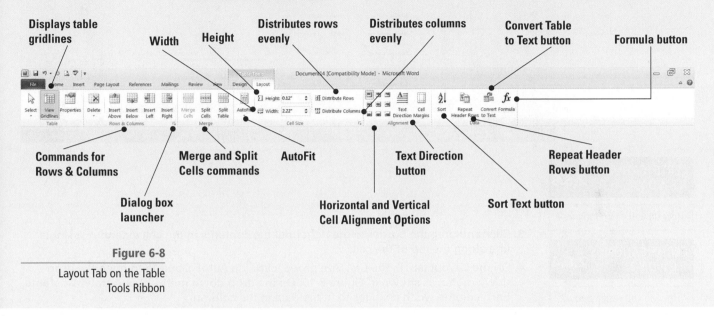

Figure 6-8

Layout Tab on the Table Tools Ribbon

MANAGING TABLES

The Bottom Line

As with any document that you edit, some adjustments are always necessary when you work with tables. After you create a table, you can resize and move its columns; insert columns and rows; change the alignment or direction of its text; set the header row to repeat on several pages; organize data through sorting by text, number, or date; convert text and tables; merge and split cells; and work with the table's properties. Word's gridlines make all such edits easier.

Resizing a Row or Column

Word offers a number of tools for resizing rows or columns. You can resize a column or row a couple of ways using the mouse. You can use commands in the Cell Size group on the Layout tab to adjust height and width, and Word's AutoFit command enables you to adjust column width to fit the size of table contents, the window, or to fit all content to a fixed column width. In addition, the Table Properties dialog box allows you to set the measurements at a precise height for rows or ideal width columns, cells, and tables. In this exercise, you practice using these techniques to resize rows and columns in a Word table.

STEP BY STEP **Resize a Row or Column**

USE the document that is open from the previous exercise.

1. On the Layout tab, in the Table group, click the **View Gridlines** button to display gridlines and enable more precise editing.
2. Click in the first column and position the mouse pointer over the horizontal ruler on the first column marker. The pointer changes to a double-headed arrow along with the ScreenTip *Move Table Column*, as shown in Figure 6-9.

Figure 6-9

Horizontal Ruler on the first
column marker

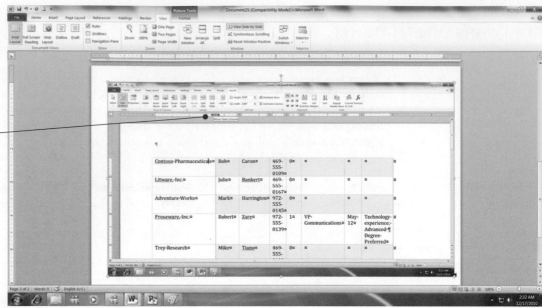

Figure 6-9

Horizontal Ruler on the first
column marker

**Column marker on
ruler. Columns can be
adjusted manually by
dragging.**

**CERTIFICATION
READY?**   **2.6.8**

How do you view gridlines?

**CERTIFICATION
READY?**   **2.6.4**

How do you resize a row?

3. Click and drag the border to the right until the contents in the cell extend in a single line along the top of the cell.

4. On the Layout tab, in the Cell Size group, click the **AutoFit** button to open the drop-down menu, as shown in Figure 6-10. On the drop-down menu, click **AutoFit Contents**. Each column width changes to fit the data in the column.

Figure 6-10

AutoFit button and menu

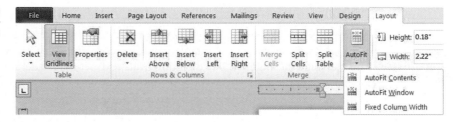

 Another Way
Position the pointer outside the table, above the column containing the phone numbers. The pointer changes to a down selection arrow. Click to select the column.

**CERTIFICATION
READY?**   **2.6.5**

How do you resize
a column?

 **Another Way**
The Table Properties dialog box can be accessed from the shortcut menu by right-clicking anywhere in the table and selecting Table Properties.

5. Position the insertion point in the phone number column of the table. In the Table group, of the Layout tab, click the **Select** button and choose **Select Column** from the drop-down menu.

6. On the Layout tab, in the Cell Size group, click the **up arrow** in the Width box until it reads **1.1"** and the column width changes.

7. Place the insertion point anywhere in the first row. In the Table group, click the **Select** button, then **Select Row** from the drop-down menu. The first row is selected.

8. On the Layout tab, in the Cell Size group, click the **dialog box launcher**. The Table Properties dialog box appears.

9. Click the **Row** tab in the dialog box. Click the **Specify height** check box. In the Height box, click the **up arrow** until the box reads **0.5"**, as shown in Figure 6-11.

10. Click the **Next Row** button to apply your changes to the row that follows the selected row in the table. Notice the selection moves down one row. Click **OK**.

11. Click in any cell to remove the selection.

12. **SAVE** the document as ***clients_table1*** in the lesson folder on your USB flash drive.

PAUSE. LEAVE the document open to use in the next exercise.

Figure 6-11

Figure 6-11

Table Properties dialog box

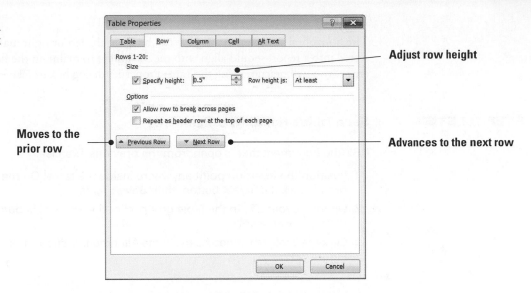

Adjust row height

Moves to the prior row

Advances to the next row

Moving a Row or Column

When working with tables, it is important to know how to rearrange columns and rows to better display your data. By selecting the entire column or row, drag and drop is used for moving data to a new area in the table. The mouse pointer changes and resembles an empty rectangle underneath with dotted lines. In this lesson, you practice moving text from rows and columns.

 Ref   The Cut and Paste commands were covered Lesson 2.

STEP BY STEP   **Move a Row or Column**

USE the document that is open from the previous exercise.

1. In the table, select the fourth row of data, which contains the information for Proseware, Inc. In the Table group, click the **Select** button, then **Select Row** from the drop-down menu.

CERTIFICATION READY?   2.6.4

How do you move a row?

2. The insertion point is positioned on the selected row, hold down the mouse button. Notice the mouse pointer changes to a move pointer with a dotted insertion point.

3. Drag the dotted insertion point down and position it before the *W* in *Wingtip Toys*. Release the mouse button and click in the table to deselect. The row is moved to the position above the Wingtip Toys row.

4. Place the insertion point in the second column of the table, which contains first names. Click the **Select** button, in the Table group, then **Select Column** from the drop-down menu.

CERTIFICATION READY?   2.6.5

How do you move a column?

5. Position the pointer inside the selected cells and right-click to display the shortcut menu. Select **Cut** to delete that column of text and move the remaining columns to the left.

6. Place the insertion point on the phone numbers column.

NEW to Office 2010

7. Right-click to display the shortcut menu, then under the Paste Options section, click **Insert as New Column**. A new Paste Options menu is displayed with the options Insert as New Column, Nest Table, Insert as New Row, and Keep Text Only. Selecting the first option to **Insert as New Column**; the first name column is pasted to the left of the phone number column. Click anywhere in the table to deselect.

8. **SAVE** the document as *clients_table2* in the lesson folder on your USB flash drive.

PAUSE. LEAVE the document open to use in the next exercise.

Take Note   Instead of using the shortcut menu, you can also use the Cut and Paste commands in the Clipboard group on the Home tab to cut and move rows and columns.

Setting a Table's Horizontal Alignment

The horizontal alignment for a table can be set to the left or right margins or centered. Tables inserted into a report should align with the document to maintain the flow of the report. In this exercise, you will practice using the Table Properties dialog box to set a table's horizontal alignment.

STEP BY STEP **Set a Table's Horizontal Alignment**

USE the document that is open from the previous exercise.

1. Position the insertion point anywhere inside the table. On the Layout tab, in the Table group, click the **Select** button, then **Select Table**.
2. On the Layout tab, in the Table group, click the **Properties** button. The Table Properties dialog box appears.
3. Click the **Table** tab, if necessary. In the Alignment section, click **Center**, as shown in Figure 6-12.

Figure 6-12

Table Properties dialog box

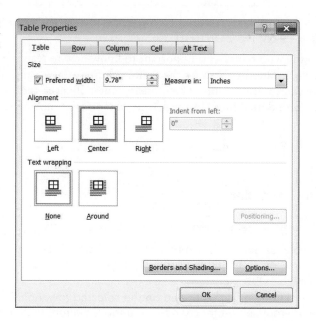

4. Click **OK**. The table is centered horizontally on the page. Click anywhere within the table to deselect.
5. **SAVE** the document on your USB flash drive in the lesson folder.

PAUSE. Leave the document open to use in the next exercise.

CERTIFICATION READY? **2.5.5**

How do you set a table's alignment?

Creating a Header Row

A **header row** is the first row of the table that is formatted differently and should be repeated for tables that extend beyond one page. When you specify a header row in the Table Style Options group, the row is distinguished from the entire table. Column headings are usually placed in the header row. In this exercise, you will practice repeating heading rows for lengthy tables.

STEP BY STEP **Create a Header Row**

USE the document that is open from the previous exercise.

1. Place the insertion point on the first row of the table.
2. On the Layout tab, in the Rows & Columns group, click **Insert Above** . A new blank row is inserted.

3. On the Design tab, in the Table Style Options group, click the Header Row check box to apply a distinctive format to the header row.

4. Key headings in each cell within the first row of the table, as shown in Figure 6-13.

Figure 6-13

Header row

Company·Name¤	Contact· Person¤	¤	Phone· Number¤	Number·of· Current·Open· Positions¤	Position·Title¤	Date· Posted¤	Notes¤
Contoso· Pharmaceuticals¤	Caron¤	Rob¤	469-555-0109¤	0¤	¤	¤	¤
Litware,·Inc.¤	Bankert¤	Julie¤	469-555-0167¤	0¤	¤	¤	¤

CERTIFICATION
READY?   2.6.2

How do you insert a row in a table?

CERTIFICATION
READY?   2.6.6

How do you define a header row?

Take Note

5. Select the first row of the table. On the Table group of the Layout tab, click the Select button and Select Row.

6. On the Home tab, in the Font group, click the Bold **B** button. The header rows are bolded.

7. On the Layout tab, in the Data group, click the Repeat Header Rows button. Scroll down and view the headings on the second page. Click anywhere in the table to deselect.

8. SAVE the document as *clients_table3* in the lesson folder on your USB flash drive.

PAUSE. LEAVE the document open to use in the next exercise.

Repeating rows are only visible in Print Layout view or on a printed document.

Sorting a Table's Contents

To **sort** data means to arrange it alphabetically, numerically, or chronologically. Sorting displays data in order so that it can be immediately located. Text, numbers, or dates can be sorted in ascending or descending order. **Ascending** order sorts text from beginning to end, such as from A to Z, 1 to 10, and January to December. **Descending** order sorts text from the end to the beginning, such as from Z to A, 10 to 1, and December to January. In this exercise, you practice sorting data in a Word table using the Sort dialog box, which you access through the Sort command on the Layout tab in the Data group.

Take Note

You can sort up to three columns of data in the Sort dialog box. Before beginning the sort process, you must select the column (or columns) to be sorted.

STEP BY STEP   **Sort a Table's Contents**

USE the document that is open from the previous exercise.

1. Place the insertion point on the first column to select the Company Name column. On the Table group of the Layout tab, click the Select button and Select Column.

2. On the Layout tab, in the Data group, click the Sort button. The Sort dialog box appears, as shown in Figure 6-14. The Company Name data is listed in the Sort By text box, with Ascending Order selected by default.

Figure 6-14

Sort dialog box

Identify data as text, numbers, or dates for easier sorting.

Identifies the order in which to sort your list

Ascending order sorts from A to Z.

Descending order sorts from Z to A.

If your table has headings, select Header row.

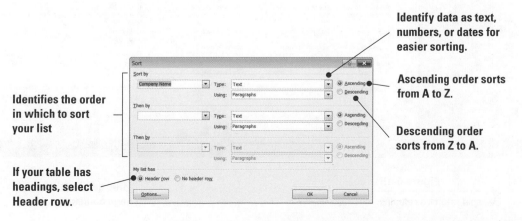

CERTIFICATION
READY?   **2.6.1**

How do you sort a
table's contents?

3. Click **OK**. Note that the table now appears sorted in ascending alphabetical order by company name.

4. **SAVE** the document as ***clients_table4*** in the lesson folder on your USB flash drive.

PAUSE. LEAVE the document open to use in the next exercise.

Merging and Splitting Table Cells

The ability to merge and split table cells provides flexibility in customizing tables. To **merge cells** means to combine two or more cells into one. Merging cells is useful for headings that extend over several columns. To **split cells** means to divide one cell into two or more cells. Cells may be split when more than one type of data needs to be placed in one cell. The Split Cells dialog box enables you to split a cell into columns or rows. In this lesson, you practice using commands in the Merge group on the Layout tab to merge and split cells.

STEP BY STEP   **Merge and Split Table Cells**

USE the document that is open from the previous exercise.

CERTIFICATION
READY?   **2.6.4**

How do you merge
rows?

1. Position the insertion point on the header row located on page 1. Select the cell that contains the Contact Person heading and the empty cell to the right of it.

2. On the Layout tab, in the Merge group, click the **Merge Cells** button. The selected columns merge into one cell.

3. In the Position Title column, on the Lucerne Publishing row, select the cell that contains the text Director Marketing VP Public Relations.

4. On the Layout tab, in the Merge group, click the **Split Cells** button.

5. Click **OK** to accept the settings as they are. A new column is inserted within the cell, as shown in Figure 6-15.

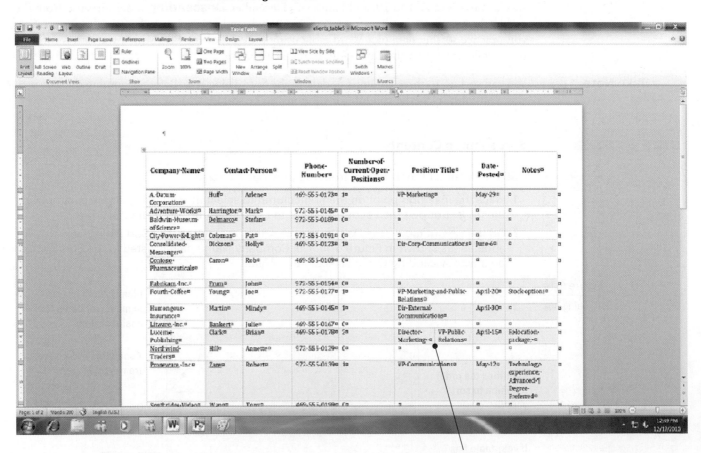

Figure 6-15

Cell split into two columns

One cell is split into two columns.

CERTIFICATION
READY?   **2.6.5**

How do you merge
columns?

6. Select the text **VP Public Relations** and drag and drop text to the new column.

7. In the Company Name column, select the Woodgrove Bank cell.

8. Click the **Split Cells** button. The default setting for the Number of columns is 2, while the Number of rows is 1. The Merge cells before split check box is checked.

9. Change the Number of columns settings to **1** and the Number of rows setting to **2** to split the cell into a single column containing two rows, as shown in Figure 6-16.

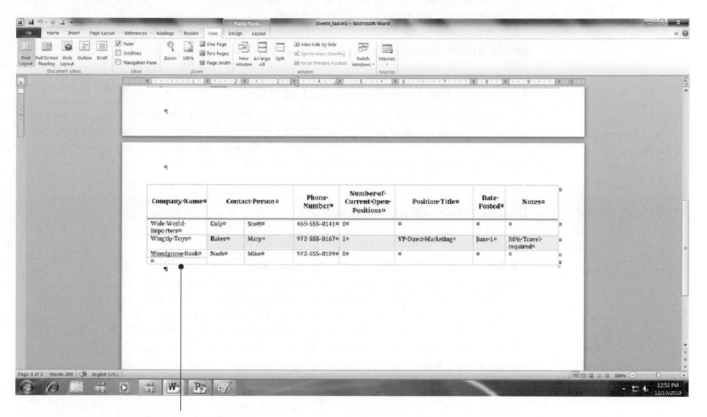

One cell is split into
two rows.

Figure 6-16

Cell split into two rows

CERTIFICATION
READY?   **2.6.4**

How do you split cells
by rows?

10. Select the split cell and merge. Place the insertion point in front of *Woodgrove Bank*. Press and hold the mouse button to select the two rows within the column. On the Merge group, click the **Merge Cells** button. The cell is now a single row.

11. Click the Undo  button.

12. **SAVE** the document as ***clients_table5*** in the lesson folder on your USB flash drive.

PAUSE. LEAVE the document open to use in the next exercise.

CERTIFICATION
READY?   **2.6.5**

How do you split cells
by columns?

Changing the Position of Text in a Cell

Word provides you with nine options for aligning text in a cell. These options enable you to control the horizontal and vertical alignment of cell text, such as Top Left, Top Center, and Top Right. To change cell text alignment, select the cell or cells you want to align and click one of the nine alignment buttons in the Alignment group on the Layout tab. In this lesson, you practice changing the text alignment within a cell.

Another Way
You can access the Merge Cells command on the shortcut menu. The Merge Cells command is visible only when you have multiple cells selected in a table.

STEP BY STEP | **Change the Position of Text in a Cell**

USE the document that is open from the previous exercise.

1. Select the table's header's row, with the headings on page 1. On the Layout tab in the Table group, click the Select button, then click Select Row.
2. In the Alignment group, click the Align Center ≡ button. The header row is centered horizontally and vertically within the cell.
3. SAVE the document in the lesson folder on your USB flash drive.

PAUSE. LEAVE the document open to use in the next exercise.

Changing the Direction of Text in a Cell

Rotating text in a cell provides additional options for creating interesting and effective tables. Changing the direction of text in a heading can be especially helpful. To change the direction of text in a cell, click the button three times to cycle through the three available directions. In this exercise, you practice changing the direction of text in a cell.

STEP BY STEP | **Change the Direction of Text in a Cell**

USE the document that is open from the previous exercise.

1. Select the cell that contains the Company Name heading.
2. On the Layout tab, in the Alignment group, click the Text Direction button three times to rotate the text direction to align to the right cell border, the left cell border, and then back to the top cell border. As you click the Text Direction button, the button face rotates to match the rotation of the text direction in the selected cell.
3. SAVE the document in the lesson folder on your USB flash drive.

PAUSE. LEAVE Word open to use in the next exercise.

Converting Text to Table or Table to Text

Text separated by a paragraph mark, tab, comma, or other character can be converted from text to a table or from a table to text. To convert text to a table, first select the text, then click the Insert tab button, then click the Table button, and finally select Convert Text to Table. The Convert Text to Table dialog box will appear, and Word will determine the number of columns needed. In this exercise, you practice using this technique to convert Word text into a table.

STEP BY STEP | **Convert Text to Table or Table to Text**

OPEN the *part_numbers* document in your lesson folder.

@ The *part_numbers* file for this lesson is available on the book companion website or in WileyPLUS.

1. Select the whole document.
2. On the Insert tab, on the Table group, click the Table button. The Table menu appears.
3. Click Convert Text to Table. The Convert Text to Table dialog box opens. Word recognizes the number columns and rows and places the number 10 in the Number of rows box—notice that it is shaded gray, making it unavailable to change. (See Figure 6-17.) Keep the default settings.
4. Click OK. The selected text was separated by paragraph marks and by selecting the default of one column, Word converts the text to a table, as shown in Figure 6-18.
5. SAVE the document as *part_numbers_table* in the lesson folder on your USB flash drive.
6. Position the insertion point anywhere in the table and click the Layout tab.
7. In the Table group, click the Select button, then click Select Table to select the entire table.

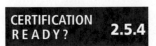

CERTIFICATION READY? 2.5.4

How do you convert text to a table?

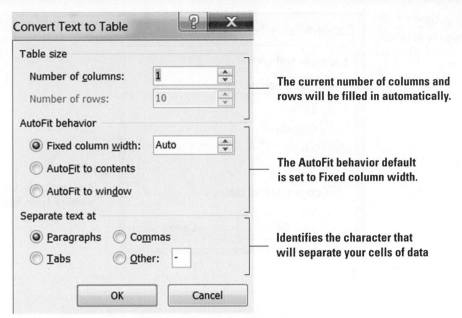

Figure 6-17

Convert Text to Table
dialog box

The current number of columns and
rows will be filled in automatically.

The AutoFit behavior default
is set to Fixed column width.

Identifies the character that
will separate your cells of data

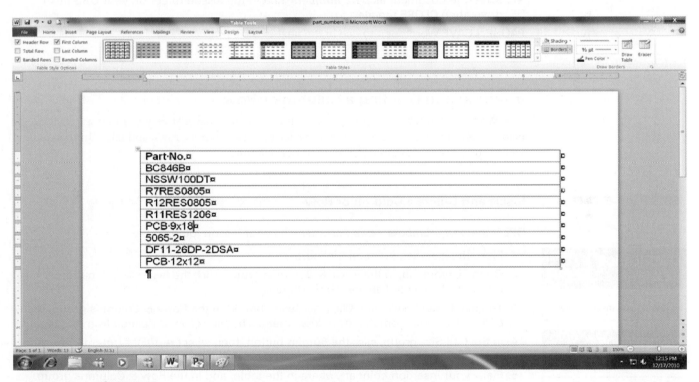

Figure 6-18

Document converted from text
to a table

8. In the Data group, click **Convert Table to Text**. The Convert Table to Text dialog box
opens. The default setting in the Convert Table to Text dialog box is Paragraph marks. A
table can be converted to text and separated by paragraph marks, tabs, commas, and
other characters (see Figure 6-19).

**CERTIFICATION
READY?** 2.6.7

How do you convert a
table to text?

Figure 6-19

Convert Table to Text
dialog box

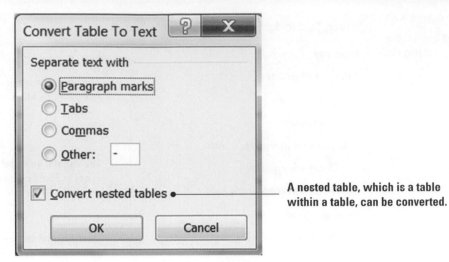

A nested table, which is a table
within a table, can be converted.

9. Click **OK**. The document is converted to text separated by paragraph marks.
10. **SAVE** the document as **part_numbers_text** in the lesson folder on your USB flash drive, then **CLOSE** the file.

PAUSE. LEAVE Word open to use in the next exercise.

Inserting and Deleting a Column or Row

The Word Layout tab in the Rows and Columns group, makes it easy to insert a row above or below a column; to the left or right; and to delete cells, columns, rows, and table. In the exercise, you learn to insert a column and row and delete a row.

STEP BY STEP | **Insert and Delete a Column or Row**

OPEN the **part_numbers_table** documents in your lesson folder.

CERTIFICATION READY? 2.6.2

How do you insert a row?

CERTIFICATION READY? 2.6.3

How do you insert a column?

CERTIFICATION READY? 2.6.4

How do you delete a row?

CERTIFICATION READY? 2.6.5

How do you delete a column?

1. Place the insertion point on the fourth row.
2. On the Layout tab, in the Rows & Columns group, click the **Insert Above** button; a blank row is inserted above the fourth row.
3. The blank row is selected. Click the **Delete** button in the Rows & Columns group, then click **Delete Row** from the drop-down menu. The blank row is deleted from the table.
4. In the Cell Size group, click the **AutoFit** button, then select **AutoFit Contents**. The data in the table automatically resizes to fit in the column width.
5. Place your insertion point anywhere in the table, and in the Row & Columns group, click **Insert Right**. A new column is inserted to the right.
6. On the Rows & Columns group, click the **Delete** button, then click **Delete Column**. The Delete button menu allows you to delete cells, rows, and the entire table.
7. **SAVE** the document in the lesson folder on your USB flash drive, then **CLOSE** the file.

CLOSE Word.

SKILL SUMMARY

In This Lesson, You Learned How To:	Exam Objective	Objective Number
Create a table	Use the Insert Table dialog box.	2.5.1
	Use Draw Table.	2.5.2
	Insert a Quick Table.	2.5.3
	Convert text to a table.	2.5.4
Format a table	Use a table to control page layout.	2.5.5
Manage tables	Sort content.	2.6.1
	Add a row to a table.	2.6.2
	Add a column to a table.	2.6.3
	Manipulate rows.	2.6.4
	Manipulate columns.	2.6.5
	Define the header row.	2.6.6
	Convert tables to text.	2.6.7
	View gridlines.	2.6.8

Knowledge Assessment

True/False

Circle T if the statement is true or F if the statement is false.

T   F   **1.** When you know how many rows and columns you need in a table, the quickest way to create the table is by dragging over the grid in the Table menu.

T   F   **2.** Turning Table Style Options on or off has no effect on the Quick Styles in the Table Styles gallery.

T   F   **3.** When Word converts text to tables, it uses paragraph marks, tabs, and commas to determine how to organize the data within the table.

T   F   **4.** You can move a column or row using Cut and Paste.

T   F   **5.** Sorting can only sort one column of data at a time.

T   F   **6.** If a hyphen exists within a section of text, and you are converting that text to a table, the hyphen will create a new column.

T   F   **7.** Text can be aligned both horizontally and vertically in a cell.

T   F   **8.** Word provides four options for changing the direction of text in a cell.

T   F   **9.** You can sort single-level lists, such as bulleted or numbered lists.

T   F   **10.** The Repeat Header Rows button is used for tables that extend to multiple pages.

Multiple Choice

Select the best response for the following statements.

1. Using the Sort feature in a table will sort selected content in what order?

    a. Ascending

    b. Descending

    c. Alphabetically order

    d. All of the above

2. Combining two or more cells into one uses a Word feature called:
   a. Split Cells.
   b. Merge Cells.
   c. Merge All Cells.
   d. Merge Selected Cells.

3. An arrangement of data made up of horizontal rows and vertical columns is called a:
   a. Menu.
   b. Heading.
   c. Table.
   d. Merge.

4. Built-in preformatted tables that can be inserted and used in your documents are called:
   a. Table Styles Options.
   b. Tables.
   c. Quick Tables.
   d. Insert Tables.

5. The rectangles that are formed when rows and columns intersect are known as:
   a. cells.
   b. merged cells.
   c. split cells.
   d. tables.

6. Which sort order sorts text from the end to the beginning?
   a. Descending.
   b. Ascending.
   c. Plunging.
   d. Downward.

7. Sorted data can consist of:
   a. text.
   b. numbers.
   c. dates.
   d. All of the above

8. Which option would you choose to arrange data alphabetically, numerically, or chronologically?
   a. Filter
   b. Group
   c. Sort
   d. Category dialog box

9. When you create a table in Word, two new Ribbon tabs appear. Which of the following are in a new Table Tools tab?
   a. Page Layout
   b. Design
   c. Insert
   d. Merge Cells

10. The first row of a table that is formatted differently than the rest of the table is called a:
    a. total row.
    b. banded column.
    c. header column.
    d. header row.

Competency Assessment

Project 6-1: Placements Table

Ms. Archer, the executive recruiter, asks you to start working on a placements table that will list the candidates that have been placed, the companies that hired them, and the date of hire.

GET READY. LAUNCH Word if it is not already running.

@ The *placements* file for this lesson is available on the book companion website or in WileyPLUS.

1. **OPEN** *placements* from the data files for this lesson.
2. Place the insertion point in the last column. Select the last column in the table. In the Layout tab, in the Table group, click the **Select** button and Select Columns.
3. On the Layout tab, in the Cell Size group, click the **down arrow** in the Width box until it reads **.9"**.
4. Place the insertion point in the first column and select the first column in the table. In the Table group, click the **Select** button and **Select Columns**.
5. On the Layout tab, in the Cell Size group, click the **down arrow** in the Width box until it reads **.9"**.
6. Select the **Company** column and change the width to **1.5"**.
7. Select the **Date of Placement** column and change the width to **1.3"**. Click in the table to deselect.
8. On the Design tab, in the Table Style Options group, click the **Header Row** check box and **Banded Rows** check box to turn on. Place your insertion point within the table.
9. On the Design tab, in the Table Styles group, select the **Medium Shading 1 - Accent 1** style in the ninth column, second row in the Built-In gallery.
10. Select the Last column in the table.
11. On the Layout tab, in the Data group, click the **Sort** button. Under the *My list has* section, select Header Row. In the Sort dialog box, click **OK**. This will sort the column by date.
12. The table is selected. On the Layout tab, in the Table group, click the **Properties** button.
13. In the Table Properties dialog box, click **Center** alignment in the Table tab and click **OK**.
14. Select the header row.
15. On the Layout tab, in the Alignment group, click **Align Center**.
16. **SAVE** the document as *placements_table* in the lesson folder on your USB flash drive, then **CLOSE** the file.

LEAVE Word open for the next project.

Project 6-2: Quarterly Sales Data

Create a table showing the quarterly sales for Coho Vineyard.

GET READY. LAUNCH Word if it is not already running.

1. Create a new blank document.
2. On the Insert tab, in the Tables group, click the **Table** button. Drag to create a table that has 5 columns and 6 rows.
3. Enter the following data in the table as shown:

20XX				
	First Quarter	*Second Quarter*	*Third Quarter*	*Fourth Quarter*
Mark Hanson	19,098	25,890	39,088	28,789
Terry Adams	21,890	19,567	32,811	31,562
Max Benson	39,400	35,021	19,789	21,349
Cathan Cook	34,319	27,437	28,936	19,034

4. Select the first row. On the Layout tab, in the Merge group, click the **Merge Cells** button.

5. With the row still selected, center the title by clicking the **Align Center** button in the Alignment group on the Layout tab.

6. On the Design tab, in the Table Styles Options group, click the **Banded Columns** check box to turn on. The Header Row, First Column, and Banded Rows options should be turned on already.

7. On the Design tab, in the Table Styles gallery, click the **More** button to display the gallery. On the seventh column, choose the orange **Dark List - Accent 6**.

8. **SAVE** the document as *quarterly_sales* in the lesson folder on your USB flash drive.

9. On the Layout tab, click the **Select** button in the Table group, and then choose **Select Table** from the drop-down menu.

10. In the Data group, select **Convert to Text**, then select the **Tabs** section.

11. **SAVE** the document as *quarterly_sales2* in the lesson folder on your USB flash drive, then **CLOSE** the file.

LEAVE Word open for the next project.

Proficiency Assessment

Project 6-3: Sales Table

Ms. Archer asks you to create a sales table including data from the past two years. She can use this table to set goals and project future income.

GET READY. LAUNCH Word if it is not already running.

1. **OPEN** *sales* from the data files for this lesson.

@ The *sales* file for this lesson is available on the book companion website or in WileyPLUS.

2. Select the columns headings containing the months and change the text direction for all the months so that they begin at the bottom of the column and extend to the top.

3. Increase the row height of the row containing the months to **0.9** inches so that the text all fits on one line.

4. Use the **AutoFit Contents** for the selected months.

5. Select the last row and Delete.

6. Make sure the Header Row, Banded Columns, and First Column Table Style Options are the only ones turned on.

7. Merge all the cells in the first row and center the heading.

8. Merge all the cells in the second row and center the subheading.

9. Choose the **Medium Shading 2 - Accent 2** Table Style format.

10. Center the table horizontally in the Tables Properties dialog box.

11. **SAVE** the document as *sales_table* in the lesson folder on your USB flash drive, then **CLOSE** the file. **Leave** Word open for the next project.

Project 6-4: Client Contact Table

Ms. Archer needs you to create a quick contact list.

GET READY. LAUNCH Word if it is not already running.

1. **OPEN** *client_table_2* from the data files for this lesson.

@ The *client_table_2* file for this lesson is available on the book companion website or in WileyPLUS.

2. Delete the last four columns: Number of Current Open Positions, Position Title, Date Posted, and Notes.

3. Change the page orientation to **Portrait**.

4. Change the width of the Company Name column to **1.9** inches.

5. Delete the Total row and turn off the Total Row option in Table Styles Options.

6. Change the style to the purple Light List –Accent 4 style.

7. Center the table horizontally on the page.

8. Change the alignment for the first row to Align Center.

9. Change the header row height to 0.4 inches.

10. **SAVE** the document as *new_client_table* in the lesson folder on your USB flash drive, then **CLOSE** the file.

LEAVE Word open for the next project.

Mastery Assessment

Project 6-5: Quarterly Sales Table Update

The Coho Winery's Quarterly Sales Table includes some formatting mistakes. Find and correct the four problems within this document.

GET READY. LAUNCH Word if it is not already running.

1. **OPEN** *problem* from the data files for this lesson.

2. Find and correct four errors in the table.

3. **SAVE** the document as *fixed_quarterly_sales* in the lesson folder on your USB flash drive, then **CLOSE** the file.

LEAVE Word open for the next project.

@ The *problem* file for this lesson is available on the book companion website or in WileyPLUS.

Project 6-6: Soccer Team Roster

As coach of your child's soccer team, you need to distribute a roster to all of your players with contact information, uniform numbers, and assigned snack responsibilities. You received a rough list from the league and you would like to convert it to table form. You haven't converted text to a table before, but you're confident you can do it.

GET READY. LAUNCH Word if it is not already running.

1. **OPEN** *soccer_team* from the data files for this lesson.

2. Select all the text.

3. On the Insert tab, in the Tables group, click the Table button. Select Convert Text to Table from the menu.

4. In the Convert Text to Table dialog box, key 4 in the Number of columns box. Click the Commas button under the Separate Text At section and click OK.

5. Use what you learned in this lesson to format the table as shown in Figure 6-20. Start by removing extra spaces or words, adjusting column widths, and aligning text. Sort the table by snack date, insert a header row with the following headings for each column (Name, Uniform, Telephone Numbers, Snacks) and choose the Medium Grid 3 – Accent 2 Table Style.

@ The *soccer_team* file for this lesson is available on the book companion website or in WileyPLUS.

Figure 6-20

Name¤	Uniform¤	Telephone·Number¤	Snacks¤	¤
Annette·Hill¤	#·4¤	806-555-0110¤	snack·responsibility· on·9/9¤	¤
Brian·Groth¤	#·3¤	806-555-0134¤	snacks·on·9/16¤	¤
Maria·Hammond¤	#2¤	806-555-0175¤	snacks·of·9/23¤	¤
Russell·King¤	#·7¤	806-555-0161¤	snacks·on·9/30¤	¤
Lee·Oliver¤	#8¤	806-555-0154¤	snacks·on·10/7¤	¤
Chris·Preston¤	#6¤	806-555-0182¤	snacks·on·10/14¤	¤
Garrett·Young¤	#9¤	806-555-0192¤	snacks·on·10/28¤	¤
Dylan·Miller¤	#1¤	806-555-0149¤	snacks·on·11/4¤	¤
Eric·Parkinson¤	#5¤	806-555-0170¤	snacks·on·11/11¤	¤

6. SAVE the document as *soccer_roster* in the lesson folder on your USB flash drive, then **CLOSE** the file.

STOP. **CLOSE** Word.

INTERNET READY

Search the Internet for job openings that interest you. Create a table to record data about at least five positions. Include columns for the job title, salary, location, contact person, and any other information that would help you in a job search. Use what you have learned in this chapter to format the table in an attractive way that you could easily maintain.

Workplace *Ready*

CREATING TABLES

Most people working in business are familiar with the many advantages of using Excel for creating tables. What some people may not realize is that Word provides many of the same capabilities. By creating a table and performing basic calculations directly within a Word document, you can turn an ordinary word processing document into a comprehensive business illustration.

Having just completed your college education, you are excited to begin your new career with Woodgrove Bank. As a Banking Associate in the Mortgage Department, one of your main responsibilities is to produce a monthly Mortgage Status memo. This memo includes monthly information on the number of new mortgage applications, the dollar amount of each, and their current status.

Presenting this information in a table format will provide for the most appealing design. However, you also need to include a brief introductory paragraph recapping the monthly information, as well as calculations for the total dollar amount of new mortgage applications. This report should be sent out in a memo format. By using Word, you can easily meet all of your objectives in just one program.

A co-worker reminds you that Word provides several memo templates, and you decide to choose one when initially creating your document. Memo templates provide replaceable text for To, From, Subject, Date, and CC information. Below this, you can enter your monthly recap paragraph. Finally, you can use Word's Table options to create and format a table with the desired number of columns and rows.

Once the table has been created and the information has been entered into the appropriate cells, you can use Word's Table Layout and Design tools to enhance your table's appearance. Word provides many of the same capabilities you would find in Excel, such as merging cells, splitting cells, aligning text, auto-fitting text, sorting, and much more.

With so many possibilities, Word is a true all-in-one business tool.

Working with Themes, Quick Parts, Page Backgrounds, and Headers and Footers

7

LESSON SKILL MATRIX

Skill	Exam Objective	Objective Number
Formatting, Creating, and Customizing a Theme	Use a theme to apply formatting.	3.2.1
	Customize a theme.	3.2.2
Using Quick Parts in a Document	Add built-in building blocks.	3.3.1
Formatting a Document's Background	Set a colored background.	3.4.2
	Format a document's background.	3.4.1
	Add a watermark.	3.4.3
	Set page borders.	3.4.4
Creating and Modifying Headers and Footers	Insert page numbers.	3.5.1
	Format page numbers.	3.5.2
	Insert the current date and time.	3.5.3
	Insert a built-in header or footer.	3.5.4
	Apply a different first page attribute.	3.5.8
	Add content to a header or footer.	3.5.5
	Change margins.	3.5.7
	Delete a header or footer.	3.5.6

KEY TERMS

- building blocks
- content controls
- document theme
- fields
- footer
- header
- watermarks

You are a content manager for Flatland Hosting Company, a position in which you are responsible for writing and editing all client material, such as hosting guidelines and agreements. When creating and revising documents, several Word commands can help you work more efficiently. In this lesson, you learn to apply a theme to a document, add content to a document using quick parts, and insert page numbers, headers, and footers.

FORMATTING, CREATING, AND CUSTOMIZING A THEME

The Bottom Line

Word provides features such as themes and Quick Parts to produce creative and professional documents. In this lesson, you learn to change the appearance of the document using the existing and customized themes and inserting building blocks in the document.

Formatting a Document with a Theme

Predefined formatting preferences allow you to change the overall appearance of the document by selecting and applying a theme. A **document theme** is a set of predefined formatting options that includes theme colors, fonts, and effects. You can apply one of the preexisting themes or create and customize a theme. Document themes contain the following elements: theme colors, theme fonts, and theme effects. In this exercise, you learn how to apply a document theme in Word.

Theme colors contain four text and background colors, six accent colors, and two hyperlink colors. Click the Theme Colors button to change the colors for the current theme, as shown in Figure 7-1.

Figure 7-1

Theme Colors menu

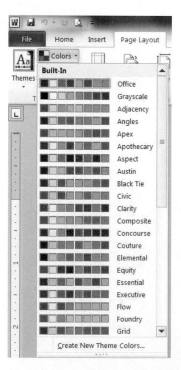

Theme fonts contain a heading font and a body text font. Click the Theme Fonts button to change the fonts for the current theme, as shown in Figure 7-2.

Figure 7-2

Theme Fonts menu

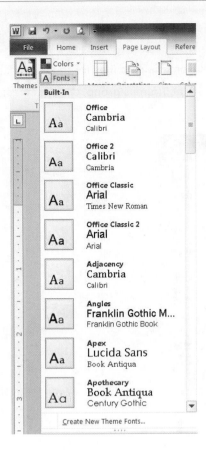

Theme effects are sets of lines and fill effects. Click the Theme Effects button to change the effects for the current theme, as shown in Figure 7-3.

Figure 7-3

Theme Effects menu

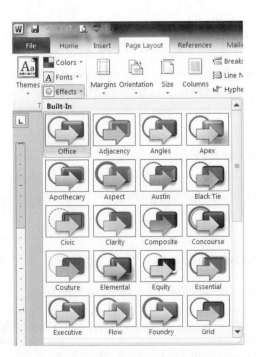

Format a Document with a Theme

OPEN the *hosting* document from the data files for this lesson.

1. On the Page Layout tab, in the Themes group, click Themes; the Themes menu opens, as shown in Figure 7-4.

Figure 7-4

Document Themes menu

The *hosting* document for this lesson is available on the book companion website or in WileyPLUS.

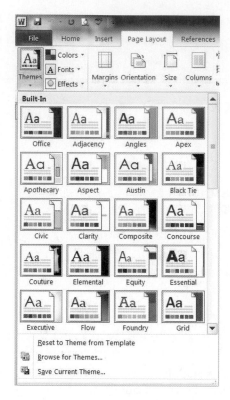

WileyPLUS Extra! features an online tutorial of this task.

2. Place your insertion point over any built-in theme and notice that the document changes to display a live preview of your document.

Take Note   Applying a theme changes the overall design of the entire document.

CERTIFICATION READY?   3.2.1

How do you apply a theme to a document?

3. Click the Grid theme and the elements are applied to the document.
4. SAVE the document as *hosting_term* in your USB flash drive in the lesson folder.

PAUSE. LEAVE the document open to use in the next exercise.

Creating and Customizing a Theme

In a business environment, the company may want to show consistency by customizing a theme to be used for reports throughout the organization. In this exercise, you create, customize, and apply a new theme to a document.

Create and Customize a Theme

USE the document that is open from the previous exercise.

1. In the Themes group, click the Theme Colors button to open the Colors menu (refer to Figure 7-1). The Theme Colors contain predefined formatting colors with text and background colors, six accent colors, and two hyperlink colors. These colors can be customized and saved with a new name.
2. At the bottom of the Colors menu, click Create New Theme Colors; the Create New Theme Colors dialog box opens (see Figure 7-5).

Figure 7-5

Create New Theme Colors
dialog box

There are 12 settings for each color
set—the defaults are displayed.

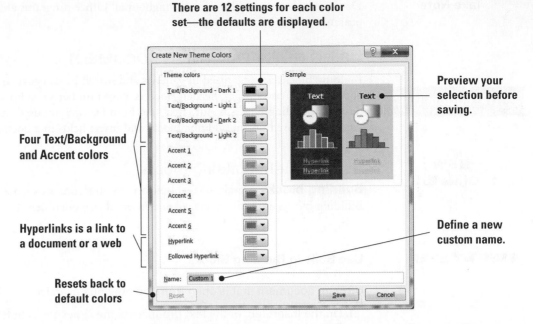

Four Text/Background
and Accent colors

Hyperlinks is a link to
a document or a web

Resets back to
default colors

Preview your
selection before
saving.

Define a new
custom name.

Take Note

Throughout this chapter you will see information that appears in black text within brackets, such as [Press Enter], or [your email address]. The information contained in the brackets is intended to be directions for you rather than something you actually type word-for-word. It will instruct you to perform an action or substitute text. Do not type the actual text that appears within brackets.

Another Way

You can edit the Colors and Fonts in the Styles group, under Change Styles.

3. In the *Name* text box, replace Custom 1 by keying **Corporate_[your initials]**. Click **Save**; the dialog box closes and you have defined a new custom theme color name based on default colors.

4. Click **Colors** and under the Custom section place your insertion point over Corporate_ [your initials]. Right-click this theme name, then click **Edit** from the pop-up menu that appears. The Edit Theme Colors dialog box appears.

5. In the list of theme colors, click the **Accent 2 drop-down arrow** to produce a menu of colors for this element. In the fourth column of the menu's sixth row select **Tan, Text 2, Darker 50%**. Click **Save**. You changed the default color to a specific color and created your own custom theme colors for your document.

6. Click the **Fonts** button to produce the Theme Fonts menu (refer to Figure 7-2). In the menu, click **Create New Theme Fonts**; the Create New Theme Fonts dialog box opens. In the Name text box, replace Custom 1 by keying **CorporateFonts_[your initials]**.

7. Change the Heading Font and Body Font to **Arial**; notice the preview of your font choices that appears in the Sample pane of the dialog box. Click **Save** to close the dialog box and apply your font choices to the document.

Take Note

A quick way to change fonts is by keying the font name.

8. Click the **Effects** button and select **Concourse** from the menu that appears (refer to Figure 7-3). When applying shapes to your document, such as a bevel shape, the shape will display based on the effect you selected. Notice the change in the bevel shape on page one by the second paragraph under the heading *Introduction* (see Figure 7-6).

Figure 7-6

Sample Bevel Shape
with Theme Effects

Applying one of the
Theme Effects produces
a different effect on the
bevel shape.

arbiter as the interpretation of the following. By utilizing Flatland Hosting's services, you agree to be bound by the terms herein outlined.↵

↵

Questions or comments regarding this document should be forwarded to Flatland Hosting at: info@flatlandhostingcompany.com¶

¶

9. **SAVE** the document as ***hosting_term1*** in your USB flash drive in the lesson folder.

PAUSE. LEAVE the document open to use in the next exercise.

Take Note

Document themes are the same throughout all Office programs and can share the same appearance.

USING QUICK PARTS IN A DOCUMENT

The Bottom Line

Building blocks are organized in galleries and sorted by category. In the Building Block gallery, you can insert cover pages, headers, footers, page numbers, text boxes, and watermarks. Another term for building blocks is AutoText, and both features are used the same way. In this exercise, you learn to use built-in building blocks and insert fields in a document.

NEW to Office 2010

Using Built-In Building Blocks

Building blocks contain several built-in reusable content such as text, graphics, and objects. Building blocks are easily managed and inserted in a document for a quick format.

STEP BY STEP   **Use Built-In Building Blocks**

USE the document that is open from the previous exercise.

1. On the Insert tab, in the Text group, click the **Quick Parts** button to display the Quick Parts menu, as shown in Figure 7-7.

Figure 7-7

Quick Parts menu

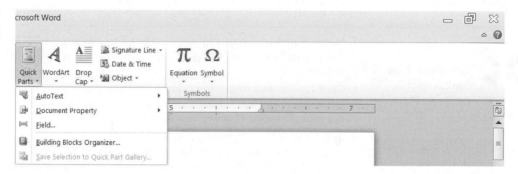

2. Click the **Building Blocks Organizer** menu option to display the Building Blocks Organizer dialog box, as shown in Figure 7-8. In the left pane of the dialog box, the preformatted elements or building blocks are listed by name; the Gallery column indicates the gallery that contains each building block, and the Category column indicates each element's general type, while the Template column indicates within which template the element is stored. You can use the buttons at the bottom of the dialog box to delete and edit selected building blocks. The right pane previews your selections.

3. Click the **Name** heading to sort the building blocks by name.

4. Scroll down the list and select **Confidential 1 Watermark**.

Troubleshooting You can adjust the Name column by dragging the resize bar to the right to change the width.

CERTIFICATION READY?   **3.3.1**

How do you insert a quote in a document using the Building Blocks Organizer?

5. Click the **Insert** button. The Confidential watermark appears behind the text on every page.

6. Display the **Building Blocks Organizer** dialog box. Click the **Gallery** heading to sort the building blocks by gallery.

7. Scroll down and select the **Austin Pull Quote** from the Text Box gallery. Click **Insert** and pull quote is inserted in the document as shown in Figure 7-9. You can key text in the placeholders or drag and drop text in the area.

Figure 7-8

Building Blocks Organizer

Easily sort list by column heading

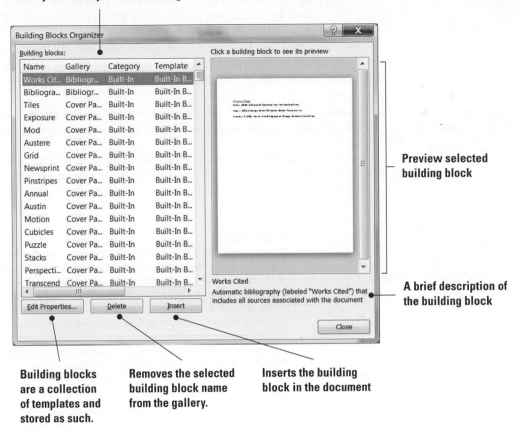

Preview selected
building block

A brief description of
the building block

Building blocks
are a collection
of templates and
stored as such.

Removes the selected
building block name
from the gallery.

Inserts the building
block in the document

Figure 7-9

Document with text
box pull quote

Place pointer on hyphenated
lines around text box to drag
and drop to the end of first
paragraph.

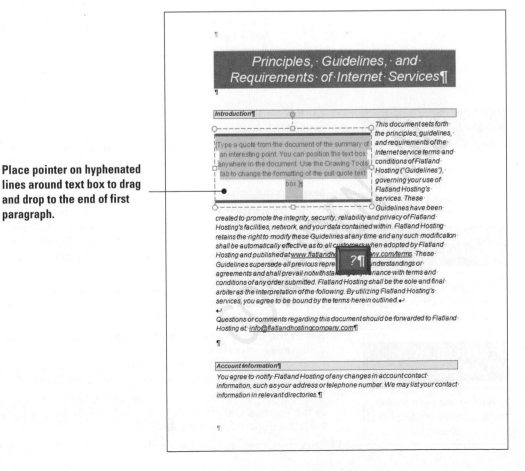

8. Under the heading, Introduction, select the second paragraph beginning with "Questions or comments. . . ." Move the selected text inside the quote area by dragging and dropping. Delete the line break and one paragraph mark after the first paragraph under *Introduction*.

9. Place your pointer on the hyphenated lines around the quote text box—the pointer changes to four arrows to allow you to drag and drop. Drag the quote to the end of the first paragraph until it wraps around the last seven lines of the paragraph.

 Troubleshooting Deselect the text box and select again to see the hyphenated lines around the text box.

10. Select the Bevel shape—the pointer changes to four arrows to allow you to drag to a new location. Drag the Bevel shape by the quote text box on the right margin (see Figure 7-10).

Figure 7-10

Document with text box pull quote wrapped around paragraph with bevel shape

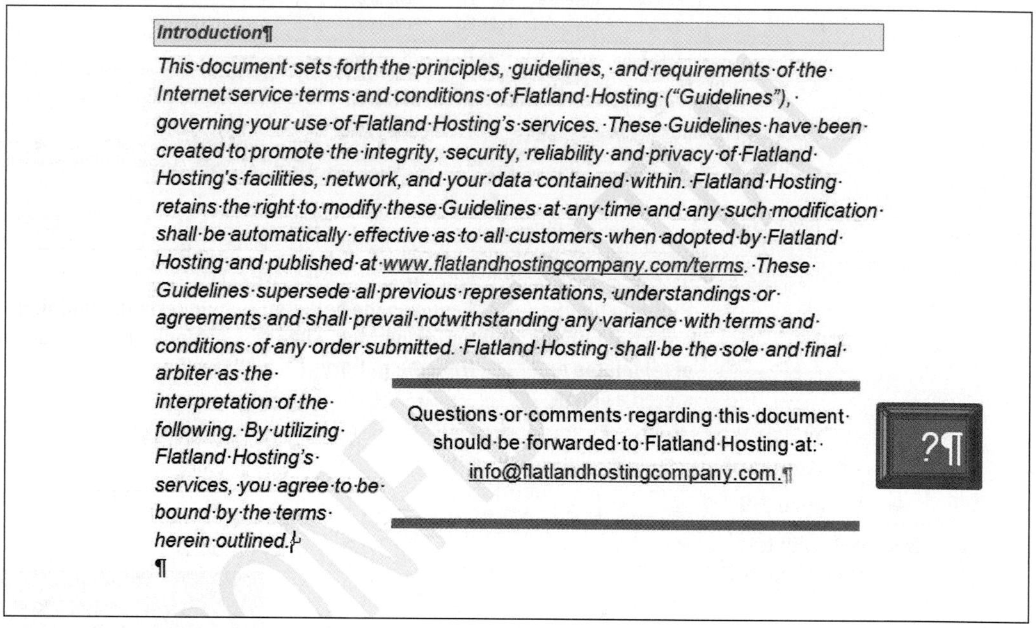

Introduction¶

This document sets forth the principles, guidelines, and requirements of the Internet service terms and conditions of Flatland Hosting ("Guidelines"), governing your use of Flatland Hosting's services. These Guidelines have been created to promote the integrity, security, reliability and privacy of Flatland Hosting's facilities, network, and your data contained within. Flatland Hosting retains the right to modify these Guidelines at any time and any such modification shall be automatically effective as to all customers when adopted by Flatland Hosting and published at www.flatlandhostingcompany.com/terms. These Guidelines supersede all previous representations, understandings or agreements and shall prevail notwithstanding any variance with terms and conditions of any order submitted. Flatland Hosting shall be the sole and final arbiter as the interpretation of the following. By utilizing Flatland Hosting's services, you agree to be bound by the terms herein outlined.¶

¶

Questions or comments regarding this document should be forwarded to Flatland Hosting at: info@flatlandhostingcompany.com.¶

CERTIFICATION READY? 3.3.1

How do you insert a building block text box using the Building Blocks Organizer?

CERTIFICATION READY? 3.3.1

How do you insert a header or footer in a document using the Building Blocks Organizer?

CERTIFICATION READY? 3.3.1

How do you insert a cover page using the Building Blocks Organizer?

11. Click outside the Bevel shape and press **Ctrl+End** to move the insertion point to the end of the document.

12. Display the Building Blocks Organizer dialog box. Scroll down and select **Alphabet Sidebar** from the Text Box Gallery. Click **Insert**. The text box is inserted at the end of the document and positioned on the left side of the document. Your next step is to insert text into the text box.

13. When selecting the paragraph, do not select the paragraph mark; this will avoid displaying the horizontal line in the Text Box twice. Select the paragraph above Refusal of Service beginning with "*You and Flatland Hosting further agree . . .*" and drag and drop the selection in the text box. Delete the two paragraph marks above the heading, Refusal of Service.

14. Click the **Building Blocks Organizer** to display the dialog box and select **Austin** in the Headers Gallery. Click **Insert**. A header with a border is inserted in every page of the document.

15. Select the text in the placeholder, *Type the document title* and key **Flatland Hosting Company** in the Header placeholder. Click the **Close Header and Footer** button located on the Header & Footer Tools Design tab. Inserting a header from the Building Block will automatically display the Header & Footer Tools tab.

16. Click the **Building Blocks Organizer** to display the dialog box and select **Conservative** in the Footers Gallery. Click **Insert**. A footer is inserted in every page of the document with the page number displayed.

17. Click the **Close Header and Footer** button from the Header & Footer Tools Design tab.

18. Click the **Building Blocks Organizer** to display the dialog box and select **Austin** in the Cover Page Gallery. Click **Insert**. The cover page is inserted as page 1.
19. Key the following information in the placeholders:

    Abstract: **Flatland Hosting Company will set guidelines and requirements for use of Flatland Hosting services.**

    Document Title: Flatland Hosting Company automatically appears

    Subtitle: Guidelines & Agreements

    Type the Author Name: A. Becker

20. **SAVE** the document as *hosting_term2* in your USB flash drive in the lesson folder and **CLOSE** the file.

PAUSE. LEAVE Word open to use in the next exercise.

Another Way
On the Insert tab, in the Pages group, click the Cover Page button to insert a cover page.

Troubleshooting If you experience problems in saving the author's name, complete one of the following actions: (1) Click the File tab, then Options. In the General category, under Personalize your copy of Microsoft Office section, key the author's name by the User name box and initials. Changing the User Name will be discussed in Lesson 9; (2) Click the File tab and in the section Prepare for Sharing, click the *Allow this information to be saved in your file link* and then save. Prepare for Sharing will be discussed in Lesson 13.

 Ref   Later in this lesson, you will learn to insert a watermark in the Page Background group.

Inserting an Equation

Microsoft Word 2010 has built-in equations, which can be inserted from the Quick Parts gallery or using the Equations command. You can use the Equation Tool Design tab, which displays when an equation is inserted in a document, to edit or construct your own equation. In this exercise, you learn to insert equations in a document.

Another Way
In the Header & Footer group, you can insert a header or footer or page number.

STEP BY STEP	**Insert an Equation**

OPEN a new blank Word document.

1. Click the **Insert** Tab and, in the Text group, click the **Quick Parts** button then click the **Building Blocks Organizer.**

2. In the Building Block Organizer dialog box, locate and click the **Expansion of a Sum** equation in the Equation Gallery. Click **Insert**. The Expansion of a Sum equation is inserted in the document. Position the insertion point after the equation placeholder and then press the **Enter** key twice to place a blank line below the placeholder.

3. In the Building Block Organizer dialog box, locate and click the **Area of Circle** equation, then click **Insert**. Position the insertion point after the equation placeholder and then press the **Enter** key twice to place a blank line below the placeholder.

4. In the Building Block Organizer dialog box, locate and click the **Binomial Theorem** equation. Click **Insert**. Click outside the equation placeholder, and press the **Enter** key twice.

5. **SAVE** the document as *equations* in your USB flash drive in the lesson folder and **CLOSE**.

PAUSE. LEAVE Word open to use in the next exercise.

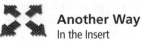

Another Way
In the Insert tab, Symbols group, click the Equation button and select an equation from the built-in menu.

Inserting a Field from Quick Parts

A **field** is a placeholder where Word inserts content in a document. Word automatically uses fields when specific commands are activated, such as those for inserting dates, page numbers, and a table of contents. When you insert a date field in a document, the date will be updated automatically each time the document is opened. In this exercise, you learn to insert a field in a document.

Fields, also called field codes, appear between curly brackets ({ }) when displayed. Field codes are turned off by default. To display field codes in a document, press Alt+F9. To edit a field, place the insertion point within the field and right-click and then click Edit Field.

STEP BY STEP   **Insert a Field from Quick Parts**

OPEN the *hosting_term2* document from the lesson folder.

@ The *hosting_term2* document file for this lesson is available on the book companion website or in WileyPLUS.

1. Press **Ctrl+End** to move to the end of the document. The insertion point is positioned on the last paragraph mark.
2. Key **Last Updated:** in bold and press the **spacebar** once after the colon.
3. On the Insert tab, in the Text group, click the **Quick Parts** button.
4. Click **Field** on the menu. The Field dialog box is displayed (see Figure 7-11).

Figure 7-11

Field dialog box

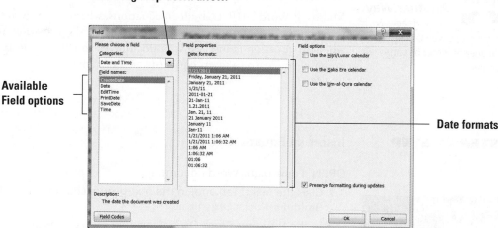

Select category by clicking drop-down arrow.

Available Field options

Date formats

5. From the Categories drop-down list, click **Date and Time**.
6. In the Field Names list, click **Date**.
7. In the Date Formats list, select the ninth option with the **Day Month Year** format and click **OK** to close the dialog box and insert the date and time field in your document. The document should look similar to the one shown in Figure 7-12, with the exception that the current date will appear.

Another Way On the Insert tab, in the Text group, click Date & Time to open the Date and Time dialog box.

8. **SAVE** document as *hosting_term3* in your USB flash drive in the lesson folder and **CLOSE**.

PAUSE. LEAVE Word open to use in the next exercise.

Figure 7-12

Document with Date field inserted

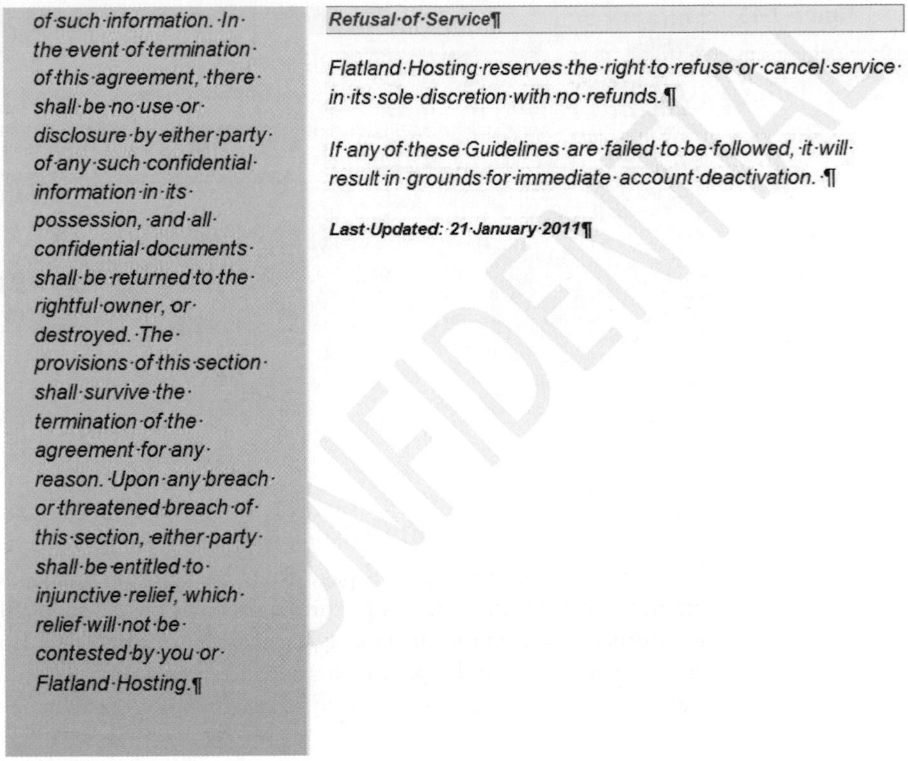

of·such·information.·In· the·event·of·termination· of·this·agreement,·there· shall·be·no·use·or· disclosure·by·either·party· of·any·such·confidential· information·in·its· possession,·and·all· confidential·documents· shall·be·returned·to·the· rightful·owner,·or· destroyed.·The· provisions·of·this·section· shall·survive·the· termination·of·the· agreement·for·any· reason.·Upon·any·breach· or·threatened·breach·of· this·section,·either·party· shall·be·entitled·to· injunctive·relief,·which· relief·will·not·be· contested·by·you·or· Flatland·Hosting.¶

Refusal·of·Service¶

Flatland·Hosting·reserves·the·right·to·refuse·or·cancel·service· in·its·sole·discretion·with·no·refunds.¶

If·any·of·these·Guidelines·are·failed·to·be·followed,·it·will· result·in·grounds·for·immediate·account·deactivation.·¶

Last·Updated:·21·January·2011¶

FORMATTING A DOCUMENT'S BACKGROUND

The Bottom Line

Word's enhanced features allow the user to produce a creatively formatted document by changing the background color, inserting a watermark, and adding a border to the document.

Inserting a Page Color

Adding a background color to the title page of a report conveys originality. You may want to distinguish your research paper from others, for example, by adding a background color to the first page. It is important to use background colors in moderation and to choose a page color that will not interfere with the text. If text is dark, for example, then the background color should be light, and if text is light, a dark background would improve the document's readability. In this exercise, you learn to insert a page color in a document.

WileyPLUS Extra! features an online tutorial of this task.

STEP BY STEP   **Insert a Page Color**

OPEN *hosting_term* from your USB flash drive for this lesson.

@ The *hosting_term* document file for this lesson is available on the book companion website or in WileyPLUS.

1. Click the **Page Layout** tab.
2. In the *Page Background* group, click the **Page Color** button to open the color menu and gallery, as shown in Figure 7-13. Click to select **White, Background 1, Darker 5%**; the page color is applied.
3. **SAVE** the document as *hosting_term4* in your USB flash drive in the lesson folder.

PAUSE. LEAVE the document open to use in the next exercise.

CERTIFICATION READY?   **3.4.2**

How do you add a page color to a document?

Figure 7-13

Page Color menu

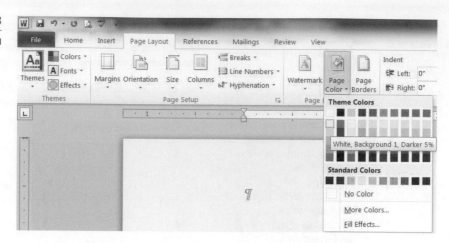

Formatting the Page Color Background

You can apply formatting to a page color background with one color or fill effect, such as, gradient, texture, pattern, or a picture. A gradient fill is a shape fill that changes from one color to another based on the shading style selected. You can select from one color or two to preset colors. The layout of the page colors provides emphasis to the document. In this exercise, you learn to format the page background using two colors and changing the shading style.

STEP BY STEP **Format the Page Color Background**

USE the document that is open from the previous exercise.

1. With the Page Layout tab active, click the **Page Color** button, and in the menu that appears, click **Fill Effects**. The Fill Effects dialog opens with the Gradient tab active.

2. Under the Colors section, select **Preset** and then click the **drop-down arrow** under the Preset colors section to view available background colors.

3. In the Gradient tab under the Colors section, select **Two colors**. Two options appear, Color 1 and Color 2. Under Color 2 click the **drop-down arrow** to produce the color palette. In the ninth column third row, select **Brown, Accent 5, Lighter 60%**. The selected color appears in the box under Color 2 (see Figure 7-14).

Figure 7-14

Fill Effects dialog box

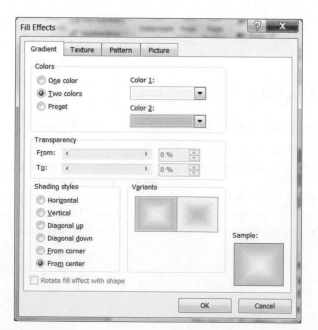

4. Under the Variants section, samples of the two colors are displayed. Under the Shading Styles section, you have choices on how the style should appear in the document. Select **From Center**. Notice the lower-right corner produces Color 1 in the center and Color 2 outside. Click **OK**.

5. **SAVE** the document as *hosting_term5* in your USB flash drive in the lesson folder.

PAUSE. LEAVE the document open to use in the next exercise.

Adding a Watermark

In business, some documents may contain sensitive information, and the nature of a document's status should be clearly conveyed on its pages. Word provides built-in text, called **watermarks**, that display lightly behind text as words, such as, *confidential*, *draft*, or *urgent*. Watermarks can be customized to include text or images, including company logos. In this lesson, you learn to customize a watermark and insert it into a document.

STEP BY STEP   **Add a Watermark**

USE the document that is open from the previous exercise.

1. In the Page Background group of the Page Layout tab, click the **Watermark** menu and scroll down to select **Custom Watermark**. The Printed Watermark dialog box opens. Select the **Text watermark** radio button and then click the **drop-down arrow** next to Text and select **Draft**. You can customize text watermarks by keying content in the text box or you can select from the drop-down menu.

2. Click the **drop-down arrow** by Font and select **Calibri**. This will change the text watermark font.

3. In the Color text box click the **drop-down arrow** and select **Gray-50%, Accent 6** in the Theme Colors (see Figure 7-15).

Figure 7-15

Printed Watermark dialog box

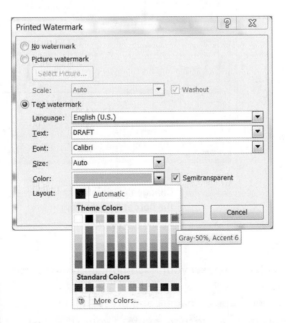

4. Click **OK**. The watermark is inserted on all pages. Note, if you click **Apply**, the dialog box remains open and you can view your watermark in the document. When you click **OK**, the dialog box closes and you're back in the document screen.

5. **SAVE** the document in your USB flash drive in the lesson folder.

PAUSE. LEAVE the document open to use in the next exercise.

 Ref   Earlier in this lesson, you learned to insert a watermark using the Building Blocks Organizer.

Adding a Page Border

The Page Borders command allows you to insert a border around a document's page. Adding a border adds to the page or frame of a page and improves the appearance of the document. Applying elements by changing the color, width, and style adds emphasis to the page. In this lesson, you learn to add elements to a page border and insert them into a document.

STEP BY STEP   **Add a Page Border**

USE the document that is open from the previous exercise.

1. In the Page Background group of the Page Layout tab, click the Page Borders button. The Borders and Shading dialog box appears.

2. In the Setting section, click the Shadow option. Notice the lower-right bottom has a shadow effect to the border.

3. Click the drop-down arrow on the Color menu and in the ninth column, first row choose Brown, Accent 5. You are applying a specific color to the border.

4. Click the drop-down arrow on the Width menu and choose 2 1/4 pt. The width of the border is increased to provide emphasis.

5. Click the drop-down arrow on the Apply To menu and click This section–First page only as shown in Figure 7-16. The page border is applied to the first page only.

Figure 7-16

Borders and Shading
dialog box

Border lines styles can give a
document a different appearance.

Allows you to
preview before
confirming
your selection

Setting contains
five options.

A specific color can
be applied to borders.

Determine where the
border will be applied
in the document.

Change the weight of
the border by selecting
one of the options.

6. Click OK. Scroll and review your document and notice that the border does not appear on other pages.

7. Select the bevel shape on page 1 and press Delete.

8. SAVE the document as *hosting_term6* to your USB flash drive in the lesson folder.

PAUSE. LEAVE the document open to use in the next exercise.

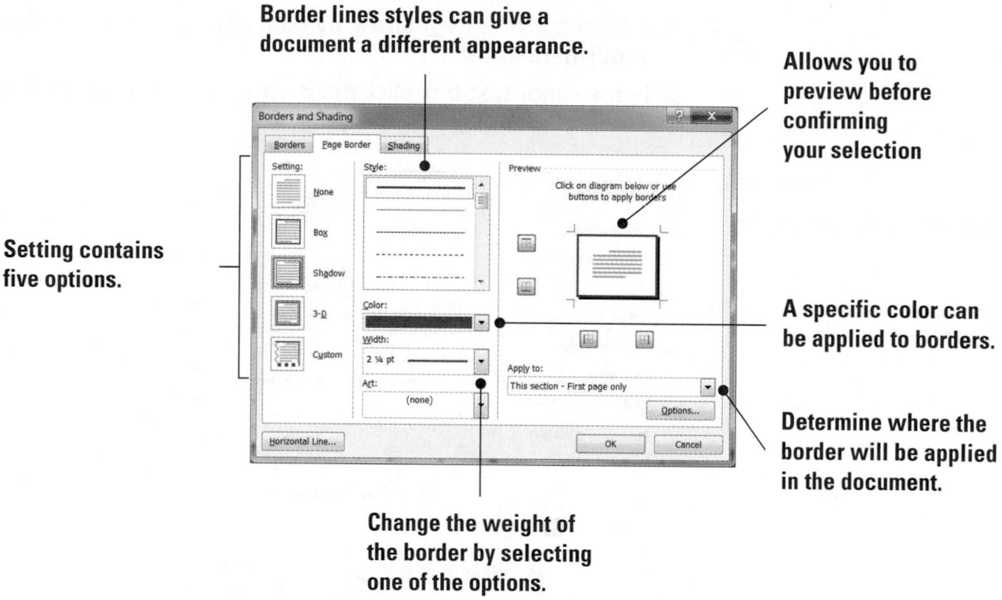

CERTIFICATION READY?   **3.4.4**

How do you add a page border to a document?

CREATING AND MODIFYING HEADERS AND FOOTERS

The Bottom Line

A **header** appears on the top of a page and a **footer** appears at the bottom of the document's page. The Header & Footer group contains commands for inserting built-in headers, footers, and page numbers into a Word document.

The Page Number button in the Header & Footer group has commands for inserting page numbers at the top, bottom, or in the margin of a page using the built-in gallery. In this exercise, you learn to insert page numbers in a document.

Adding Page Numbers

USE the document that is open from the previous exercise.

1. Place the insertion point anywhere on the first page.
2. Click the **Insert** tab.
3. In the Header & Footer group, click the **Page Number** button, and in the menu that appears, point to Bottom of Page; in the pull-down menu, select **Plain Number 2**, as shown in Figure 7-17. Page numbers are inserted on all pages. Notice that the Headers & Footer Tools opens with the Design tab active.

Figure 7-17

Page Number menu

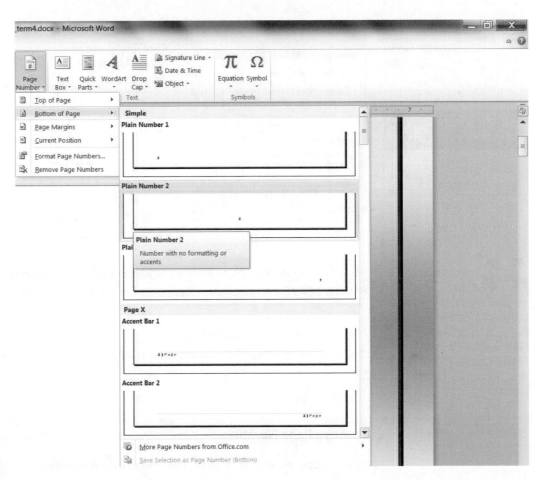

CERTIFICATION READY? 3.5.1

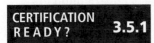

How do you add page numbers to every page?

4. In the Design tab, in the Close group, click the **Close Header and Footer** button. The Header & Footer Tools closes.
5. **SAVE** the document in your USB flash drive in the lesson folder.

PAUSE. LEAVE the document open to use in the next exercise.

Formatting Page Numbers

Word provides various types of numbering formats to choose from, such as, *1, 2, 3 . . .; i, ii, iii . . .;* or *a, b, c. . . .* In addition to choosing a numbering style, Word's page number formatting commands enable you to decide where page numbering will begin, pause, and continue. In this exercise, you learn to change the page number format.

STEP BY STEP **Format Page Numbers**

USE the document that is open from the previous exercise.

1. In the Headers & Footers group in the Insert tab, click the Page Number button to display the menu.
2. Click Format Page Numbers. The Page Number Format dialog box appears.
3. In the Number Format text box, click the drop-down arrow and select the lowercase roman numerals option (i, ii, iii, . . .) as shown in Figure 7-18. Selecting this option will change the number format to lowercase Roman numerals on all pages.

Figure 7-18

Page Number Format dialog box

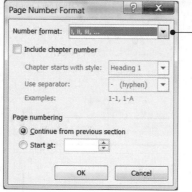

Click drop-down arrow to select format.

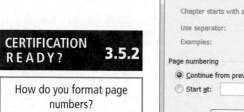

CERTIFICATION READY?   **3.5.2**

How do you format page numbers?

4. Click OK.
5. **SAVE** the document as *hosting_update* in your USB flash drive in the lesson folder.

PAUSE. LEAVE the document open to use in the next exercise.

Another Way
Scroll down to the first footer on page 1 and double-click on the footer; the Header & Footer Tools display. Click Page Number and then Format Page Numbers to open the Page Number Format dialog box.

Removing Page Numbers

The Remove Page Numbers command will remove all page numbering in the document. In this exercise, you will remove all page numbers from the document.

STEP BY STEP **Remove Page Numbers**

USE the document that is open from the previous exercise.

1. In the Headers & Footers group in the Insert tab, click the Page Number button to display the menu.
2. Click Remove Page Numbers. All page numbers are removed from the document.
3. Click Undo to restore all page numbers.
4. **SAVE** the document in your USB flash drive in the lesson folder.

PAUSE. LEAVE the document open to use in the next exercise.

Inserting the Current Date and Time

Word's Insert tab contains a number of command groups that enable you to insert charts, graphs, images, and other elements into Word documents. In this exercise, you learn to use commands in the Insert tab to insert the date in a document.

STEP BY STEP   **Insert Current Date and Time**

USE the document that is open from the previous exercise.

1. Position the insertion point in the third line on page 1, under the heading. Key **Date Submitted:** and press the **spacebar** once after the colon.

2. In the Text group, in the Insert Tab, click **Date & Time**. The Date and Time dialog box opens, as shown in Figure 7-19.

Figure 7-19

Date and Time dialog box

Available format options

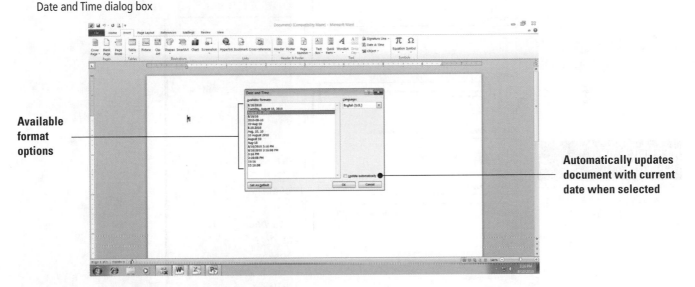

Automatically updates document with current date when selected

3. In the Available Formats list, select the ninth option, which displays the Day Month Year date format. Click **OK**. The selected format with the current date is inserted in the document.

4. Press **Ctrl+End**. The insertion point is on the last paragraph mark. Key **Time Submitted:** and press the **spacebar** once after the colon.

5. Click the **Date & Time** command, and in the Date and Time menu that appears, select the fourth option from the bottom of the Available Formats list, which displays time in hours and minutes, using the 12-hour clock format.

6. **SAVE** the document in your USB flash drive in the lesson folder.

PAUSE. LEAVE the document open to use in the next exercise.

Inserting a Built-In Header or Footer

The Header and Footer commands provide options for inserting content at the top and bottom of pages and enable you to edit, remove, save, and view additional headers and footers online. You can choose to make the first page header and/or footer different from those on subsequent pages and place these elements on odd or even pages only using the Headers and Footers tools from the Design tab that appears when you insert one of these elements into your document. In this exercise, you learn to insert a built-in header and footer.

 Ref   Earlier in this lesson, you learned how to insert headers and footers using Quick Parts.

STEP BY STEP   **Insert a Built-In Header or Footer**

USE the document that is open from the previous exercise.

1. In the Header & Footer group in the *Insert* tab, click the Header button, and in the drop-down menu that appears, scroll down to select the Pinstripes option, as shown in Figure 7-20. The header is inserted on every page and the Header & Footer Design tab opens.

Figure 7-20

Header menu

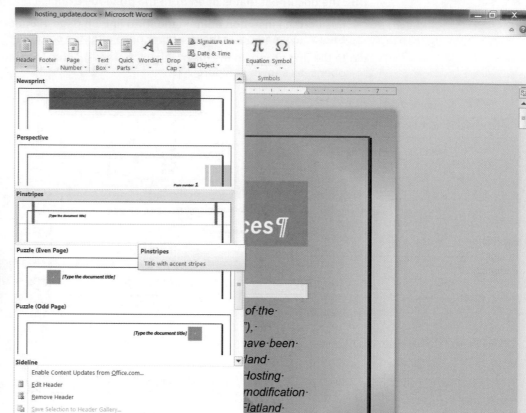

2. In the Options group of the Header & Footer Design tab, shown in Figure 7-21, click the Different First Page box. In the Navigation group, click Previous to go to the first page and notice the header is removed from the first page.

Figure 7-21

Header & Footer Tools

Takes you to the preceding header or footer

Advances to the next header or footer

Options group allows you to turn off the page number, header, or footer.

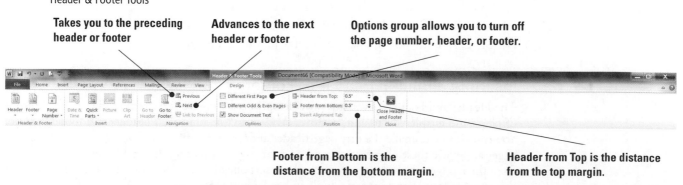

Footer from Bottom is the distance from the bottom margin.

Header from Top is the distance from the top margin.

3. In the Navigation group, click Next to go to the header area of page 2.

4. In the Header & Footer group, click the Footer button and scroll down to click Pinstripes from the menu that appears. Notice the new footer inserts the word Page by the formatted page number that you inserted in a previous exercise (see Figure 7-22).

Figure 7-22

Footer with formatted page number

Formatted page number

CERTIFICATION
READY? **3.5.8**

How do you apply a different first page?

5. Click the **Close Header and Footer** button on the Design tab.

6. **SAVE** the document as *hosting_update1* in your USB flash drive in lesson folder.

PAUSE. LEAVE the document open to use in the next exercise.

Adding Content to a Header or Footer

Content controls are individual programs that allow you to add information in a document, such as a header or footer. Content controls are used for templates, forms, and documents and are identified by a border and temporary text. In this exercise, you learn to add content to a placeholder in a header and footer.

STEP BY STEP   **Add Content to a Header or Footer**

USE the document that is open from the previous exercise.

Another Way
Click the Insert tab and in the Header & Footer group, click Edit Header.

1. Position the insertion point on the second page of the document and double-click the header to activate.

2. The placeholder [Type the document title] is selected.

3. Key **Guidelines and Requirements**, as shown in Figure 7-23, to create the text that will appear in your document's header.

Figure 7-23

Title in header

Content added to header

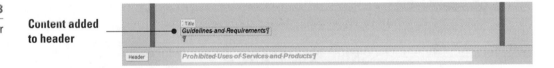

CERTIFICATION
READY? **3.5.5**

How do you add content to a header or footer?

4. On the Navigation group on the Design tab, click **Go to Footer**; the insertion point moves to the page ii footer. Click **[Type text]** and key **Flatland Hosting Company** to replace the placeholder.

5. Select the text in the footer, including the page number. Display the Mini toolbar by right-clicking. Click the **drop-down arrow** at the Font box and change the Font to **Arial**.

6. Click the **Grow Font** button on the Mini toolbar to increase the font size to **12**.

7. Click the **Italic** button to turn off.

8. Click the footer to deselect.

9. Click the **Close Header and Footer** button on the Design tab to close. The Header & Footers Tools Design tab closes.

10. **SAVE** the document in your USB flash drive in the lesson folder.

PAUSE. LEAVE the document open to use in the next exercise.

Changing the Position of a Header or Footer

The header and footer default location is .5" from the top and bottom margins. The Position commands option on the Header & Footer Tools enable you to change this default setting. In this exercise, you learn to modify the header and footer position.

STEP BY STEP   **Change the Position of a Header or Footer**

USE the document that is open from the previous exercise.

1. Point to the header on the second page and double-click to activate the Header & Footer tools.

2. In the Position group, in the Header & Footer Design tab, click the Header from Top scroll arrow until the measurement in the selection box changes to .2″.

3. In the Position group, click the Footer from Bottom scroll arrow until the measurement in the selection box changes to .2″.

4. SAVE the document in your USB flash drive in the lesson folder.

PAUSE. LEAVE the document open to use in the next exercise.

Removing a Header or Footer

In this exercise, you learn to use the Remove Header or Footer command to remove all headers and footers from the document.

STEP BY STEP   **Remove a Header or Footer**

USE the document that is open from the previous exercise.

1. In the Design tab, in the Header & Footer group, click the Header button and the menu appears.

Another Way
Double-click the Header or Footer and press Delete. This will remove all headers or footers.

2. Click Remove Header. The headers are removed from the document.

3. To remove all footers in the document, click the Footer button in the Header & Footer group. The menu appears.

4. Click Remove Footer and footers are removed from the document.

5. SAVE and CLOSE the document as *hosting_final* in your USB flash drive in the lesson folder.

CLOSE Word.

SKILL SUMMARY

In This Lesson, You Learned How To:	Exam Objective	Objective Number
Format, create, and customize a theme	Use a theme to apply formatting.	3.2.1
	Customize a theme.	3.2.2
Use Quick Parts in a document	Add built-in building blocks.	3.3.1
Format a document's background	Set a colored background	3.4.2
	Format a document's background.	3.4.1
	Add a watermark.	3.4.3
	Set page borders.	3.4.4
Create and modify headers and footers	Insert page numbers.	3.5.1
	Format page numbers.	3.5.2
	Insert the current date and time.	3.5.3
	Insert a built-in header or footer.	3.5.4
	Apply a different first page attribute.	3.5.8
	Add content to a header or footer.	3.5.5
	Change margins.	3.5.7
	Delete a header or footer.	3.5.6

Knowledge Assessment

True/False

Circle T if the statement is true or F if the statement is false.

T   F   **1.** A watermark is a text or graphic printed behind text.

T   F   **2.** To edit a header or footer, you must triple-click to activate a header or footer.

T   F   **3.** The Header & Footer Tools display in the Ribbon after a header or footer is inserted.

T   F   **4.** Built-in headers and footers provide instant design.

T   F   **5.** If you make any changes to the colors, fonts, or effects of the current theme, you can save it as a custom version and apply it to future documents.

T   F   **6.** A picture can be inserted as a page background.

T   F   **7.** A header and footer cannot be used in the same document.

T   F   **8.** You can specify a different header for odd and even pages.

T   F   **9.** Page colors are the background color of a page.

T   F   **10.** A footer can contain text or graphics.

Multiple Choice

Select the best response for the following statements.

1. Building blocks can be sorted by all EXCEPT which of the following?
   a. Name
   b. Creator
   c. Gallery
   d. Category

2. _____ is a new option within the Quick Parts menu.
   a. AutoComplete
   b. Auto Organizer
   c. AutoText Insert
   d. AutoText

3. Identify the tiny program that includes a label for instructing you on the type of text to include and a placeholder that reserves a place for your new text.
   a. Placeholder
   b. Fields
   c. Content Control
   d. All of the above

4. A document theme includes sets of which of the following?
   a. Colors
   b. Fonts
   c. Effects
   d. All of the above
   e. None of the above

5. A line inserted around the page is called a _____.
   a. Document page border
   b. Border
   c. Page border
   d. None of the above

6. To preview a style or a theme, you must do which of the following?
   a. Place your pointer over the choice
   b. Print the document
   c. Set up the document properties
   d. It is not possible to preview a style or theme.

7. The _____ provides a way to manage building blocks by editing, deleting, and/ or inserting them.
   a. Quick Organizer
   b. Cover Page
   c. Text box
   d. Organizer

8. A _____ is a placeholder that tells Word to insert changeable data into a document.
   a. Field name
   b. Field
   c. Data field
   d. Data source

9. Customized company logos applied to a page background is called a(n)_____.
   a. MarkArt
   b. Insert picture command
   c. Watermark
   d. SmartArt

10. In the _____dialog box, you can specify to insert a page border on only the first page of a document.
    a. Page Border
    b. Borders and Shading
    c. Page Border tab
    d. Line Border

Competency Assessment

Project 7-1: Elevator Communications

Montgomery, Slade & Parker uses elevator communications for in-house announcements, invitations, and other employee relations documents. In each elevator, a durable 8¹/₂" × 14" clear plastic frame has been installed in which announcements can be inserted and changed on a regular basis. Create a document for approval that recognizes employee award winners and invites employees to a reception to honor these award winners.

GET READY. LAUNCH Word if it is not already running.

1. **OPEN** *congratulations* from the data files for this lesson and **SAVE AS** *elevator_com* in your USB flash drive in the lesson folder.

@ The *congratulations* document file for this lesson is available on the book companion website or in WileyPLUS.

2. In the Page Background group, in the Page Layout tab click the Page Color menu. In the Theme Colors section, select Olive Green, Accent 3, Lighter 60%.

3. Click the Page Borders button. In the Borders and Shading dialog box, click Shadow in the Setting section. Click the Width menu and choose 3 pt. In the Color section, select Olive Green, Accent 3, Darker 50%. Click OK.

4. In the Page Setup group in the Page Layout tab, click the Size menu and select Legal.

5. Launch the Page Setup dialog box and click the Layout tab. In the Page section, change the Vertical Alignment to Center.

6. **SAVE** the document in your USB flash drive in the lesson folder and then **CLOSE**.

LEAVE Word open for the next project.

Project 7-2: Reference Letter

A former employee at Flatland Hosting Company has asked for a reference letter.

GET READY. LAUNCH Word if it is not already running.

@ The *reference letter* document file for this lesson is available on the book companion website or in WileyPLUS.

1. **OPEN** *reference_letter* from the data files for this lesson and **SAVE AS** *jasmine_reference* in your USB flash drive in the lesson folder.

2. In the Page Layout tab, in the Themes group, click Themes and click Origin from the gallery menu.

3. **SAVE** the document in your USB flash drive in the lesson folder and then **CLOSE**.

LEAVE Word open for the next project.

Proficiency Assessment

Project 7-3: Letterhead

Create a new letterhead for the Flatland Hosting Company.

GET READY. LAUNCH Word if it is not already running.

1. **OPEN** a new blank document and **SAVE AS** *FHCletterhead* in your USB flash drive in the lesson folder.

2. In the Insert tab, in the Header & Footer group, insert the Tiles built-in header and key the document title as Flatland Hosting Company. Bold the text and change the size to 18 pt.

3. Right-click the Content Control, Year, and click Remove Content Control.

4. Insert the Tiles built-in footer and key the company address as 1234 Grand Street, Forest Grove, OR 97116. Select the page number and press the Delete key. Close the Header and Footer.

5. **SAVE** the document in your USB flash drive in the lesson folder and then **CLOSE**.

LEAVE Word open for the next project.

Project 7-4: Two-Page Resume

Your friend Mike has revised and added some information to his resume, and it is now two pages long. Update the formatting to include a header and footer.

GET READY. LAUNCH Word if it is not already running.

@ The *mzresume2* document file for this lesson is available on the book companion website or in WileyPLUS.

1. **OPEN** *mzresume2* from the data files for this lesson and **SAVE AS** *mzresume2updated* in your USB flash drive in the lesson folder.

2. In the Page Layout tab, click the Margins menu and select Custom Margins. In the Page Setup dialog box, change the top, bottom, left, and right margins to 1.25".

3. Click OK.

4. In the Insert tab, in the Header & Footer group, click the Header menu and select Stacks.

5. In the header document title, key Resume of Michael J. Zuberi.

6. In the Options group, click the Different First Page box.

7. In the Navigation group, click Next. In the Header & Footer group, click the Footer button and select Stacks.

8. Select the Content Control, [Type the Company Name], and right-click and Remove Content Control. Close the Header and Footer.

9. **SAVE** the document in your USB flash drive in the lesson folder and then **CLOSE**.

LEAVE Word open for the next project.

Mastery Assessment

Project 7-5: Postcard

It's soccer season again, and the YMCA is sending out postcards to all participants who played last season.

GET READY. LAUNCH Word if it is not already running.

 The *soccer* document file for this lesson is available on the book companion website or in WileyPLUS.

1. **OPEN** *soccer* from the data files for this lesson and **SAVE AS** *postcard* in your USB flash drive in the lesson folder.
2. Customize the page size to **4" x 6"**, the orientation to **Landscape**, and the margins to **Narrow**.
3. Insert a page border and add a red double-line page border with a box setting and set the width to **3/4 pt**.
4. In the Fill Effects dialog box select **One Color** in the Color 1 section and select **Red, Accent 2, Lighter 80%**. In the Shading styles section, select **Diagonal up**. Under Variants, click the sample **horizontal** pattern in the lower-right corner.
5. Add a **Custom Watermark** in the Text watermark section and replace ASAP with **YMCA SOCCER**. Click the **Horizontal** button and click **OK**.
6. **SAVE** the document in your USB flash drive in the lesson folder and then **CLOSE**.

LEAVE Word open for the next project.

Project 7-6: Thank-You Card

Create thank-you notes that match the style of Mike's new two-page resume.

GET READY. LAUNCH Word if it is not already running.

1. Create a new blank document and **SAVE AS** *thankyou* in your USB flash drive in the lesson folder.
2. Customize the page size to **5.5" x 8.5"**, leave the orientation at the default, and change the margins to **narrow**. The goal is to format the document appropriately and fold the document in the middle so that the text, *Thank You,* will be on the front of the note card.
3. Refer to the built-in footer used in the *mzresume2updated* document and insert that footer in your current document. In the *Content Controls* placeholder, key **Thank You**. For consistency, use the same font, size, and style as Michael J. Zuberi's name on the resume.
4. **SAVE** the document in your USB flash drive in the lesson folder and then **CLOSE**.

CLOSE Word.

INTERNET READY

Studies have identified which cities are the "Best Places to Live." Choose one of the top ten and find out why it ranked high. Create a promotional document touting the positive ranking and listing reasons for the ranking. The document could be a flyer, postcard, or letter that city officials could mail to prospective businesses and families who request information about the city.

Workplace *Ready*

CREATING A FLYER AND APPLYING THEMES AND QUICK PARTS

You are the assistant to two managers at Flatland Hosting Company. They have decided to distribute monthly flyers to all employees on new happenings within the company.

They have asked you to format the monthly flyer using the new skills you have learned in Word. Create a flyer promoting Internet services to employees at a discounted rate and include security and privacy issues. Be innovative; incorporate features such as adding a customized theme, watermark, page color, and page border, and apply an appropriate building block to produce a flyer that will capture employees' attention. Insert the current date as a footer.

8 Using Illustrations and Graphics

LESSON SKILL MATRIX

Skill	Exam Objective	Objective Number
Inserting and Formatting Pictures in a Document	Add captions.	4.1.1
	Adjust position and size.	4.1.6
	Modify a shape.	4.1.5
	Apply picture styles.	4.1.3
	Apply artistic effects.	4.1.2
	Insert screenshots.	4.1.7
Inserting and Formatting Shapes, WordArt, and SmartArt	Add text to a shape.	4.2.1
	Add captions.	4.2.3
	Modify text on a shape.	4.2.2
	Set shape styles.	4.2.4
	Adjust position and size of shapes.	4.2.5
Inserting and Formatting Clip Art	Adjust position and size of clip art.	4.3.5
	Add captions.	4.3.2
	Apply artistic effects.	4.3.3
	Organize clip art.	4.3.1
Compressing and Resetting Images	Compress pictures.	4.1.4
	Compress clip art pictures.	4.3.4
Making Text Graphically Appealing		
Applying and Manipulating Text Boxes	Format text boxes.	4.4.1
	Apply text box styles.	4.4.3
	Change text direction.	4.4.4
	Apply shadow effects.	4.4.5
	Apply 3 D effects.	4.4.6
	Save a selection to the text box gallery.	4.4.2

KEY TERMS

- caption
- clip art
- Clip Organizer
- compress
- crop
- drawing canvas
- drop cap
- embedded object
- floating object
- inline object
- linked object
- pull quote
- resetting
- scale
- screen clippings
- screenshot
- shapes
- SmartArt graphics
- text box
- WordArt

Margie's Travel is a full-service travel agency that specializes in providing services associated with tours, cruises, adventure activities, group travel, and vacation packages all geared toward seniors. Agents at Margie's Travel frequently need to enhance a document with graphics, pictures, or drawings. Word provides eye-catching travel information, signs, brochures, and flyers using SmartArt, clip art, and shapes. In this lesson, you learn how to insert SmartArt graphics, clip art, pictures, screenshots, and shapes and apply artistic art in a document. You will work with pictures to resize; scale; crop; rotate; apply a Quick Style; adjust color, brightness, and contrast; compress a resetting; and work with text boxes.

SOFTWARE ORIENTATION

Insert Tab and Picture Tools

The Insert tab, shown in Figure 8-1, contains a group of features that you can use to add graphics to your document in Word 2010. Commands in the Illustrations group enable you to add several types of graphics to enhance your Word documents, including pictures, clip art, shapes, SmartArt, charts, and screenshots. The Text group contains options to improve the appearance of the document by adding a text box, WordArt, drop cap, or other text object.

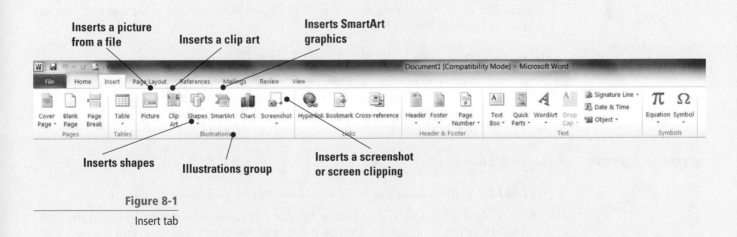

Figure 8-1

Insert tab

The Picture Tools tab, shown in Figure 8-2, is a contextual command tab that appears after you have added a picture to the Word document. Formatting options on the Picture Tools tab enable you to make changes to the graphic object, including removing its background; applying corrections to improve brightness, sharpness, and contrast to the picture; applying color; adding artistic effects; adding borders; enhancing the image with picture effects; cropping; and resizing.

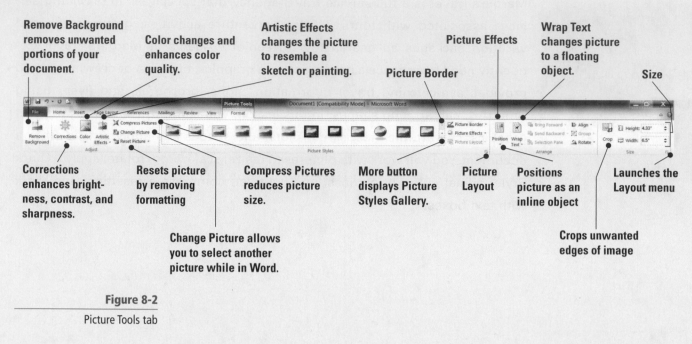

Figure 8-2

Picture Tools tab

Use these figures as a reference throughout this lesson, as well as the rest of the book.

INSERTING AND FORMATTING PICTURES IN A DOCUMENT

Word offers a number of tools to help you capture your readers' attention with illustrations that include pictures, clip art, shapes, SmartArt, charts, and screenshots. You can format images in a number of ways, including converting them to SmartArt; adding captions; resizing, cropping, and rotating them; applying styles; adjusting color and tone; and applying Artistic Effects, which are new in Word 2010. Word also enables you to insert a screenshot and screen clipping and compress and reset the pictures that you've added to your documents. The ability to capture a screenshot or screen clipping from within Word and automatically insert and edit it in the document is new in Word 2010.

The Bottom Line

Inserting Pictures

When you insert a picture into a document, Word marks it as an **embedded object** by default—which means it becomes part of the document. Inserting a picture is very similar to opening a document file. In this exercise, you learn to insert a picture.

STEP BY STEP **Insert Pictures**

GET READY. Before you begin, be sure to **LAUNCH** Microsoft Word.

1. On a blank page, key **Visit the Palm Trees of California**. Select the text and right-click to display the Mini toolbar. Change the font of the title to **Cambria**, and the font size to **28 pt.**, and then center on the page. Deselect the text.

 Ref

In Lesson 3, you learned to change fonts and font sizes, and alignments were covered in Lesson 4.

2. Press **Enter**.
3. Click the Insert tab, in the Illustrations group, then click the **Picture** button. The Insert Picture dialog box appears.

4. Click the dialog box's drop-down directory to navigate to your USB flash drive for the data files for this lesson and click to select the picture file named *palms* (see Figure 8-3).

Figure 8-3

Insert Picture dialog box

Insert Picture dialog box drop-down directory

Change your view to display image.

USB flash drive

Preview area

The *palms* picture file for this lesson is available on the book companion website or in WileyPLUS.

5. Click Insert. The picture appears within your document at the cursor location, and the Format tab opens with the Picture Tool command groups.

6. **SAVE** the document as *palm_trees* in your USB flash drive in the lesson folder.

PAUSE. LEAVE the document open to use in the next exercise.

Take Note Another option is to insert a picture as a **linked object**, which creates a connection between the document and picture, but doesn't combine them in the same file. Using linked objects can help minimize the file size of your final document, while still including pictures, photographs, and other objects that can eat up file space.

Formatting Pictures

The Formatting tab with Picture Tools appears whenever you insert a picture into a document or click on an existing picture within the document. The Picture Tools provide many options, such as cropping, resizing, scaling, and rotating. When you **crop** a picture, you trim the horizontal or vertical edges to get rid of unwanted areas. **Scale** increases or decreases the original picture's height and width by percentage. In this exercise, you will crop, resize, scale, and rotate a picture within a document.

STEP BY STEP **Crop, Resize, Scale, and Rotate a Picture**

USE the document you left open from the previous exercise.

1. The picture should be selected. In the Size group, click the Crop button. The insertion point becomes a cropping tool, and cropping handles appear on the edges of the picture, as shown in Figure 8-4.

2. Position the cropping tool over the top-right cropping handle. Then click and drag down and left until it is past the street sign in the picture. Release the mouse button and then click the Crop button again to remove the cropping handles. The image is trimmed to remove the unwanted area and displays only the cropped area. You can also use the Height and Width buttons in the Size group to crop by precise measurements. The picture height should be **4.33"** and the picture width **2.86"**. If the measurements do not match, edit the settings in the Size group.

Figure 8-4

Cropping a picture

Cropping handles
appear on the edges
of the picture.

3. In the Size group, launch the **dialog box launcher** to display the Layout dialog box, as shown in Figure 8-5. In the Layout dialog box, you can resize the picture by changing the exact measurements of the height and width or rescale it by changing the height and width percentages.

Figure 8-5

Layout dialog box

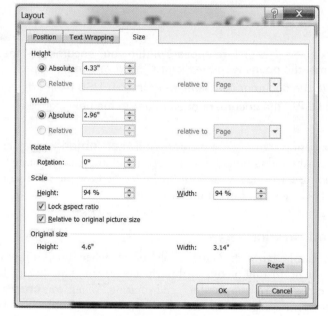

 **Another Way**
You can also rotate a picture by selecting it and dragging the rotation handle—the round green arrow that appears at the top of a selected picture or shape—in the direction you want to rotate the picture.

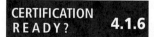
**CERTIFICATION
READY?** **4.1.6**

How do you resize a picture?

Take Note

**CERTIFICATION
READY?** **4.1.5**

How do you modify a picture's shape?

4. Key **3.91″** in the Height Absolute text box. In the Rotate section, key **350** in the text box. The whole height of the picture will be slightly altered and the position of the picture will rotate 350 degrees.

5. In the Scale section, both the **Lock Aspect Ratio** and **Relative To Original Picture Size** check boxes should be selected. When the Lock Aspect Ratio box is selected, you will be able to scale the picture in proportion by height and width by the same percentage. When the Relative To Original Picture Size box is selected, the scaling is comparative to the original size. The original size of the picture is listed below the Layout dialog box under the Original Size section.

In cropping, you remove unwanted portions of the picture, and in scaling, the original picture is increased or decreased in size to fit in the document.

6. Under the Scale section, click the **Height downward pointing arrow** until **62%** appears. The width of the active picture automatically changes to 62%. The Absolute Height dimension also changes to 3.71″, to maintain the picture's original size.

7. Click **OK** to apply your changes and close the dialog box. Deselect the picture.

8. **SAVE** the document as *travel_palms* in your USB flash drive in the lesson folder.

PAUSE. LEAVE the document open to use in the next exercise.

Applying a Picture Style to a Picture

Applying a Picture Style to a picture allows you to select from various designs and give the picture an added appeal. Choosing from the available options and the More button provided in the gallery adds interest to your picture. **Captions** consist of few descriptive words and are used for figures, tables, and equations. Adding a caption to a picture provides readers with information regarding the image. Formatting a picture using the Picture Layout enables you to use one of the built-in SmartArt graphics with a caption placeholder. SmartArt graphics will be covered later in this lesson. In this exercise, you learn to apply a Quick Style, insert a border, add effects, and add a caption by applying a Picture Style to a picture.

STEP BY STEP   **Apply a Picture Style to a Picture**

USE the document that is open from the previous exercise.

1. To display the Picture Tools, select the picture.

2. Click the Format tab, and in the Picture Styles group, click the More ▼ button to display the Picture Style gallery, shown in Figure 8-6.

Figure 8-6

Picture Style gallery

More button displays the Picture Styles gallery.

3. Click **Bevel Rectangle** in the second row, ninth option to apply that style to the image.

4. In the Picture Styles group, click the **Picture Border** button to display the menu shown in Figure 8-7. Click the **Weight** submenu, then **2 ¼**. The border weight is increased and is more noticeable. Click the **Picture Border** button again, and under the Theme Colors section, select **Dark Blue Text 2**. The picture is now surrounded by a colored border.

Figure 8-7

Picture Border menu

Picture Border displays the menu.

5. In the Picture Styles group, click the **Picture Effects** button to display the menu shown in Figure 8-8. Scroll through each Effects option to preview how it changes the appearance of your picture. Click the **Shadow** effect option, and in the Perspective section of the pop-up menu that appears, select **Perspective Diagonal Lower Left** (the first option in the second row of the section) to apply that shadow effect to your image. The picture displays with a shadow on the lower-left side.

Figure 8-8

Picture Effects menu

Picture Effects options

CERTIFICATION READY? **4.1.3**

How do you apply an effect to a picture and modify its appearance?

NEW
to Office 2010

6. **SAVE** the document as *travel_palms1* in your USB flash drive in the lesson folder.

PAUSE. LEAVE the document open for the next exercise.

Converting a Picture to a SmartArt Graphic

SmartArt graphics have preformatted designs with placeholders that allow you to enter text as a caption. In this exercise, you learn to convert a picture to a SmartArt graphic with a caption.

USE the document that is open from the previous exercise.

1. The picture should be selected to display the Picture Tools.

2. In the Pictures Styles group on the Format tab, click the **Picture Layout** button, and select the **Bending Picture Caption List** in the second row, fifth option (see Figure 8-9). The preset layout appears—each layout enables you to apply a picture with text. You can add a caption in the text area by adding a short description to your picture. The Picture Layout button automatically converts the picture to a SmartArt graphic and the picture is resized to accommodate a caption. The SmartArt Tools Design tab is activated.

Figure 8-9

Picture Layout gallery

Documents with pictures must be saved before converting them to a SmartArt graphics.

Take Note   The Picture Layout tab is inactive until the document is saved.

3. Key **Sunny California** in the placeholder [Text], shown in Figure 8-10. Text is automatically adjusted to fit in the placeholder, which is the caption for the picture. Click outside of the graphic to deselect.

Figure 8-10

SmartArt with caption

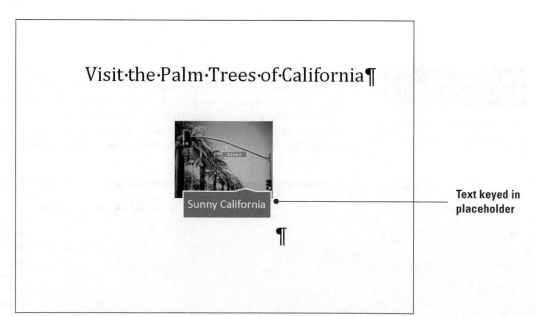

Text keyed in placeholder

CERTIFICATION READY?   **4.1.1**

How do you apply a picture with a caption using the Picture Layout feature?

4. **SAVE** the document as *travel_palms_caption* in your USB flash drive in the lesson folder and close the file.

PAUSE. LEAVE the document open to use in the next exercise.

 Troubleshooting Before you can use the Picture Layout feature in a new document, you must save the file.

Adjusting a Picture's Brightness, Contrast, and Color and Adding Artistic Effects

Although Word does not have all the advanced features of a stand-alone photo-editing program, it does offer many ways for you to adjust pictures—including correcting a picture's brightness, contrast, and color and adding an artistic effect (see Table 8-1). The Artistic Effects feature can give the picture the appearance of a drawing, sketch, or painting. In this exercise, you will adjust the picture's brightness, contrast, and color and apply an artistic effect.

Table 8-1

Adjust Group—Provides Options to Enhance or Return Your Picture to Its Original Form

Type	Purpose
Remove Background	Removes unwanted portions of a background.
Corrections	Sharpen and Soften adjusts picture by highlighting the pixel colors. Brightness and Contrast alters the adjustment between the brightness and darkness of a picture.
Color	Color Saturation can be an intense deep color or a dim color. Color Tone adjusts the color cast of a picture that contains a dominance of one color by adjusting the color temperature to enhance the details. Recolor adjusts the image by changing the color to a gray scale or sepia tone for an added impact.
Artistic Effects	Applies distinct changes to an image to give it the appearance of a pencil drawing, line drawing, blur, watercolor sponge, film grains photocopy, texturizer, and more.
Compress Picture	Reduces the size of an object.
Change Picture	Changes the image while maintaining the size of the current image.
Reset Picture	Removes all formatting from the picture or resets picture and size back to its original size.

STEP BY STEP   Adjust a Picture's Brightness, Contrast, and Color and Add Artistic Effects

OPEN the *travel_palms1* document completed earlier in the lesson.

1. To display the Picture Tools, select the picture.
2. Click the *Format tab*, and in the *Adjust group*, click the **Corrections** button to display the menu shown in Figure 8-11.
3. In Brightness and Contrast section, select the fourth option in the fourth row (**Brightness: +20% and Contrast: +20%**) to increase the brightness and contrast of your image by 20%. Notice the difference in the picture with an increased brightness and contrast.

WileyPLUS Extra! features an online tutorial of this task.

Figure 8-11

Corrections gallery

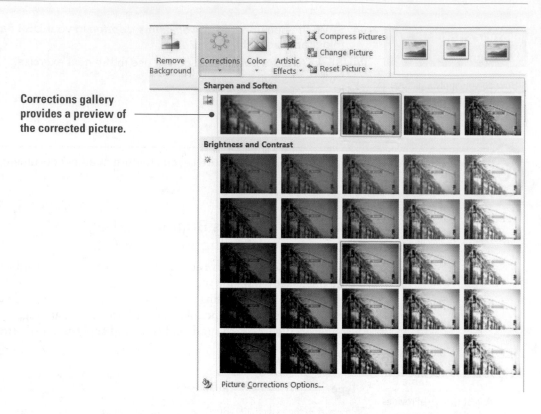

Figure 8-11

Corrections gallery

Corrections gallery
provides a preview of
the corrected picture.

4. On the Format tab, in the Adjust group, click the **Color** button to display the menu shown in Figure 8-12.

Figure 8-12

Color gallery

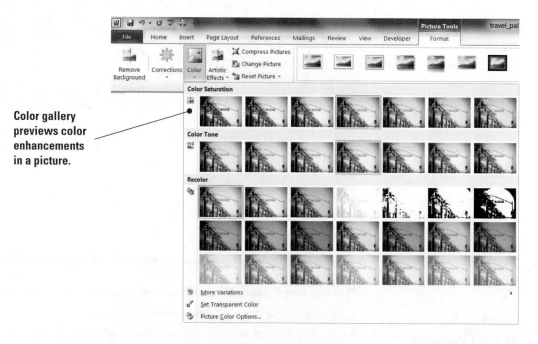

Color gallery
previews color
enhancements
in a picture.

5. Scroll through the options and notice how your picture changes. In the Color Saturation section, select **Saturation 200%**. The higher the saturation percentage, the more vibrant the colors appear in the picture, consequently making the nature's color in the picture more noticeable. Click the **Color** button again to display the menu. In the Color Tone section, select **Temperature 5300 K**. The lower temperature tone creates a picture with a slight tint blue color, while the higher temperature makes the picture appear with an orange tint color. Under *Recolor*, No Recolor is selected by default.

6. SAVE the document as ***travel_palms2*** in your USB flash drive in the lesson folder.

7. On the Format tab, in the Adjust group, click the Artistic Effects button to display the menu shown in Figure 8-13.

Figure 8-13

Artistic Effects gallery

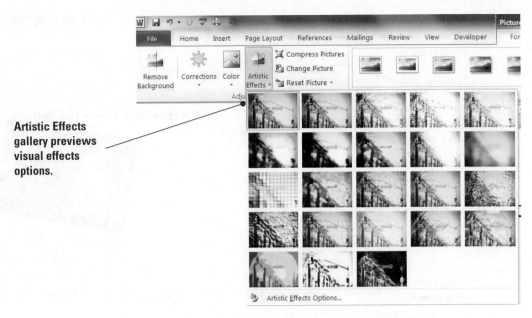

Artistic Effects gallery previews visual effects options.

8. Select the Crisscross Etching option from the Artistic Effects gallery; the effect is applied to the selected image in the fourth row, third option. The impression of the picture is now of an etching sketch. Deselect the picture.

9. SAVE the document as *travel_palms3* in your USB flash drive in the lesson folder.

PAUSE. LEAVE the Word document open to use in the next exercise.

Removing Backgrounds

NEW to Office 2010

Remove Background is a new feature in Word 2010 that removes portions of images you have inserted into documents. You can use the Remove Background options either to automatically remove the image background or to mark and remove specific portions of the image. In this exercise, you learn to use the Remove Background features.

STEP BY STEP   **Remove Background**

USE the document that is open from the previous exercise.

1. To display the Picture Tools, select the picture.

2. Click the Format tab, and in the Adjust group, click the Remove Background button. The Background Removal tab opens, as shown in Figure 8-14, and the picture is surrounded by a color selection marquee. A magenta color overlays the image, marking everything that is to be removed from the image.

3. To change the area of the picture that will be kept, resize the marquee by dragging the upper-left handle up until it meets the upper-left corner of the picture. Then drag the middle-bottom handle down to the bottom of the picture, and drag the right-middle handle to the left until it rests immediately beside the street light. Everything outside these boundaries will be removed from the image.

Take Note   Removing a background may take practice; therefore, you may need to use the Undo button to begin again.

Background Removal will remove unwanted portions of the document automatically or by marking.

Mark changes by drawing with the mouse pointer

Confirm changes and click Keep Changes

Mark areas to keep with the mouse pointer

Mark areas to remove with the mouse pointer

Document is surrounded by a marquee selection – magenta color marks everything to remove.

Handles allow you to resize

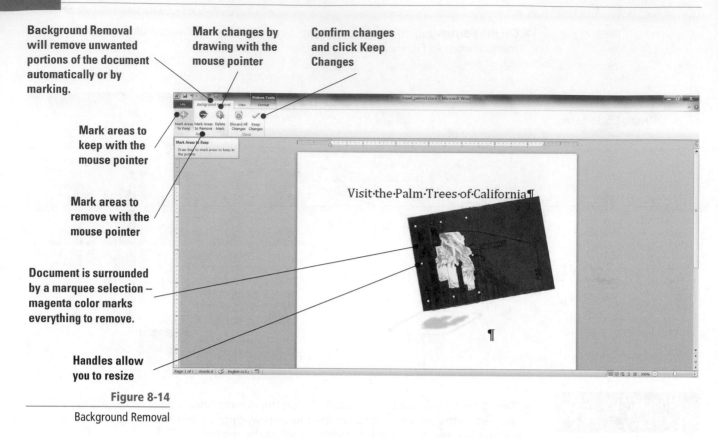

Figure 8-14

Background Removal

4. In the Close group, click **Keep Changes** to remove the designated area of the image, and then click outside the image to deselect. Your edited image should be similar to the one shown in Figure 8-15. Removing the background of a picture is similar to cropping except that the background removal focuses on the picture you wish to point out. In this exercise, the sky, palm trees, and light pole have been removed.

Figure 8-15

Document without background

5. **SAVE** the document as ***palms_no_background*** in your USB flash drive in the lesson folder.

6. The palm picture is still selected. To keep the top and bottom parts of the palm tree, click the Remove Background button in the Adjust group. In the Refine group, click the Mark Areas To Keep button, press and hold the left mouse button and draw around the palm tree to the right and below the street light. As you mark the area of keep, a circle with a plus symbol marks an area to keep.

7. Click the Mark Areas Remove button, press and hold the left mouse button and draw around the mark area to keep, and then continue marking the palm tree until it is completely marked. As you mark the area, the magenta color will appear and the smaller palm trees will be marked.

8. Click the Keep Changes button. Your document should match Figure 8-16.

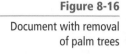

Figure 8-16

Document with removal
of palm trees

9. **SAVE** the document as ***palms_removed*** in your USB flash drive in the lesson folder and close the file.

PAUSE. LEAVE the Word document open to use in the next exercise.

Arranging Text around a Picture

Arranging pictures and text together on the page is simple using Word's Positioning and Text Wrap commands. The Positioning command automatically positions the object in the location you select on the page. The Wrap Text command determines the way text wraps around the picture or other objects on the page, depending on the option you select. To configure the picture as an **inline object** that moves along with the text that surrounds it, select the In Line with Text option. If you choose to format the picture as a **floating object**, Word positions the image precisely on the page, and allows the text to wrap around it in one of several available formats. In this exercise, you learn to position text around a picture.

STEP BY STEP   **Arrange Text around a Picture**

OPEN the ***travel_palms2*** document completed earlier in the lesson.

1. Place the insertion point on the line below the picture and press Enter. Key the following text:

   Our charming desert cities, warm sun, and hot mineral springs make California the perfect vacation destination. So come visit the palm trees and experience this magical place.

2. Select the text; right-click to use the Mini toolbar to change the font size to **14 pt**. Deselect the text.

3. To display the Picture Tools, select the picture.

4. On the Format tab, and in the Arrange group, click the **Position** button to display the menu shown in Figure 8-17.

Figure 8-17

Position menu

Position gallery previews several text and picture positioning options.

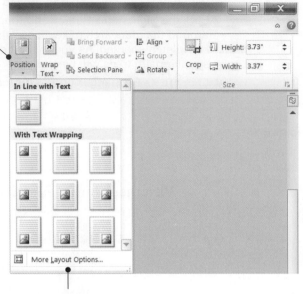

More Layout Options

Another Way
The Wrap Text feature in the Arrange group on the Format tab provides additional options for text wrapping.

5. Select **Position in Middle Center with Square Text Wrapping**. Delete the extra blank line below the heading. Place your insertion point anywhere in the paragraph you keyed in step 1, and press **Ctrl+L** to align text left. The text is now positioned at the top of the page and the picture is centered, as shown in Figure 8-18. If you were to add more text to this document, it would wrap around the image, which would remain centered in the middle of the page.

Figure 8-18

Image positioned around text

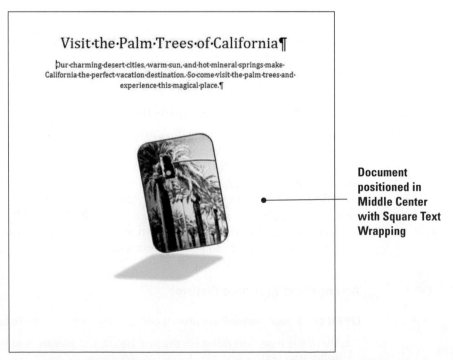

Visit·the·Palm·Trees·of·California¶

Our·charming·desert·cities,·warm·sun,·and·hot·mineral·springs·make·
California·the·perfect·vacation·destination.·So·come·visit·the·palm·trees·and·
experience·this·magical·place.¶

Document positioned in Middle Center with Square Text Wrapping

CERTIFICATION READY? **4.1.6**

How do you position an image on the page?

6. **SAVE** the document as **_travel_palms5_** in your USB flash drive in the lesson folder.

PAUSE. LEAVE the document open to use in the next exercise.

Inserting a Screenshot or Screen Clipping

NEW to Office 2010

Word 2010 has added new features to the Illustrations group. The new Screenshot feature will capture a picture of the whole screen or part of the screen and save it in the format of your choice. **Screenshots** are images of the entire current display on your computer screen. **Screen clippings**, however, are image captures of only the part of your screen that you have selected. In this exercise, you learn to insert a screenshot and a screen clipping.

STEP BY STEP   **Insert a Screenshot or Screen Clipping**

USE the document that is open from the previous exercise.

1. On the View tab, in the Zoom group, click the One Page button so that the entire page is displayed on your computer screen for the image capture. Do not minimize the display, or the screenshot will not capture the image of this document.

2. Press **Ctrl+N** to open a new blank document.

3. On the Insert tab, in the Illustrations group, click the Screenshot button; the Available Windows gallery opens, displaying the **travel_palms5** document, as shown in Figure 8-19. If you have more than one window open, you will see images from all open documents in the Screenshot Available Windows area. Minimize or close the other windows.

Figure 8-19

Screenshot displaying Available Windows

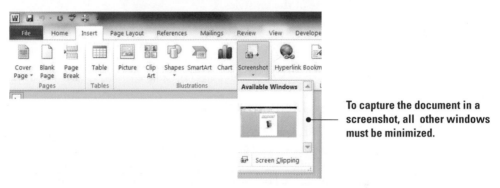

To capture the document in a screenshot, all other windows must be minimized.

4. Under the Available Windows area, click the travel_palms5 document to insert a screenshot of that document, as currently displayed, into the blank document.

5. **SAVE** the new document as **screenshot_palms** in your USB flash drive in the lesson folder (it remains the active document). Click below the image to deselect it, and then press the Enter key twice.

CERTIFICATION READY?   **4.1.7**

How do you insert a screenshot in a document?

6. Click the Insert tab, in the Illustrations group, click the Screenshot button drop-down arrow, then select Screen Clipping from the menu that appears. The active document fades away, the **travel_palms5** document appears, and the mouse pointer changes to a crosshair (+).

7. Click and drag the mouse pointer over the heading, Visit the Palm Trees of California. When you release the mouse button, the heading is placed in the **screenshot_palms** document as shown in Figure 8-20. Click outside the heading to deselect it.

Figure 8-20

Document with screen clipping

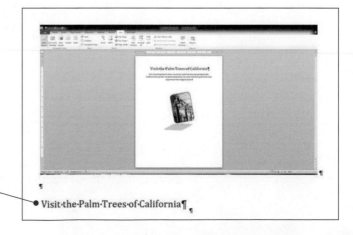

Screen clipping enables you to select portions of text or a picture.

8. **SAVE** the document as *screen_clipping* in your USB flash in the lesson folder and close the file.

9. **CLOSE** the *travel_palms5* document.

PAUSE. LEAVE the document open to use in the next exercise.

INSERTING AND FORMATTING SHAPES, WORDART, AND SMARTART

The Bottom Line

Word provides illustrations to enhance your document with different preset shapes, SmartArt, and WordArt. **Shapes** are figures such as lines, rectangles, block arrows, equation shapes, flowcharts, stars and banners, and callouts. You may also insert a drawing canvas. The Drawing Tools make it possible for you to change the shape, add text, apply styles, fill with theme or standard colors, gradient, texture colors, and apply preset effects. **SmartArt graphics** are graphical illustrations available from a list of various categories, including List diagrams, Process diagrams, Cycle diagrams, Hierarchy diagrams, Relationship diagrams, Matrix diagrams, and Pyramid diagrams. The Smart Tools enable you to manipulate the shape by adding shapes, bullets, and text; changing the layout and colors; and applying special effects using styles. **WordArt** is a feature that creates decorative effects with text. The Drawing Tools allow you to format the WordArt by adding special effects to the text or outline, applying preset effects, and transforming the shape using one of the set styles.

SOFTWARE ORIENTATION

Shapes Menu and Drawing Tools

When you click the Shapes button in the Illustrations group of the Insert tab, the Shapes menu is displayed, as shown in Figure 8-21. The menu contains options for an assortment of ready-made shapes, including lines, arrows, stars, and banners. After you insert a shape into a Word document, the Format tab opens containing the Drawing Tools shown in Figure 8-22. You use these tools to format a shape's style, fill, color, outline, and many other attributes.

Figure 8-21

Shapes menu

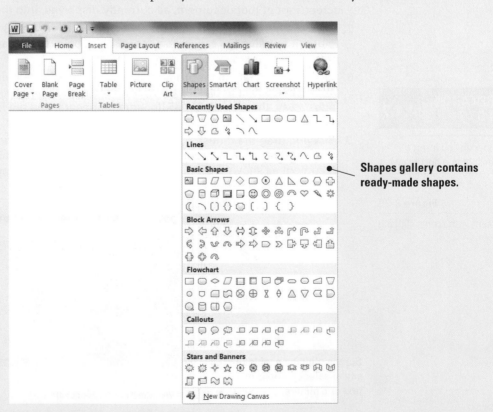

Shapes gallery contains ready-made shapes.

Edit Shape: Points in the shape can be reshaped or you can change the shape. Note, new document shapes must be saved before this feature is activated.

Adds text to shape

Adds color within shape

Adds color or changes the width of the outline

Height button

Launches the Layout dialog box

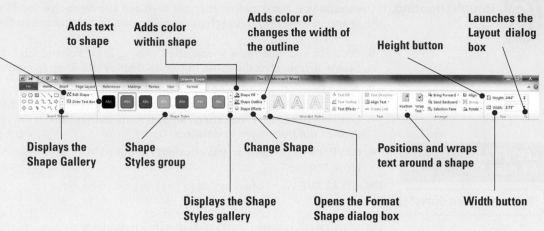

Displays the Shape Gallery

Shape Styles group

Change Shape

Positions and wraps text around a shape

Displays the Shape Styles gallery

Opens the Format Shape dialog box

Width button

Figure 8-22

Drawing Tools

Use these figures as a reference throughout this lesson, as well as the rest of the book.

Inserting Shapes

Word provides many different ready-made shapes to choose from such as lines, rectangles, arrows, equation shapes, callouts, stars, banners, and more. Inserting a shape in a document opens the Format tab containing Drawing Tools in several command groups. You can use these tools to insert shapes, apply shape styles, add a shadow or 3-D effect to inserted shapes, arrange the shape on the page, and size it. In this exercise, you learn to insert a shape, add a style from the gallery, and add a 3-D effect to the shape.

| STEP BY STEP | **Insert Shapes** |

OPEN *travel* from the data files for this lesson.

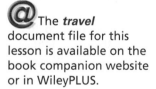

The *travel* document file for this lesson is available on the book companion website or in WileyPLUS.

WileyPLUS Extra! features an online tutorial of this task.

1. Click and drag to select the text **Picture Yourself Here** and the picture below it. On the Home tab, in the Paragraph group, click the **Align Text Right** button and deselect.

2. Click the **Insert** tab, in the Illustrations group, then click the **Shapes** button to display the Shapes menu.

3. In the Block Arrows section, click the **Curved Right Arrow** shape. The cursor turns into a crosshair (+).

4. Place the crosshair in front of the word Picture. Click and drag down toward the chairs on the left of the photograph to create the arrow shown in Figure 8-23. Click in a blank area of the document screen to deselect.

Figure 8-23

Block arrow shape

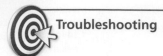

Troubleshooting If the shape you are drawing does not turn out the right size the first time, you can adjust the shape by selecting it and then dragging one of the sizing handles.

5. Because you inserted a shape, the Drawing Tools Format tab is open. In the Insert Shape group, click the **More** button to display the Shapes menu.

6. In the Basic Shapes section, click the **Smiley Face** shape.

7. Place the crosshair (+) inside the curve of the arrow. Click and drag to insert and position the smiley face shape so that it fits within the curved space. Click in a blank area of the document to deselect.

8. **SAVE** the document as **travel_update** in your USB flash drive in the lesson folder and close the file.

PAUSE. LEAVE Word open to use in the next exercise.

CERTIFICATION READY? **4.2**

How do you insert shapes?

Grouping Shapes into a Single Drawing

A drawing can be a single object or multiple objects grouped together, and it can include lines, rectangles, arrows, equation shapes, callouts, stars, banners, and more. The Shapes menu contains a number of shapes you can use to draw a flowchart—a type of drawing that presents a diagram of the tasks and timelines involved in completing a process, or that shows the hierarchy of personnel within an organization. In this exercise, you learn to use the Shapes menu to create a flowchart, using connecting lines to show the personnel organization within Margie's Travel and the Drawing Canvas to arrange the flowchart elements.

Take Note   A **drawing canvas** is a frame-like boundary that keeps multiple drawing objects together. By default, the drawing canvas is off, but you can display it easily by clicking the Shapes button on the Insert tab, and then choosing the New Drawing Canvas option from the Shapes menu that appears.

STEP BY STEP   **Create a Flowchart**

OPEN a new blank Word document.

1. At the top of the document, key **Margie's Travel**. Select the text and use the Font command group tools on the Home tab to change the font to **Cambria** and font size to **24 pt**. In the Paragraph group, click the **Center** button to center the text horizontally on the page. Deselect text and press **Enter**.

2. Key **Organization Chart**. Select the text and in the Home tab, change the font size to **20 pt**. Deselect the text and press **Enter**. The text is centered and inserted in the document.

3. Click the **Insert** tab, and in the Illustrations group, click the **Shapes** button to display the Shapes menu.

4. At the bottom of the Shapes menu, click **New Drawing Canvas**. The drawing canvas frame appears on the document and the Drawing Tools Format tab (see Figure 8-24).

Another Way   Click the File tab, then Options to open the Word Options dialog box. In the left side category, click Advanced, then under the Editing options section, click the check box at Automatically create drawing canvas when inserting AutoShapes to enable.

Figure 8-24

Drawing canvas

Margie's·Travel¶

Organization·Chart¶

Drawing canvas

CERTIFICATION
READY?   4.2

How do you insert shapes?

Another Way
The SmartArt gallery includes a number of formatted Process and organizational Hierarchy flowcharts that are ready to insert into your document. Learn more in "Using SmartArt Graphics" later in this lesson.

Figure 8-25

Flowchart shapes and connector

5. On Format tab, in the Insert Shapes groups, click the **More** button to display the Shapes menu.

6. In the Flowchart section, click the **Flowchart: Alternate Process** symbol (the second option in the first row).

7. At the top center of the drawing canvas, click and drag the crosshair (+) to create a shape that is approximately 2 inches wide by 1 inch high. The Drawing Tools Format tab opens.

8. Repeat steps 5–7 to draw the same shape in the bottom left of the drawing canvas.

9. On the Format tab, in the Insert Shapes group, click the **More** button.

10. In the Lines section, click the **Elbow Arrow Connector** symbol (fifth in the row).

11. Click the **crosshair** (+) on the bottom center of the top shape and drag to the top center of the bottom shape. Click the **green circle** to turn the arrow downward and drag to connect to the bottom box, as shown in Figure 8-25.

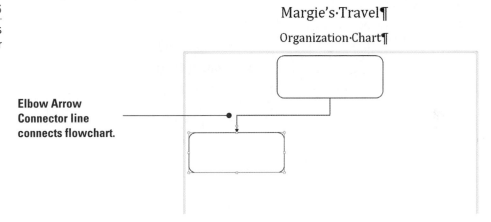

Margie's·Travel¶

Organization·Chart¶

Elbow Arrow Connector line connects flowchart.

12. **SAVE** the document as ***travel_flowchart*** in your USB flash drive in the lesson folder.

PAUSE. LEAVE the document open to use in the next exercise.

Adding Text and a Caption to a Shape

You can add, edit, and format text in shapes, just as you do in any part of the Word document. Adding text to a flowchart, symbol, or any shape opens the Drawing Tools Format tab. In this exercise, you will add text and a caption to the shapes within the organizational chart you created in the previous exercise.

STEP BY STEP   **Add Text and Caption to a Shape**

USE the document that is open from the previous exercise.

1. Select the **top box**.

2. Key **Josh Barnhill**, press **Enter** to move down to the next line, and key **President**.

3. Select the text for both lines; right-click and use the Mini toolbar to change the font size to **14 pt**.

4. Select the **bottom box**.

5. Key **Jeanne Bourne**, press **Enter**, and key **Vice President**.

6. Select the text for both lines, right-click and use the Mini toolbar to change the font size to **12 pt**.

7. Click outside the drawing canvas to deselect the drawing.

8. Click to place your insertion point below the flowchart and press **Enter** to create a blank line.

9. Click the **References** tab and, in the Caption group, click the **Insert Caption** button. The Caption dialog box opens. Your insertion point is located to the right of the default

CERTIFICATION
READY?   4.2.1

How do you add text to shapes?

caption text, Figure 1. Press the spacebar once and key Organizational Chart for 20XX (see Figure 8-26). Click OK. A caption with Figure 1 and the description appears on the left margin below the organizational chart. The document should resemble Figure 8-27.

Figure 8-26

Caption dialog box

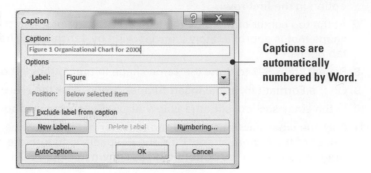

Captions are automatically numbered by Word.

Figure 8-27

Document with text and caption

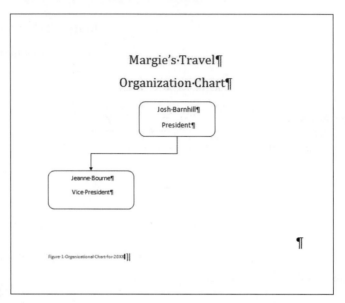

CERTIFICATION READY? **4.2.3**

How do you add a caption to a shape?

10. **SAVE** the document as *travel_flowchart_caption* in your USB flash drive in the lesson folder.

PAUSE. LEAVE the Word document open to use in the next exercise.

Take Note   A shape cannot be converted to a SmartArt graphic like a picture because it is not an image. Adding a caption to a shape would require you to add the caption using the References tab.

Formatting Shapes

The Drawing Tools include a number of options for changing the appearance of shapes. In this exercise, you learn to use the shape styles and to position and size shapes, working within the flowchart you have created in preceding exercises.

STEP BY STEP   **Format Shapes**

USE the document that is open from the previous exercise.

1. Select the top box. In the Shape Styles group of the Format tab, click the More button to display the gallery of preformatted styles available for the selected shape, as shown in Figure 8-28.

Figure 8-28

Shape Styles gallery

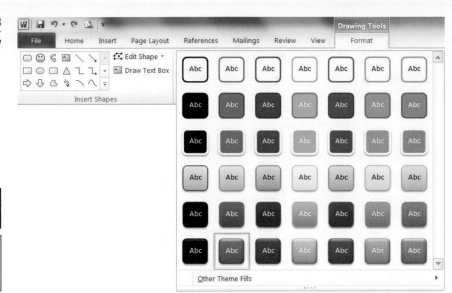

2. Select the **Intense Effect – Blue Accent 1** for the first box (second column, sixth option).

3. Select the **bottom box** and click the **More** button in the Shape Styles group to display the gallery. Select the **Colored Fill – Blue, Accent 1** from the menu that appears. Notice this style has a border (second column second option).

4. The bottom box is still selected. Click the **Shape Outline** button in the Shape Styles group to display the menu. In the Theme Colors section, select **Dark Blue, Text 2, Darker 50%**. The outline of the border becomes darker.

5. In the Shape Styles group, click the **Shape Outline** button again, and change the **Weight** for the bottom box to **3 pt** to change the thickness of the box's border.

6. Select the **top box**. In the Size group of the Format tab, change the Height to **1.1"** and Width to **2.28"** by keying the dimensions in the box. The top box height and width have been modified.

7. Select the **bottom box** and change the Height to **.9"** by repeating step 6. The bottom box is modified with its new dimensions. Click outside the drawing canvas to deselect.

8. **SAVE** the document as ***travel_flowchart1*** in your USB flash drive in the lesson folder.

PAUSE. LEAVE Word open to use in the next exercise.

Inserting WordArt

WordArt has been enhanced for Word 2010 with more vibrant colors and shapes and a gallery of text styles. When you insert a WordArt object, the Drawing Tools Format tab opens. In this exercise, you learn to insert WordArt in a document.

STEP BY STEP   **Insert WordArt**

USE the document that is open from the previous exercise.

1. Select **Margie's Travel**. Click the **Page Layout** tab and, in the Paragraph group, click the **up arrow** button in the After box to change the Spacing After to **66 pt**. This creates spacing between the heading and subheading.

2. Click the **Insert** tab and, in the Text group, click the **WordArt** button to display the menu, as shown in Figure 8-29.

Figure 8-29

WordArt menu

WordArt Gallery
previews ready-made
decorative effects.

3. In the WordArt gallery select **Fill – White, Drop Shadow** (first row, third option). The Drawing Tools Format tab opens. The lettering of the Margie's Travel heading takes on a new appearance and style.

4. The WordArt heading, Margie's Travel, is selected. A box appears around the WordArt; place your insertion point to the center-right sizing handle until it changes to a double-headed arrow, and drag to the right margin. The subheading automatically moves down one line as you resize the heading.

**CERTIFICATION
READY?**   **4.2**

How do you insert
WordArt?

5. In the WordArt Styles group of the Format tab, click the **Text Effects** button, then select **Transform**, and under the Warp section select **Inflate** in the first column, sixth option.

6. The WordArt, Margie's Travel, is still selected. In the WordArt Styles group, click the **Text Fills** button. In the Theme Colors, select **Dark Blue, Text 2, Darker 25%**. The text is outlined in white while the text coloring is dark blue.

7. In the WordArt Styles group, click the Text Outline button. Under the Theme Colors section of the Text Outline select **Red, Accent 2, Darker 50%**. The document should resemble Figure 8-30. The WordArt is formatted with a red outline.

Figure 8-30

Formatted Document
with WordArt

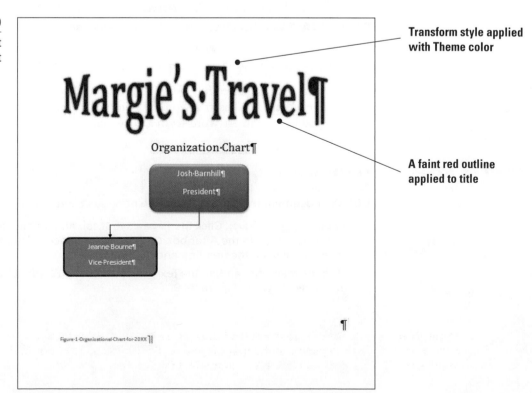

Transform style applied
with Theme color

A faint red outline
applied to title

8. **SAVE** the document as *travel_flowchart2* in your USB flash drive in the lesson folder and close the file.

PAUSE. LEAVE the document open to use in the next exercise.

Using SmartArt Graphics

SmartArt graphics are visual representations of information that can help communicate your message or ideas more effectively. SmartArt graphics and designer-quality illustrations can contribute to eye-catching documents that draw the attention of the target audience. Table 8-2 gives some examples of the type of information you can display with each category of SmartArt graphics. Earlier in this lesson, you learned to convert pictures to SmartArt with captions. In this exercise, you learn to insert SmartArt graphics into Word documents and add a caption to the graphics.

Table 8-2

SmartArt Graphic Categories

Type	Purpose
List	Show nonsequential or grouped blocks of information
Process	Show a progression of steps in a process, timeline, task, or workflow
Cycle	Show a continuing sequence of stages, tasks, or events in a circular flow
Hierarchy	Show a decision tree or create an organization chart
Relationship	Illustrate connections or interlocking ideas; show related or contrasting concepts
Matrix	Show how parts relate to a whole
Pyramid	Show proportional, foundation-based, containment, overlapping, or interconnected relationships

STEP BY STEP   **Use SmartArt Graphics**

OPEN a new, blank document.

1. Click the **Insert** tab, in the Illustrations group, click the **SmartArt** button. The Choose a SmartArt Graphic dialog box appears.

2. Click the **Relationship** category and then select **Equation** as shown in Figure 8-31. Use the scroll bar to locate the equation graphic in the third column, sixth option.

Figure 8-31

Choose a SmartArt Graphic dialog box

Several categories of SmartArt are available with preview option.

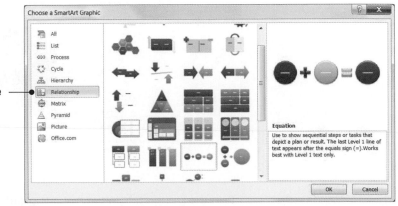

Another Way
Select the SmartArt graphic and double-click to insert.

3. Click **OK** to insert the Equation SmartArt graphic into your document. The placeholders are placed in the graphic and ready for you to key information. Text can be keyed in the placeholders or in the Text Pane.

4. On the Design tab, click the **Text Pane** button to enable—the text pane appears enabling you to key text in each element of the graphic equation. The first placeholder is selected by default and ready for you to key text, as shown in Figure 8-32.

Figure 8-32

The Text Pane

Enable or disable Text Pane button

The Text Pane makes entering text easy.

Description of SmartArt graphic

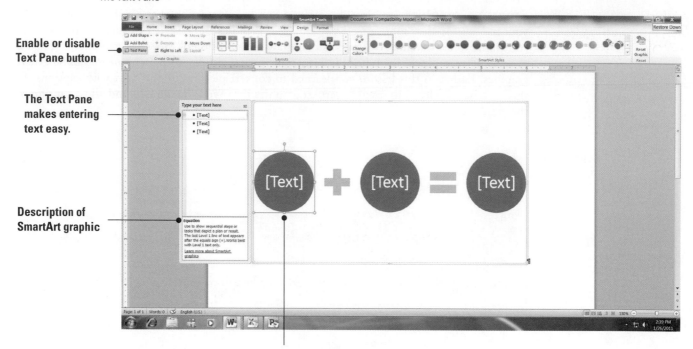

Placeholder for text

5. Key the information as displayed in Figure 8-33. Click to move to the next element and key the remaining text. As you key text, Word automatically adjusts the text to fit in the graphic. If you press the **Enter** key at the end, another element is added to the equation. Click the **Close** button in the Text Pane or in the Create Graphic group; click the **Text Pane** button to close.

Figure 8-33

Text added to SmartArt graphic

The Text Pane makes entering text easy.

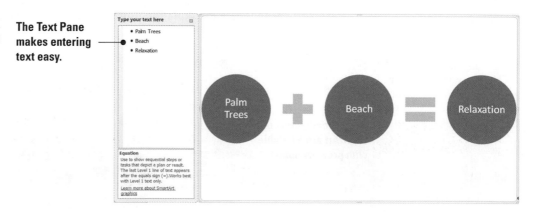

6. In the Design tab, in the Layouts group, click the drop-down arrow at the **More** arrow to produce the Layouts gallery, then select **More Layouts**. The Choose a SmartArt Graphic dialog box appears. Select **Picture**, then select **Bubble Picture List** (fourth column, seventh position) from the menu that appears. Click **OK**. The equation's graphic is replaced with the Bubble Picture List, and text is carried over to the new layout. The text you added in step 5 now appears as captions beside the bubbles in the SmartArt graphic. An image icon appears in the middle of each circle.

7. To add an image to a bubble, click the first image icon for the Palm Trees; the default Insert Pictures dialog box opens. Use the scroll bar to locate your USB flash drive and click the lesson folder. Click the image for the palms to select, then click **Open** or double-click on image. The image is inserted in the first bubble and is automatically resized and adjusted.

8. Click the image in the bubble for the second image by Beach. The Insert Picture dialog box opens. Select the beach picture, and click **Open** or double-click on the image. The beach image is inserted in the bubble by the caption, Beach.

9. For the Relaxation Bubble List, click the image in the bubble. The Insert Picture dialog box opens. Select the relaxing at the beach picture and click **Open** or double-click on the image. The relaxing at the beach image is inserted in the bubble by the caption, Relaxation. The document should resemble Figure 8-34.

CERTIFICATION
READY?   4.2

How do you insert SmartArt
graphics in a document?

Figure 8-34

SmartArt with captions
and images

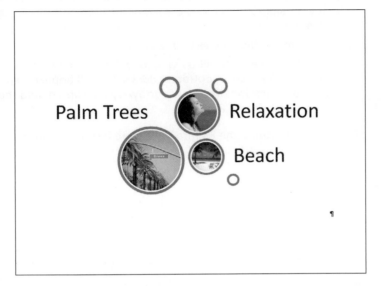

CERTIFICATION
READY?   4.2.3

How do you add a caption to
a SmartArt graphic?

10. On the Design tab, in the SmartArt Styles group, click the **Change Colors** button. Then under the Primary Theme Colors section, click **Dark 2 Outline**. The Bubble graphic now has an outline style applied. Click outside the Bubble graphic layout to deselect.

11. **SAVE** the document as *travel_sign* in your USB flash drive in the lesson folder and close the file.

PAUSE. LEAVE Word open to use in the next exercise.

INSERTING AND FORMATTING CLIP ART

The Bottom Line

Clip art is a collection of media files available for you to insert in Microsoft Office documents that can include illustrations, photographs, video, or audio content. You can search the entire Microsoft Office Clip Art Gallery, or you can limit your search by using the Clip Organizer. The **Clip Organizer** collects and stores clip art, photos, animations, videos, and other types of media to use. You can categorize clips into a collection for easy access. After you insert a clip art object into your document, you can position it within text on the page, add a caption, resize the clip art, apply artistic effects, compress the clip art, and more.

Inserting, Resizing, and Adding a Caption to Clip Art

Clip art refers to picture files and are inserted in a document. The clip can be resized for better management within the document so that you can position it correctly. In this exercise, you learn how to insert a clip art graphic image file, resize the image, and add a caption to it.

STEP BY STEP   **Insert, Resize, and Add a Caption to a Clip Art**

OPEN a new, blank Word document.

1. Key **Explore the World** and select text. On the Home tab, Font group, change the font to **Cambria** and font size to **36 pt**. In the Paragraph group, click the **Center** button. Deselect the text.

2. Press **Enter**.

3. Click the **Insert** tab and, in the Illustrations group, click **Clip Art**. The Clip Art pane appears to the right of your document.

4. In the Search For box, key **travel**. Clip art appears in the results box.

5. In the Results Should Be box, click the **drop-down arrow** to view the four types of media searches. Maintain the default selection: All Media Types (if you wanted to limit your search, you could click to deselect this check box then click the check boxes beside the collections you wish to search).

6. Click **Go** to produce the search results.

7. In the Results pane, scroll down and in the first column sixth option click the **airliners, airplanes, concepts . . . option**. A ScreenTip will appear displaying the keywords for the clip art. Click the drop-down arrow by the clip art, and then click **Insert**. The image should match Figure 8-35.

 Ref   Earlier in this lesson, the Picture Tools were introduced for pictures. They are used the same way for clip art.

Opens the Clip Art pane

Type text to search.

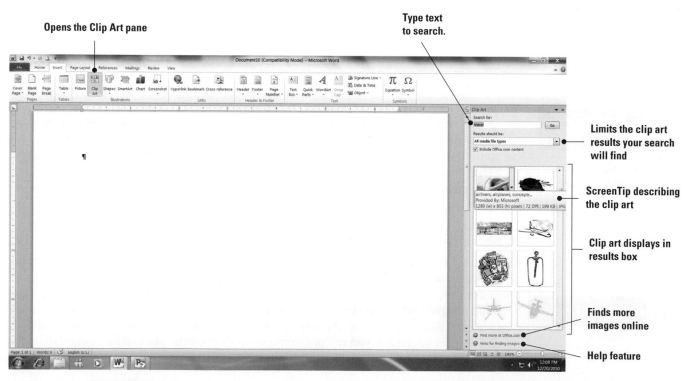

Limits the clip art results your search will find

ScreenTip describing the clip art

Clip art displays in results box

Finds more images online

Help feature

Figure 8-35

Clip Art pane with search results on travel

CERTIFICATION READY?   **4.3**

How do you insert clip art?

8. With the clip art selected, hold the **Shift** key (to maintain the proportions of the clip art picture) as you click and drag the bottom-right sizing handle of the clip art to make it smaller—2.11" in height and 3.17" wide. You can also use the Height and Width buttons in the Size group to crop by precise measurements.

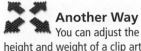

Another Way
You can adjust the height and weight of a clip art picture in the Size group of the Format tab in the Picture Tools.

CERTIFICATION READY?   **4.3.5**

How do you resize clip art?

Figure 8-36

Document with SmartArt and caption

9. Close the Clip Art pane.

10. **SAVE** the document as *travel_overseas* in your USB flash drive in the lesson folder.

11. Select the travel clip art image you have inserted in your document to display the Picture Tools Format tab.

12. In the Picture Styles group, click the **Picture Layout** button and, in the menu that appears, select **Snapshot Picture List** (first row, fourth option). The original image is carried over into the new layout with a [Text] placeholder.

13. The Snapshot Picture List contains a placeholder for text. In the *text* placeholder, key **Traveling by Air**. *Traveling by Air* is a caption describing the picture. Click outside the SmartArt graphic to deselect. Your document should match Figure 8-36.

14. **SAVE** the document with the same filename in your USB flash drive in the lesson folder.

PAUSE. LEAVE the document open to use in the next exercise.

CERTIFICATION READY?   **4.3.2**

How do you add a caption to clip art using the Picture Tools?

Formatting Clip Art

As you've seen in earlier exercises, the Picture Tools Format tab provides a number of commands for enhancing your document's appearance. You can use these tools to apply Artistic Effects features to a clip art picture, and then position the clip art automatically around the text. Compressing reduces the file size of clip art. In this exercise, you learn to add Artistic Effects to clip art, reposition the clip art, and compress the clip art image.

STEP BY STEP   **Format Clip Art**

USE the document that is open from the previous exercise.

1. Place the insertion point after the Snapshot Picture List layout SmartArt graphic and press **Enter** twice to create blank lines.

2. Select the clip art image you inserted into the document during the preceding exercise to display the Picture Tools Format tab.

3. Click the Format tab, and click the **Adjust group drop-down arrow** to display the Artistic Effects menu.

4. Select the **Pencil Sketch** option from the menu in the first row, fourth option, and click outside the image to deselect it. The picture changes to a sketch, making it appear as though it was hand drawn.

5. Move the insertion point to the first blank line below the Pencil Sketch SmartArt image. Key the following text:

    Word 2010 has enhanced the Illustration and Graphics commands by adding the Artistic Effects feature. Applying an artistic effect to a picture or clip art gives it a compelling new look. This feature might not have all the photo-editing capabilities but it can change an original picture to make it look like a sketch, drawing, or painting.

6. Select the text and in the Font group of the Home tab, change the font size of the text you've keyed to **14 pt**, then click the **Align Text Left** button.

7. Select the Pencil Sketch SmartArt image layout, and then click the Format tab. In the Arrange group, click the **drop-down arrow** to display the Position menu.

8. Select **Position in Top Left with Square Text Wrapping**. The image is positioned in the top-left margin with the heading to the right side and text below (see Figure 8-37).

Explore the World

Traveling by Air

Word 2010 has enhanced the Illustration and Graphics commands by adding the Artistic Effects feature. Applying an artistic effect to a picture or clip art gives it a compelling new look. This feature might not have all the photo-editing capabilities but it can change an original picture to make it look like a sketch, drawing or painting.

CERTIFICATION READY? 4.3.3

How do you apply an artistic effect to clip art?

CERTIFICATION READY? 4.3.5

How do you position a picture within the document?

9. **SAVE** the document as *exploring_world_flyer* in your USB flash drive in the lesson folder and close file.

PAUSE. LEAVE the program open for the next exercise.

Organizing Clip Art

The Microsoft Clip Organizer collects and stores clip art, photos animations, videos, and other types of media to use. You can use the organizer to add, delete, copy, and move clips, and to change keywords and captions. You also can take clips from a file, scanner, or camera, or online and place them in a personalized folder or in one of the existing folders in the organizer. These folders are categorized into collections for easy access. In this exercise, you learn to expand and collapse folders and add an image from a target location to the Clip Organizer in a specific folder. Table 8-3 displays the types of media files you can add to the Clip Organizer and their file extensions.

Table 8-3

Types of Media Files

File Type	Extension
Microsoft Windows Metafile	.emf, .wmf
Windows Bitmap	.bmp, .dib, .rle
Computer Graphics Metafile	.cgm
Graphics Interchange Format	.gif
Joint Photographic Experts Group	.jpg
Portable Network Graphics	.png
Macintosh PICT	.pct
Tagged Image File Format	.tif
Vector Markup Language	.vml
Microsoft Windows Media	.avi, .asf, .asx, .rmi, .wma, .wax, .wav

STEP BY STEP **Organize Clip Art**

OPEN a blank document.

1. On the task bar, click the Start button.

2. In the Search box, key **Microsoft Clip Organizer**. The Microsoft Clip Organizer will open on your screen, as shown in Figure 8-38. In the left pane of the Organizer, a folder named My Collections contains two subfolders—Favorites and Unclassified Clips.

Ref

Launching Microsoft Office programs was covered in Lesson 1.

Figure 8-38

Microsoft Clip Organizer

By default, two subfolders appear under My Collections: Favorites and Unclassified Clips.

In the Office Collections folder, additional categories are available with clips.

The Web Collections folder also contains clips by categories for use in web pages.

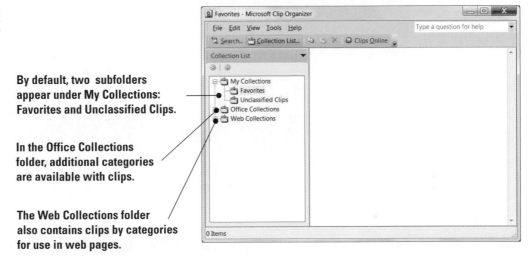

3. Click the plus (+) symbol beside the Office Collections folder to expand the folder, and then notice the subfolders it contains. Scan through some of the subfolders to view the categories of clips they contain. Click the minus (–) symbol to collapse the Office Collections folder contents.

4. Click the plus (+) symbol to expand the Web Collections folder, and then scan through the subfolders to view the categories of clips they contain. Click the minus (–) symbol to collapse the Web Collections folder contents.

5. To begin the process of inserting a picture from your data files in the lesson folder and adding it to the Favorites folder, select the **Favorites** folder from the *Collection* list. The Favorites folder is the active folder.

6. On the Menu bar, click **File**, then click the **right arrow** at Add Clips to Organizer, to select **On my Own**. The Add to Clips Organizer dialog box opens.

7. Locate your lesson folder and select the **beach** picture. In the Add Clips to Organizer dialog box, the filename is added to the Clip Name text box. Click the **Add** button. The picture is added to the Favorites folder, as shown in Figure 8-39.

8. Click the Word document to minimize the Clips Organizer. On the Insert tab, in the Illustrations group, click the **Clip Art** button to produce the Clip Art pane on the right side of the window. In the Search For box, key **beach**, and then click **GO**. The beach picture appears in the results box at the bottom of the pane. Close the Clip Art pane.

@The **beach** picture file for this lesson is available on the book companion website or in WileyPLUS.

Take Note Table 8-3 displays the type of media files you can add to the Clip Organizer and their file extensions. In the above exercise, you inserted a .jpg file from your lesson folder to the Clip Organizer.

9. **CLOSE** the Microsoft Clip Organizer.

PAUSE. LEAVE Word open for the next exercise.

CERTIFICATION READY? **4.3.1**

How do you insert clip art into a folder in the Clip Organizer?

Drop-down arrow contains
additional commands.

Figure 8-39

My Favorites folder
with image

Take Note   To remove the picture from the Clip Organizer, open the Microsoft Clip Organizer (repeat step 2 earlier), select the picture, and then click the drop-down arrow and select Delete from Clip Organizer. A prompt will appear that states, "This will delete the selected clip(s) from all collections in Clip Organizer." Click OK.

COMPRESSING AND RESETTING IMAGES

When you compress an image, it reduces the file size, thereby reducing the resolution and making the documents more manageable to share. You can compress images for clip art and pictures. Larger images may take up space on your USB flash drive. When you **compress** an image, you can make it occupy less space on your hard drive or USB flash drive, which will allow you to open and save your document more quickly and reduces the download time for file sharing. **Resetting** a picture will discard all formatting changes you made to the picture, including changes to contrast, color, brightness, and style.

Compressing Images

Compressing and resetting images will save space when sharing images by email. In this exercise, you learn to compress and reset an image in preparation for sharing by email.

STEP BY STEP   **Compress Images**

OPEN the *travel_palms2* document competed in an earlier exercise.

1. To display the Picture Tools, select the *travel_palms2* picture.
2. Click the Format tab, and in the Adjust group, and click the Compress Pictures button to display the *Compress Pictures* dialog box, shown in Figure 8-40.

Figure 8-40

Compress Pictures dialog box

Identify your target output for this document (print, web, etc.) and Word will recommend an ideal compression size.

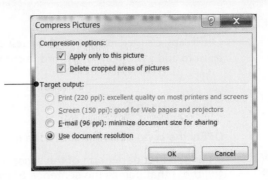

CERTIFICATION READY? 4.1.4

How do you compress a picture?

CERTIFICATION READY? 4.3.4

How do you compress clip art?

3. In the Compress Options section, check marks indicate which features are activated.

4. In the Target Output section, select the **E-mail (96 ppi): minimize document size for sharing** radio button. By selecting the radio button, the picture file size will be compressed to make the document ready for sharing via email. The other Target Outputs compress the picture to print correctly on printers and screens and to view on web pages and projectors.

5. Click **OK** to apply your choices.

6. **SAVE** the document as *travel_pic_compress* in your USB flash drive in the lesson folder.

PAUSE. LEAVE the document open to use in the next exercise.

Troubleshooting You will not see the compression take place. To verify that the file is smaller after compressing pictures, you can compare the document's properties before and after performing the command. Keep in mind that if your picture is already smaller than the compression option chosen, no compression will occur.

Resetting an Image

When resetting a picture's brightness and contrast, the color is reset using the Reset Picture command. You may also choose to Reset Picture and Size. In this exercise, you learn to reset an image.

STEP BY STEP   **Reset an Image**

USE the document that is open from the previous exercise.

1. To display the Picture Tools, select the **travel palms** picture.

2. Click the **Format** tab, and in the Adjust group, click the **drop-down arrow** to display the Reset Picture menu; then select **Reset Picture**. Formatting changes you made to the picture earlier are discarded.

3. **SAVE** the document as *travel_reset* to your USB flash drive in the lesson folder and close the file.

PAUSE. LEAVE the document open to use in the next exercise.

MAKING TEXT GRAPHICALLY APPEALING

The Bottom Line

Word's Text Box command lets you insert professionally formatted text elements such as pull quotes and drop caps quickly. A **drop cap** is a large initial letter that drops down two or more lines at the beginning of a paragraph to indicate that a new block of information is beginning and to give interest to newsletters or magazine articles. A **pull quote** is a sentence or other text displayed within a box on the page for emphasis and for ease of movement, and they are often used along with drop caps in newsletters, advertisements, and magazines.

Creating a Drop Cap

Drop caps are used to add visual interest to newsletters or magazine articles. In this exercise, you learn to add a drop cap to a Word document.

STEP BY STEP **Create a Drop Cap**

 The *coho* file for this lesson is available on the book companion website or in WileyPLUS.

OPEN the *coho* document from the data files for this lesson.

1. In the first paragraph of the second column of the article written by John Kane, select the **S** that begins the sentence *Since wine is my business*.

2. Click the **Insert** tab, and in the Text group, click the **Drop Cap** button; the Drop Cap menu appears, as shown in Figure 8-41.

Figure 8-41

Drop Cap menu

WILEY **PLUS** *EXTRA*

WileyPLUS Extra! features an online tutorial of this task.

3. Select **Dropped** from the menu. A drop cap is inserted and extends down three lines in the paragraph—the default line drop length.

4. In the Text group, click the **drop-down arrow** to display the Drop Cap menu, and select **Drop Cap Options** to produce the Drop Cap dialog box. You can use the options in this dialog box to change the position, font, and size of the drop cap. The default settings for Font, number of Lines to drop, and Distance from text are shown in Figure 8-42.

Figure 8-42

Drop Cap dialog box

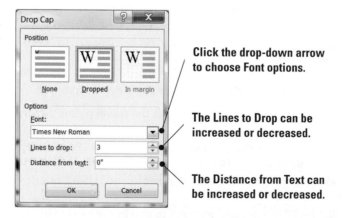

Click the drop-down arrow to choose Font options.

The Lines to Drop can be increased or decreased.

The Distance from Text can be increased or decreased.

5. Click the Font **drop-down arrow** to change the font to **Bookman Old Style**. Click **OK** to apply your changes and close the dialog box. Click outside the drop cap to deselect it. The drop cap font is set to Bookman Old Style for the selected text, while the remaining text is unaffected.

6. **SAVE** your document as *coho_newsletter* in your USB flash drive in the lesson folder.

PAUSE. LEAVE the document open to use in the next exercise.

Creating a Pull Quote

Word has built-in pull quotes that can be inserted in a document. The pull quotes are preformatted and shown within a box. In this exercise, you learn to insert a pull quote and add existing text from the document and place it in the pull quote.

STEP BY STEP   **Create a Pull Quote**

USE the document that is open from the previous exercise.

1. On the Insert tab, in the Text group, click the **Text Box** button. A menu of built-in quotes and sidebars appears.

2. Scroll down and select **Contrast Quote**, as shown in Figure 8-43. The pull quote box is inserted into the document.

Figure 8-43

Text Box button and built-in
Quotes and Sidebars menu

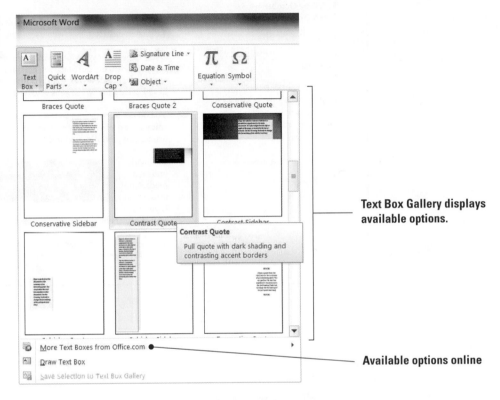

Text Box Gallery displays available options.

Available options online

3. Select the text below the first paragraph beginning with *You should drink whatever wine . . . you like.* Do not select the hidden paragraph mark; this will help you avoid adding an extra blank line in the text box. Press and hold the **left mouse button** and drag and drop in the text box.

4. Position the insertion point on the bottom border of the pull quote box until the pointer becomes a four-sided move arrow.

5. Click and drag the quote down until the pull quote box is about ²/₃ of the way down to the bottom of the page, as shown in Figure 8-44.

6. **SAVE** the document as *coho_newsletter_draft* in your USB flash drive in the lesson folder.

PAUSE. LEAVE the document open to use in the next exercise.

Take Note   After you insert a pull quote, you can select the text and use the Mini toolbar to change its font, size, color, alignment, or effects.

Figure 8-44

Pull quotes in document

You're invited to our Harvest Celebration and Barbecue at Johnny's vineyard. The view is fabulous! Enjoy an afternoon of delicious barbecue and fine wine at the prettiest vineyard in the West.¶

October 17↵
$25 per person↵
RSVP by October 1↵
356-555-1045¶

¶

Wine Facts¶
¶
An open bottle of wine can stay fresh for 3 to 5 days. After enjoying a glass or two, re-cork the bottle and refrigerate.¶
¶

................Column Break................

By John Kane, Winemaker¶

Since wine is my business, I am often asked about which foods go best with which wines. The general rule is to drink white wine with fish and chicken and red wine with beef, but that is only a general guide. And although I do have my favorite pairings, which I will be glad to discuss with you at length, I want to impart a bit of wisdom to you that will make all these decisions much easier from now on. ¶

¶

I know it is a radical concept. Wine snobs everywhere must be gasping in disbelief. But, who cares what people think?¶

Don't stress out over which wines to have with the foods you are serving. If you are hosting a formal dinner party or an outdoor barbecue, provide a variety of wines for people to choose from and have a great time. Wine goes great with everything. ¶

You do not have to wait for a special occasion and a gourmet meal to enjoy a glass of wine. Of course, you should drink moderately and responsibly. But it's okay to enjoy a glass of wine at home on ordinary days with ordinary foods. Life is too short. If you want a glass of wine with your frozen burrito, you should have it.¶

You should drink whatever wine you like with whatever foods you like. ¶

It is a great idea to try new wines. You never know when you'll find a new favorite. Attend a wine tasting event, like the ones offered at Coho Winery, or invite a few friends over with their favorite wines. ¶

SOFTWARE ORIENTATION

Text Box Tools in the Ribbon

Before you begin working with text boxes, it is a good idea to become familiar with the new tools available in the Ribbon. When you insert a text box, the Text Box Tools appear in the Ribbon, as shown in Figure 8-45.

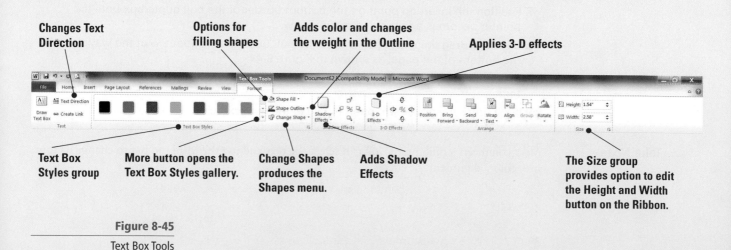

Changes Text Direction

Options for filling shapes

Adds color and changes the weight in the Outline

Applies 3-D effects

Text Box Styles group

More button opens the Text Box Styles gallery.

Change Shapes produces the Shapes menu.

Adds Shadow Effects

The Size group provides option to edit the Height and Width button on the Ribbon.

Figure 8-45

Text Box Tools

The Text Box Tools provide commands for editing text boxes. Use this figure as a reference throughout this lesson as well as the rest of this book.

APPLYING AND MANIPULATING TEXT BOXES

A **text box** is an invisible, formatted box in which you can insert and position text and/or graphic objects. Text boxes can be used for a variety of purposes. Most often, they are used to insert text within other document text or to lay out text for specific emphasis or visual interest. After you insert a text box, you can format it.

Inserting a Text Box

Word provides a gallery of built-in text boxes with pull quotes and sidebars that you can insert in a document. When you need a different kind of text box, you can draw and insert your own empty, unformatted text box. In this exercise, you will insert a preformatted text box and draw a text box.

STEP BY STEP   **Insert a Text Box**

USE the document that is open from the previous exercise.

1. At the top-left of the document, click before the H in *Harvest Celebration . . .* to position the insertion point at the beginning of the document.

2. On the Insert tab, in the Text group, click the Text Box button. A menu of built-in quote and sidebar text box styles appears.

3. Click the Contrast Sidebar option. The text box, containing placeholder text, is inserted at the top of the document.

4. The placeholder text is selected; key Coho Winery. Press Ctrl+E to center. Press Enter.

5. Key September 20XX Newsletter and press Enter.

6. Key Daily tours with complimentary. Press Shift+Enter to create a line break. Then key wine tasting. Press Enter. Creating a line break keeps lines together. For instance, if you were to align text to the left, both lines would automatically align to the left.

7. Key Monday–Saturday: 10 am to 5 pm and press Shift+Enter to create a line break.

8. Key Sunday: Noon to 5 pm. Press Ctrl+R to Align Text Right. Both lines automatically align right. Notice that you didn't need to select the lines of text; they aligned to the right together.

9. In the first column, above the Wine Facts heading, place your insertion point on the blank line.

10. Click the Insert tab, in the Text group, and click the Text Box button, then Draw Text Box. A crosshair (+) appears. Press and hold the left mouse button to draw a text box in the blank line above the Wine Facts heading. It should be approximately 2.22" wide and .95" in height. For the precise measurements, change the height and width on the Size group of the Format tab.

11. Select the four lines beginning with October 17 (do not select the hidden paragraph mark—if selected, this will extend the selection to the text box). Press and hold the left mouse button and drag and drop the text into the text box, then press Ctrl+E to center the text within the text box.

12. Select the text box until you see the four-sided move arrow to move the text box above Wine Facts and below the first paragraph. Deselect the text box.

13. Click the Insert tab, in the Text group, click the Text Box button, then Draw Text Box. A crosshair (+) appears. Draw a text box in the upper-left corner of the document. It should be approximately 1.1" wide and 2.7" in height. Key Newsletter in the text box. Your document should look similar to the one shown in Figure 8-46.

14. **SAVE** the document as *coho_newletter_draft1* in your USB flash drive in the lesson folder.

PAUSE. LEAVE the document open to use in the next exercise.

Figure 8-46

Document
with text boxes

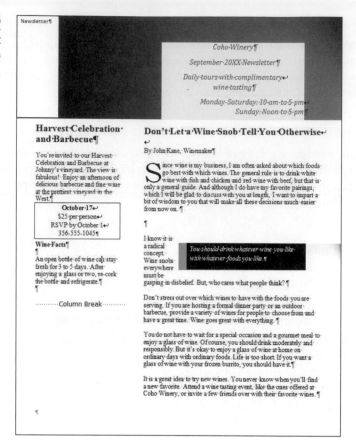

Formatting a Text Box

After you insert a text box, the Text Box Tools appear on the Format tab. In this exercise, you practice using these tools to format a text box.

STEP BY STEP　　**Format a Text Box**

USE the document that is open from the previous exercise.

1. In the first column, above Wine Facts, select the text box that contains the date, cost, and RSVP information.

CERTIFICATION READY?　**4.4.1**

How do you format a text box?

2. Click the **Format** tab, and in the Arrange group, of the Drawing Tools, click the **Position** button and select **Position in Bottom Left with Square Text Wrapping** from the drop-down menu that appears. The text box is moved to the lower-left corner of the document in the first column.

3. The text box is still selected. On the Format tab, in the Shape Styles group, click the **More** button to display the gallery of styles.

CERTIFICATION READY?　**4.4.3**

How do you apply text box styles?

4. Click the **Subtle Effect – Black Dark 1** style in the Shape Styles gallery. The text box is formatted with the preformatted style.

5. In the Shape Styles group, click the **Shape Outline** button, and then select **No Outline**. The lines around the text box are removed.

6. Click the **Edit Shape** button in the Insert Shape group to display the menu; then click **Change Shape** to display the Shapes menu.

7. Under the Basic Shape section, select the **Hexagon** shape in the first row, eighth option. The text box shape takes on a Hexagon shape.

CERTIFICATION READY?　**4.4.4**

How do you change text direction in a text box?

8. In the Size group, click the **Height** box and key **1.36"** to increase the height and display all text.

9. Remove the two blank lines above Wine Facts in the first column and the blank line in column two between the first and second paragraph.

10. Select the **Hexagon** shape, click the **Format** tab, and in the Shapes Styles group, click the **Shapes Effects** button to display the menu; then click **3D Rotation** to display the additional options in the menu. Under the Perspective section, click **Perspective Contrasting Right** (third row, first option). The shape object acquires more depth.

11. The Hexagon shape should still be selected. In the Shapes Styles group, click the **Shapes Effects** button to display the menu. Click **Shadow**, and then in the Inner section, select the second option in the third row, **Inside Bottom**. Notice the shadow toward the bottom of the Hexagon shape.

12. Select the text box that contains the Newsletter text. In the Format tab, in the Text group, click the **Text Direction** button to display the menu. Click **Rotate all Text 270°** to rotate the text in the text box.

13. The text Newsletter should be selected. Right-click and change the Font size to **36 pt** using the Mini toolbar.

14. Select the text box that contains the Newsletter text. In the Shapes Styles group, click the **Shapes Effects** button to display the menu. Click **Shadow**, and then in the Inner section, select the second option in the second row, **Inside Center**. A shadow appears inside the text box shape. Your document should resemble Figure 8-47.

Figure 8-47

Formatted document

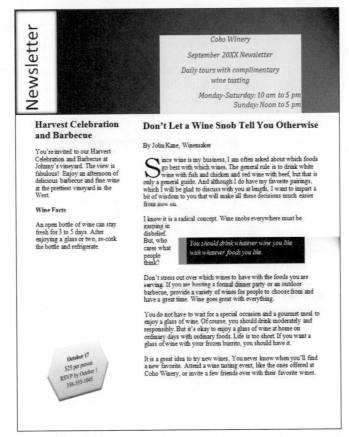

15. **SAVE** the document as *coho_newsletter_final* in your USB flash drive in the lesson folder.

PAUSE. LEAVE the document open for the next exercise.

Saving a Selection to the Text Box Gallery

After you have customized a text box style by changing the color, weight, and so on, you can save the customized style to the Text Box gallery for reuse. In this exercise, you will learn to save the newsletter text box in the gallery.

STEP BY STEP   **Save a Selection to the Text Box Gallery**

USE the document that is open from the previous exercise.

1. Select the text box that contains the Newsletter heading and winery hours information. When you click the text box, a hyphenated line appears. Click until the line changes to a single border line.

2. Click the *Insert* tab, and in the Text group, click the *Text Box* button; then choose *Save Selection to Text Box Gallery* from the menu that appears. The Create New Building Block dialog box opens, as shown in Figure 8-48.

Figure 8-48

Create New Building Block dialog box

Name box will automatically place text in box or you can key name.

Add short description of new building block.

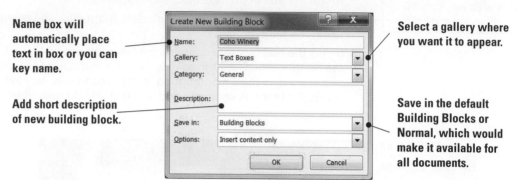

Select a gallery where you want it to appear.

Save in the default Building Blocks or Normal, which would make it available for all documents.

3. Keep the defaults as listed. Click *OK*. The saved selection of the Newsletter text box is saved in the gallery under the General section. To view, click in a blank area of the document. In the Text group, click the *Text Box* button, then scroll down to the end of the scroll bar, as shown in Figure 8-49.

Figure 8-49

Text Box gallery

Saved selections for Coho Newsletter can be found in the Text Box gallery under the General section.

Take Note   Under the General section menu of the Text Box, both text boxes appear separately. To have them appear together, the text boxes would have to be linked. Linking is an advanced feature of Word 2010 and not covered in this book.

 Ref   Building blocks were covered in Lesson 7.

4. When closing Word, a prompt will appear stating, "You have modified styles, building blocks (such as cover pages or headers), or other content that is stored in 'Building Blocks.' Do you want to save changes to 'Building Blocks'?" Click *Save*. This will allow you to continue using the customized text box that you saved.

5. **SAVE** the document with the same filename in your USB flash drive in the lesson folder and close the file.

CLOSE Word.

CERTIFICATION READY?   **4.4.2**

How do you save a selection to the Text Box gallery?

SKILL SUMMARY

In This Lesson You Learned How To:	Exam Objective	Objective Number
Insert and format pictures in a document	Add captions.	4.1.1
	Adjust position and size.	4.1.6
	Modify a shape.	4.1.5
	Apply picture styles.	4.1.3
	Apply artistic effects.	4.1.2
	Insert screenshots.	4.1.7
Insert and format shapes, WordArt, and SmartArt	Add text to a shape.	4.2.1
	Add captions.	4.2.3
	Modify text on a shape.	4.2.2
	Set shape styles.	4.2.4
	Adjust position and size of shapes.	4.2.5
Insert and format clip art	Adjust position and size of clip art.	4.3.5
	Add captions.	4.3.2
	Apply artistic effects.	4.3.3
	Organize clip art.	4.3.1
Compress and reset images	Compress pictures.	4.1.4
	Compress clip art pictures.	4.3.4
Make text graphically appealing		
Apply and manipulate text boxes	Format text boxes.	4.4.1
	Apply text box styles.	4.4.3
	Change text direction.	4.4.4
	Apply shadow effects.	4.4.5
	Apply 3D effects.	4.4.6
	Save a selection to the text box gallery.	4.4.2

Knowledge Assessment

True/False

Circle T if the statement is true or F if the statement is false.

T   F   **1.** A text box can be rotated within the document.

T   F   **2.** Images shared by email should be compressed to avoid a long download time.

T   F   **3.** A new document with a text box should be saved prior to saving to the Text Box gallery.

T   F   **4.** In a new document, images can be converted to SmartArt with captions.

T   F   **5.** By default, a drop cap will drop four lines down beside the text.

T   F   **6.** Text boxes can be saved in the gallery for later use.

T   F   **7.** Modifying a shape will open the Drawing Tools Format tab.

T   F   **8.** You can use the Remove Background tool to select what areas of an inserted image to keep and what areas to discard.

T   F   **9.** Resetting a picture will remove formatting that you have applied to it.

T   F   **10.** WordArt has new features and enhancements in Word 2010.

Multiple Choice

Select the best response for the following statements.

1. In the Clip Art pane, you can search for which media type?
   a. Illustrations
   b. Photographs
   c. Videos
   d. Audio
   e. All of the above

2. Decreasing the size of a picture file by reducing the resolution is called _____.
   a. Compressing
   b. Rotating
   c. Cropping
   d. Resizing

3. Lines, block arrows, stars, and banners are examples of what?
   a. Diagrams
   b. Shapes
   c. Flowcharts
   d. Quick Styles

4. Which tools provide options for formatting shapes?
   a. Drawing
   b. Picture
   c. Text
   d. Effects

5. The _____ will capture a picture of the whole program window.
   a. Copy button
   b. Print Screen button
   c. Screenshot button
   d. None of the above

6. Which command enables you to remove unwanted parts from a picture?
   a. SmartArt
   b. Contrast
   c. Rotate
   d. Crop

7. The Artistic Effect is available on which tool?
   a. Picture
   b. Drawing
   c. Recolor
   d. Format

8. What element can you use to provide a short descriptive label for an image in a newsletter or magazine?
   a. Caption
   b. Text
   c. Drop cap
   d. All of the above

9. Which command allows you to change the appearance of an inserted image without the use of photo-editing programs?
   a. Artistic Effect
   b. Corrections
   c. Color
   d. None of the above

10. Which command would you use to discard all the formatting changes made to a picture?
   a. Original
   b. Undo
   c. Reset
   d. Discard

Competency Assessment

Project 8-1: House for Sale

In your position at Tech Terrace Real Estate, you are asked to add a photo to a flyer that is advertising a house for sale and format it attractively.

GET READY. LAUNCH Word if it is not already running.

@ The *tech_house* document file for this lesson is available on the book companion website or in WileyPLUS.

1. **OPEN** *tech_house* from the data files for this lesson.
2. Place the insertion point on the first line of the document.
3. On the Insert tab, in the Illustrations group, click Picture.
4. Navigate to the data files for this lesson and select the housephoto file.
5. On the Format tab, in the Size group, click the Crop button.
6. Click the bottom-right cropping handle and drag up until the sidewalk is outside the selection area and release the mouse button to crop out the sidewalk.
7. On the Format tab, in the Picture Styles group, click the More button.
8. Click Center Shadow Rectangle in the gallery.
9. On the Format menu, in the Adjust group, click the Color button.
10. In the Recolor section, click Sepia.
11. **SAVE** the document as *house_flyer* in your USB flash drive in the lesson folder and **CLOSE** the file.

PAUSE. LEAVE Word open for the next project.

Project 8-2: CD Case Insert

Your friend's birthday is coming up and you have decided to burn a CD of his favorite songs. Create an insert for the front of the CD case.

GET READY. LAUNCH Word if it is not already running.

1. Create a new blank document.
2. Click the Page Layout tab, then click the Size button to open the Page Setup dialog box. Under the Paper size, change the width to 5" and height to 5". Click OK.
3. Click the Margins tab in the Page Setup group, and then click Narrow margins.
4. On the Insert tab, in the Text group, click the Text Box button and select Draw Text Box from the menu.
5. Draw a square box 4" × 4" on the page at the margins, leaving approximately half an inch of margin space on all sides.
6. On the Format tab, in the Arrange group, click the Position button and select Position in Middle Center with Square Text Wrapping.
7. Click the Shape Fill button and select Picture from the menu. Double-click the Public Picture folder, select Desert, and click Insert.
8. Click outside the text box.
9. **SAVE** the document as *cd_insert* in your USB flash drive in the lesson folder.
10. At the blank line in the text box, key My Favorite Tunes and select the text.
11. On the Insert tab, in the Text group, click the WordArt button and select Gradient Fill – Orange, Accent 6, Inner Shadow.

12. In the Text group, click the Text Effects button, select Transform, then Cascade Up.

13. **SAVE** the document in your USB flash drive in the lesson folder and then close the file.

PAUSE. LEAVE Word open for the next project.

Proficiency Assessment

Project 8-3: House for Sale Flyer

You need to make some additions and changes to the flyer completed in Project 8-1.

GET READY. LAUNCH Word if it is not already running.

1. **OPEN** the *house_flyer* you completed for Project 8-1.

2. Convert the picture to a SmartArt graphic and select Titled Picture Blocks. In the text placeholder, key House for Sale.

3. **SAVE** the document as *house_for_sale* in your USB flash drive in the lesson folder and close the file.

PAUSE. LEAVE Word open for the next project.

Project 8-4: Happy Birthday Card

Create a birthday card for your friend.

GET READY. LAUNCH Word if it is not already running.

1. Create a new blank document.

2. Change the orientation to Landscape with Narrow margins.

3. Key Happy Birthday! Insert WordArt with Gradient Fill – Purple, Accent 4 Reflection.

4. Position the WordArt graphic Middle Center with Square Text Wrapping.

5. Change the Text Effects by selecting the Shadow Effects button and Offset Top.

6. **SAVE** the document as *birthday_card* in your USB flash drive in the lesson folder and close the file.

PAUSE. LEAVE Word open for the next project.

Mastery Assessment

Project 8-5: Formatting a Flyer

A coworker at Keyser Garden & Nursery tried to create a sales flyer about roses, but was not familiar with formatting tools and ran into trouble. She asks if you can open the file and try to correct the problems and help format it.

@ The *rose_bushes* document file for this lesson is available on the book companion website or in WileyPLUS.

GET READY. LAUNCH Word if it is not already running.

1. **OPEN** *rose_bushes* from the data files for this lesson.

2. Use the skills learned in this lesson to correct the problems and format the document to look like Figure 8-50.

Figure 8-50

Rose Bush document

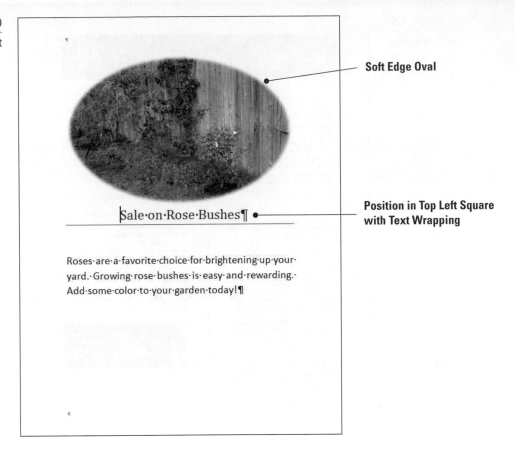

Soft Edge Oval

Position in Top Left Square
with Text Wrapping

3. **SAVE** the document as *rose_sale* in your USB flash drive in the lesson folder and close the file.

PAUSE. LEAVE Word open for the next project.

Project 8-6: Update the YMCA Newsletter

Now that you have improved your Word skills, update the YMCA newsletter created in an earlier lesson.

GET READY. LAUNCH Word if it is not already running.

@ The *ymcanewsletter* document file for this lesson is available on the book companion website or in WileyPLUS.

1. **OPEN** *ymcanewsletter* from the data files for this lesson.

2. Apply WordArt for the Fall Soccer Registration heading, using Gradient Fill – Red, Accent 1. Change the shape fill to red. Apply the Chevron Up effects. Reduce font size to 16 pt, and position as shown in Figure 8-51.

3. Create a drop cap for the *Mother's Day Out* article and the *Get Movin' Challenge* article. Change the color of the drop cap to red.

4. Replace the title of the newsletter with the Transcend Sidebar. Key the title in the sidebar and change the text color to red. Change font size to 36 pt, center.

5. Replace the membership box in the lower-right corner with the Transcend Quote text box. Change the text color to red.

Figure 8-51

YMCA newsletter

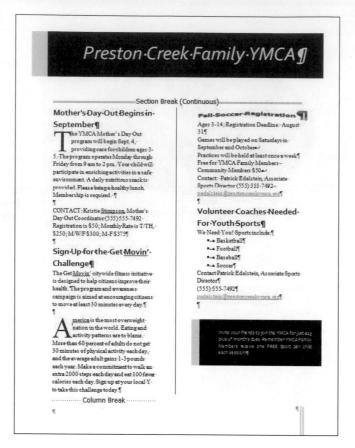

6. The newsletter should fit on one page.

7. **SAVE** the document as *ymca_newsletter_final* in your USB flash drive in the lesson folder and close the file.

CLOSE Word.

 INTERNET READY

When creating a document, you are not limited to inserting only the clip art and other media that comes installed with Word. A single click can open up a whole new world of options. At the bottom of the Clip Art pane, notice the Find more at Office.com link. You can click the link to browse dozens of categories and download clips. Next time you need to enhance your document with clip art or other media, expand your options by going online.

Search the Internet for tips on how to create reader-friendly, professional-looking newsletters, brochures, and other types of desktop publishing documents. Use the information you find to create a newsletter. Include a pull quote, drop cap, text box, and WordArt in your newsletter.

Workplace *Ready*

USING SMARTART AND WORDART

There was a time when doing anything other than simply typing sentences and paragraphs in a word processing document was unheard of. Enhancing a document with graphics used to require a separate desktop publishing programs, which were costly to purchase and often difficult to master. Word provides you with many of the same graphical capabilities you find in today's desktop publishing programs, but without the added cost or the learning curve.

As the marketing director for Alpine Ski House, a nonprofit organization that provides discounted ski equipment to underprivileged children, you are often called on to create promotional materials. These materials are used to promote your organization's mission, as well as to solicit

donations. Being a nonprofit organization, your company tries to keep its operating costs as low as possible, so you work within an extremely tight budget.

You need to create several different promotional pieces for your upcoming annual donation drive. These materials include items such as brochures, flyers, and pledge cards. Outsourcing the design work to a professional desktop publisher or printer is absolutely out of the question, so put your knowledge of Word's many formatting options to use and design the items yourself.

Circling Back 2

Create a postcard to announce the date of the conference to members and to solicit early registrations.

Project 1: Postcard

GET READY. LAUNCH Word if it is not already running.

1. Create a new blank document.

2. Click the Page Layout tab. Then, in the Page Setup group, use the Size command to create a custom paper size of **4.25″** wide by **5.5″** high.

3. Change the document setup to landscape orientation with narrow margins.

4. **SAVE** the document as *napc_postcard* in the lesson folder on your USB flash drive.

5. Click the Insert tab. Then, in the Header & Footer group, insert the Transcend (Even) header.

6. Select the Date placeholder text and key **20XX**. Change the font size and style to **18 pt bold**.

7. Select the Title placeholder text and key **NAPC PROFESSIONAL CONFERENCE**. Change the font size and style to **18 pt, bold**.

8. Double-click the body of the postcard, then key the following text:

   September 14–16

   Lakeview Towers in South Lake Tahoe, California

   Early Bird Registration $329; Regular Rate $389

   Admission to all keynotes, seminars, and breakout sessions

   Ticket to Saturday night banquet

   All meals included

   Early Bird Deadline is August 1, 20XX

   Register online at www.napc20XX.com or call 800-555-5678

9. *Do not* press Enter after the last line of keyed text.

10. Select September 14–16, change the font size and style to **20 pt Bold**, and center the text.

11. Select the Lakeview Towers. . . line of text. Change the font size to **14 pt** and center the text.

12. Click the View Ruler button to display the ruler (if it isn't displayed already).

13. Place the insertion point before the E in Early Bird Registration. Then click on the **0.5″** position to insert a left tab.

14. Press the Tab key to indent the paragraph.

15. Select the three lines of text under the registration costs information and format them as a bulleted list.

16. Select $329. Change the font color and style to Purple, Accent 4, Darker 50%, and bold.

17. On the Home tab, in the Clipboard group, use the Format Painter to copy the format of **$329** and apply it to **$389**, **August 1, 20XX**, **www.napc20XX.com**, and **800-555-5678**.

18. Beginning with Lakeview Towers, select all the remaining text. On the Page Layout tab, in the Paragraph group, adjust the spacing after the paragraph to **6 pt**.

19. Select the last two lines of text and center them.

20. In the Page Background group, use the Page Borders command to insert a 1½ pt wide box page border, using the color Purple, Accent 4, Darker 25%.

21. Use the Watermark command to create a custom horizontal watermark with the text SAVE THE DATE using Times New Roman font.

22. **SAVE** the document as *napc_postcard_draft* in the lesson folder on your USB flash drive.

23. Apply a Page Color, making sure to select, Purple, Accent 4, Lighter 80%.

24. Select the last paragraph, which begins Register online. . . .

25. On the Home tab, in the Paragraph group, use the Shading command to insert shading using the color Purple, Accent 4, Lighter 40%.

26. In the Page Layout tab, in the Themes group, use the Theme Colors menu to change the color to Median.

27. Your document should look similar to Figure 1. Make any necessary adjustments.

Figure 1

NAPC Postcard

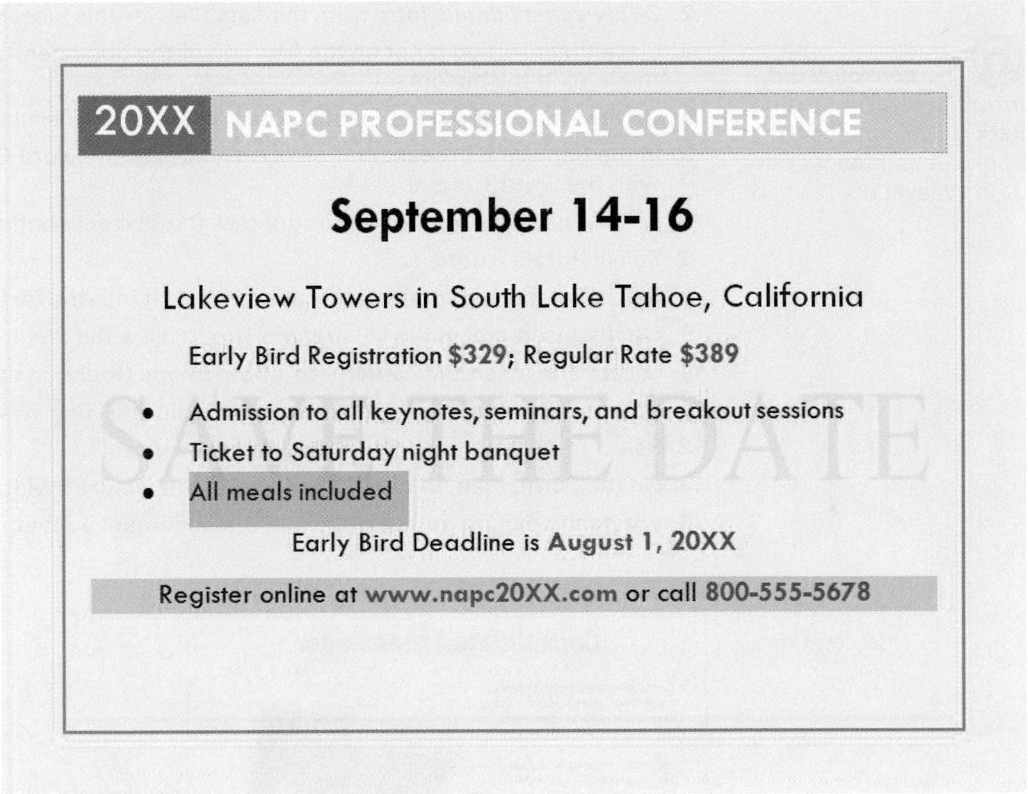

28. **SAVE** the document as *napc_postcard_final* in the lesson folder on your USB flash drive, then **CLOSE** the file.

PAUSE. LEAVE Word for the next project.

Project 2: Creating a Logo

As the scheduling manager for Consolidated Messenger, a full-service conference and retreat center, you use Word to create and revise all documents and forms used when coordinating the facility's events.

In recent years, the conference center has expanded and changed its focus. The owner needs your help in creating a new logo for all of the business' documents.

GET READY. LAUNCH Word if it is not already running.

1. **OPEN** a new, blank document and key Consolidated Messenger.

2. **SAVE** the document as *consolidated_letterhead* in the lesson folder on your USB flash drive.

3. Insert the Fill-Red A 2 Warm Matte Beval WordArt.

4. Decrease the font size to 28 pts, and right align the watermark to the right corner of the document.

5. Change the watermark width to 6.78".

6. Insert a blank footer, then key Conference and Retreat Center in the footer.

7. Change the font of the footer text to Bookman Old Style, the font size to 14 pts, and the font color to Dark Red.

8. **SAVE** the document with these changes.

PAUSE. LEAVE the *consolidated_letterhead* document open for the next project.

Project 3: Editing a Document

You are working on a promotional piece for the conference center, but you need to make some changes and add the logo.

USE the document that is open from the previous project.

1. Select the logo and copy it to the Clipboard.
2. **OPEN** ***consolidated_intro*** from the data files for this lesson.
3. Place the insertion point on the first line of the document you just opened, then paste the logo in the document.
4. On the Home tab, in the Editing group, click the **Replace** button.
5. In the Replace tab, search for all occurrences of the word Gallery and replace them with the word **Theatre**.
6. On the Insert tab, in the Text group, click the **Text Box** button.
7. Select **Puzzle Quote**.
8. Select the last paragraph, and cut and paste it into the Text Box.
9. On the Insert tab, in the Illustrations group, click the **Picture** button.
10. Locate and insert the ***conference_photo*** image (found in the data files for this lesson).
11. On the Format tab, in the Arrange group, click the **Text Wrapping** button.
12. Select **More Layout Options**, then **Square**, **left only**.
13. On the Format tab, in the Size group, set the picture's width to **2.53.**"
14. Rotate the picture and position it in the document so that it looks similar to Figure 2.

@ The ***consolidated_intro*** file for this Circling Back is available on the book companion website or in WileyPLUS.

Figure 2

Consolidated Promo

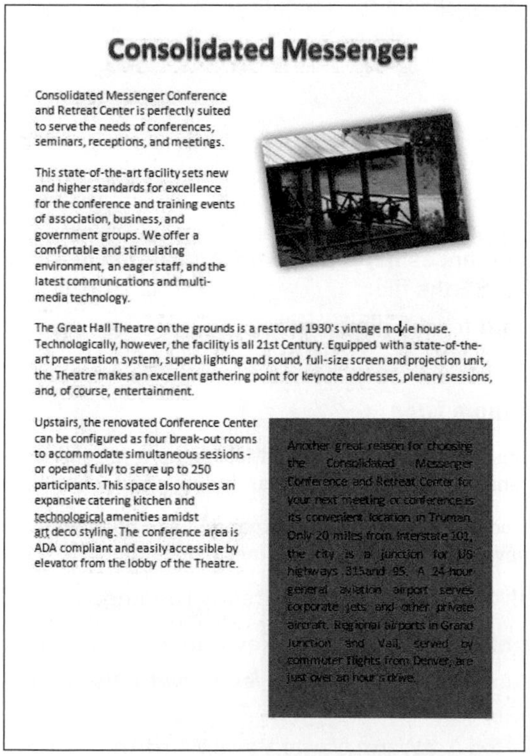

Consolidated Messenger

Consolidated Messenger Conference and Retreat Center is perfectly suited to serve the needs of conferences, seminars, receptions, and meetings.

This state-of-the-art facility sets new and higher standards for excellence for the conference and training events of association, business, and government groups. We offer a comfortable and stimulating environment, an eager staff, and the latest communications and multi-media technology.

The Great Hall Theatre on the grounds is a restored 1930's vintage movie house. Technologically, however, the facility is all 21st Century. Equipped with a state-of-the-art presentation system, superb lighting and sound, full-size screen and projection unit, the Theatre makes an excellent gathering point for keynote addresses, plenary sessions, and, of course, entertainment.

Upstairs, the renovated Conference Center can be configured as four break-out rooms to accommodate simultaneous sessions - or opened fully to serve up to 250 participants. This space also houses an expansive catering kitchen and technological amenities amidst art deco styling. The conference area is ADA compliant and easily accessible by elevator from the lobby of the Theatre.

Another great reason for choosing the Consolidated Messenger Conference and Retreat Center for your next meeting or conference is its convenient location in Truman. Only 20 miles from Interstate 101, the city is a junction for US highways 315and 95. A 24-hour general aviation airport serves corporate jets and other private aircraft. Regional airports in Grand Junction and Vail, served by commuter flights from Denver, are just over an hour's drive.

15. On the Format tab, in the Picture Styles group, click the **More** button.
16. Select the **Center Shadow Rectangle**.
17. In the Adjust group, click the **Color** button; then, under Color Tone, select **Temperature: 11200K**.
18. In the Adjust group, click the **Artistic Effects** button, then select **Texturizer**.
19. **SAVE** the document as ***consolidated_promo***.

PAUSE. LEAVE the document open to use in the next project.

Project 4: Audio-Visual Equipment Table

Create a table that contains a list of the audio and visual equipment available for rent at the conference center.

USE the ***consolidated_logo*** document that is open from the previous project.

1. Place the insertion point below the logo.
2. In Cambria, 24 pt font, key the title **Audio Visual Equipment Rental**.
3. Create a table that has three columns and eight rows.
4. Change column widths as necessary and key the information shown in Figure 3 into the table.

Figure 3

Consolidated Equipment

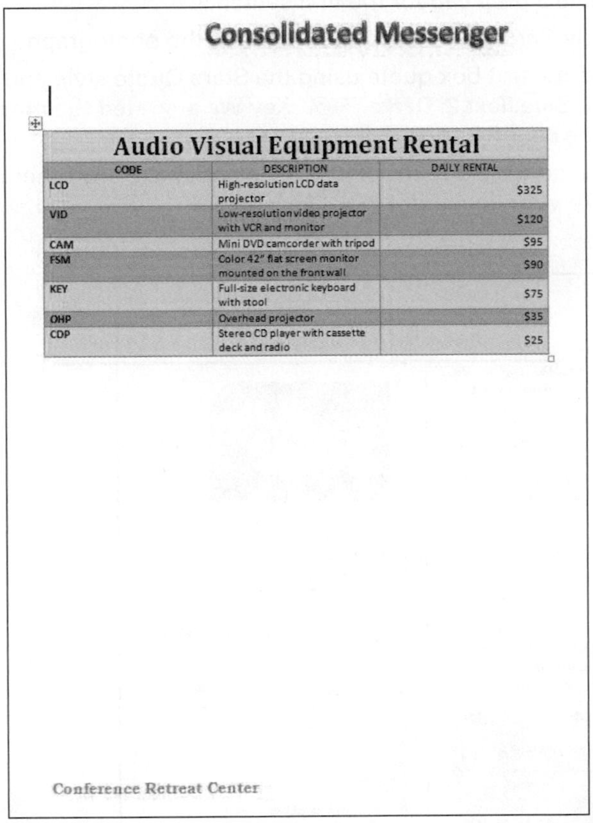

Consolidated Messenger

Audio Visual Equipment Rental		
CODE	DESCRIPTION	DAILY RENTAL
LCD	High-resolution LCD data projector	$325
VID	Low-resolution video projector with VCR and monitor	$120
CAM	Mini DVD camcorder with tripod	$95
FSM	Color 42" flat screen monitor mounted on the front wall	$90
KEY	Full-size electronic keyboard with stool	$75
OHP	Overhead projector	$35
CDP	Stereo CD player with cassette deck and radio	$25

Conference Retreat Center

5. Place the insertion point anywhere in the table.
6. On the Design tab, in the Table Styles group, click the **More** button to view a gallery of Quick Styles.
7. Scroll down and click the **Medium Grid 1 - Accent 2** option.
8. On the Layout tab, in the Data group, click the **Sort** button. Sort by the Daily Rental column in descending order.
9. Select the first row of the table.
10. On the Layout tab, in the Alignment group, click **Align Top Center**.
11. Select all numbers in the Daily Rental column.
12. On the Layout tab, in the Alignment group, click **Align Center Right**.
13. Insert a row above the first row and merge cells.
14. Drag and drop the title in the row.
15. **SAVE** the document as ***consolidated_equipment*** and **CLOSE** the file.

PAUSE. LEAVE Word open for the next project.

Project 5: Formatting a Document

You began creating a document to serve as a guide for introducing guests to the conference center. Open and format the document.

GET READY. LAUNCH Word if it is not already running.

@ The **consolidated_ guests** document file for this Circling Back is available on the book companion website or in WileyPLUS.

1. **OPEN** *consolidated_guests* from the data files for this lesson.
2. Use what you learned in this unit to complete the following tasks. You do not have to complete them in this order, but your goal is to make the document look similar to Figure 4.

   a. Use section breaks to create a section for the text, then arrange the text in two columns.

   b. Create a drop cap for the first sentence.

   c. Apply Snip Diagonal corner, White to the photograph.

   d. Create a text box quote using the Stars Quote style and change the font color to Dark Blue, Text 2, Darker 50%. Key We are rated the most unique conference center in the country.

   e. Arrange the elements on the page and make any other necessary adjustments to make your document look like Figure 4.

Figure 4

Consolidated Guide

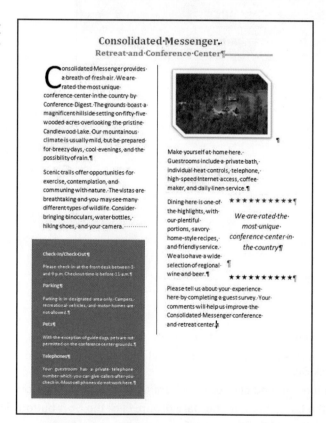

3. **SAVE** the document as *consolidated_guide* and **CLOSE** the file.

STOP. CLOSE Word.

Proofing Documents 9

LESSON SKILL MATRIX

Skill	Exam Objective	Objective Number
Validating Content by Using Spelling and Grammar Checking Options	Set grammar. Set style options.	5.1.1 5.1.2
Configuring AutoCorrect Settings	Add or remove exceptions. Turn AutoCorrect on and off.	5.2.1 5.2.2
Inserting and Modifying Comments in a Document	Insert a comment. Edit a comment. Delete a comment.	5.3.1 5.3.2 5.3.3
Viewing Comments	View comments.	5.3.4

KEY TERMS
- AutoCorrect
- balloons
- inline
- markup

BlueYonder Airlines is a large company with hundreds of employees. In your job as a human resources specialist, you are involved in hiring, employee benefit programs, and employee communications. Many of the documents you work with relate to employee issues, and you need to ensure that these documents are error free. In this lesson, you will learn to use the spelling and grammar feature, insert comments, and change the AutoCorrect settings.

SOFTWARE ORIENTATION

The Proofing and Language Groups

The Proofing group contains commands for launching Word's spelling and grammar functions, searching through references, using the Thesaurus, and counting words by characters, paragraphs, and lines. The Language group contains commands for translating words or paragraphs and an option to select a language. These and other commands for reviewing and editing Word documents are located on the Review tab, shown in Figure 9-1.

Figure 9-1

Proofing and Language groups

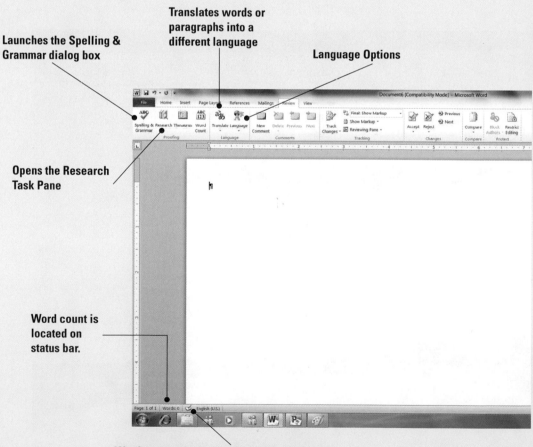

Launches the Spelling & Grammar dialog box

Translates words or paragraphs into a different language

Language Options

Opens the Research Task Pane

Word count is located on status bar.

Word automatically checks the document for errors. A blue check mark indicates the document is error free; a red check mark indicates there are errors.

Use this figure as a reference throughout this lesson and the rest of this book.

VALIDATING CONTENT BY USING SPELLING AND GRAMMAR CHECKING OPTIONS

It is a good business practice to proof a document to ensure it is error free before sharing or printing it. Word provides proofing tools such as a Spelling and Grammar checking function, Thesaurus, Word Count tracker, and a Research tool that provides searchable access to reference books and online research and business sites. All of these tools and commands are located on the Ribbon on the Review tab. The status bar also contains Word Count and Proofing Error buttons that give you quick access to some proofing features. On the status bar, Word automatically displays the document's word count.

Using the Spelling and Grammar Feature

Word's Spelling and Grammar feature automatically checks the spelling and grammar in a document. Word underlines misspelled words with a wavy red line and underlines grammatical errors with a wavy green line. Word will also detect if words are used inappropriately and it underlines the word with a wavy blue line. In other words, the word is in the dictionary but not used correctly in the context. In this exercise, you learn to use Word's automatic Spelling and Grammar feature and its options to proof and correct your document.

STEP BY STEP   **Check Spelling and Grammar**

 The *employ_offer* document file for this lesson is available on the book companion website or in WileyPLUS.

WILEY PLUS EXTRA

WileyPLUS Extra! features an online tutorial of this task.

GET READY. Before you begin these steps, **LAUNCH** Microsoft Word and **OPEN** the *employ_offer* document that is in your lesson folder.

1. Click the Review tab and, in the Proofing group, click the Spelling & Grammar button. The Spelling and Grammar dialog box opens.

2. Click the Options button in the Spelling and Grammar dialog box; the Word Options dialog box opens in Backstage view, as shown in Figure 9-2. Select Proofing in the left pane and, in the *When Correcting Spelling and Grammar in Word* section, click the Writing Style drop-down arrow and use the Grammar Only default to set the tool for checking the document's grammar, but not its writing style. Click OK to apply your changes and to launch the Spelling and Grammar tool.

Figure 9-2

Word Options in Backstage view Spelling and Grammar dialog box

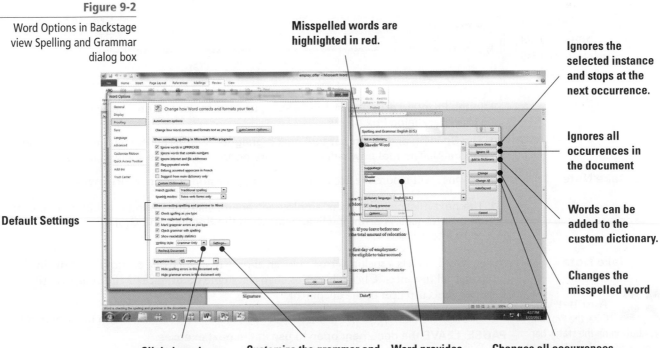

Misspelled words are highlighted in red.

Ignores the selected instance and stops at the next occurrence.

Ignores all occurrences in the document

Default Settings

Words can be added to the custom dictionary.

Changes the misspelled word

Click drop-down arrow to change Writing Style.

Customize the grammar and set style guidelines.

Word provides suggested corrections.

Changes all occurrences of the misspelled word throughout the document

3. The first word the tool highlights is Sheela, a proper noun not contained in the tool's dictionary. The Spelling and Grammar dialog box opens, with the potential error identified in the upper pane as Not in Dictionary (see Figure 9-3). With the correct spelling highlighted in the Suggestions pane, click the **Change All** button to correct all occurrences of the misspelling.

Figure 9-3

Spelling and Grammar dialog box

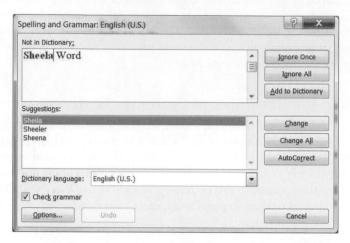

4. The word *confim* is misspelled; with the correct spelling highlighted in the Suggestions pane, click the **Change All** button.

5. The next misspelled word is *begining*. Click the **Change All** button.

6. The next misspelled word is *asistance*. Click the **Change All** button. A prompt will appear when the Spelling and Grammar check is complete. Click **OK**.

7. Word has the option for users to ignore misspelled words. In this case, the previous user ignored misspellings. You will be rechecking the document to ensure you have captured all errors. Click the **File** tab, then **Options** to open the Word Options dialog box in Backstage.

8. Select **Proofing** in the left pane and, in the *When Correcting Spelling and Grammar in Word* section, click the **Recheck Document** button. A prompt appears stating *This operation resets the spelling checker and the grammar checker so that Word will recheck words and grammar you previously checked and chose to ignore. Do you want to continue?* Click **Yes** (see Figure 9-4). The document flags misspellings.

Figure 9-4

Microsoft Word resets spelling and grammar checker

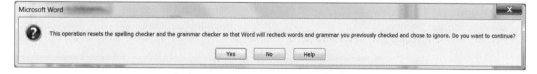

9. In the Proofing group, click the **Spelling and Grammar** button. The Spelling and Grammar dialog box opens.

10. The Spelling and Grammar tool next highlights **Suurs**. This spelling is correct, so click **Ignore All**. The tool now will ignore every occurrence of this spelling in the document.

Take Note   Ignore Once will ignore the occurrence once and will stop at the next occurrence.

11. The next misspelled work is *employmet*; again, click the **Change All** button to correct all occurrences. A prompt will appear when the Spelling and Grammar check is complete. Click **OK**.

Take Note   When Word detects a spelling error, you can choose to change one occurrence of the instance or change all instances. Click Change to change a single occurrence or click Change All to Change all occurrences in the document.

Another Way
Click the Proofing Error button on the status bar (or press the keyboard shortcut, F7). Word displays a shortcut menu with suggested words.

12. **SAVE** the document as *employment_offer* in your USB flash drive in the lesson folder.

PAUSE. LEAVE the document open to use in the next exercise.

Take Note   If you run the Spelling and Grammar command in the middle of the document, it will check from that point to the end of the document. A prompt will appear asking if you want to continue checking the document from the beginning.

Changing the Grammar Settings

Word's grammar settings enable you to determine the punctuation and other stylistic guidelines by which the program will check for and detect errors. You can change the writing style to check for grammar only or check stylistic rules, such as contractions, hyphenated and compound words, sentence length (more than 60 words), and more. In this exercise, you learn to change the style settings and customize them to meet your needs.

STEP BY STEP   **Change the Grammar Settings**

USE the document from the previous exercise.

1. Click the **File** tab and then **Options** to open the Word Options dialog box in Backstage.

2. Select **Proofing** in the left pane and in the *When Correcting Spelling and Grammar in Word* section, click the **Settings** button to open the Grammar Settings dialog box. This dialog box lists the writing style where you can customize the Grammar Only or Grammar & Style (see Figure 9-5).

Figure 9-5

Grammar Settings
dialog box

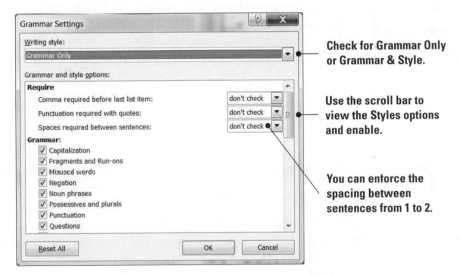

Check for Grammar Only
or Grammar & Style.

Use the scroll bar to
view the Styles options
and enable.

You can enforce the
spacing between
sentences from 1 to 2.

3. Click the **drop-down arrow** in the Writing Style section and select **Grammar & Style**.

4. Under the Require section, the *Spaces required between sentences* setting is set to **don't check**. Click the **drop-down arrow** and select **2**. You are changing the style to reflect two spaces after the punctuation between each sentence. Click **OK**.

5. In the Word Options dialog box, under *When Correcting Spelling and Grammar in Word* section, click the **Recheck Document** button, then click **OK**. A prompt appears stating that *This operation resets the spelling checker and the grammar checker so that Word will recheck words and grammar you previously checked and chose to ignore. Do you want to continue?* Click **Yes**. Click **OK** to close the Word Options dialog box. Word flags and marks the punctuation at the end of sentences with a green wavy line. Notice in the second paragraph, the document flags "are issued." Right-click on the phrase and a pop-up menu appears. It states "Passive Voice (consider revising)."

6. Repeat steps 1 and 2 to open the Grammar Settings dialog box.

7. Under the Require section, click the **drop-down arrow** to change the Spaces required between sentences setting to **don't check**.

8. Scroll down and disable all styles with the exception of **Clichés, Colloquialisms, and Jargons**. One style is kept active. Click **OK**.

9. In the Word Options dialog box, under the *When Correcting Spelling and Grammar in Word* section, click the **Recheck Document** button. A prompt appears stating that

This operation resets the spelling checker and the grammar checker so that Word will recheck words and grammar you previously checked and chose to ignore. Do you want to continue? Click **Yes**. Click **OK** to close the Word Options dialog box. Notice "are issued" in the second paragraph is no longer flagged. In the third paragraph, the phrase "in the amount of" is flagged with a wavy line.

10. When you right-click on the phrase, the pop-up menu appears. Click **About This Sentence**. The Help menu appears, indicating this is a cliché and the marked word or phrase may be overused or unnecessary to the meaning of your sentence. To remove it, you would repeat steps 6–9 to disable Clichés, Colloquialisms, and Jargons.

11. Click the **Options** button in the Spelling and Grammar dialog box; the Word Options dialog box opens in Backstage view. Select **Proofing** in the left pane and, in the *When Correcting Spelling and Grammar in Word* section, click the **Writing Style** command box **drop-down arrow** and select **Grammar Only** to set the tool for checking the document's grammar. Click **OK** to apply your changes.

12. **SAVE** your document in your USB flash drive in the lesson folder.

PAUSE. LEAVE the document open to use in the next exercise.

CERTIFICATION READY? 5.1.1

How do you set grammar options?

CERTIFICATION READY? 5.1.2

How do you change the style options?

The Bottom Line

CONFIGURING AUTOCORRECT SETTINGS

The Proofing pane of the Word Options dialog box also contains Word's AutoCorrect setting options. **AutoCorrect** is a feature that replaces symbols, commonly misspelled words, and abbreviations for specific text strings. For instance, to add the Trademark symbol, key **(TM)** and it automatically inserts the symbol ™. The bottom line, AutoCorrect saves time in keying text. You can manage the list of exceptions in the AutoCorrect Exceptions dialog box, such as not capitalizing the first letter of an abbreviation; for example, etc. You can disregard two initial caps, such as a student ID, or you can customize and add or delete text. AutoCorrect is on by default, but you can use the AutoCorrect options to disable or enable the feature. In this lesson, you learn to use AutoCorrect to replace text and insert symbols in your document, and you practice turning the AutoCorrect feature on and off.

STEP BY STEP **Configure AutoCorrect Options**

USE the document from the previous exercise.

1. Click the **File** tab to open the Backstage view.
2. Click the **Options** button to display the Word Options dialog box.
3. Click **Proofing** on the left pane to display the Proofing options in the right pane of the screen.
4. Click the **AutoCorrect Options** button to display the AutoCorrect dialog box with the AutoCorrect tab open, as shown in Figure 9-6. Notice that the dialog box title indicates that the program is set to check and correct text based on U.S. English.

Figure 9-6

AutoCorrect dialog box

Default settings for AutoCorrect. To disable, click the appropriate check box.

As you key text, it will automatically be corrected.

When keying a text string, it automatically changes in your document.

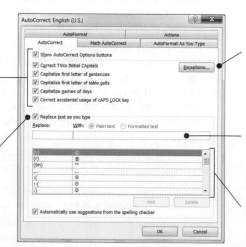

AutoCorrect Exceptions dialog box allows you to manage the exceptions.

You can add your own AutoText elements here.

All AutoText (common misspellings, acronyms, symbols, etc.) and replacements are listed here.

CERTIFICATION READY? 5.2.1

How do you add a word to AutoCorrect?

 Another Way
You also can use the Find and Replace command to replace words or phrases.

CERTIFICATION READY? 5.2.1

How do you delete a word or phrase from AutoCorrect?

5. You want AutoText to replace the typed abbreviation BYA, with the full name, Blue Yonder Airlines, so you can save time keying in text. In the Replace box, key **BYA**. In the *With* box, key **Blue Yonder Airlines**.

6. Check that you have spelled the replacement text correctly, then click the **Add** button to add your AutoText replacement to the list. Click **OK** to close the AutoCorrect dialog box, and then click **OK** to close the Word Options dialog box and return to your document.

7. In the first paragraph at end of the first sentence, place your insertion point after *r* in *for* and press the **Spacebar** once.

8. Key **BYA** and press the **Spacebar** once. BYA is replaced with Blue Yonder Airlines. Delete the extra space before the punctuation.

9. Repeat steps 1–4 to open the AutoCorrect Options dialog box.

10. In the Replace box, key **BYA**. BYA and Blue Yonder Airlines are highlighted in the list of AutoText exceptions, as shown in Figure 9-7. Click the **Delete** button to remove the highlighted entries. Now, if you key BYA in your document and press the **Spacebar**, no action will occur.

Figure 9-7

AutoCorrect dialog box

BYA. Notice it appears below.

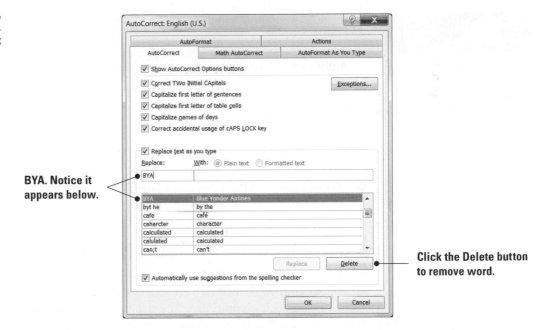

Click the Delete button to remove word.

11. **SAVE** the file as *employment_offer1* in your USB flash drive in the lesson folder.

12. Double-click the Blue Yonder Airlines header to open the *Header and Footer Tools Design* tab. Place your insertion point after the *s* in Airlines in the heading. Blue Yonder Airlines is the trademark name for the company and requires the trademark symbol after the name.

13. Key **(TM)** to insert the trademark symbol after Airlines. Insert the trademark symbol in the document.

14. By default, the AutoCorrect Options are enabled. To disable AutoCorrect, repeat steps 1–4 to open the AutoCorrect Options dialog box. Click to **clear the check mark** from *Replace text as you type*. The feature is off and the *Automatically Use Suggestions from the Spelling Checker* option is shaded gray to show that it's unavailable. To enable the AutoCorrect function, click the **check box** again; a check mark appears in the box and the Automatically Use Suggestions from the Spelling Checker option again becomes available. (Check with your instructor to determine whether you should leave AutoCorrect disabled or enabled.)

CERTIFICATION READY? 5.2.2

How do you enable or disable AutoCorrect?

Figure 9-8

AutoCorrect Exceptions dialog box

You can add and delete your own abbreviations.

You can add and delete your own personalized initial caps in words.

You can add other corrections with an option to delete.

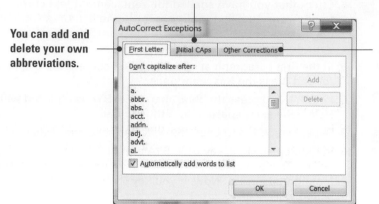

CERTIFICATION
READY? **5.2.1**

How do you add or delete text in the AutoCorrect Exceptions dialog box?

15. Click the Exceptions button. The AutoCorrect Exceptions dialog box opens (see Figure 9-8).

16. Click the INitial CAps tab and key IDs, then click the Add button. Click OK to close the AutoCorrect Exceptions dialog box.

17. Click OK to close the AutoCorrect dialog box, and then click OK to close the Word Options dialog box.

18. At the end of the fourth paragraph, key Employee IDs will be provided to you on location. Adding IDs to the exceptions will avoid flagging the word.

19. Click OK to close the AutoCorrect Options dialog box. Click OK to close the Word Options dialog box.

20. **SAVE** the document in your USB flash drive in the lesson folder.

PAUSE. LEAVE the document open to use in the next exercise.

INSERTING AND MODIFYING COMMENTS IN A DOCUMENT

The Bottom Line

Word's Comment feature enables reviewers to insert comments or questions in documents without interrupting the flow of existing text. A **markup** keeps the original document along with changes made, such as comments. The right side of the document is shaded in gray and is the markup area. **Balloons** are markups used for comments made in the document and appear as colored balloons on the right side of the document. On the Review tab, using the Comments group (Figure 9-9), comments can be placed **inline** with text, which is another form for displaying the markup. Word labels each comment balloon with your initials and the sequential comment number.

Figure 9-9

Comments group

Move to Previous Comment

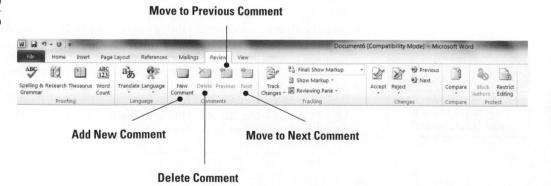

Add New Comment

Move to Next Comment

Delete Comment

Inserting, Editing, and Deleting a Comment

You use the commands in the Comments group to insert and delete comments, and to move among comments in a document. You can edit or delete comment text by clicking and typing directly in the comment or by using the shortcut menu. In this exercise, you learn to insert, edit, and delete comments.

STEP BY STEP   **Insert, Edit, and Delete a Comment**

USE the document from the previous exercise.

1. In the first sentence of the second paragraph, select $55,000.

2. Click the Review tab and, in the Comments group, click the New Comment button. A comment balloon appears in the right margin of the document, labeled with initials and the comment number. (Later in this lesson, you will learn how to change these initials to match your initials.)

3. Key Will you please confirm if the salary is correct? (see Figure 9-10).

Figure 9-10

Document with comment

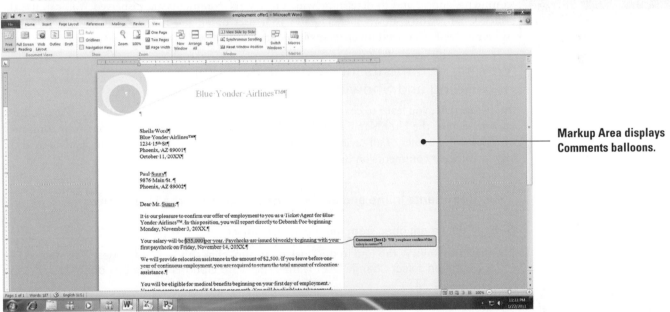

Markup Area displays Comments balloons.

CERTIFICATION READY?   **5.3.1**

How do you insert a comment?

CERTIFICATION READY?   **5.3.2**

How do you edit a comment?

4. In the first sentence of the third paragraph, select $2,500.

5. In the Comments group, click the New Comment button; a second comment balloon appears in the right margin, labeled with initials and a number.

6. In the new comment balloon, key The relocation amount is $5,000.

7. Click the Previous button in the Comments group to move back to the first comment.

8. Place the insertion point at the end of the text in the first comment, and key I need a response by 5 pm today. You have edited the comment by adding more information.

9. Click the Next button in the Comments group to move to the second comment balloon. Click the Delete button drop-down arrow in the Comments group, and then select Delete from the drop-down menu, as shown in Figure 9-11. The comment is removed, and Word renumbers any subsequent comments in your document.

Figure 9-11

Comment Delete menu

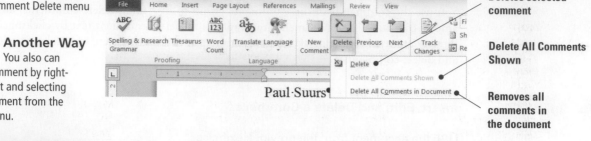

Deletes selected comment

Delete All Comments Shown

Removes all comments in the document

Another Way
You also can delete a comment by right-clicking on it and selecting Delete Comment from the shortcut menu.

10. **SAVE** the document as *employment_offer_comments* in your USB flash drive in the lesson folder.

PAUSE. LEAVE the document open to use in the next exercise.

CERTIFICATION READY?   **5.3.3**

How do you delete a comment?

The Bottom Line

VIEWING COMMENTS

By default, Word displays comments in balloons, but it also can display **inline** comments in ScreenTips or in a separate reviewing pane. Inline comments are hidden; the reviewer's initials appear in brackets beside the selected text. The Show Markup menu allows you to change how comments appear and to determine which reviewers' comments are displayed. You can use the Track Changes drop-down menu to add your user name and initials to the list of reviewers. When in Draft view, certain elements in a document are not visible.

Viewing Comments Inline and as Balloons and Hiding and Showing Reviewer Comments

In this exercise, you learn to change the comments display from inline to balloons. You also learn how to change the User Name that Word displays with comments added from your computer, to display the names of all reviewers who insert comments in your document, and to turn the display of their comments on or off.

STEP BY STEP   **View Comments Inline and as Balloons and Change the User Name**

USE the document open from the previous exercise.

1. Click the **Review** tab and in the Tracking group, click the **Track Changes drop-down arrow**, then select **Change User Name**. The Word Options dialog box opens, as shown in Figure 9-12.

Figure 9-12

Word Options

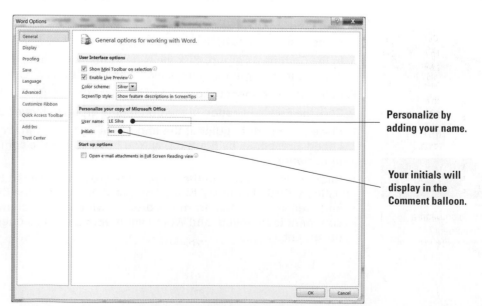

Personalize by adding your name.

Your initials will display in the Comment balloon.

2. In the Personalize Your Copy Of Microsoft Office section, key [your name] in the User Name box, then key [your initials] in the box below. Click **OK** to apply your changes and close the Word Options dialog box.

3. By default, Word displays comments and formatting in balloons, as shown in Figure 9-13. Deletions and additions to text appear inline and when in Draft view, these are also shown inline.

Figure 9-13

Show Markup

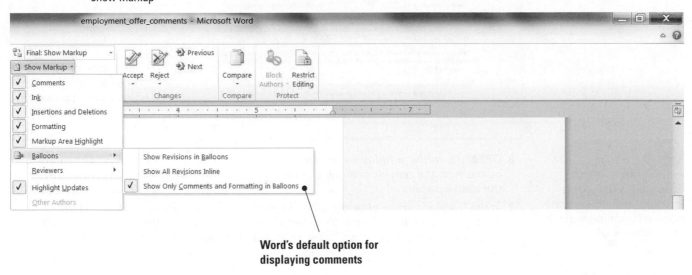

Word's default option for displaying comments

4. In the Tracking group, click the **Show Markup button drop-down arrow** to display the menu. Options are available on how markup should display in the document. Select **Balloons**, then **Show All Revisions Inline**. Inline comments are hidden and indicated by bracketed reviewer initials beside the selected text, as shown in Figure 9-14.

Figure 9-14

Reviewer initials

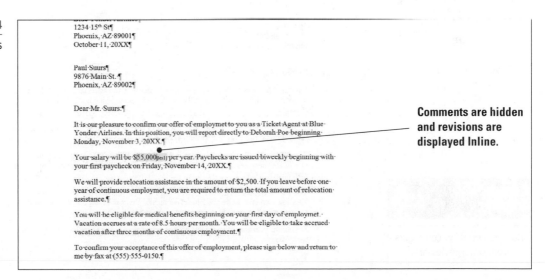

Comments are hidden and revisions are displayed Inline.

5. Position the mouse pointer over your initials. The comment appears in a ScreenTip, as shown in Figure 9-15.

6. In the Tracking group, click the **drop-down arrow** in the Show Markup button; select **Balloons**, then **Show Revisions in Balloons**. The comment is shown in a balloon in the Markup area. If there are formatting revisions and text changes in this document, only the comments will display in balloons.

7. **SAVE** the document as *employment_offer_comments2* in your USB flash drive in the lesson folder and close the file.

Figure 9-15

Comment displayed
in ScreenTip

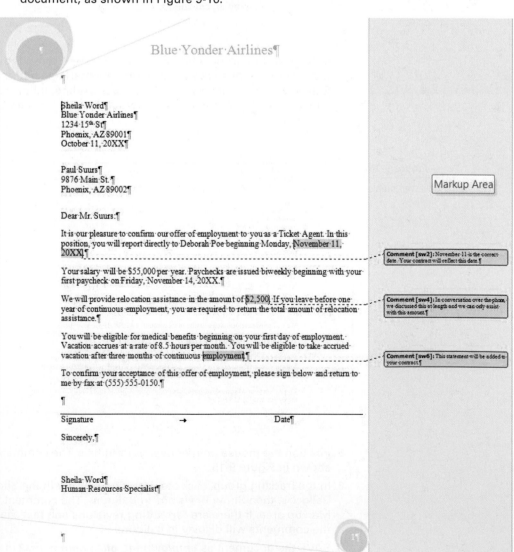

Hover the cursor over
reviewer's initials to
read hidden comments.

@ The *initial_
employment_offer*
document file for this
lesson is available on the
book companion website
or in WileyPLUS.

8. **OPEN** the *initial_employment_offer* document in the lesson folder. The document opens with the default settings displaying comments and formatting changes in the markup area.

9. In the Tracking group, click the Show Markup button drop-down arrow and select Reviewers; then in the drop-down list of All Reviewers, click the check box beside LE Silva to remove the check mark. His comments no longer are displayed in the document, as shown in Figure 9-16.

Figure 9-16

Document displaying only
one reviewer's comments

CERTIFICATION
READY?   **5.3.4**

How do you view comments
from other reviewers?

CERTIFICATION
READY?   **5.3.4**

How do you view
comments inline?

CERTIFICATION READY? 5.3.4

How do you view comments as balloons?

10. **SAVE** the document in your USB flash drive in the lesson folder.

PAUSE. LEAVE the document open to use in the next exercise.

Displaying the Reviewing Pane

Comments are listed in sequence and tracked on the Reviewing Pane either vertically or horizontally on your screen. When the Reviewing Pane opens, a summary displays the number of insertions, deletions, moves, formatting, and comments that have been made in the document. In this lesson, you learn to change the review pane's display from vertical to horizontal.

STEP BY STEP **Display the Reviewing Pane**

USE the document that is open from the previous exercise.

1. Click the Review tab and in the Tracking group, click the Reviewing Pane drop-down arrow, and select Reviewing Pane Horizontal from the drop-down menu. The comments now display in a horizontal pane across the bottom of the Word window, as shown in Figure 9-17.

Figure 9-17

Reviewing Pane Horizontal

Summary detail number of revisions made in document

Resize Reviewing Pane to view additional revisions.

Reviewer's full name appears

Date and time comments were modified and saved

Comments by (sw) and numbered

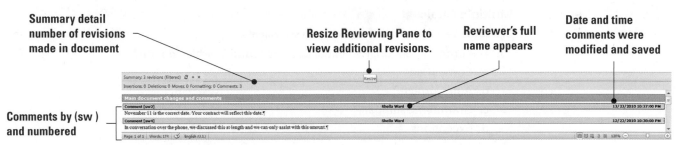

2. To view the Reviewing Pane vertically, repeat step 1 and select Reviewing Pane Vertical. The Reviewing Pane will display vertically along the left side of the document.

3. Click the X on the Vertical Reviewing Pane to close or click the Reviewing Pane button to close.

4. **SAVE** the document in your USB flash drive in the lesson folder and close the file.

STOP. CLOSE Word without saving.

SKILL SUMMARY

In This Lesson You Learned How To:	Exam Objective	Objective Number
Validate content by using spelling and grammar checking options	Set grammar. Set Style options.	5.1.1 5.1.2
Configure AutoCorrect settings	Add or remove exceptions. Turn AutoCorrect on and off.	5.2.1 5.2.2
Insert and modify comments in a document	Insert a comment. Edit a comment. Delete a comment.	5.3.1 5.3.2 5.3.3
View a comment	View comments.	5.3.4

Knowledge Assessment

True/False

Circle T if the statement is true or F if the statement is false.

T   F   **1.** The proofing screen contains options to change how Word corrects and formats text.

T   F   **2.** You can change your name and initials in the Tracking group.

T   F   **3.** You should always proof documents before sharing them.

T   F   **4.** AutoCorrect can be found in the Backstage view Display option.

T   F   **5.** By default, comments are shown inline.

T   F   **6.** AutoCorrect cannot be turned off.

T   F   **7.** Inline comments are placed in curly brackets.

T   F   **8.** You can right-click on a comment and use the shortcut menu to delete the comment.

T   F   **9.** The default Writing Styles setting is Grammar and Styles.

T   F   **10.** The status bar contains a proofing error button for quick access.

Multiple Choice

Select the best response for the following statements.

1. The proofing option, Two Initial Caps, is found in which option?

   a. CorrectCaps

   b. AutoCorrect

   c. Grammar Settings

   d. Exceptions

2. Which command(s) open the Spelling and Grammar feature?

   a. F7

   b. Shift+F7

   c. Spelling and Grammar button

   d. a and c

3. Exceptions can be added to AutoCorrect

   a. By not capitalizing the first letter of an abbreviation

   b. By ignoring the INitial CAps

   c. Other Corrections

   d. All of the above

4. Comments are used to add _____ to Word documents.

   a. Concerns

   b. Questions

   c. Reminders

   d. All of the above

5. The Comments ScreenTips appear in which view?

   a. Showing Revisions in Balloons

   b. Show All Revisions Inline

   c. Show Only Comments and Formatting in Balloons

   d. ScreenTips display only on the Ribbon

6. How do you display only one reviewer's comments in a Word document containing multiple reviewers' comments?

   a. Leave the check mark in the All Reviewers check box.

   b. Deselect the All Reviewers check box and place a check mark beside only that one reviewer's name.

   c. This feature only displays all reviewers' comments.

   d. This feature cannot display one reviewer's comments.

7. The Vertical Reviewing Pane displays

   a. To the right of the document

   b. Below the Ribbon

   c. To the left of the document

   d. Above the status bar

8. A summary of the total number of comments in a document will appear in the

   a. Vertical Reviewing Pane

   b. Horizontal Reviewing Pane

   c. Status bar

   d. a and b

9. The Personalizing Your Copy Of Microsoft Office options

   a. Are located in Backstage view

   b. Are located in the Tracking group

   c. Cannot be changed

   d. Automatically change when Word is launched

10. You can insert comments in which of the following types of documents?

   a. Research papers

   b. Resumes

   c. Marketing plans

   d. All of the above

Competency Assessment

Project 9-1: Research Paper

You are writing a paper about the health benefits of wine and are ready to check the spelling in your document.

GET READY. LAUNCH Word if it is not already running.

@ The *benefits_of_ wine* document file for this lesson is available on the book companion website or in WileyPLUS.

1. **OPEN** the *benefits_of_wine* document from the lesson folder.

2. On the Review tab in the Proofing group, click the Spelling and Grammar button.

3. Click the Options button in the Spelling and Grammar dialog box to change the Writing Style. The Word Options screen opens in Backstage view. Select Proofing and under the section *When correcting spelling and grammar in Word*, click the drop-down arrow beside the Writing Style command box and select Grammar Only. Click OK.

4. The Spelling and Grammar check will stop on the words/phrases listed in the following table; for each misspelled word, take the action indicated in the table.

Misspelled Word	Corrected Word	Action to Take
Choleterol	cholesterol	Change All
polyphenl	Polyphenol	Change All
But what about white wine?		Ignore Rule
Stuttaford		Ignore All
Healthspan		Ignore All
Teissedre		Ignore All
The USDA makes it clear. . .		Ignore All
cancers		Ignore All
Agatston		Ignore All

5. When the prompt appears stating that the spelling and grammar check is completed, click **OK**.

6. **SAVE** the document as *benefits_of_wine_final* in your USB flash drive in the lesson folder.

LEAVE Word open for the next project.

Project 9-2   Books and Beyond Handbook

You work for Books and Beyond and the manager needs your assistance in using the AutoCorrect Options in Word. Your task is to manually proof the document and locate the six occurrences of Books and Beyond. You will be using the AutoCorrect to add © after Books and Beyond for each occurrence.

GET READY. LAUNCH Word if it is not already running.

@ The *handbook_ acknowledge* document file for this lesson is available on the book companion website or in WileyPLUS.

1. **OPEN** the *handbook_acknowledge* document in the lesson folder.

2. In the first paragraph, first sentence, place your insertion point after d in Beyond. Key **(C)** to insert the copyright symbol in the document.

3. In the first paragraph, second sentence, place your insertion point after d in Beyond. Key **(C)** to insert the copyright symbol in the document.

4. In the second paragraph, second sentence, place your insertion point after d in Beyond. Key **(C)** to insert the copyright symbol in the document.

5. **SAVE** the document as *handbook_acknowledge_update* in your USB flash drive in the lesson folder.

LEAVE the document open for the next project.

Proficiency Assessment

Project 9-3: Books and Beyond Handbook Review

Sonny is one of the managers at Books and Beyond and has asked you to comment on the document.

GET READY. LAUNCH Word if it is not already running.

1. For every occurrence of Books and Beyond, add the following comments: The document should be consistent throughout. Consider using B & B throughout or spell out.

2. Locate the title The Vice President of Operations and add the following comment: The Vice President of Operations is replaced with the new title, Vice President of Support Services.

3. **SAVE** the document as *handbook_mycomments* in your USB flash drive in the lesson folder.

LEAVE Word open for the next project.

Project 9-4: Showing Comments as Inline

Sonny is out of town and is interested in reviewing any comments you may have regarding the handbook. You will be emailing this document to him with comments displayed as inline. You will be working with the previous document from Project 9-3.

GET READY. LAUNCH Word if it is not already running.

1. Change the Show Markup settings to display comments as *inline* only.
2. SAVE the document as *handbook_inline_comments* in your USB flash drive in the lesson folder and close the file.

LEAVE Word open for the next project.

Mastery Assessment

Project 9-5: Blue Yonder Airlines Stock Agreements

Blue Yonder Airlines employs you, and one of your recent responsibilities is proofing all documents. The stockholders agreement document contains many misspelled words. Use the Spelling and Grammar check to correct the misspellings.

GET READY. LAUNCH Word if it is not already running.

1. **OPEN** the *stock_agreement* document from the lesson folder.
2. Locate all errors and correct them.
3. **SAVE** the document as *stock_agreement_final* in your USB flash drive in the lesson folder and close the file.

LEAVE Word open for the next project.

 The *stock_agreement* document file for this lesson is available on the book companion website or in WileyPLUS.

Project 9-6: Job Description

The job descriptions for flight attendants have been emailed to all flight attendants for their comments. Review the comments and display comments inline with the vertical reviewing pane.

GET READY. LAUNCH Word if it is not already running.

1. **OPEN** the *flightattendant* document from the lesson folder.
2. Change the comments to display as inline.
3. Display the reviewing pane vertically.
4. **SAVE** the document as *flight_attendant_comments* in your USB flash drive in the lesson folder.

CLOSE Word.

The *flightattendant* document file for this lesson is available on the book companion website or in WileyPLUS.

INTERNET READY

In this lesson, you learned how to configure AutoCorrect. You would like to find additional information about this tool that Microsoft may have. Access the Microsoft website and select three links of your choice and prepare a short two-page report to provide to your instructor.

10 Applying References and Hyperlinks

LESSON SKILL MATRIX

Skill	Exam Objective	Objective Number
Applying a Hyperlink	Apply a hyperlink to text or graphic.	6.1.1
	Use a hyperlink as a bookmark.	6.1.2
	Link a hyperlink to an email address.	6.1.3
Creating Endnotes and Footnotes in a Document	Demonstrate the difference between endnotes and footnotes.	6.2.1
	Configure footnote and endnote format.	6.2.3
	Manage footnote and endnote locations.	6.2.2
	Change footnote and endnote numbering.	6.2.5
	Presentation.	6.2.4
Creating a Table of Contents in a Document	Use default formats.	6.3.1
	Set tab leaders.	6.3.4
	Set alignment.	6.3.3
	Set levels.	6.3.2
	Modify styles.	6.3.5
	Update a table of contents.	6.3.6

KEY TERMS

- **bookmark**
- **endnote**
- **footnote**
- **hyperlink**
- **tab leader**
- **table of contents**

You have just begun a new career as a project manager at Proseware, Inc., a web development company. One of the responsibilities of this position includes meeting with new clients who want to develop new websites or redesign existing sites. To help make this process easier, you decide to create a template that you can use to plan website development for each client. Although the template is only about seven pages long, you know it will get longer as the sections are filled in and completed for each client. In this lesson, you will apply a hyperlink to text and graphics, apply bookmarks in a document, link to an email address, create endnotes and footnotes, and create a table of contents so that all sections of the document can be referred to easily among client representatives and coworkers during the planning and development of websites.

UNDERSTANDING HYPERLINKS

The Bottom Line

A **hyperlink** is a location to an internal or external page that readers follow when opening a new page. To access the page, you would press the left mouse button on the hyperlink. Hyperlinks can be applied to text or graphics and these can be in the document where the link would jump from one page to the next. Hyperlinks can be external links to a web page on the Internet. The hyperlink follows a specific target location within the document as a bookmark, as an email address, or to an external location. Hyperlinks can be applied to text or graphics. In this exercise, you learn to apply a hyperlink to text and an image, remove a hyperlink and ScreenTip, add a bookmark, and add an email as a hyperlink.

Applying a Hyperlink

Working with hyperlinks quickly takes you to the location within the document, web page, bookmark, or email address. In this exercise, you learn to insert a hyperlink in text and an image, add a ScreenTip, and remove a hyperlink and ScreenTip.

STEP BY STEP   **Apply a Hyperlink**

The *proseware_weblayout* document file for this lesson is available on the book companion website or in WileyPLUS.

GET READY. Before you begin these steps, be sure to launch Microsoft Word.

1. **OPEN** the *proseware_weblayout* document from the lesson folder.
2. On the Home tab, in the Paragraph group, click the Show/Hide button to enable.
3. Select the company name, Proseware, Inc.
4. On the Insert tab, in the Links group, click the Hyperlink button to open the Insert Hyperlink dialog box as shown in Figure 10-1. The Insert Hyperlink dialog box opens.

Figure 10-1

Insert Hyperlink dialog box

WILEY **PLUS** *EXTRA*

WileyPLUS Extra! features an online tutorial of this task.

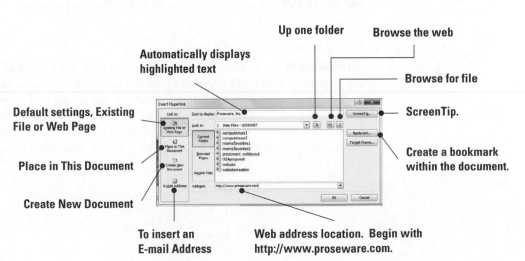

Automatically displays highlighted text

Up one folder   Browse the web

Browse for file

Default settings, Existing File or Web Page

Place in This Document

Create New Document

ScreenTip.

Create a bookmark within the document.

To insert an E-mail Address

Web address location. Begin with http://www.proseware.com.

5. In the Address box, key http://www.proseware.com/. Click OK. You have created a link for the company to link directly to the external website.

6. In text, the company name appears underlined in blue and is linked. Since this is a fictitious company, the link will direct you to the Microsoft official website. To check the link, press the Ctrl key and click to go directly to the website. Notice the ScreenTip appearing above the hyperlink. When you click on the link, the hyperlink changes to another color. Also, when you hover over the link, you will see the ScreenTip.

7. Select the first image to the top left. The next step is to link the graphic to the company website.

8. In the Links group, click the Hyperlink button. With the dialog box open, key http://www.proseware.com. As you begin keying, Autofill recognizes text and completes the entry for you.

9. Click the ScreenTip button. The Set Hyperlink ScreenTip dialog box appears. Key PWI. Click OK to close the Set Hyperlink ScreenTip dialog box. Click OK to close the Edit Hyperlink dialog box.

10. Place your insertion point over the first image and notice the ScreenTip PWI appears.

11. Repeat steps 6–8 for the second image and test your links.

12. **SAVE** the document as *proseware_weblayout_links* in your USB flash drive in the lesson folder.

PAUSE. LEAVE the document open to use in the next exercise.

CERTIFICATION READY?   6.1.1

How do you apply a hyperlink to text?

CERTIFICATION READY?   6.1.1

How do you apply a hyperlink to a graphic?

Another Way
Using the shortcut Ctrl+K will open the Insert Hyperlink dialog box.

Removing a Hyperlink and ScreenTip

Once a hyperlink is removed, it will no longer be linked to a document or external web location. Hyperlinks are removed the same way for text and images. After a ScreenTip is deleted, it will not display in the hyperlink. In this exercise, you learn to remove a hyperlink and ScreenTip.

STEP BY STEP   **Remove a Hyperlink and ScreenTip**

USE the document open from the previous exercise.

1. Select the second image.

2. Use the shortcut keyboard command Ctrl+K to access the Insert Hyperlink dialog box.

3. Click Remove Link to remove the hyperlink.

4. Select the first image and on the Links group, click the Hyperlink button.

5. Click the ScreenTip button and delete PWI. Click OK.

6. Place your insertion point over the first image and notice the ScreenTip no longer appears.

7. **SAVE** the document as *proseware_weblayout_links1* in your USB flash drive in the lesson folder.

PAUSE. LEAVE the document open to use in the next exercise.

Adding a Bookmark

A **bookmark** is a location or a selection of text that you name and identify for future reference. For instance, you may like to revisit a page in a document and locate text; in this case, you could use the Bookmark dialog box and get there quickly using the name of the bookmark you created. Bookmark names can contain numbers, but they must begin with a letter. You cannot have any spaces in a bookmark name, so use an underscore to separate words or put the words together—for example, Trade_Secrets or TradeSecrets. In this exercise, you learn to add a bookmark inside a document.

STEP BY STEP   **Add Bookmark**

USE the document open from the previous exercise.

1. Select the Web Site Creation Strategy text.

2. On the Insert tab in the Links group, click the Hyperlink button. In the Insert Hyperlink dialog box, click the Bookmark button. The Select Place in Document dialog box opens.

3. Scroll up and select Top of the Document as shown in Figure 10-2. Click OK to close the Select Place in Document dialog box. Notice the Address bar in the Insert Hyperlink dialog box displays in the box #Top of the Document—this will link to the beginning of the document. Click OK to close the Insert Hyperlink dialog box.

Figure 10-2

Select Place in Document dialog box

Bookmark is set to link to top of document.

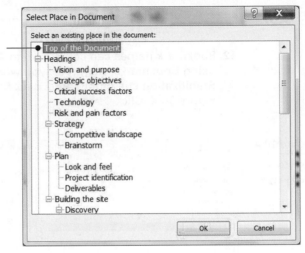

4. Press Ctrl+End to move to the end of the document.

5. Press Enter after the email image and key Back to Top.

6. Select Back to Top then press Ctrl+K to open the Insert Hyperlink dialog box.

7. Click the Bookmark button and scroll up and select Top of the Document. Click OK twice. The Back to Top link changes to a Bookmark link.

8. Test the Bookmark by pressing and holding the Ctrl key and clicking the Back to Top link. Notice that it automatically goes to the top of the document.

9. **SAVE** the document as *proseware_weblayout_links2* in your USB flash drive in the lesson folder.

10. The next step is to create bookmarks based on headings and use the Go To command to go directly to the bookmark.

11. On page 2, double-click to select the word Strategy. In the Links group, click the Bookmark button and key the word Strategy in the box. Click Add and the word Strategy is added, as shown in Figure 10-3. Complete step 11 again for the headings listed in the table below until the additional five text items are bookmarked. In the last item after clicking Add, click OK to close the Bookmark dialog box.

Plan
Discovery
Design
Implementation
Stabilization

Figure 10-3

Bookmark dialog box

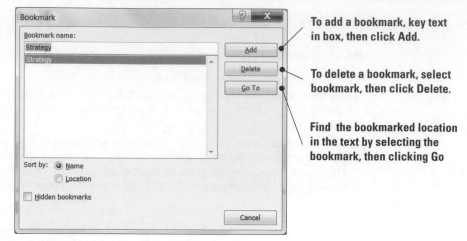

To add a bookmark, key text in box, then click Add.

To delete a bookmark, select bookmark, then click Delete.

Find the bookmarked location in the text by selecting the bookmark, then clicking Go

12. Bookmark names can contain up to 40 characters and spaces are not allowed when using Bookmarks; therefore, you would use an underscore to separate words. With Stabilization still highlighted, click **Bookmark** again. Your screen should match Figure 10-4. Click **Cancel**.

Figure 10-4

Bookmark dialog box with bookmarks added

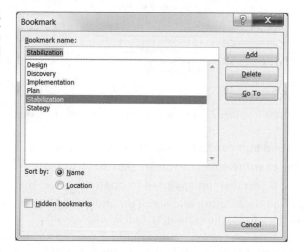

13. Position the insertion point at the beginning of the document by pressing **Ctrl+Home**. In the Links group click the **Bookmark** button. Test each link by selecting the bookmark name and then click the **Go To** button. Select **Design** and then click **Go To**, and the word is automatically highlighted in the document. After testing all bookmarks, click **Close**.

14. **SAVE** the document in your USB flash drive in the lesson folder.

PAUSE. LEAVE the document open to use in the next exercise.

CERTIFICATION
READY? **6.1.2**

How do you insert a bookmark in a document?

Ref

You can access the Go To command in one of the following ways: (1) use the Select Browse Object, (2) click the shortcut key F5, or (3) click the Edit group, and then click the Find Button. Using any one of these commands will open the Find and Replace dialog box, as you learned in Lesson 2.

Troubleshooting If your bookmark does not run properly, delete the bookmark, select the text, key the same text, and then click Add.

Adding an Email as a Hyperlink

An email address link is used to provide contact information, elicit feedback, or request information. In this exercise, you learn to add an email as a hyperlink.

STEP BY STEP   **Add an Email as a Hyperlink**

USE the document open from the previous exercise.

1. Press **Ctrl+End** to move to the end of the document.

2. Click the email image to select it.

Take Note   Email links can be applied to text or images.

3. In the Links group of the Insert tab, click the **Hyperlink** button or press **Ctrl+K**. The Insert Hyperlink dialog box opens.

4. Under the Link to section, click **E-mail Address**. Notice the middle portion of the dialog box changes. In the E-mail address section, key **manager@proseware.com** in the box. Mail to automatically appears when you begin keying the email address. For the Subject box, key **Web Design** as displayed in Figure 10-5. Click the **ScreenTip** button to open the Set Hyperlink ScreenTip dialog box; then in the ScreenTip text box, key **Manager**. Click **OK** twice.

Key email address.
Mailto: automatically
displays.

To create a ScreenTip

Select image or text to create an e-mail link.

Key a subject in the box.

Select E-mail Address to insert link.

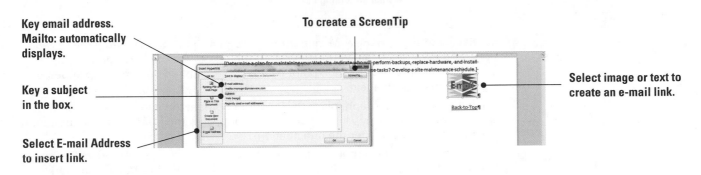

Figure 10-5

Insert Hyperlink dialog box
E-mail Address link

5. Hover your mouse over the E-mail image and the ScreenTip Manager appears. Test your email link by pressing the **Ctrl** key and clicking the left mouse button once. Outlook automatically opens with the email address and subject line inserted. This type of hyperlink is known as a mailto link.

6. **SAVE** the document in your USB flash drive in the lesson folder and close the file.

PAUSE. LEAVE Word open to use in the next exercise.

CREATING FOOTNOTES AND ENDNOTES

The Bottom Line

Both endnotes and footnotes are citations in a document. A **footnote** is placed at the bottom of the page in the document on which the citation is located, while an **endnote** is at the end of document. Footnotes and endnotes are automatically numbered. Edits to a footnote or endnote are made within the text. Deleting a footnote or endnote will automatically renumber the remaining footnotes or endnotes. As a student, you will use these in your research papers. In this lesson, you learn to insert a footnote and endnote into a document.

Creating Footnotes in a Document

| STEP BY STEP | Create Footnotes and Endnotes |

GET READY. Before you begin these steps, be sure to launch Microsoft Word.

1. **OPEN** the *firstladies* document from the lesson folder.
2. Place the insertion point at the end of the third paragraph.
3. On the References tab, click the Insert Footnote button in the Footnotes group, as shown in Figure 10-6. A superscript 1 is placed after the paragraph and at the end of the document.

The *firstladies* document file for this lesson is available on the book companion website or in WileyPLUS.

Figure 10-6

References tab

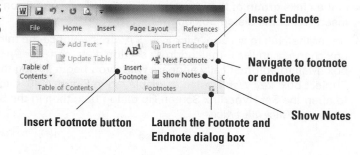

WileyPLUS Extra! features an online tutorial of this task.

4. Key **Mayo, Edith and Denise, Meringolo. First Ladies: Political Role and Public Image. Washington: Smithsonian Institute, 1994.** At the end of the third paragraph is a superscript 1, place the insertion point by the superscript and a ScreenTip appears displaying the footnote text.
5. On page 1, fourth paragraph, place the insertion point at the end of the second sentence (before Anthony). In the Footnotes group, click the Insert Footnote button. A superscript 2 is placed after the punctuation.
6. At the bottom of the document page, key **Anthony, Carl Sferrazza. American's First Families: An Inside View of 200 Years of Private Life in the White House. New York: Simon & Schuster, Inc., 2000.** The bottom of page 1 should resemble Figure 10-7.

Figure 10-7

Unformatted footnotes

Unformatted footnote at bottom of page. A border line automatically appears above footnote.

Second footnote added

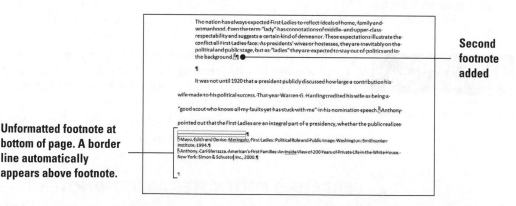

7. On page 2, fifth paragraph, end of third sentence, in the Footnotes group, click the Insert Footnote button. A superscript 3 is placed after the punctuation.
8. At the bottom of the document page, key **Gutin, Mayra G. The President's Partner: The First Lady in the Twentieth Century. Westport: Greenwood Press, 1989.**
9. **SAVE** the document as *firstladies_footnotes* in your USB flash drive in the lesson folder.

PAUSE. LEAVE the document open to use in the next exercise.

CERTIFICATION READY? 6.2.1

How do you create a footnote?

Formatting Footnotes and Endnotes

According to the Modern Language Association (MLA), a bottom-of-the-page footnote in MLA Style is single spaced with a hanging indent and double spacing between each footnote, whereas an endnote is double-spaced with no hanging indent. The dialog box contains additional options to change the numbering format and location for both footnotes and endnotes. In this lesson, you learn to format a footnote and endnote.

STEP BY STEP   **Format Footnotes**

USE the document open from the previous exercise.

1. Press and hold the left mouse button to select the first footnote beginning with Mayo. . . 1994.

2. On the Home tab, in the Paragraph group, launch the Paragraph dialog box and change the indent to a **hanging indent** and spacing after to **12**. Click **OK**.

3. Press and hold the **left mouse button** to select the second footnote and repeat step 2 to create a hanging indent.

4. For footnote number 3, repeat steps 1 to select and 2 to create a hanging indent. The footnotes have been formatted with a hanging indent and spaced appropriately.

5. Place your insertion point after the superscript 1 at the bottom of the document on page 1. On the References tab in the Footnotes group, click the **arrow** to launch the Footnote and Endnote dialog box. The Footnote and Endnote dialog box opens. In the Format section by Number format, click the **drop-down arrow** and select the uppercase Roman numerals, as shown in Figure 10-8. Click **Apply**. Notice the numbering format has changed.

Figure 10-8

Footnote and Endnote dialog box

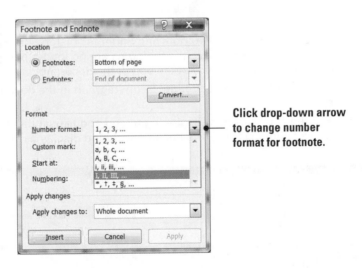

Click drop-down arrow to change number format for footnote.

6. In the third paragraph, place your insertion point before the first footnote superscript on page 1, press and hold the left mouse button to select the footnote. Launch the Footnote and Endnote dialog box. The Footnote and Endnote dialog box opens. In the Location section, by Footnotes, click the **drop-down arrow** and select **Below text**. Click **Apply**. The first footnote is moved below the third paragraph with a continuous section break.

7. Repeat the same steps for the second and third footnote to place them below text.

8. **SAVE** the document as ***firstladies_footnotes1*** in your USB flash drive in the lesson folder.

9. Place the insertion point behind the second footnote on the fourth paragraph, at the end of the second sentence. Delete the footnote. Notice the footnote number 3 is now 2. Footnotes are automatically renumbered and rearranged when one is deleted. Click **Undo** ↰.

10. **SAVE** the document in your USB flash drive in the lesson folder.

PAUSE. LEAVE the document open to use in the next exercise.

Converting Footnotes and Endnotes

It is easy to convert from a footnote to an endnote. The process is the same for both types of notes. In this exercise, you learn to convert from footnotes to endnotes and to format the endnote.

OPEN the *firstladies_footnotes* document completed earlier in this lesson.

1. The insertion point is at the beginning of the first footnote below the horizontal line.

2. On the References tab in the Footnotes group, click the **arrow** to launch the Footnote and Endnote dialog box. The Footnote and Endnote dialog box opens.

3. Click the **Convert** button. The Convert Notes dialog box opens. The first option *Convert all footnotes to endnotes* is selected, as shown in Figure 10-9. Click **OK** to convert the notes and close the Convert Notes dialog box.

Figure 10-9

Convert Notes dialog box

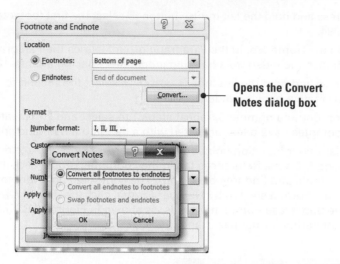

Opens the Convert Notes dialog box

4. Click **Insert** to close the Footnote and Endnotes dialog box. Scroll through to the end of the document and notice the footnotes are no longer positioned at the end of the page. The endnotes display at the end of the document in lowercase Roman numerals.

5. Place the insertion point after the last paragraph in the document and insert a page break.

6. Select the endnotes from beginning to end and format them by double spacing and create a hanging indent. The document should display as Figure 10-10.

CERTIFICATION READY? **6.2.1**

How do you format an endnote?

Figure 10-10

Formatted endnote

Endnotes appear at the end of the document and are formatted with a hanging indent and double space.

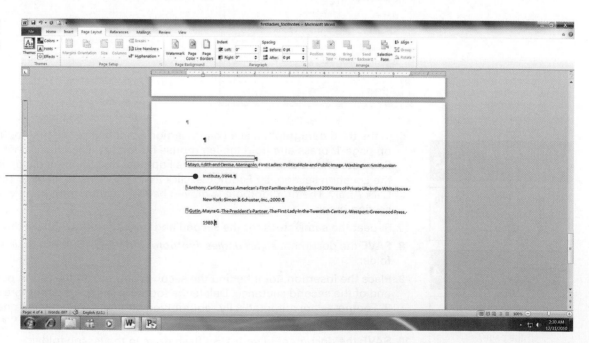

7. SAVE the document as *firstladies_endnotes* in your USB flash drive in the lesson folder and close the file.

PAUSE. LEAVE the document open to use in the next exercise.

CREATING A TABLE OF CONTENTS

The Bottom Line

A table of contents is usually found at the beginning of a long document to help readers quickly locate topics of interest. A **table of contents** is an ordered list of the topics in a document, along with the page numbers on which they are found. In this exercise, you learn to add a heading style and insert a table of contents.

Creating a Table of Contents from Heading Styles

Word makes inserting a table of contents easy using the built-in gallery of styles on the Table of Contents menu. The menu includes an automatic format and a manual format. Word automatically builds your table of contents using the Heading 1, Heading 2, and Heading 3 styles. In this exercise you will choose one of the automatic formats to create a table of contents (TOC).

STEP BY STEP   **Create a Table of Contents**

 The *website* document file for this lesson is available on the book companion website or in WileyPLUS.

WILEY **PLUS** *EXTRA*

WileyPLUS Extra! features an online tutorial of this task.

1. **OPEN** the *website* document from the data files for this lesson.
2. On the first page, fourth line, select Planning the site.
3. On the Home tab, in the Styles group, click the Heading 1 style.
4. On the next line, select Research. Click the Heading 2 style.
5. On the next line, select Research and Scheduling. On the Home tab, in the Styles group, click the Heading 3 style.
6. Scroll through the document to verify that all the other headings have the correct styles applied to them. Before you can create a table of contents, heading styles must be applied to headings in the document as listed in Table 10-1.

Table 10-1

Headings and Styles Applied

Vision and Purpose	Heading 3	Risk Assessment	Heading 3
Strategic Objectives	Heading 3	Design	Heading 2
Critical Success Factors	Heading 3	Conceptual Design and Prototypes	Heading 3
Technology	Heading 3	Technology Architecture	Heading 3
Risk and Pain Factors	Heading 3	Quality Assurance	Heading 3
Strategy	Heading 2	Implementation	Heading 2
Competitive Landscape	Heading 3	Content Development	Heading 3
Brainstorm	Heading 3	Graphic Assets	Heading 3
Plan	Heading 2	Templates	Heading 3
Look and Feel	Heading 3	Functionality Testing	Heading 3
Project Identification	Heading 3	Updated Project Plan	Heading 3
Deliverables	Heading 3	Stabilization	Heading 2
Building the Site	Heading 1	Testing	Heading 3
Discovery	Heading 2	Bug Fixes	Heading 3
Team Structure	Heading 3	Deployment	Heading 3
Content	Heading 3	Maintenance Plan	Heading 3
Project Plan	Heading 3		

7. Return to page 1 by pressing **Ctrl+Home** and click on a blank line above the Web Site Creation Strategy title.

8. On the References tab, in the Table of Contents group, click the **Table of Contents** button. A gallery of built-in styles and a menu appears, as shown in Figure 10-11.

Figure 10-11

Table of Contents menu

9. Select the **Automatic Table 2** style. The table of contents is inserted in the document—scroll up to see the table of contents (see Figure 10-12). The table of contents is shaded in gray and each heading is linked to the document and follows the link.

10. Press the **Ctrl** key and click the mouse button to follow the link for Research.

11. **SAVE** your document as **website_template** in your USB flash drive in the lesson folder.

PAUSE. LEAVE the document open to use in the next exercise.

Figure 10-12

Automatic Table 2 style applied to document

Table of Contents button. The drop-down arrow will produce the Table of Contents menu.

Update Table button will open the Update Table of Contents dialog box.

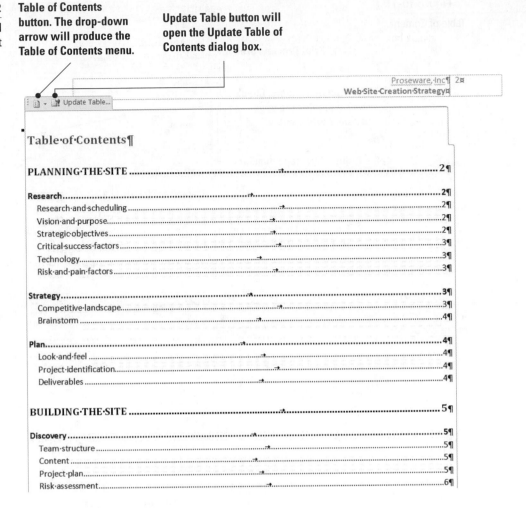

Formatting a Table of Contents

You can use styles other than Heading 1, Heading 2, and Heading 3 to create a table of contents. The Table of Contents Options dialog box provides options for choosing which styles you want to include and at what level you would like them to appear in the table of contents.

The Table of Contents dialog box has other options you can specify, including whether to show page numbers or right-align page numbers. You can also specify **tab leaders**, which are the symbols that appear between the table of contents topic and the tab set for the corresponding page number. In this lesson, you learn to format a table of contents by changing the alignment tab leaders and levels.

STEP BY STEP   **Format a Table of Contents**

USE the document that is open from the previous exercise.

1. On the References tab, in the Table of Contents group, click the Table of Contents button.

2. Select Insert Table of Contents from the menu. The Table of Contents dialog box appears, as shown in Figure 10-13. The Print Preview box lists the styles used to create the table of contents. The Table of Contents dialog box offers options for you to specify whether to show page numbers and whether to right-align those page numbers. Tab leaders are symbols that serve as a visual guide from the headings to the page numbers. These can appear as periods, hyphens, lines, or none. The format for the Table of Contents can be changed to display different heading levels in the Table of Contents.

Figure 10-13

Table of Contents
dialog box

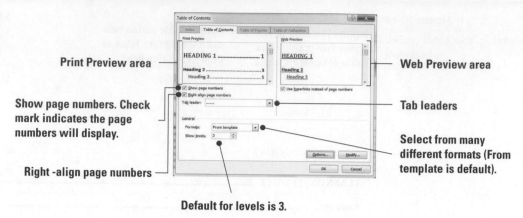

Print Preview area

Web Preview area

Show page numbers. Check
mark indicates the page
numbers will display.

Tab leaders

Select from many
different formats (From
template is default).

Right -align page numbers

Default for levels is 3.

3. Click the **Options** button. The Table of Contents Options dialog box appears, as shown in Figure 10-14. The Options dialog box provides options for choosing which styles to include and at what level you want them to appear in the table of contents.

Figure 10-14

Table of Contents
Options dialog box

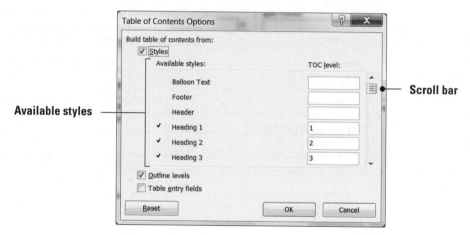

Available styles

Scroll bar

4. In the *Build table of contents from* section, scroll through the TOC level list. Notice the styles and their levels marked for inclusion in the table of contents.

5. Add a TOC level 4 by keying **4** in the box by Heading 4; a check mark is automatically placed by the heading. Click **OK** to close the Table of Contents Options dialog box, then click **OK** to close the Table of Contents dialog box.

6. If prompted to replace the selected table of contents, click **Yes**.

7. On the Home tab in the Styles group, notice that **Heading 4** is now available. Scroll down to page 3 and select the RISK AND PAIN FACTORS heading. On the Styles group, select **Heading 4**—the format for the selected text automatically changes and the Heading 4 style is applied.

Take Note   To remove Heading 4, open the Table of Contents dialog box and delete 4.

8. Press **Ctrl+Home** to return to the beginning of the document. Click the **References** tab in the Table of Contents group, click the **Table of Contents** button, and then select **Insert Table of Contents** from the menu. The Table of Contents dialog box opens. Under the General section, click the **drop-down arrow** on the Formats menu and select **Formal**.

9. In the Print Preview section, click the **drop-down arrow** on the Tab leader drop-down menu and select **hyphens**. By default, the Tab leader uses periods.

10. In the General section, notice that under the Show levels option, 4 levels is displayed. Therefore the preview screen displays four levels.

11. Click **OK** to close the Table of Contents dialog box. Word displays a prompt asking you if you want to replace the selected table of contents. Click **Yes**.

12. The new format for the table of contents displays four levels. The Risk and pain factors heading is listed as a level four, so it now displays in the table of contents.

13. **SAVE** the document as *website_template1* in your USB flash drive in the lesson folder.

**CERTIFICATION
READY?**   **6.3.3**

How do you set alignments
for a table of contents?

**CERTIFICATION
READY?**   **6.3.4**

How do you set tab leaders
for a table of contents?

14. On the Table of Contents group, click the Table of Contents button, and then select Insert Table of Contents from the menu.

15. Click the check box for Right align page numbers to remove the check and turn off the right alignment. Notice that the Print Preview area displays no leaders. Click OK. A prompt box will appear asking if you want to replace the selected table of contents. Click Yes. The table of contents is updated with no alignment set.

16. SAVE the document as *website_template2* in your USB flash drive in the lesson folder.

PAUSE. LEAVE the document open to use in the next exercise.

Modifying a Table of Contents

Modifying a table of contents allows you to change the properties and formatting and to decide whether you want to apply the changes to the present document or the Quick Style list, or add to the template to reapply. Any changes made will allow you to automatically update the document. In this lesson, you learn to modify a table of contents by changing the formatting and turning off the Quick Style list.

STEP BY STEP   **Modify a Table of Contents**

USE the document that is open from the previous exercise.

1. Position the insertion point in the table of contents. On the References tab in the Table of Contents group, click the Table of Contents button, click Insert Table of Contents, and then click the Modify button in the lower right of the Table of Contents dialog box. The Style dialog box opens with TOC 1 selected, as shown in Figure 10-15.

Figure 10-15

Style dialog box

TOC 1 paragraph formats

Modify

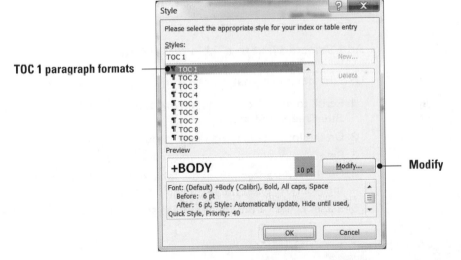

2. Click the Modify button from the Style dialog box. The Modify Style dialog box opens, as shown in Figure 10-16.

3. The alignment for TOC 1 is set to align text left; change this to center. Change the Font from Calibri to Arial and Size from 10 to 16. The commands shown in the Modify Style dialog box resemble the commands on the Home tab, in the Font and Paragraph groups.

4. At the bottom of the dialog box, click the Add to Quick Style list check box to remove the check and turn off. Modifications made to the style will apply only to this document and automatically update the table of contents.

5. Click OK to accept your changes and close the Modify Style dialog box. Click OK to close the Style dialog box. Click OK to close the Table of Contents dialog box.

6. A prompt will appear asking if you want to replace the selected table of contents. Click Yes. Notice the changes made to the Heading 1 style.

Figure 10-16

Modify Style dialog box

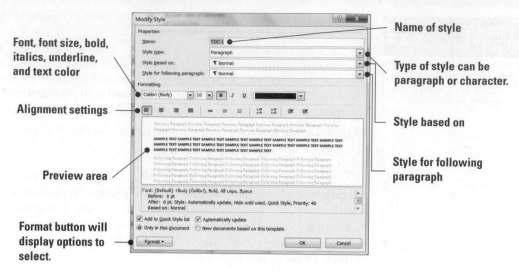

Figure 10-16

Modify Style dialog box

Name of style

Font, font size, bold, italics, underline, and text color

Type of style can be paragraph or character.

Alignment settings

Style based on

Preview area

Style for following paragraph

Format button will display options to select.

7. SAVE the document as **website_template3** in your USB flash drive in the lesson folder.
PAUSE. LEAVE the document open to use in the next exercise.

Adding Selected Text to a Table of Contents

Sometimes in a table of contents you might want to include text that has not been formatted with a heading style. The Add Text menu enables you to choose the level at which the new text will appear. The levels available in the previous exercise were Do Not Show in Table of Contents, Level 1, Level 2, and Level 3. When working with tables of contents in other documents that have more levels, additional options may be available on the menu.

STEP BY STEP   **Add Selected Text to a Table of Contents**

USE the document that is open from the previous exercise.

1. Scroll to page 2 of the document and position the insertion point before the W in Web Site Creation Strategy.
2. On the Insert tab, in the Pages group, click the Page Break button.
3. Select the Web Site Creation Strategy text.
4. On the References tab, in the Table of Contents group, click the drop-down arrow by the Add Text button to display the menu.
5. Select Level 1 from the menu, as shown in Figure 10-17. Deselect the text.

Figure 10-17

Add Text button and menu

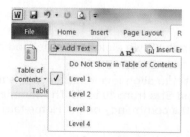

6. SAVE the document in your USB flash drive in the lesson folder.
PAUSE. LEAVE the document open to use in the next exercise.

Updating a Table of Contents

After adding new text, a new page, or modifying the table of contents, the next step is to update the table of contents. In this exercise, you learn to update the table of contents.

STEP BY STEP   **Update a Table of Contents**

USE the document that is open from the previous exercise.

Another Way
You can also use the shortcut key F9 to open the Update the Table of Contents dialog box.

1. Scroll to the beginning of page 1 and click in the Table of Contents to select it. On the References tab, in the Table of Contents group, click the Update Table button.

2. The Update Table of Contents dialog box appears. The default, Update page numbers only, is selected, as shown in Figure 10-18; just click OK. Notice that the page numbers for the table of contents have been updated.

Figure 10-18

Update Table of Contents dialog box

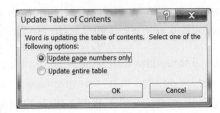

3. Click Update Table, and the Update Table of Contents dialog box appears. Click the Update entire table button, and click OK. Notice that *Web Site Creation Strategy 3* is added to the table of contents.

4. **SAVE** the document in your USB flash drive in the lesson folder.

PAUSE. LEAVE the document open to use in the next exercise.

CERTIFICATION READY?   **6.3.6**

How do you update a table of contents by page numbers only?

CERTIFICATION READY?   **6.3.6**

How do you update the entire table of contents?

Removing a Table of Contents

Remove a table of contents from the document.

USE the document that is open from the previous exercise.

1. On the References tab, in the Table of Contents group, click Remove Table of Contents.

2. Delete the page break.

3. **SAVE** the document as *website_template_final* in your USB flash drive in the lesson folder.

CLOSE Word.

Another Way
You can also update a table of contents using the shortcut key, F9.

SKILL SUMMARY

In This Lesson You Learned How To:	Exam Objective	Objective Number
Apply a hyperlink	Apply a hyperlink to text or graphic.	6.1.1
	Use a hyperlink as a bookmark.	6.1.2
	Link a hyperlink to an email address.	6.1.3
Create endnotes and footnotes in a document	Demonstrate the difference between endnotes and footnotes.	6.2.1
	Configure footnote and endnote format.	6.2.3
	Manage footnote and endnote locations.	6.2.2
	Change footnote and endnote numbering.	6.2.5
	Presentation.	6.2.4
Create a table of contents in a document	Use default formats.	6.3.1
	Set tab leaders.	6.3.4
	Set alignment.	6.3.3
	Set levels.	6.3.2
	Modify styles.	6.3.5
	Update a table of contents.	6.3.6

Knowledge Assessment

True/False

Circle T if the statement is true or F if the statement is false.

T F **1.** A table of contents is usually found at the end of document.

T F **2.** The manual table of contents option allows you to create a table of contents on your own.

T F **3.** You can choose a hyphen as tab leaders for a table of contents.

T F **4.** Only text formatted with a heading style can be included in a table of contents.

T F **5.** You can choose to update only the page numbers in a table of contents.

T F **6.** Hyperlinks can be applied to text or graphics.

T F **7.** When you create an email link, the Outlook application will automatically open.

T F **8.** A bookmark is a reference point in a document.

T F **9.** An endnote is a citation and placed at the end of the document.

T F **10.** Deleting a footnote or endnote will automatically renumber the remaining footnotes or endnotes.

Multiple Choice

Select the best response for the following statements.

1. A table of contents is located at the _____ of the document.
   a. Middle
   b. End
   c. Beginning
   d. None of the above

2. Tab leaders can be changed into what types of symbols for use in a table of contents?
   a. Periods
   b. Hyphens
   c. Lines
   d. All of the above

3. Which menu will allow you to add content to the table of contents?
   a. Update Table
   b. Add Text
   c. Add Bookmark
   d. None of the above

4. When adding a page or text to a table of contents, it is recommended that you
   a. Click the Update Table button on the Ribbon
   b. Press F9
   c. Click the Update Table button above the table of contents
   d. All of the above

5. By default, a footnote is placed
   a. At the beginning of the document
   b. At the end of the document
   c. At the end of the page
   d. Below text

6. Formatting a footnote in a document, per MLA style, should be
   a. single spaced with a hanging indent and triple spaced
   b. single spaced with a hanging indent and doubled spaced between each footnote
   c. doubled spaced with a hanging indent and single spaced between each footnote
   d. No format is needed.

7. Hyperlinks can be linked
   a. From one page to another page
   b. As a website
   c. As email
   d. All of the above

8. Reference points in a document are created using which command?
   a. Bookmark
   b. Hyperlink
   c. Email
   d. All of the above

9. The Footnote and Endnote dialog box contains an option to change the page number format to
   a. Uppercase Roman numerals
   b. A1, A2, A3, etc.
   c. a and b
   d. It is not an option.

10. Endnotes can be converted to which of the following?
    a. Table of contents
    b. Footnote
    c. Hyperlink
    d. They cannot be converted.

Competency Assessment

Project 10-1: Mom's Favorite Recipes

You know that your mom will be sending you more recipes for her cookbook. You decide to create a table of contents using headings in the cookbook, making it easy to update as recipes are added.

GET READY. LAUNCH Word if it is not already running.

@ The *momsfavorites1* document file for this lesson is available on the book companion website or in WileyPLUS.

1. **OPEN** *momsfavorites1* from the data files for this lesson. On the Home tab, turn on your Show/Hide command.

2. Use the Go To command to go to page 3. Select the Breads heading and apply the Heading 1 style to it.

3. Select the Banana Nut Bread/Chocolate Chip Muffins heading and apply the Heading 2 style.

4. Apply the Heading 2 style to the remaining recipe headings.

5. On page 1, position the insertion point before the M in Main Dishes.

6. On the References tab, in the Table of Contents group, click the Table of Contents button. Select Automatic Table 1 from the menu.

7. Center Contents and apply the Title style.

8. Select the table and click the Update Table button. Update the page numbers only.

9. **SAVE** the worksheet as *moms_recipes_toc* in your USB flash drive and **CLOSE** the file.

PAUSE. LEAVE Word open for the next project.

Project 10-2: Margie Travel

You will be updating the Explore the World flyer created in an earlier lesson. Since this flyer will be shared by email, you want to insert hyperlinks and Margie's email address.

GET READY. LAUNCH Word if it is not already running.

@ The *exploring_world_flyer* document file for this lesson is available on the book companion website or in WileyPLUS.

1. **OPEN** the *exploring_world_flyer* document from the lesson folder.
2. Select the Explore the World text. On the Insert tab in the Links group, select Hyperlink.
3. In the address box, key http://www.margiestravel.com. Click OK.
4. Place the insertion point at the end of the paragraph, press Enter. Key Contact: Margie and align right.
5. Select Margie and in the Links group, click Hyperlink, then select E-mail address.
6. For the E-mail address, key Margie@margiestravel.com. Click OK.
7. **SAVE** the document as *world_flyer_update* in your USB flash drive and close the file.

LEAVE Word open for the next project.

Proficiency Assessment

Project 10-3: First Ladies

You will be modifying the First Ladies document by formatting the footnotes and changing the number format.

GET READY. LAUNCH Word if it is not already running.

@ The *firstladies4* document file for this lesson is available on the book companion website or in WileyPLUS.

1. **OPEN** the *firstladies4* document from the lesson folder.
2. At the end of page 1, select the first footnote and format the footnote with a hanging indent, single space and spacing after to 12 pts. between each footnote.
3. Complete the same process in step 2 for the second and third footnote.
4. Place the insertion point after the first footnote below the horizontal line. On the References tab in the Footnotes group, launch the Footnote and Endnote dialog box and change the number format to lowercase Roman numerals.
5. **SAVE** the worksheet as *firstladies4_update* in your USB flash drive in the lesson folder and **CLOSE** the file.

LEAVE Word open for the next project.

Project 10-4: Computer Use Policy Contents

Add a table of contents to the Computer Use Policy document.

GET READY. LAUNCH Word if it is not already running.

@ The *computeruse2* document file for this lesson is available on the book companion website or in WileyPLUS.

1. **OPEN** *computeruse2* from the data files for this lesson.
2. Select the title, Computer Use Policy, and apply the Title style.
3. Select Section One and apply the Heading 1 style.
4. Select Purpose and apply the Heading 2 style.
5. In the same manner, continue applying the Heading 1 and Heading 2 styles to the headings for the remainder of the document.
6. On page 1, position the insertion point before the C in Computer Use Policy and insert a built-in table of contents using the Automatic Table 1 style.
7. With the insertion point in front of the C in Computer Use Policy, insert a page break.
8. **SAVE** the document as *computer_use_toc* in your USB flash drive and **CLOSE** the file.

PAUSE. LEAVE Word open for the next project.

Mastery Assessment

Project 10-5: USA Proposal

You need to add a table of contents to the USA Proposal document. However, the document was created without using heading styles, and you cannot change the format of the document. Use the Add Text command to create a table of contents.

GET READY. LAUNCH Word if it is not already running.

The *USAproposal* document file for this lesson is available on the book companion website or in WileyPLUS.

1. **OPEN** *USAproposal* from the data files for this lesson.
2. Use the Add Text command to create a table of contents with three levels. Level 1 will be the Proposal Description, Level 2 will be the three Options, and Level 3 will be the cities listed under each option.
3. Add a page break at the beginning of the document and select the hidden mark and Clear Formatting and create a blank line.
4. Key Table of Contents. Change the font to Arial, font size to 20 pts, and spacing after to 12 pts and center.
5. Create a manual table of contents using the Formal format.
6. **SAVE** the document as *USA_proposal_toc* in your USB flash drive in the lesson folder and **CLOSE** the file.

PAUSE. LEAVE Word open for the next exercise.

Project 10-6: Computer Use Policy Contents Update

You will be using Project 10-4 to update a table of contents.

GET READY. LAUNCH Word if it is not already running.

1. **OPEN** the *computer_use_toc* completed in Project 10-4.
2. Delete all of Section Seven by selecting text beginning at Section Seven to the end of the paragraph under Encryption.
3. Renumber Section Eight to Section Seven, renumber Section Nine to Section Eight, and renumber Section Ten to Section Nine.
4. Return to the table of contents and update the entire table of contents.
5. **SAVE** the worksheet as *computer_toc_update* and **CLOSE** the file.

CLOSE Word.

INTERNET READY

The skills you are learning from this book are giving you a good foundation for using Word in the workplace. There may be times when you want to perform a task that goes beyond what you have already learned. The Internet can be a great resource for finding additional information. Use the Internet to search for information about one of the following bookmark topics and then write a brief paragraph answering the topic's question or explaining how to accomplish the task. Document your sources by including the URL in your answer.

- The Bookmark dialog box has a Hidden Bookmarks check box. What is the purpose of this check box? Is it possible to hide a bookmark? If so, how?

- It is easy to delete a bookmark using the Bookmark dialog box. Suppose you want to protect bookmarks from being deleted. Is this possible? If so, how? If not, why not?

- List the steps you would follow to create a hyperlink in an HTML page to a bookmark in a Word document.

- You want to highlight the bookmarks in your document by making them bold so you can see them better. Is this possible? If so, how?

11 Performing Mail Merges

LESSON SKILL MATRIX

Skill	Exam Objective	Objective Number
Setting Up Mail Merge	Perform a mail merge using the Mail Merge Wizard.	7.1.1
	Preview and print a mail merge operation.	7.2.1
	Perform a mail merge manually.	7.1.2
Executing Mail Merge	Use Auto Check for errors.	7.1.3

KEY TERMS

- chevrons
- data source
- field name
- main document

You are employed at Graphic Design Institute as an admissions officer in the Office of Enrollment Services. Because you frequently send out letters containing the same content to different recipients, it is essential that you know how to perform mail merges. In this lesson, you will learn how to create merged documents and merge data into form letters.

SOFTWARE ORIENTATION

Mailings Tab

Commands on the Mailings tab are used to perform mail merges, as well as to create envelopes and labels for a group mailing.

Figure 11-1

Mailings tab

Use Figure 11-1 as a reference throughout this lesson as well as the rest of this book.

SETTING UP MAIL MERGE

The Bottom Line

Mail merges are useful for creating multiple documents that have the same basic content, and personalizing them with unique information from a data source—for example, a form letter, sent to multiple customers using different recipient names and addresses. In essence, mail merges are used for internal and external correspondence such as memorandums, labels, invitations, and more. The mail merge document contains the same information that everyone will receive. The individuals receiving the document are created in a data source, which is the list of recipients and contains information for each individual with variable data, such as the person's first and last name, address, city, state, zip code, phone number, etc. The data source can be created as a database using Word, where Word provides the fields and you key the data in them. You also customize the fields to fit your document. Other programs can be used for the data source such as an Excel worksheet, an Access table or query, or your Outlook contacts list.

Setting Up a Main Document Using the Mail Merge Wizard

To begin a mail merge, the main document is set up from a new or an existing document. The **main document** contains the text and graphics that are the same for each version of the merged document. In this exercise, you learn to set up a main document using the Mail Merge Wizard, setting up mail merge manually, using the Auto Check for Errors, and previewing and printing the merge document.

STEP BY STEP   Set Up a Main Document Using the Mail Merge Wizard

WileyPLUS Extra! features an online tutorial of this task.

GET READY. Before you begin these steps, be sure to launch Microsoft Word.

1. On the Mailings tab, in the Start Mail Merge group, click the drop-down arrow to display the Start Mail Merge menu, as shown in Figure 11-2.

Figure 11-2

Start Mail Merge menu

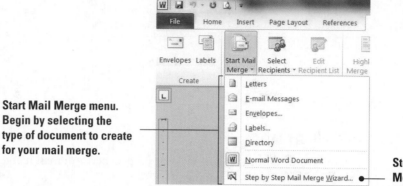

Start Mail Merge menu. Begin by selecting the type of document to create for your mail merge.

Step by Step Mail Merge Wizard opens the Mail Merge Pane.

2. Click Step by Step Mail Merge Wizard. The Mail Merge pane opens, as shown in Figure 11-3. The mail merge wizard has six steps to complete.

Figure 11-3

Mail Merge Step 1

Using the Step by Step Mail Merge Wizard walks you through six steps beginning with selecting a document type.

Mail Merge Wizard Steps

Click link to go to next step.

STEP 1:

1. Under the section *Select document type*, Letters is the default. You will be using the default for the main document.
2. Click the link below the Mail Merge pane, Next: Starting document.

STEP 2:

1. This step contains three options on setting up the letter. You will open an existing document in the lesson folder. Below the section *Select starting document*, click the radio button Start from existing document. Below the section, *Start from existing*, click the Open button, as shown in Figure 11-4.

Figure 11-4

Mail Merge Step 2

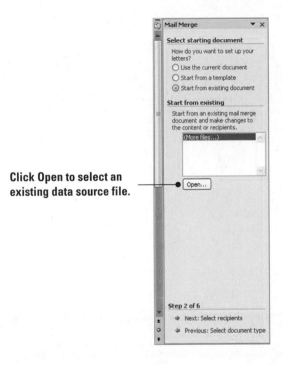

Click Open to select an existing data source file.

2. The Open dialog box displays. Use the scroll bar to locate your USB flash drive and open data files from your lesson folder. Select the *scholarship* document and double-click to open it or click the Open button. The document is inserted in the document screen.
3. At the bottom of the Mail Merge pane, click the link Next: Select recipients.

@ The *scholarship* file for this lesson is available on the book companion website or in WileyPLUS.

STEP 3:

1. Under the *Select recipients* section (Figure 11-5) you will use the default setting, Use an existing list. The existing list is located in the data lesson folder in your USB flash drive.
2. Under the *Use an existing list* section, click the Browse link. The Select Data Source dialog box opens—this is the default location for data source files (see Figure 11-6). Use the scroll bar to navigate to the location of your data lesson folder in your USB flash drive.

Figure 11-5

Mail Merge Step 3

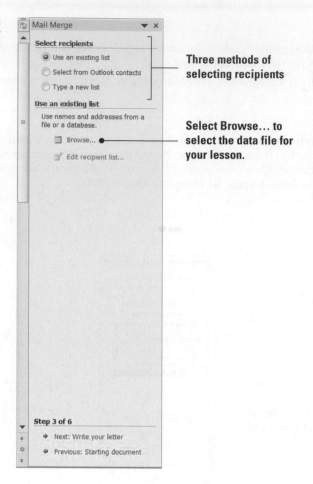

Three methods of selecting recipients

Select Browse… to select the data file for your lesson.

Figure 11-6

Select Data Source dialog box

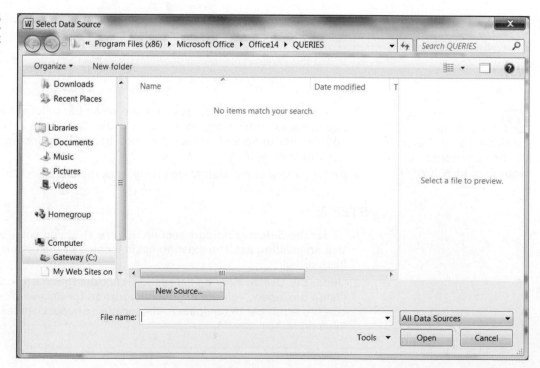

3. A **data source** is a file that contains information to be merged in the main document. A data source can be from an Excel spreadsheet, an Access database, an HTML file, or a Word document containing a single table, an electronic address book such as Outlook, or any text that has data fields. **Field names** provide a description for the specific data, such as a person's first name, last name, address, city, state, and zip code, to be merged from the data source.

@ The *student_list* file for this lesson is available on the book companion website or in WileyPLUS.

4. Select the *student_list* as shown in Figure 11-7 and double-click or click the Open button. The icon listed for the *student_list* is a database file. A **database** is a collection of information that is organized so that you can retrieve information quickly. The *student_list* file is the data source that will be merged with the letter in the document screen.

Figure 11-7

Target location for data file

Select Data Source

Target location of data lesson files. Your screen will not resemble the screen displayed.

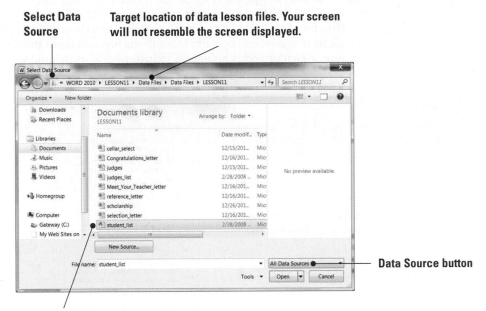

Data Source button

Data Source file.

5. The Mail Merge Recipients dialog box opens as displayed in Figure 11-8. The Mail Merge Recipients dialog box has been expanded to display all fields and records. The check mark indicates that all recipients' fields will merge with the document. You can choose not to send a recipient a letter by unchecking the check box. When the document merges, all recipients with a check mark by their name will be merged with the document. Click OK to close the Mail Merge Recipients dialog box and return to the document screen.

Figure 11-8

Mail Merge Recipients dialog box

Check mark indicates recipients will merge with document.

Field names

Data Source file indicates the type of file it is. For example, a file with a file extension of .mdb is an Access database.

When selecting the data source file, the Edit and Refresh button will be activated.

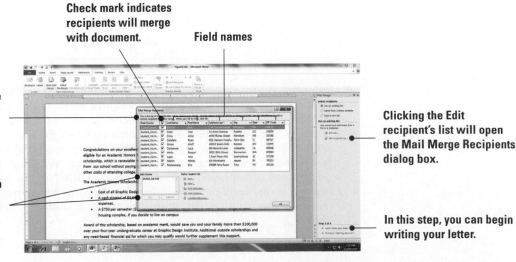

Clicking the Edit recipient's list will open the Mail Merge Recipients dialog box.

In this step, you can begin writing your letter.

STEP 4:

1. At the bottom of the Mail Merge pane, click the link, **Next: Write your letter**. Since you have already opened an existing document, the document is ready for fields to be inserted.

2. Your insertion point is already positioned on the blank line above the first paragraph to insert the current date.

3. Click the **Insert** tab, in the Text group, and click the **Date & Time** button. When the Date & Time dialog box opens, click the **third option** and click **OK**. The current date is inserted in the document.

4. Press **Enter** once.

5. In the Mail Merge pane, under the *Write your letter* section, it shows four links (see Figure 11-9). The Address block link contains the fields from the recipients list, the Greeting line link contains the salutation, the Electronic postage link will insert the electronic postage, and the More items link will open the Insert Merge Field dialog box, which provides an option to insert fields individually.

Figure 11-9

Mail Merge Pane, Write your letter

Step 4 is adding the Address block and Greeting line.

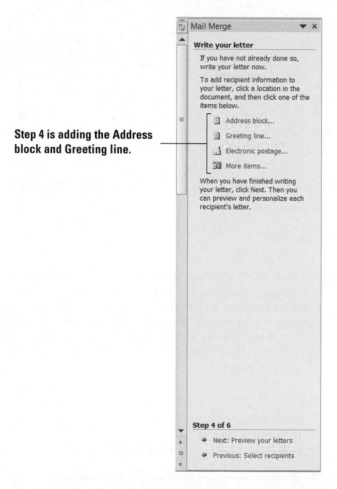

6. Under the *Write your letter* section, click the **Address block** link. The Insert Address Block dialog box opens, as shown in Figure 11-10. Under *Specify address elements*, the fifth option is selected with a specific format as displayed on the Preview section. On the Preview side, there are four arrows: **First**, **Previous**, **Next**, and **Last**. Notice that the First and Previous arrow buttons are grayed out. When these arrow buttons are shaded in gray, it indicates that they are not available. The first recipient's name and address is displayed and when you click the Next or Last arrow, the First and Previous arrows will become available. Click the **Next** arrow and preview the ten records in the recipient list, then click the **First** button to return to the first recipient. Click **OK**.

Figure 11-10

Insert Address Block dialog box

Directional arrows under the Preview section allows you to preview each record.

Options for how the Address Block should display

Preview address block

If fields are missing or out of order in the Address block, click the Match Fields button to correct.

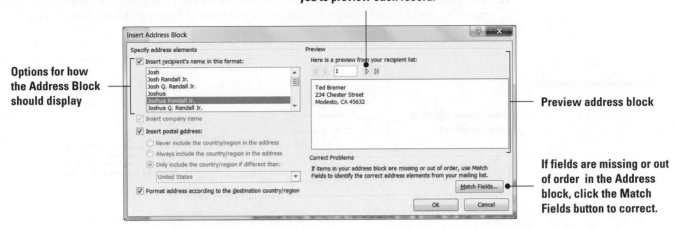

7. A field code <<Address Block>> is inserted in the document, as shown in Figure 11-11. The field name is surrounded by **chevrons** (<< >>) and will not display in the merged document. When the document is merged, the Address Block will display the recipients' first and last name, address, city, state, and postal code.

Figure 11-11

Address Block inserted in document

The Address Block contains all recipient's information and will display once you preview your results and merge.

Chevrons <<   >> surround the field name and will not print in your document.

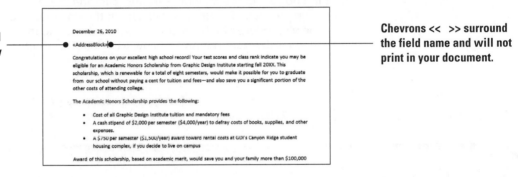

8. Press the Enter key once.

9. Click the Greeting line link to open the Insert Greeting Line dialog box, as shown in Figure 11-12. The drop-down arrows under the *Greeting line format* provide options to select the salutation, name, and punctuation. You will use the salutation **Dear** for the letter.

Figure 11-12

Insert Greeting line dialog box

Greeting line format: drop-down arrows contain options to select

Additional Greeting Line options

Preview of Greeting Line

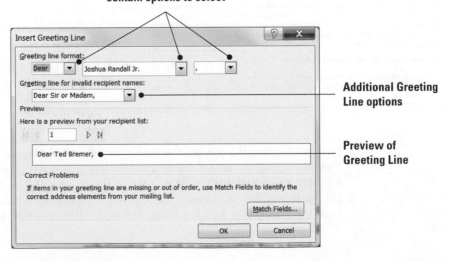

10. Click the **drop-down arrow** next to Joshua Randal Jr. to view the options. Keep the default as the selection.

11. Click the **drop-down arrow** next to the comma and select the colon (:). Click **OK**. Your document should match Figure 11-13. You have inserted two field codes in your document.

Figure 11-13

Document with field codes

Field codes inserted into document

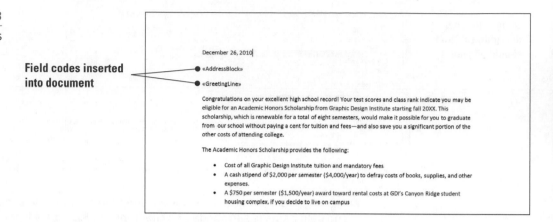

STEP 5:

1. At the bottom of the Mail Merge pane, click the link, **Next: Preview your letters**. Notice the first recipient, Ted Bremer, appears in the document. On the Mail Merge pane, preview each letter in the document screen by using the buttons as shown in Figure 11-14. Click the **Next** button, preview each letter, and return to the first recipient.

Figure 11-14

Preview your letter

Previous button

Preview each recipient by clicking the Previous or Next arrows.

Next button

Edit Recipient List will allow you to make corrections of different fields, such as address, city, state, or zip code.

Select to exclude the currently displayed recipient.

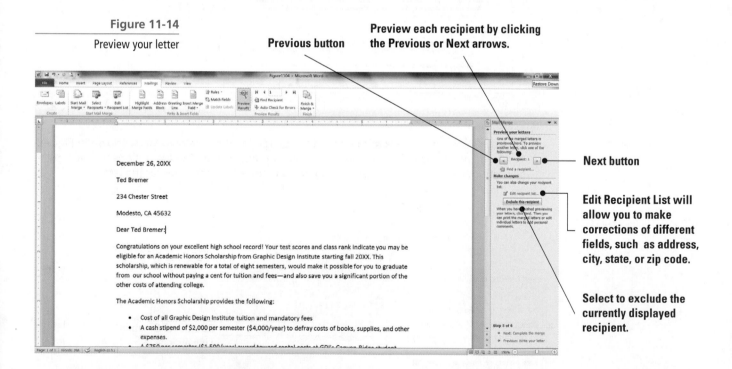

2. Before finalizing the merge, the mailing address contains extra spaces between the lines that need correction. Select the text beginning with Ted Bremer, including the address through the zip code, 45632.

3. On the Home tab, in the Paragraph group, click the **drop-down arrow** to display the Line and Paragraph Spacing menu and select **Remove Space Before Paragraph**.

4. Place the insertion point in the date. In the Paragraph group on the Home tab, click the **drop-down arrow** to display the Line and Paragraph Spacing menu and select **Add Space After Paragraph.** This separates the date from the Address Block. The document should display as Figure 11-15. Preview each letter again by using the **Next** and **Previous** buttons on the Mail Merge pane and return to the first recipient. Each recipient should be in the correct format.

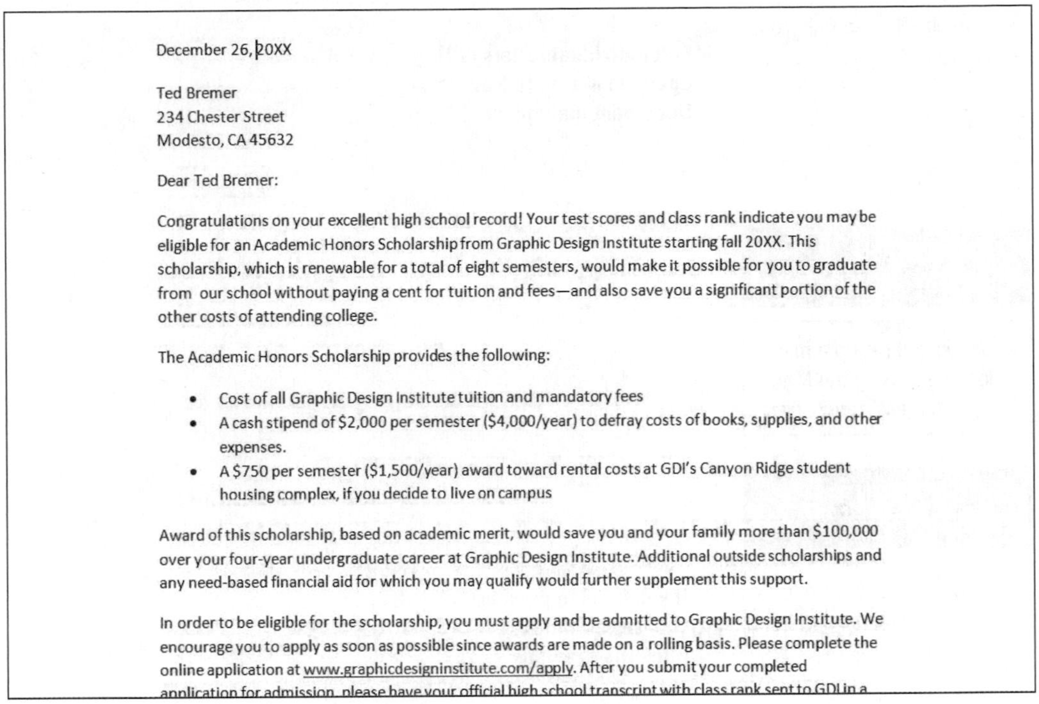

Figure 11-15

Formatted document

December 26, 20XX

Ted Bremer
234 Chester Street
Modesto, CA 45632

Dear Ted Bremer:

Congratulations on your excellent high school record! Your test scores and class rank indicate you may be eligible for an Academic Honors Scholarship from Graphic Design Institute starting fall 20XX. This scholarship, which is renewable for a total of eight semesters, would make it possible for you to graduate from our school without paying a cent for tuition and fees—and also save you a significant portion of the other costs of attending college.

The Academic Honors Scholarship provides the following:

- Cost of all Graphic Design Institute tuition and mandatory fees
- A cash stipend of $2,000 per semester ($4,000/year) to defray costs of books, supplies, and other expenses.
- A $750 per semester ($1,500/year) award toward rental costs at GDI's Canyon Ridge student housing complex, if you decide to live on campus

Award of this scholarship, based on academic merit, would save you and your family more than $100,000 over your four-year undergraduate career at Graphic Design Institute. Additional outside scholarships and any need-based financial aid for which you may qualify would further supplement this support.

In order to be eligible for the scholarship, you must apply and be admitted to Graphic Design Institute. We encourage you to apply as soon as possible since awards are made on a rolling basis. Please complete the online application at www.graphicdesigninstitute.com/apply. After you submit your completed application for admission, please have your official high school transcript with class rank sent to GDI in a

STEP 6:

1. At the bottom of the Mail Merge pane, click the link, **Next: Complete the merge,** to advance to Step 6, as shown in Figure 11-16. The letter is already merged and ready to **Print** or you can edit each letter individually. When you click the link **Edit individual letters** under the Merge section, the Merge to New Document dialog box opens. When you select the **All** radio button, then all letters will open as a new document, and Letters1 will display on the title bar. When you finish editing the letters, you are ready to save the letters—all letters will be saved as one document. If your insertion point is on the third letter, and you click the link **Edit individual letters** and then select the radio button for **Current Record,** the document will open in a new screen with the third document as a new document, and Letters followed by a number will appear on the title bar. Edit the document and when you save the document, only the third letter will be saved with the changes made. Selecting the third radio button **From,** you key the beginning number to the end number of the document you wish to edit. For example, if you wish to edit letter 3 through 5, you would key **3** to **5** in the From boxes.

2. Under Mail Merge pane, in the Merge section, click **Print** to print each letter. The Merge to Printer dialog box opens with three options to select. Selecting the **All** radio button will print all letters, the Current record will print the record where your insertion point is located, and From is where you specify which records to print. For example, if you specify records 2 to 4—only those two records will print. Make sure the All radio button is selected and click **OK** to print.

Figure 11-16

Mail Merge pane Step 6 of 6

Print will open the Merge to Printer dialog box.

Edit individual letters will open the Merge to New Document dialog box.

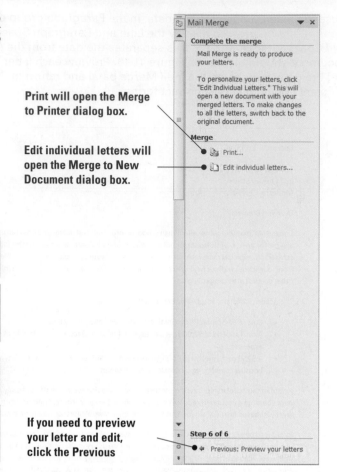

Mail Merge

Complete the merge

Mail Merge is ready to produce your letters.

To personalize your letters, click "Edit Individual Letters." This will open a new document with your merged letters. To make changes to all the letters, switch back to the original document.

Merge

Print...

Edit individual letters...

If you need to preview your letter and edit, click the Previous

Step 6 of 6

Previous: Preview your letters

CERTIFICATION READY? **7.1.1**

How do you set up a main document using the Mail Merge Wizard?

CERTIFICATION READY? **7.2.1**

How do you finalize a merge document using the Mail Merge Wizard?

CERTIFICATION READY? **7.2.1**

How do you preview and print a merge document using the Mail Merge Wizard?

3. Close the Mail Merge pane.

4. **SAVE** the merge document as ***congratulation_letter_merged*** in your USB flash drive in the lesson folder and **CLOSE** the file.

PAUSE. LEAVE Word open to use in the next exercise.

Setting Up a Main Document Manually

You can begin working with Mail Merge by keying your letter and using an existing data source, creating your own data source list and keying your recipients' information, or using Outlook to get your contacts from. You don't need to have the Access program installed on your computer because Word makes it easy to create your list of recipients. It is easy to create a database in Word because the fields are already identified for you. After setting up your document, the address block and greeting line are inserted the same way they were in the Step by Step Mail Merge Wizard. You can preview your results and check for errors using the tools available in the Preview Results group, and then perform the merge. In this exercise, you will create a document, key information, insert an existing data source, insert the address block and greeting line, check for errors in the document, preview the letters, and merge.

STEP BY STEP   **Set Up a Main Document Manually**

1. Create a new blank document, click the File tab, then click New, and click Create.

2. Click the Mailings tab in the Start Mail Merge group; click the drop-down arrow to display the Start Mail Merge menu.

WILEY **PLUS** *EXTRA*

WileyPLUS Extra! features an online tutorial of this task.

3. Choose Letters. (The same letter and data source used in the previous exercise will be used to perform the mail merge manually.)

PAUSE. LEAVE Word open to use in the next exercise.

STEP BY STEP   **Select Recipients**

1. In the Start Mail Merge group, click the **drop-down arrow** to display the Select Recipients menu as shown in Figure 11-17. There are three options available. (You will be opening an existing data source file from your lesson folder. Notice the commands on the Ribbon are faded and therefore not available until a data source file is opened).

Figure 11-17

Select Recipients menu

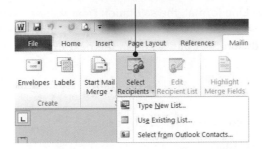

Using the Ribbon to create a Mail Merge manually

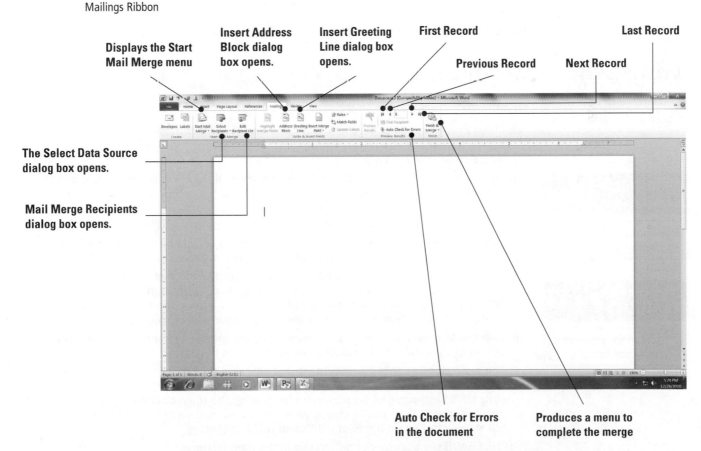

The *student_list* file for this lesson is available on the book companion website or in WileyPLUS.

2. Select **Use Existing List.** The Select Data Source dialog box opens. Use the scroll bar to locate your USB flash drive and navigate to your data files for the lesson folder.

3. **OPEN** the *student_list* data source file from the lesson folder. The *student_list* file is a database. After opening the data source file, the commands on the Ribbon become active (Figure 11-18). When selecting a data source file, this file can be a database, an Excel spreadsheet, a table in Word, or it can be opened from your Outlook contacts.

Figure 11-18

Mailings Ribbon

4. At the insertion point, key **March 19, 2011.** Press the **Enter** key twice.

PAUSE. LEAVE the document open to use in the next exercise.

STEP BY STEP   Prepare Merge Fields

USE the document open from the previous exercise.

1. On the Mailings tab, in the Write & Insert Fields group, click the Address Block button. The Insert Address Block dialog box opens. Click OK. Refer to Figure 11-10. When using the Mail Merge Wizard or completing the Mail Merge manually, the same dialog boxes are opened.

2. Press the Enter key once.

3. On the Mailings tab, in the Write & Insert Fields group, click the Greeting Line button. The Insert Greeting Line dialog box opens.

4. For the Greeting Line format, the salutation Dear will be used. You will use the default where Joshua Randal Jr. is shown. Click OK. Press the Enter key once.

PAUSE. LEAVE the document open to use in the next exercise.

STEP BY STEP   Write the Letter

USE the document open from the previous exercise.

1. **Key** the following letter:

   The President of the College, Dr. Jose A. Torres, is extending an invitation to all students who received scholarships for the next academic semester. The Graphic Design Institute recognizes all students for their academic excellence. A reception is being held in your honor on March 29 at 12 noon in the President's Conference Room 19. [Press Enter once.]

   Please confirm your attendance by calling 915-999-9999. [Press Enter once.]

   Regards, [Press Enter twice.]

   Jerry Wright [Press Shift+Enter to insert a line break.]

   Scholarship Committee Chair

PAUSE. LEAVE the document open to use in the next exercise.

STEP BY STEP   Preview the Document

USE the document open from the previous exercise.

1. In the Preview Results group, click the Preview Results button. The first recipient appears. Click the Next Record arrow button to preview the letters for each recipient. Turn Preview Results off.

2. Place the insertion point in the <<AddressBlock>> field. Click the Home tab, and then in the Paragraph group, click the Line and Paragraph Spacing button and then click Remove the Spacing After Paragraph.

3. Place the insertion point in the Greeting line and click the Page Layout tab. In the Paragraph group, click the up arrow until you see 6 pt. The Spacing Before is increased by 6 pts and separates the address block and greeting line.

4. On the Page Layout tab, in the Page Setup group, click the Margins button, then Custom Margins. Key 2 in the Top box to change the top margin. Customized letterheads are used by organizations to print their letters. The top margin must be adjusted to avoid text printing over the organization's logo. Click OK.

5. Click the Mailings tab, and in the Preview Results group, click the Preview Results button to view the formatting changes made to the document. Turn Preview Results off.

6. The main document is the document that contains the body of the letter as well as the Address Block and Greeting Line. Save the main document as *reception_letter* in your USB flash drive in the lesson folder. Saving the main document as a separate document will allow you to merge with a new data source file—when you need to use the same letter again but with a different recipient listing.

PAUSE. LEAVE the document open to use in the next exercise.

CERTIFICATION READY? 7.1.2

How do you perform a mail merge manually?

CERTIFICATION READY? 7.1.2

How do you preview using the Ribbon?

Take Note   Once the main document has been set up, you can format at the beginning of the mail merge process.

EXECUTING MAIL MERGE

The Bottom Line

The final steps in a mail merge are to check for errors, preview the merge, and finalize the merge.

STEP BY STEP **Check for Errors**

USE the document open from the previous exercise.

1. On the Preview Results group, click the Auto Check for Errors button. The Checking and Reporting Errors dialog box opens as shown in Figure 11-19. Select the first option, Simulate the merge and report errors in a new document.

Figure 11-19

Checking and Reporting Errors dialog box

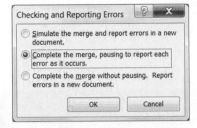

2. A prompt will appear indicating *No mail merge errors have been found* in the *reception_letter*. Click OK.

PAUSE. LEAVE the document open to use in the next exercise.

STEP BY STEP **Complete the Merge**

USE the document open from the previous exercise.

1. In the Finish group, click the drop-down arrow to display the Finish & Merge menu, as shown in Figure 11-20.

Figure 11-20

Finish & Merge menu

2. Select Edit Individual Documents. The Merge to New Document dialog box opens, as shown in Figure 11-21. The All option will merge all letters to a new document, Current record will merge only that record from where your insertion point is positioned, and in the From option, you key the first record and end record to merge. For instance, if you wanted to merge only records 2 and 3, you would key 2 to 3.

Figure 11-21

Merge to New Document dialog box

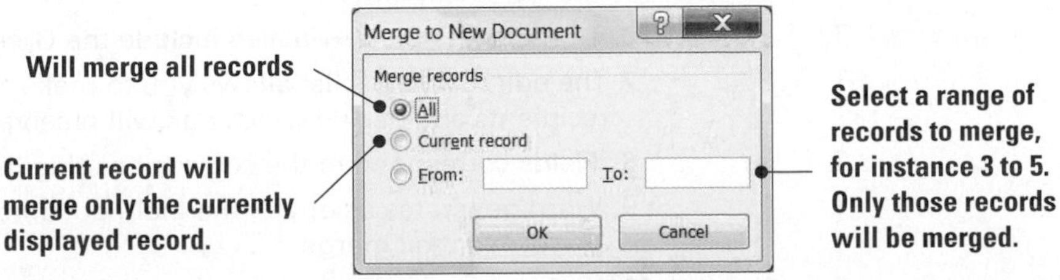

Will merge all records

Current record will merge only the currently displayed record.

Select a range of records to merge, for instance 3 to 5. Only those records will be merged.

3. For this exercise, in the From section key 3 in the first box and in the To box, key 5. Click OK. A new document is produced that displays letters for records 3 through 5 in one document. Scroll through the document to preview that the document is ready to print.

4. SAVE the merged document as *receptionletter_merged* in your USB flash drive in the lesson folder and **CLOSE** the file.

5. CLOSE the mail document *reception_letter* and a prompt will appear asking, *Do you want to save changes made to reception_letter?* Click **Yes**. When you save the main document with the field codes, you will be able to return to your document and recipient list and use the tools available in the Mailings tab. You can also edit the list of recipients and open another data source to send the same letter to another group.

CLOSE Word.

Troubleshooting A document must be opened in Word for the mail merge commands to be available.

<table>
<tr><td>CERTIFICATION READY?</td><td>7.2.1</td></tr>
</table>

How do you print the merge document?

SKILL SUMMARY

In This Lesson You Learned How To:	Exam Objective	Objective Number
Set up a Mail Merge	Perform a mail merge using the Mail Merge Wizard.	7.1.1
	Preview and print a mail merge operation.	7.2.1
	Perform a mail merge manually.	7.1.2
Execute a Mail Merge	Use Auto Check for Errors.	7.1.3

Knowledge Assessment

True/False

Circle T if the statement is true or F if the statement is false.

T F **1.** The main document does not contain the same text or graphics for each merged document.

T F **2.** The data source is a file that contains the information to be merged into a document, for example, names and addresses.

T F **3.** Mail merge fields are inserted in a document using a data source file.

T F **4.** It is a good practice to check for errors before completing the merge process.

T F **5.** Word makes it easy to use an existing list of recipients in a new mail merge document.

T F **6.** The Address Block will also include the Greeting Line.

T F **7.** The edit recipient's list allows you to make changes to the list of recipients and decide which one will receive your letter.

T F **8.** Fields correspond to the column heading in the data file.

T F **9.** Word generates a copy of the main document for reach record when you perform a mail merge.

T F **10.** You cannot preview a document before merging.

Multiple Choice

Select the best response for the following statements.

1. Which tab contains the commands used to perform mail merges?
   a. Merge
   b. Mailings
   c. Mail Merge
   d. Insert

2. What is the first step in performing a mail merge?
   a. Set up the main document
   b. Insert merge fields
   c. Preview the results
   d. Select the recipients

3. Which type of document can be merged with a data source file?
   a. Letter
   b. Label
   c. Envelope
   d. All of the above

4. Which is NOT an option for selecting a list of recipients for the mail merge?
   a. Download from an online directory
   b. Type a new list
   c. Use an existing list
   d. Use your Outlook contacts

5. To merge information into your main document, you must first connect the document to a(n)
   a. Address validator
   b. Form letter
   c. Data source
   d. Website

6. When mail merge fields have been inserted into a document, Word will automatically replace them with information from a data source when the
   a. Main document is saved
   b. Recipients are selected
   c. Merge fields are inserted
   d. Mail merge is performed

7. Mail merge fields are enclosed by
   a. Quotation marks (" ")
   b. Chevrons (<< >>)
   c. Apostrophes (' ')
   d. Brackets ([ ])

8. When previewing the mail merge document, Word replaces the merge fields with
   a. Sample data
   b. Blank spaces
   c. Actual data
   d. Highlighted headings

9. When a user selects the Current Record under the Finish & Merge menu, which document will appear in a new document screen?
   a. All documents
   b. From where your insertion point is placed in the main document
   c. Records 1 and 3
   d. It will not appear in a new document screen.

10. When you save the main document, you also save
    a. All the data in an Excel spreadsheet
    b. Any other open file
    c. The default return address for Word
    d. Its connection to the data file

Competency Assessment

Project 11-1: Judges for Business Student's Contest

As the director of business and marketing education at the School of Fine Arts, you have recruited professional members of the local business community to serve as volunteers for judging a state contest for high school business students. You are sending a mail merge letter that contains necessary information for the judges and want to set up the main document.

GET READY. LAUNCH Word if it is not already running.

@ The *judges* document file for this lesson is available on the book companion website or in WileyPLUS.

1. Click the File tab, then Open. Use the scroll bar to locate your data files for this letter and select the *judges* document and click the Open button.
2. Click the Mailings tab, in the Start Mail Merge group, click the drop-down arrow and select the Step by Step Mail Merge Wizard.
3. At the bottom of the Mail Merge pane, click the link Next: Starting document.
4. Under the Select starting document section, Use the current document is already selected. At the bottom of the pane, click the link Next: Select recipients.
5. Under the Select recipients section, you will be using the default, Use an existing list. Click the Browse link under the Use an existing list section.

@ The *judges_list* document file for this lesson is available on the book companion website or in WileyPLUS.

6. Navigate to the data source file in the lesson folder. Select *judges_list*, and click Open.
7. The Mail Merge Recipients dialog box opens. Click the check box for Houston, Peter to remove the check from the check box and click OK. Turning off the check mark for Peter Houston will remove him as a recipient; therefore, he will not receive a letter. His name will still remain in the data source file.
8. Advance to the next step, and click the Next: Write your letter link at the bottom of the Mail Merge pane. The letter is the current document.
9. The insertion point should be resting in front of the T in *Thank*. Press Enter twice and move your insertion point to the first blank line.
10. Key March 29, 2011. Press the Enter key once.
11. On the Mail Merge pane, click the Address block link. Keep the default settings and click OK.
12. Move the insertion point to the blank line below address block. On the Mail Merge pane, click the Greeting line link. In the Greeting line format, keep the first options the same and change the comma to a colon. Click OK.
13. At the bottom of the Mail Merge pane, click the Next: Preview your letters link.
14. Beginning with the first recipient, select the text from Ms. Karen Archer through the zip code, 44511. The whole address is now selected; click the Home tab, and in the Paragraph group, click the Line and Paragraph Spacing button and select Remove the Spacing After Paragraph.
15. Place your insertion point in the salutation, Dear Ms. Archer. In the Paragraph group, click the Line and Paragraph Spacing button and select Add Space Before Paragraph.
16. At the bottom of the Mail Merge pane, click the Next: Complete the merge link.
17. SAVE the main document as *judges_letter* in your USB flash in the lesson folder.

LEAVE the document open for the next project.

Project 11-2: Judges for Business Student's Contest

You are ready to complete the mail merge to the list of professional members of the local business community volunteering to judge a state contest for high school business students.

GET READY. USE the document that is open from the previous exercise.

1. On the Mail Merge pane, click the Next: Complete the merge link.
2. Under the Merge section of the Mail Merge pane, click the Edit Individual letters. The default All is selected. Click OK.
3. A new document (Letters1) opens; it consists of all four merged letters.
4. **SAVE** the merged document as *judges_merged* in your USB flash drive in the lesson folder and **CLOSE** the file.
5. **SAVE** the main document as *judges_main_letter* in your USB flash drive in the lesson folder and **CLOSE** the file.

LEAVE Word open for the next project.

Proficiency Assessment

@ The *advertising_letter* document file for this lesson is available on the book companion website or in WileyPLUS.

@ The *committee_members* document file for this lesson is available on the book companion website or in WileyPLUS.

@ The *welcome_cellar_letter* document file for this lesson is available on the book companion website or in WileyPLUS.

@ The *cellar_select* document file for this lesson is available on the book companion website or in WileyPLUS.

Project 11-3: Advertising Letter

The marketing representative, Isabel Diaz, has asked you to prepare a short letter to the committee reminding them of the deadline. Use the Step by Step Mail Merge Wizard to create the merge document.

GET READY. OPEN the *advertising_letter* document from the lesson folder.

1. Set up the letter as the main document.
2. Select the *committee_members* document as the recipient's list from the lesson folder.
3. Key May 29, 20XX.
4. Insert the Address Block and Greeting Line. Use the colon in place of the comma.
5. Place your insertion point in the Address Block, and click the Home tab. In the Paragraph group, click the Line and Paragraph Spacing button and select Remove the Spacing After Paragraph.
6. Place your insertion point in the Greeting Line. In the Paragraph group, click the Line and Paragraph Spacing button and select Add Space Before Paragraph.
7. Click Auto Check for Errors and Preview the document before printing.
8. **SAVE** the merged document as *advertising_merged_letter* in your USB flash drive in the lesson folder and **CLOSE** the file.
9. **SAVE** the main document as *advertising_main_letter* in your USB flash drive in the lesson folder and **CLOSE** the file.

LEAVE Word open for the next project.

Project 11-4: Welcome Letter

You are the office manager at Coho Winery & Vineyard where a select group of customers are invited to join the Cellar Select Friends, who receive special promotions and offers. Open an existing letter and data source and merge.

GET READY. LAUNCH Word if it is not already running.

1. **OPEN** the *welcome_cellar_letter* document and set up as the main document.
2. **OPEN** the *cellar_select* document as the recipient list.

3. Insert the Address Block and Greeting Line. Use the comma in the Greeting Line format.

4. Click Auto Check for Errors and Preview the document before printing.

5. **SAVE** the merged document as *cellar_merged_letter* in your USB flash drive in the lesson folder.

6. **SAVE** the main document as *welcome_cellar_mainltr* in your USB flash drive in the lesson folder.

LEAVE Word open for the next project.

Mastery Assessment

@ The *selection_letter* document file for this lesson is available on the book companion website or in WileyPLUS.

@ The *candidate_list* document file for this lesson is available on the book companion website or in WileyPLUS.

Project 11-5: Office Manager Position

As the assistant to the office manager at Tech Terrace Real Estate, you have been asked to set up a main document. There were many candidates who applied for the office manager's position.

GET READY. LAUNCH Word if it is not already running.

1. **OPEN** the *selection_letter* and set up as the main document.

2. **OPEN** the *candidate_list* as the recipient list.

3. Insert the Address Block and Greeting Line. Use the colon in the Greeting Line format.

4. Change the top margin to 2″ to accommodate the logo on the company's letterhead. Remove the spacing before and after in the address block and greeting line.

5. **SAVE** the main document as *selection_mainltr* in your USB flash drive in the lesson folder.

LEAVE the document open for the next project.

Project 11-6: Merging the Office Manager Position Letters

You are continuing with the previous project and are ready to complete the merge process.

GET READY. USE the document that is open from the previous exercise.

1. Edit the recipient's list and remove the check mark from Ted Bremer and Eric Rothenberg. Removing the check mark by the recipient's name will not add them to the merge document. Their names will remain in the recipients data source file.

2. Insert the Address Block and Greeting Line. Use the comma for the Greeting Line format.

3. Click Auto Check for Errors and Preview the document before printing.

4. **SAVE** the merged document as *selection_merged_letter* in your USB flash drive in the lesson folder.

5. **SAVE** the main document in your USB flash drive in the lesson folder.

CLOSE Word.

INTERNET READY

Microsoft's website (Figure 11-22) is a good tool for keeping up-to-date with the latest applications. Use the Microsoft website and learn more about mail merge. The website is http://office.microsoft.com/en-us/word-help/use-mail-merge-to-create-and-print-letters-and-other-documents-HA101857701.aspx.

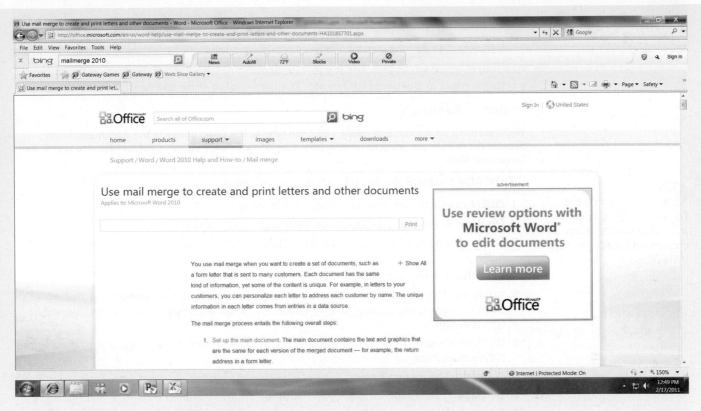

Figure 11-22

Microsoft website Word 2010 How-to Mail Merge

Workplace *Ready*

USING WORD'S MAIL MERGE

Creating correspondence is likely the most popular business use for Word. Often, companies create standard business letters that they can personalize with individual contact names, addresses, company names, and more. As the Director of Charities for Children's Hospital, you need to send out thank-you letters to the nearly 200 corporate donors for this year's toy drive. To create each personalized letter, you have two choices: manually inserting the personalized information into individual letters for all of the donors, or using Word's Mail Merge.

The first option would require manually searching through each letter, finding the appropriate spot where each piece of personalized information should be inserted, and then typing in the information. If several copies of this letter need to be sent to different individuals or companies, this process would need to be completed for each letter—a very cumbersome task.

You decide that a much better choice is using the Mail Merge option found in Word. This option provides the ability to insert text placeholders for personalized information into a letter. An existing Word document can be selected during the Mail Merge process, or you can choose to create a new letter. You already have an Access database containing the necessary information for all donors, such as company name, contact name, and address, so you choose to import this information from the database. At the end of the process, you preview how the letters will appear and click to complete the task.

By using Word's Mail Merge, you saved yourself a great deal of time and aggravation. Now, if only all your business decisions could be so obvious!

Circling Back 3

As a fourth-grade writing teacher at a private elementary school, you have been asked to present a research paper at a national conference. You use Word to write and edit the research paper.

Project 1: Bookmarks

While working on the research paper, you often refer to the same places in the document. Insert bookmarks to help you jump to specific text more quickly. Apply styles to the headings to create the Document Map.

@ The *research* file for this Circling Back is available on the book companion website or in WileyPLUS.

GET READY. LAUNCH Word if it is not already running.

1. **OPEN** *research* from the data files for this lesson.
2. On page 1, select the Introduction heading.
3. On the Home tab, in the Styles group, click the More button to display the Quick Styles gallery.
4. Click the Heading 1 option.
5. Apply the Heading 1 style to the remaining headings in the document: Community in the Classroom, Technology within Literature Circles, Computer-Mediated Discussion Groups, and Conclusion.
6. On the View tab, in the Show group, click the Navigation Pane check box to display the Navigation Pane.
7. Close the Navigation Pane.
8. On page 1, select the Introduction heading.
9. On the Insert tab, in the Links group, click the Bookmark button.
10. In the Bookmark dialog box, key Introduction in the Bookmark name box.
11. Click the Add button.
12. Create a bookmark for each of the remaining headings in the document. Use the following abbreviated headings as bookmark names: Community, Technology, Discussion, and Conclusion.
13. Insert a comment by Conclusion and key Test each bookmark.
14. **SAVE** the document as *research_navigate* in your USB flash drive in the lesson folder.

PAUSE. LEAVE Word and the document open for the next project.

Project 2: Table of Contents

A table of contents helps readers quickly locate topics of interest, and an index helps readers find the location of specific topics, words, and phrases. Because your research paper is a long document, both of these would be helpful. Insert a table of contents and an index so that all sections of the document can be referred to easily.

GET READY. LAUNCH Word if it is not already running.

USE the document that is open from the previous project.

1. Delete the comment by Conclusion.
2. Place the insertion point on page 1 on a line after the author's name.
3. Insert a blank page.
4. On the References tab, in the Table of Contents group, click the Table of Contents button to display the gallery of built-in styles.
5. Click the Automatic Table 2 style to insert a table of contents on its own page.
6. On the View tab, in the Show group, click the check box at the Navigation Pane.
7. In the Navigation Pane box, key literature circles.
8. Use the Advance Find and Highlight All occurrences.
9. Run the Spelling and Grammar tool. Ignore all the proper nouns and field codes.

10. **SAVE** the document as ***research_contents*** in your USB flash drive in the lesson folder and **CLOSE** the file.

PAUSE. LEAVE Word open for the next project.

Project 3: Main Document

Insert merge fields to create a main document.

GET READY. LAUNCH Word if it is not already running.

@ The ***speakerthankyou3*** file for this Circling Back is available on the book companion website or in WileyPLUS.

@ The ***speakerlist*** file for this Circling Back is available on the book companion website or in WileyPLUS.

1. **OPEN** ***speakerthankyou3*** from the data files for this lesson.
2. On the Mailings tab, in the Start Mail Merge group, click the Select Recipients button. Then select Use Existing List from the menu.
3. Navigate to the data files for this lesson and select ***speakerlist***.
4. Select the text beginning with Jo Berry through 64163, and delete.
5. Click the Address Block button and click OK to accept the format.
6. Move the insertion point down two lines.
7. Click the Greeting Line button and click OK to accept the Dear Mr. Randall format.
8. Position the insertion point at the end of the first sentence, after the blank space following the word *on* and key September 24.
9. **SAVE** the main document as ***speaker_thank_you_main***.
10. In the Preview Results group, click the Auto Check for Errors button. Preview each letter for errors and close.
11. In the Preview Results group, click the Preview Results button.
12. On the Mailings tab, in the Preview Results group, click Next Record and continue until you have previewed each letter.
13. Click the Preview Results button again.
14. On the Mailings tab, in the Finish group, click the Finish & Merge button.
15. Click Edit Individual Documents.
16. In the Merge to New Document dialog box, select All and click OK.
17. Save the merged document as ***thank_you_merge*** and **CLOSE** the file.
18. **CLOSE** the ***speaker_thank_you_main*** file without saving.

PAUSE. CLOSE Word.

12 Maintaining Documents and Working with Templates

LESSON SKILL MATRIX

Skill	Exam Objective	Objective Number
Arranging Document Views	Reorganize a document outline, master documents, and subdocuments.	1.1.4
Working with Templates	Find templates.	1.6.1

KEY TERMS

- **master document**
- **subdocument**
- **template**

You are the president of the Lakeville.NET User's Group, a group of students, faculty, and professionals in the community whose purpose is to educate, help build development skills, and provide a forum for networking. This group meets monthly and schedules regular workshops and speakers on relevant topics. In this role, you are discovering that you use many of the same types of documents on a regular basis, and you would like to streamline the process of creating similar documents. In this lesson, you will learn to work with outlines and arrange master documents and subdocuments and locate a template on the computer and Internet.

SOFTWARE ORIENTATION

Outline View

The Outlining tab contains buttons for working with long documents and arranging the document into smaller sections. The Outlining tab is shown in Figure 12-1.

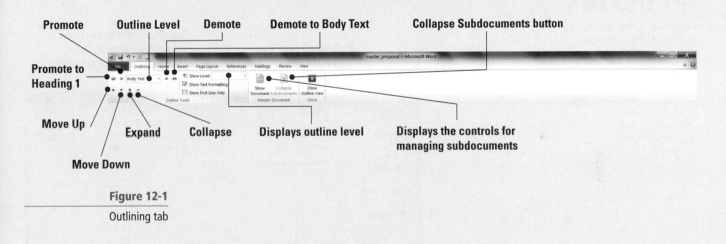

Figure 12-1

Outlining tab

Use this figure as a reference throughout this lesson as well as the rest of this book.

ARRANGING DOCUMENT VIEWS

The Bottom Line

Creating master documents enables you to work efficiently with large reports such as your research paper. Creating sections in a long document makes it more manageable and easy to edit.

Working with a Master and Subdocuments

The **master document** is the main document from a Word file and is organized into smaller sections. **Subdocuments** are the sections within the master document that have been separated into smaller sections. The subdocuments exist within the master document and as a separate file. For example, you would create a master document for long reports and research papers. Master documents are formatted with heading styles and then separated into subdocuments using the Outlining Tools. As a student, you have research papers to complete for your classes. You outline a research paper to make it more manageable for you to work with a section at a time. Working with the master and subdocuments is similar to how you work on sections of your paper. You can edit from your master document or work in the subdocument as a separate individual document. When you edit and save subdocuments independently, the master document automatically gets updated. When you need to review the master document, all editing changes will appear in the document.

Saving the Master Document

You must save the master document first before creating subdocuments. In this exercise, you will learn to save the master document.

STEP BY STEP **Save the Master Document**

OPEN the *hosting* document from the lesson folder.

The *hosting* document file for this lesson is available on the book companion website or in WileyPLUS.

1. Click the File tab, then Save As. In the Save As dialog box, use the scroll bar to locate your USB flash drive.

2. Click the New folder button located under the address bar and Key MASTER_DOCUMENT, and press Enter. Then click the Open button to place the MASTER_DOCUMENT folder in the address bar, or double-click. You are creating a folder in which to save the master document file.

3. In the File name box, key master_proposal. Figure 12-2 displays the file in the folder.

WileyPLUS Extra! features an online tutorial of this task.

Figure 12-2

Save As dialog box

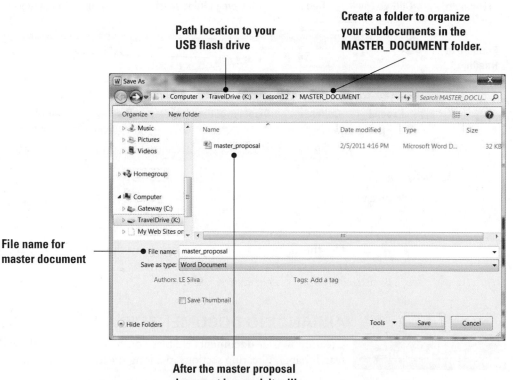

Path location to your USB flash drive

Create a folder to organize your subdocuments in the MASTER_DOCUMENT folder.

File name for master document

After the master proposal document is saved, it will appear in the MASTER_ DOCUMENT folder.

4. Click the Save button to save the document in the MASTER_DOCUMENT folder.

PAUSE. LEAVE the document open for the next exercise.

 Ref

Creating and saving documents was covered in Lesson 1.

Creating Subdocuments

A subdocument is part of the master document and separated into small sections. This feature would be useful for a large research paper—you could work on one subdocument section at a time rather than having the whole document opened. The first step is identifying the levels within the subdocuments. A heading style should be identified within the document first to determine the outline level. Editing subdocuments automatically updates the master document. The Outlining tab contains the Collapse and Expand subdocument buttons that correlate with the master document. In this exercise, you will save the document as a master document in a specific folder and create subdocuments that are saved separately.

STEP BY STEP **Create Subdocuments**

USE the document open from the previous exercise.

1. Click the **View** tab in the Document Views group, then click the **Outline** button. The Outlining tab is now available on the Ribbon.

2. In the Outline Tools group, click the **drop-down arrow** at Show Level and select **Level 1** to make the document more manageable. This document has already been formatted with heading styles; when you change the levels, the document collapses and only Level 1 displays on the screen, as shown in Figure 12-3.

Select the plus symbol (+) to select a heading.

Click the Expand (+) button to display content within a heading.

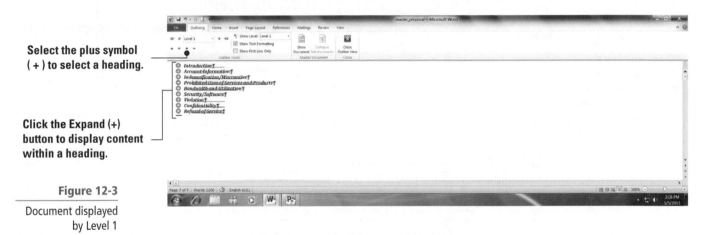

Figure 12-3

Document displayed by Level 1

3. On the Master Document group, click **Show Document**. Additional commands appear on the Ribbon, as displayed in Figure 12-4.

Click to display additional commands.

Creates a subdocument

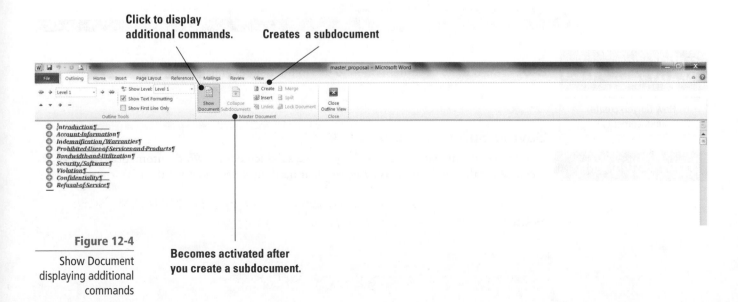

Figure 12-4

Show Document displaying additional commands

Becomes activated after you create a subdocument.

4. Click the **plus (+)** symbol next to Introduction to select the heading. The paragraph within the heading is also selected automatically.

5. On the Master Document group, click the **Create** button to create a subdocument. Notice that Introduction is surrounded by a border. The border indicates this is a subdocument. Also, it automatically places a continuous section break and the *Collapse* button is activated in the Master Document group.

 Ref   Section breaks were covered in Lesson 5.

6. Select the **plus (+)** symbol next to the Account Information heading, then click the **Create** button on the Master Document group. A border is placed around the subdocument, Account Information, heading.

7. Repeat your steps for the remaining headings: Indemnification/Warranties, Prohibited Uses of Services and Products, Bandwidth and Utilization, Security/Software, Violation, Confidentiality, and Refusal of Service. The document should display as shown in Figure 12-5. A border appears around each subdocument.

Figure 12-5

Document with subdocuments

Collapse button is activated.

A border is placed around the subdocument after you create.

Continuous section breaks are automatically inserted to separate subdocuments.

Subdocument icon. When you click the subdocument icon, the subdocument heading and contents are selected.

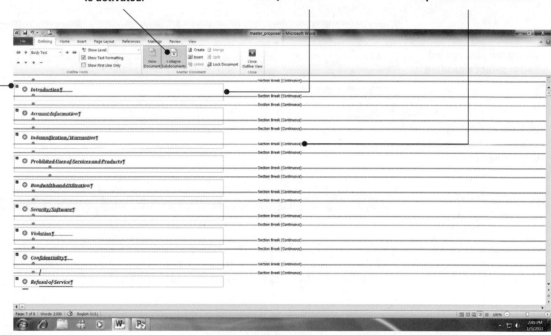

CERTIFICATION READY? 1.1.4

PAUSE. LEAVE the document open to use in the next exercise.

How do you create subdocuments?

Saving Subdocuments

The Bottom Line

The master document will be saved with the subdocuments. Word automatically creates the filename for the subdocuments based on their heading styles and saves them as separate files.

Save Subdocuments

USE the document that is open from the previous exercise.

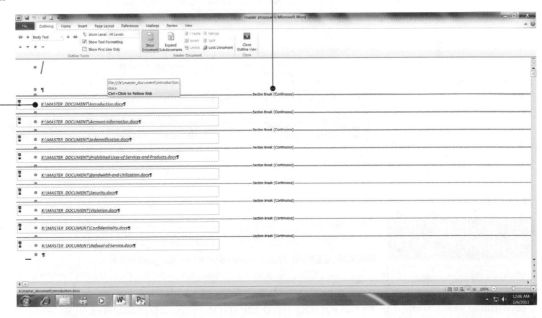

<table>
<tr><td>

CERTIFICATION READY? 1.1.4

How do you save a master document with subdocuments?

</td><td>

1. Click the SAVE 💾 button on the Quick Access Toolbar to save the ***master_proposal*** document with the updated changes made to the document. Word saves each subdocument as a separate file based on the heading.

2. Click the File tab and then close.

</td></tr>
</table>

PAUSE. LEAVE the document open to use in the next exercise.

View the Subdocuments in the Master Document

USE the document that is open from the previous exercise.

1. Click the File tab and click Open. The MASTER_DOCUMENT folder is already opened. Word automatically saves each subdocument as separate files based on their headings. You started with one file in your MASTER_DOCUMENT folder and now you have several subdocuments.

2. Select the ***master_proposal*** document and click open or double-click. When opening a master document, the subdocuments will show the target location of the saved master document in a hyperlink. By default the subdocuments are locked and collapsed.

3. Figure 12-6 displays the document with the target location of the saved subdocuments with hyperlinks. Each hyperlink will go directly to the subdocument when opened.

Figure 12-6

Master document with subdocuments

Continuous section breaks inserted automatically

Target location for each subdocument within the Master_Document folder

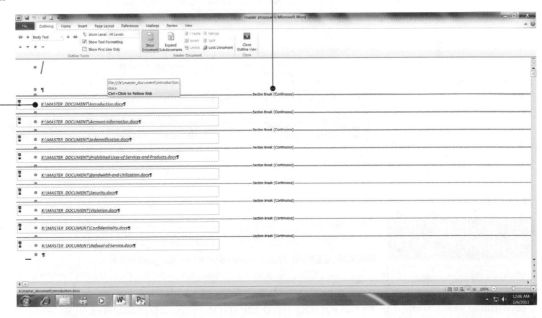

PAUSE. LEAVE Word open for the next exercise.

Expanding and Collapsing Subdocuments

To view the master document with its contents, click the Expand subdocuments button. The Collapse subdocuments button will close the subdocuments. In this exercise, you will expand and collapse subdocuments.

STEP BY STEP   **Expand and Collapse Subdocuments**

1. Click the Expand Subdocuments button in the Master Document group and notice that all subdocuments are expanded, as shown in Figure 12-7. Each heading and its contents now appear within a border.

Troubleshooting If you do not see the headings and contents in a border, click the Show Documents button in the Master Document group.

Figure 12-7

Subdocument expanded

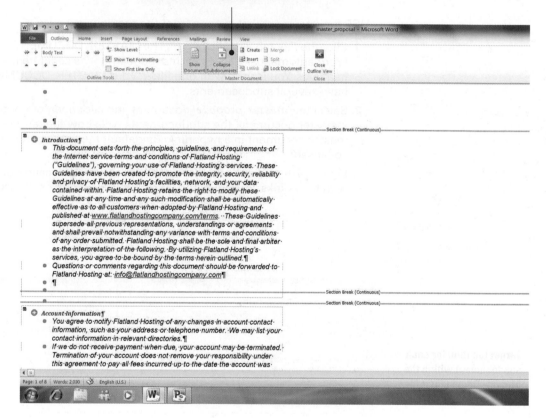

2. Click the Collapse Subdocument button in the Master Document group. Subdocuments are now collapsed.

PAUSE. LEAVE Word open for the next exercise.

CERTIFICATION READY? **1.1.4**

How do you expand subdocuments in a master document to view contents?

CERTIFICATION READY? **1.1.4**

How do you collapse subdocuments in a master document?

Promoting and Demoting Subdocuments

Rearrange the levels in Word by promoting and demoting subdocuments just like you would in an outline for a research paper. For instance, to demote the Level 1 heading to a Level 2, you would use the Outline Tools groups. In this lesson, you learn to promote and demote levels.

STEP BY STEP **Promote and Demote Subdocuments**

USE the document that is open from the previous exercise.

1. Click the Expand Subdocuments button in the Master Document group to expand all subdocuments.

2. Point at the plus (+) symbol next to the Account Information heading—when the mouse pointer changes to the four move arrows, click once.

3. In the Outline Tools groups in the Outlining tab, click the Demote button once. The Account Information has been demoted to a Level 2, as shown in Figure 12-8.

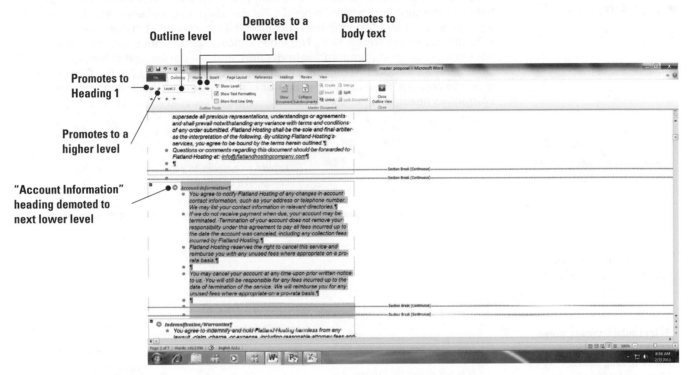

Figure 12-8

Heading demoted

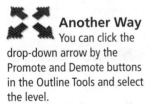

Another Way
You can click the drop-down arrow by the Promote and Demote buttons in the Outline Tools and select the level.

4. Click the Promote arrow once. The Account Information has been promoted back to a Level 1. Click the Demote button again to demote back to a Level 2.

PAUSE. LEAVE Word open for the next exercise.

Reorganizing Subdocuments

Subdocuments can be rearranged within the master document. Subdocuments can be moved from one location to another by using the command buttons on the Outlining tab or by dragging and dropping. Or you can merge two or more subdocuments into one subdocument. In this exercise, you will reorganize subdocuments.

STEP BY STEP   Reorganize Subdocuments

USE the document that is open from the previous exercise.

1. Deselect Account Information by clicking in a blank area of the document screen.

2. On the Outline Tools, click the **check box** to add a check mark next to Show First Line Only. The subdocuments now display only the first line and hide the remaining contents, which makes the subdocuments more manageable to work with.

Another Way
Click the subdocument icon to select heading and contents.

3. Click the **plus (+)** symbol by the Indemnification/Warranties subdocument to select. Position the insertion point over the plus (+) symbol until you see the move arrows (four arrows).

4. Press and hold the mouse button and drag and drop above Account Information in between the continuous section breaks. As you drag, you will see a solid arrow on the left side and a gray horizontal line—position the move arrow between the continuous section breaks (see Figure 12-9). The Indemnification/Warranties subdocument now follows the first paragraph, Introduction, and the border that surrounded the subdocument has been removed. Click the **Create** button in the Master Document group to create a subdocument. A border is placed around the Indemnification/Warranties heading. Deselect.

Figure 12-9

Moving selected subdocument

A horizontal line will appear as a guide as you reorganize headings.

A solid arrow along with a horizontal line indicates section breaks.

Select subdocument, press and hold the left mouse button to drag above "Account Information."

Select the heading and its content by clicking on the subdocument heading or the plus (+) symbol.

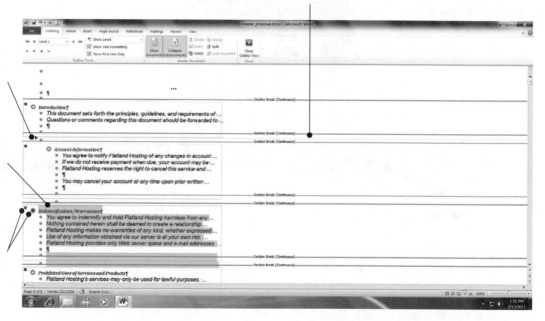

5. Scroll down and click to select the subdocument icon 🖳 to view *Security/Software* subdocument heading and its contents.

6. On the Outline Tools group, click the **Move Down** 🡇 button until it is positioned below the continuous section break below **Violation**.

7. The Security/Software subdocument is no longer surrounded by a border. Click the **Create** button on the Master Document group to create the selection as a subdocument. A border appears around the Security/Software heading and its content.

8. Click the **Save** button in the Quick Access Toolbar and click the **File** tab, then click **Close** to close the *master_proposal* document.

9. Click the **File** tab, then **Open**. Select the *master_proposal* document and double-click to open. The document opens with hyperlinks. The updated changes to the subdocuments are shown in the hyperlinks. The Indemnification/Warranties subdocument new filename has been changed to Indeminification1 and Security/Software has been changed to Security1.

10. Click the **Expand Documents** button in the Master Document group.

11. Click the **View** tab, and in the Document Views, click **Print Layout**. Scroll through the document and review the changes made. Indemnification/Warranties is listed as the second heading following Introduction, followed by the Account Information, and Security/Software is positioned below Violation.

PAUSE. LEAVE Word open for the next exercise.

CERTIFICATION READY? **1.1.4**

How do you rearrange subdocuments?

Editing an Individual Subdocument

Subdocuments can be managed in the master document or you can open the document in its own window. In this exercise, you will edit a subdocument while in the master document and edit a subdocument separately.

1. In the Documents Views group, click the **Outline** button to open the Outlining tab.

2. Click the **Collapse** button to display the hyperlinks for the subdocuments.

3. Point to the Introduction subdocument hyperlink, press the **Ctrl** key and click to open in a separate window. The subdocument opens in a new window and is ready for editing and formatting.

4. In the first sentence, double-click to select *principles*, then press and hold the **Ctrl** key and double-click **guidelines and requirements**. Then in the second sentence, double-click **integrity**, **security** and **reliability** and **privacy**.

5. On the Home tab, in the Font group, click the **Bold** button, then click the **drop-down arrow** next to the Font Color button to open the menu. In the Standard Colors, select **Dark Red**.

6. Click the **Save** button on the Quick Access Toolbar and close the Introduction subdocument file.

7. Click the Outlining tab to make it available with its commands.

8. In the Master Document group, click the **Expand Subdocument** button. Notice the bolded Dark Red text under the Introduction heading. Changes made in the *Introduction* subdocument automatically updated the master document. Click the **Collapse Subdocuments** button to close.

9. Click the **Save** button on the Quick Access Toolbar and close the *master_proposal* document.

10. Click the **File** tab, then **Open**. The *Open* dialog box opens and the MASTER_DOCUMENT folder is opened on the address bar. Select the *Prohibited Uses of Services and Products* subdocument and click **Open** or double-click. Editing a subdocument in its own window makes it more manageable to format the document.

11. Triple-click to select the second paragraph, and then click the **Page Layout** tab. In the Page Background group, click the **Page Borders** button. Click the **Borders** tab, and under the *Setting* section, select **Shadow**. Click the **drop-down arrow** in the Width section and select 2¼; then under the Color section, click the **drop-down arrow** and select **Red, Accent 2** color (first row, sixth option) under Theme colors. A colored border with a 2¼ width will be applied to the paragraph.

12. Click the **Shading** tab, then under the Fill section, click the **drop-down arrow** and select the **Red, Accent 2, Lighter 80%** color (second row, sixth option) in *Theme colors*. A shading will be applied to the paragraph within the border. Click **OK**.

13. Under the headings General, System, and Network and Billings, select the contents with the bullets and on the Home tab, Paragraph group, click the **drop-down arrow** on the Bullets button and select the **solid diamond**. The bullets have been replaced with the new bullets on the selected text.

14. Scroll down to the end of the document, last paragraph, and select the **Next Page Section break**. Press the **Delete** key to remove the blank page at the end of the document.

15. Click the **Save** button on the Quick Access Toolbar to save the Prohibited Uses of Services and Products subdocument. **CLOSE** the subdocument. The master document is automatically updated after you save the subdocument.

16. Click the **File** tab, then **Open**. The MASTER_DOCUMENT folder is opened; select the *master_proposal* and click **Open** or double-click to open the document.

17. Click the **Expand Subdocument** button on the Master Document group to expand the contents within the headings.

18. Scroll down and notice the bullets under the headings *General, System,* and *Network and Billings.*

19. On the Close group, click the **Close Outline View** button. The document is now in **Print Layout** view; scroll down and notice the border and shading in the second paragraph under the *Prohibited Uses of Services and Products.* (See Figure 12-10.) You were not able to view the border and shading while in the Outlining tab but you can view them in Print Layout.

Figure 12-10

Print Layout view of document with formatting changes

Move slide

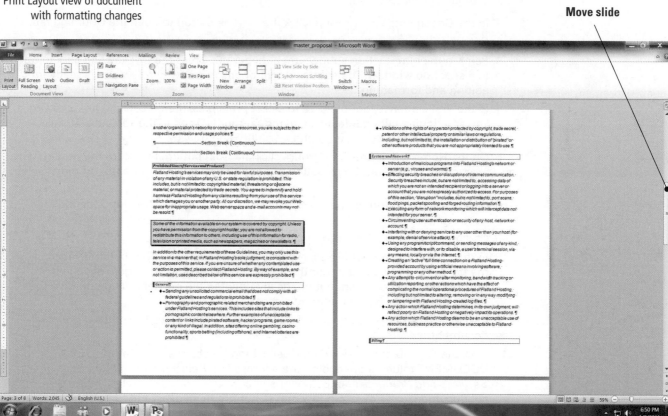

20. On the Document Views group, in the View tab, click the **Outline** button. **CLOSE** the file. If prompted to save changes, click **Save** and the document will close.

PAUSE. LEAVE the document open for the next exercise.

SOFTWARE ORIENTATION

Template Options in Backstage

You can work more efficiently by basing many of your new documents on templates that Word provides—there are many choices available for working with different templates, as shown in Figure 12-11.

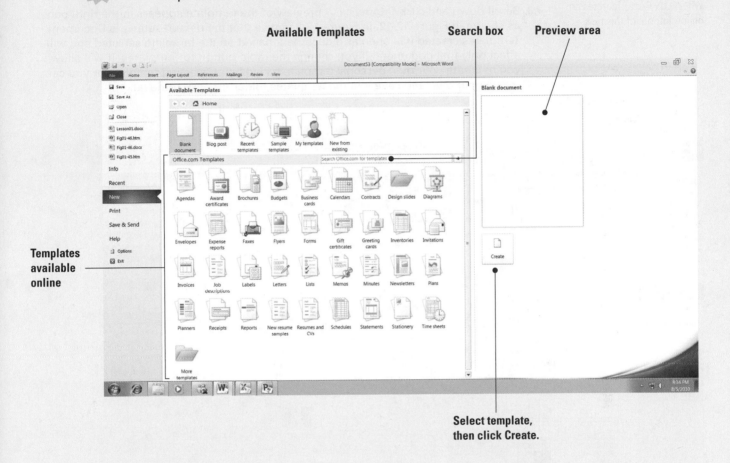

Available Templates   **Search box**   **Preview area**

Templates available online

Select template, then click Create.

Using templates keeps you from having to re-create documents such as interoffice memorandums, monthly newsletters that you share with employees, recordings of minutes from meetings, and more. In Backstage, the New command allows you to work with templates that are already installed, search for a template online, open a blank template, or create your own template.

WORKING WITH TEMPLATES

The Bottom Line

You can choose from many different categories of templates, such as letters, memos, resumes, flyers, forms, and more. Some templates are preinstalled with Word and more options are available online. A **template** is a master document with predefined page layout, fonts, margins, and styles that is used to create new documents that will share the same basic formatting. Templates are reusable even if you saved the document with a different filename. In this exercise, you will locate an installed template.

Locating a Template Installed on Your Computer

STEP BY STEP   **Locate a Template Installed on Your Computer**

GET READY. If necessary, before you begin these steps, launch Word.

WILEY PLUS EXTRA

WileyPLUS Extra! features an online tutorial of this task.

1. Click the **File** tab, then select **New**.
2. In the Available Templates categories, click **Sample Templates**. Sample Templates are stored on your computer with many different options from which to select.
3. Scroll down and click **Origin Fax**. A preview of the template appears in the right pane, as shown in Figure 12-12. In Figure 12-2, notice that the default setting is Document. Templates created will open as a document based on the template selected and will affect only that document. If you change the radio button to **Templates**, it will allow you to create your own personal template based on an existing template or you can create your own and save it in the Templates folder for easy retrieval.

Figure 12-12

Sample Templates

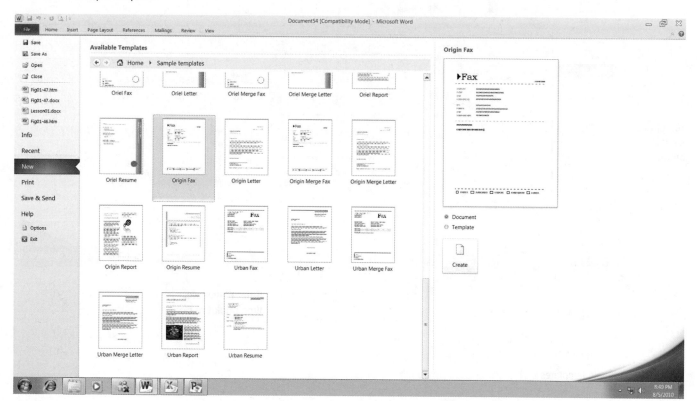

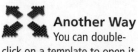

Troubleshooting If your computer does not have this preinstalled template under Sample Templates, simply choose another one.

4. To see additional templates, use the vertical scroll bar to scroll through the list and click to preview.

Another Way
You can double-click on a template to open it.

5. Select the **Oriel Report** and then click **Create**. The report is displayed on your screen. Notice that this document contains features covered in previous lessons such as placeholders, quotes text boxes, and styles.

6. **CLOSE**; do not save the report.

PAUSE. LEAVE the program open for the next exercise.

CERTIFICATION
READY?   **1.6.1**

How do you open a preinstalled template?

Finding Templates on the Internet

Microsoft offers numerous templates online and these are also available from third-party providers, as well as other users in the community. You can select from a category using the Office.com Templates section or search for a template using the Search bar and searching by keywords. You can also use the Help feature and search for additional information on templates on your computer or online. You must be connected to the Internet to search for templates online. In this exercise, you will select a template category and view a listing of templates online.

STEP BY STEP   **Find Templates on the Internet**

1. Click the **File** tab, then **New**.
2. In the Office.com Template section, click **Agendas**. Notice the additional agenda templates available.

Take Note   You must be connected to the Internet to view online templates.

3. Locate **Agenda (Capsules design)** and click on it to preview. The preview pane displays download size and the user rating for that template in the upper-right pane, as shown in Figure 12-13. The agenda is predesigned with bullets and is ready to use.

Figure 12-13

Online template

The preview pane displays the template download size and rating.

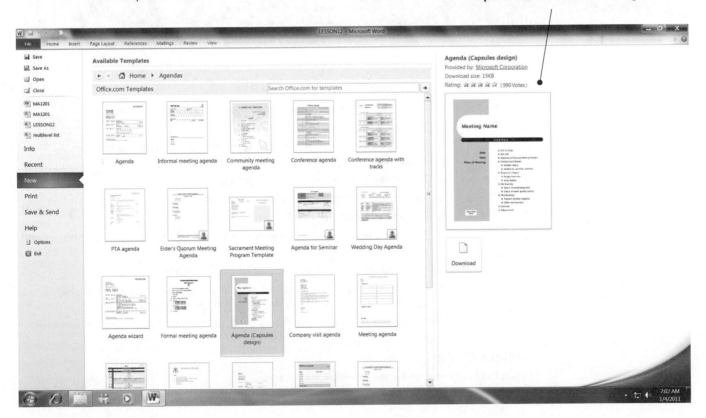

4. Below the Available Templates, click the **Home** 🏠 **Home** button. In the Office.com Templates section, click the **Flyers** category and notice the subcategories options.
5. Click the **Event flyers** folder to see the templates in that subcategory and scroll and preview.
6. In the Search Office.com for templates box, key **marketing** and press **Enter**. You can search for templates in the search box.

CERTIFICATION READY?   **1.6.1**

How do you find an online template?

7. Click **Event marketing brochure (Accessory design)** and click **Download** or double-click. View the template and close the document without saving.

CLOSE Word.

Take Note

To find additional information on templates, use the Help feature by pressing the F1 button or click the Help icon.

SKILL SUMMARY

In This Lesson You Learned How To:	Exam Objective	Objective Number
Arrange document views	Reorganize a document outline, master documents, and subdocuments.	1.1.4
Work with templates	Find a template.	1.6.1

Knowledge Assessment

True/False

Circle T if the statement is true or F if the statement is false.

T F **1.** A subdocument contains the whole document.

T F **2.** Templates are located in the Insert tab.

T F **3.** When creating subdocuments these are saved with the master document.

T F **4.** Templates are arranged by categories.

T F **5.** Templates cannot be saved as a separate file.

T F **6.** A master document can be reorganized.

T F **7.** Moving a subdocument to another location in the master document still retains it as a subdocument.

T F **8.** Short essays should be separated into sections.

T F **9.** Identifying heading styles in a document should be your first step to complete especially if the document does not contain a style.

T F **10.** Under the Available Templates section, Sample Templates are available.

Multiple Choice

Select the best response for the following statements.

1. Templates are organized by category and can also be located by keying a keyword in the

    a. Template search box

    b. Search for a template online box

    c. Open a blank template box

    d. Create your own template box

2. How many times can you use a template?
   a. Once
   b. Ten
   c. 100
   d. As many as needed

3. By default, how many levels does the Outlining View contain?
   a. Nine
   b. Eight
   c. Seven
   d. Five

4. Clicking the Show Document button displays
   a. Backstage view
   b. More commands
   c. Create
   d. None of the above

5. Clicking the Expand Document button will
   a. Open the subdocument
   b. Close the subdocument
   c. Will open only the selected content
   d. a and c

6. To view the hyperlinks in the subdocuments, you must
   a. Open the master document after creating and saving the subdocument in the master document
   b. Open the original document
   c. Open the individual subdocuments separately
   d. None of the above

7. Using which of the following commands will allow you to create a resume quickly?
   a. Tables
   b. SmartArt
   c. Templates
   d. None of the above

8. Additional information on templates can be found using
   a. Help icon
   b. F1
   c. F9
   d. a and b

9. Which template would you find in the Template category?
   a. Letters
   b. Memos
   c. Resumes
   d. All of the above

10. Where would you preview a template before downloading?
    a. Office.com
    b. Backstage view
    c. Template screen
    d. Not listed here

Project 12-1: Add a Cover Page

In your job at Books and Beyond, you continue to work on documents that will be part of the employee handbook. You will look for a template cover page and add text to the placeholders.

GET READY. LAUNCH Word if not already running.

1. **OPEN** a blank document.
2. Click the File tab, then New.
3. In the Search Office.com for templates box, key cover page. Click the Start searching right arrow or press the Enter key.
4. Select Word Cover Page Template and then click the Download button. A cover page is inserted in the document.
5. Key Books and Beyond as the company name.
6. Key Employee Handbook as the document title.
7. Key First Edition as the document subtitle.
8. Key Isabel Silver.
9. For the current year, key, 20XX.
10. **SAVE** the document as *handbook cover* and then **CLOSE** the file.

LEAVE Word open for the next project.

Project 12-2: Books and Beyond

You work at Books and Beyond and your manager has asked you to work with this document and create separate files. In your computer class, you learned about master and subdocuments and are aware that separate files are automatically created when creating subdocuments.

GET READY. LAUNCH Word if not already running.

@ The *booksbeyond* document file for this lesson is available on the book companion website or in WileyPLUS.

1. **OPEN** *booksbeyond* from the lesson folder.
2. Click the File tab, then Save As. Use the scroll bar to locate your USB flash drive. In the Save As dialog box, click the New Folder button and create a new folder in your USB flash drive and name it BOOKS BEYOND.
3. In the File name box, key master_books and click the Save button to save in the BOOKS BEYOND folder.
4. Select the heading, Acknowledgement. In the Styles group of the Home tab, select Heading 1.
5. Select the Introduction heading. In the Styles group, select Heading 1.
6. Select the General Performance Expectations Guidelines heading. In the Styles group, select Heading 1.
7. Click the View tab, and in the Document Views group click the Outline button.
8. In the Outline Tools group of the Outlining tab, click the drop-down arrow by Show Level to display Level 1.
9. Click the plus (+) symbol next to General Performance Expectation Guidelines.
10. On the Outline Tools group, click the Demote button. The General Performance Expectation Guideline heading is now a Level 2.
11. On the Master Document group, click the Show Document button.
12. Select the plus (+) symbol by next to Acknowledgement to select the heading and contents under that header. Click the Create button in the Master Document group.
13. Select the plus (+) symbol by Introduction to select the heading and contents under that heading. Click the Create button in the Master Document group.
14. Click the Save button on the Quick Access Toolbar and then close the file.

15. **OPEN** the *master_books* document and preview your document in the *Outlining* tab, and then **CLOSE** the file.

LEAVE Word open for the next project.

Proficiency Assessment

Project 12-3: Interview Thank-You Letter

As the assistant to the Director of Human Resources at Whitbeck Technologies, one of your responsibilities is preparing letters for candidates for a second interview. You decide to find a template in Word to help you with the wording and format.

GET READY. LAUNCH Word if not already running.

1. **OPEN** the Templates screen in Backstage.
2. Browse to the Letters: Employment and resignation letters: Interview Letters category.
3. Download the Confirmation of Second Interview letter.

   Replace the other fields in the document by keying the following information where indicated:

   [Your Name]: Hazel Loera

   [Street Address]: 1243 Angel Drive

   [City, ST ZIP Code]: Modesto, CA 45632

   [Recipient Name]: Joe Villanueva

   [Title]: Marketing Manager

   [Company Name]: Contoso Pharmaceuticals

   [Street Address]: 5683 Boston Street

   [City, ST ZIP Code]: Jasper, IN 70023

   [Recipient Name]: Mr. Villanueva

   [Date]: January 10, 20XX

   [Time]: 9:00 am

   [Date]: January 20

   [Time]: 8:30 am

   [Phone Number]: 999-999-9999

   [Your Name]: Hazel Loera

   [Title]: Director of Human Resources

4. **SAVE** the document as *interview_thanks* in your USB flash drive in the lesson folder and **CLOSE** the file.

LEAVE Word open for the next project.

Project 12-4: Computer Use Policy

You are putting your computer skills to use and feel more confident in creating subdocuments. Your task is to create and rearrange the subdocuments.

GET READY. LAUNCH Word if not already running.

@ The *comuterusepolicy* document file for this lesson is available on the book companion website or in WileyPLUS.

1. **OPEN** the *computerusepolicy* document from the lesson folder.
2. Create a new folder in your USB flash drive and name it COMPUTER_POLICY.
3. Save the document in the COMPUTER_POLICY folder as *master_policy*.
4. Change the view to Outline View.
5. Click the Show Level drop-down arrow in the Outline Tools group of the Outlining tab to display two levels.
6. Click the Show Documents button on the Master Document group to display the additional commands.

7. Select the individual headings by clicking the plus (+) symbol, then click the Create button to create subdocuments for each section.

8. Click the Save button on the Quick Access Toolbar to save the *master_policy* document.

9. Select the plus (+) symbol by Section Four. Click the Move Up arrow in the Outline Tools group until Section Four is above Section Two. (Hint: Make sure you see two continuous section breaks above Section Four and below Section One.)

10. Select the plus (+) symbol in Section Four, then click the Create button in the Master Document group to create a subdocument. Section Four and Section Two are in a border.

11. Select the text FOUR in SECTION FOUR and key TWO in uppercase.

12. Renumber each section appropriately and key in uppercase. Section TWO is now Section THREE, and Section THREE is now Section FOUR.

13. **SAVE** the *master_policy* document in your USB flash drive in the COMPUTER_POLICY folder and close the file.

14. **OPEN** the *master_policy* document and view document with hyperlinks.

15. **SAVE** the document in your USB flash drive in the COMPUTER_POLICY folder.

LEAVE Word open for the next project.

Mastery Assessment

Project 12-5: Fax Cover Sheet

In your position at Tech Terrace Real Estate, you frequently have to fax documents and need an attractive cover sheet. You decide to see what templates are available for faxes.

GET READY. LAUNCH Word if not already running.

1. Click the File tab, then New.

2. Under the Faxes category, select Fax cover sheet (Blue Gradient design).

3. Replace the fields in the fax document by keying the following information where indicated:

   To: Leonard Lachmann

   From: Aggie Becker

   RE: Update on Property

   Fax: 999-999-9989

   Pages: 3

4. **SAVE** the document as *fax_cover* and then **CLOSE** the file.

LEAVE Word open for the next project.

Project 12-6: Stock Agreement

You are preparing the stock agreement document for a committee. The committee will be working on this document during a scheduled meeting time. Your task is to prepare the document and separate it into seven sections and rearrange the document before the meeting.

GET READY. LAUNCH Word if not already running.

1. **OPEN** the *stock_agreement* document from the lesson folder.

@ The *stock_agreement* document file for this lesson is available on the book companion website or in WileyPLUS.

2. Create a new folder in your USB flash drive and name it AGREEMENTS.

3. Save the document in the AGREEMENTS folder as *master_agreement*.

4. Select Section One, Section Two, Section Three, Section Four, Section Five, Section Six, Section Seven, and identify as a Heading 1 style. Center each heading.

5. Under each of the sections is a subheading; select and add as a Heading 2 style. Center each subheading.

6. Create a subdocument for Sections One through Seven.

7. **SAVE** the document in your USB flash drive in the AGREEMENT folder and close the *master_agreement* file.

8. OPEN the *master_agreement* document.

9. Format Sections One through Seven by increasing the font size to **16** pts and selecting Dark Blue in the Standard Colors.

10. Move Section Four below Section Six and renumber.

11. **SAVE** the document in your USB flash drive in the AGREEMENTS folder.

CLOSE Word.

INTERNET READY

For more information about template options, visit the Microsoft Office Online Templates site: http://office.microsoft. com/en-us/templates/. A web browser opens with Microsoft templates. Locate a template that can be applied to research papers.

Workplace*Ready*

WORKING WITH TEMPLATES IN WORD

In today's business world, coming up with new ideas for various business documents can be easy. Actually trying to produce those documents may prove slightly more challenging. Time equals money in the workplace. Using any one of the many templates available in Word is the best way to quickly create a new document. The use of templates can also help you avoid the frustrations often associated with creating documents from scratch.

Your family owns and operates Tailspin Toys, a company that sells vintage and collectible toys. You decide to take on the task of streamlining the company's packing and shipping process. When doing this, you find that the packing slips currently accompanying your company's shipments do not contain all of the necessary information for each shipment.

With Word, you can choose from a wide variety of templates, such as, business letters and calendars to packing slips. Although two or more templates may contain the same information, each has a unique style of formatting. You can choose not only the appropriate type of template, but also the style that best fits your needs. You can also create your own template to include customized information and formatting.

Once you have chosen an appropriate packing slip template, you can add standard information, such as your company logo, company name, address, phone number, and email address. You can then save this template with a unique name, such as Tailspin Toys Packing Slip, so it will be easily recognizable when you later need to locate the file. Then, for each individual shipment, you can enter the appropriate information into preset fields, such as the ship to and bill to addresses, order date, order number, job, item number, description, and quantity.

13 Protecting and Sharing Documents

LESSON SKILL MATRIX

Skill	Exam Objective	Objective Number
Applying Protection to a Document	Apply protection by using the Microsoft Office Backstage view commands.	1.2.1
	Apply protection by using the Ribbon commands.	1.2.2
	Use Protected Mode.	1.5.2
Managing Document Versions	Recover draft versions.	1.3.1
	Delete all draft versions.	1.3.2
Sharing Documents	Create a shared document.	1.4.6
	Send documents via email.	1.4.1
	Send documents via SkyDrive.	1.4.2
	Send documents via Internet fax.	1.4.3
	Change file types.	1.4.4
	Register a blog account.	1.4.8
	Publish a blog post.	1.4.7
	Create PDF documents.	1.4.5

KEY TERMS

- blog
- SkyDrive

Blue Yonder Airlines is a large company with hundreds of employees. In your job as a human resources specialist, you are involved in hiring, employee benefit programs, and employee communications. Because many of the documents you work with relate to employee issues, you have to be careful about keeping documents confidential and available only to those who are authorized to have access. In this lesson, you learn different ways to guard the security of documents. You will prepare an employee evaluation for sharing with a supervisor and work together with a colleague to create an offer letter.

SOFTWARE ORIENTATION

Backstage View

When you click the File tab, Backstage view provides commands to grant permission, secure documents, share documents, and manage versions, as shown in Figure 13-1.

Figure 13-1

Backstage View

Backstage view provides commands to grant permission, secure documents, share documents, and manage versions.

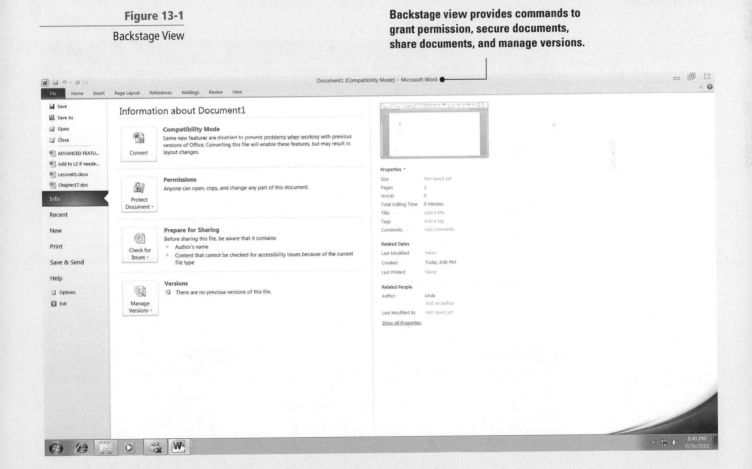

Use Figure 13-1 as a reference for this lesson.

NEW
to Office 2010

PROTECTING A DOCUMENT

When you are working in a business setting, there will be times when you are asked to create or review sensitive documents, such as budgets, employee evaluations, or hiring correspondence, that others may be unauthorized to access. To help you manage these tasks and maintain security, Word has commands you can use to restrict access to a document. You can set an access password for a document, protect a document, and mark a document as final. The Restrict Permissions command makes it possible to limit another user's ability to read or make changes to a document.

Setting an Access Password for a Document

You can protect a document with a password so that only people with access to the password can open or modify the document.

STEP BY STEP   **Set an Access Password for a Document**

OPEN the *peerreview* document from the lesson folder.

@ The *peerreview* document file for this lesson is available on the book companion website or in WileyPLUS.

1. Click the File tab and then click the Save As button. The Save As dialog box appears.
2. Click the Tools button, as shown in Figure 13-2. Select General Options from the menu. The General Options dialog box appears.

Figure 13-2

Tools menu

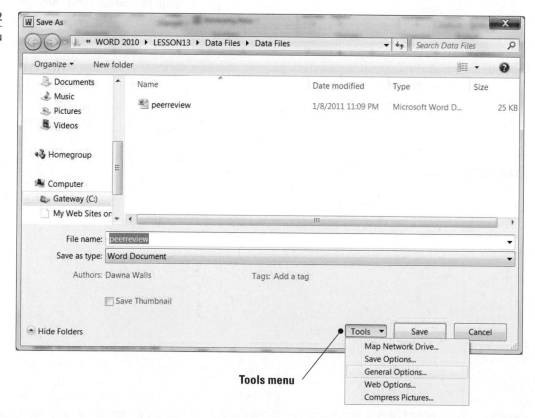

Tools menu

3. Key **HR%form$#** in the *Password to open* box (Figure 13-3). Word enables you to specify two different passwords—one to open a document and one to modify a document—both are optional. You can specify passwords for both actions—just specify a different password for each action. Passwords are case-sensitive, which means you can specify upper and/or lowercase letters. For this exercise, use the same password to open and modify. Click in the Password to modify box and Key **HR%form$#**. Click **OK**.

Figure 13-3

General Options dialog box

Read-only recommended —off by default

Protect Document

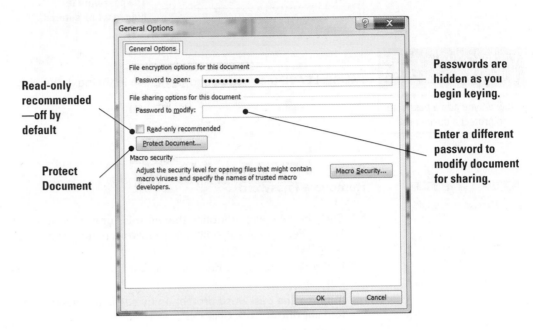

Passwords are hidden as you begin keying.

Enter a different password to modify document for sharing.

4. The Confirm Password dialog box appears. Reenter the password to open the document.

5. Key **HR%form$#** in the Reenter password to open box and click **OK**. The Confirm Password dialog box opens, reenter the same password to modify the document. When entering passwords, it is recommended that you enter a strong password that is mixed with characters and symbols.

6. Click **Save** in the Save As dialog box and **CLOSE** the file.

7. **OPEN** the document and a Password dialog box appears to open the document, as shown in Figure 13-4.

Figure 13-4

Password dialog box

Enter password to open document.

8. Key **HR%form$#** in the box and click **OK**.

9. The Password dialog box opens again because it is reserved by the original user. Reenter the same password—the password will allow you to modify, or open read only (see Figure 13-5).

Figure 13-5

Password dialog box to modify or open read only

The password is hidden when entered.

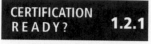

CERTIFICATION READY? 1.2.1

How do you add a password to protect a document?

PAUSE. LEAVE the document open to use in the next exercise.

STEP BY STEP **Remove a Password**

1. Click the **File** tab and notice that Permissions is highlighted in a light orange color. Under Permissions it states, "A password is required to open this document." Click **Save As**.

2. In the Save As dialog box, click the **Tools** button and then select **General Options** from the menu.

3. Remove the password protection by selecting the hidden Passwords in both boxes and clicking **Delete**. Click **OK**.

4. **SAVE** the document as *peerreview_1* in your USB flash drive in the lesson folder.

PAUSE. LEAVE the document open to use in the next exercise.

Take Note   It is very important for you to remember your password. If you forget your password, Microsoft cannot retrieve it for you. Record and store your password in a safe location, such as, placing it in your security safe or a secure place at home. Use strong passwords that combine uppercase and lowercase letters, numbers, and symbols. Weak passwords do not mix these elements. Strong password: W5!dk8. Weak password: CAR381. Passwords should be 8 or more characters in length. A pass phrase that uses 14 or more characters is better.

Protecting a Document as Read Only

You can safeguard document from formatting changes and restrict editing by protecting it. A document can be set as read only, comments only, and limited formatting styles. In this exercise, you will learn to set a document as read only, limit the document to comments only, and restrict formatting in the document.

STEP BY STEP **Protect a Document as Read Only**

USE the document open from previous exercise.

1. In the File tab, in the Permissions category, click the **Protect Document** button to display the menu. Click **Restrict Editing** as displayed in Figure 13-6.

Mark as Final   **Permission command**   **Encrypt with Password**

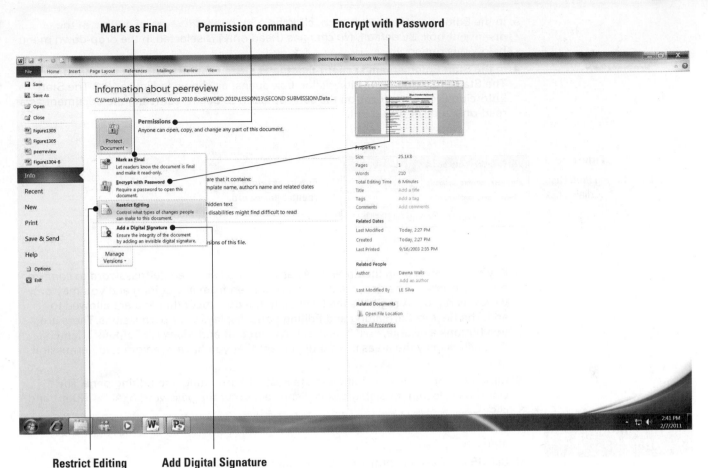

Restrict Editing   **Add Digital Signature**

Figure 13-6

Protect Document menu

2. The Restrict Formatting and Editing pane displays on the right pane your screen as shown in Figure 13-7.

Figure 13-7

Restrict Formatting and Editing pane

Off by default. Clicking the Settings link opens the Formatting Restrictions dialog box.

Adding a check mark will provide options to select, such as Tracked changes, Comments, Filling in forms, No changes (Read only).

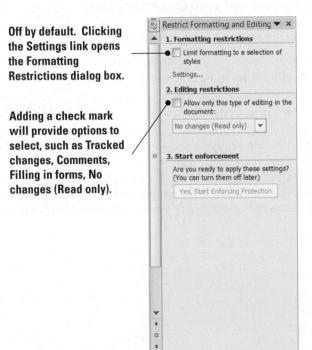

3. In the Editing restrictions section, click the Allow only this type of editing in the document box. By default, No changes (Read only) is selected in the drop-down menu below this option.

4. In the Start Enforcement section, click the Yes, Start Enforcing Protection button. The Start Enforcing Protection dialog box opens, as shown in Figure 13-8. The Start Enforcing Protection turns on the set restriction to begin restricting the document as a read-only type of document.

Figure 13-8

Start Enforcing Protection dialog box

Enter password, then reenter password.

5. Key BYA$%HRDept in the *Enter new password* box and *Reenter password to confirm* box and click OK. The document is now protected from any editing and you may only view this region. A region is the location in the document that you are allowed to edit. The Restrict Formatting and Editing pane displays your permissions. There are two buttons available, Find Next Region I Can Edit and Show All Regions I Can Edit. This will display the areas in your document that you have been granted permission to edit.

6. Click the Stop Protection button in the Restrict Formatting and Editing pane. The Unprotect Document dialog box is displayed. Enter the password BYA$%HRDept and click OK.

7. Click the Allow only this type of editing in the document box to remove the check mark.

8. **CLOSE** the Restrict Formatting and Editing pane.

9. **SAVE** the document with the same filename as *peerreview_1* in your USB flash drive in the lesson folder.

PAUSE. LEAVE the document open to use in the next exercise.

CERTIFICATION READY? 1.2.1

How do you apply restrictions and set the document as read only?

STEP BY STEP   **Restrict a Document with Comments Only**

USE the document open from the previous exercise.

1. On the Review tab in the Protect group, click the Restrict Editing button.

2. The Restrict Formatting and Editing pane displays.

3. In the Editing Restrictions section, click the Allow only this type of editing in this document box. Click the drop-down arrow and select Comments.

4. In the Start Enforcement section, click the Yes, Start Enforcing Protection button. The Start Enforcing Protection dialog box opens, which turns on the set restriction for comments only.

5. Key BYA$%HRDept in the Enter new password box and in the Reenter password *to confirm* box and click OK. Only comments can be added to the region. A region is the area in the document where you are allowed to make changes (see Figure 13-9).

Figure 13-9

Restrict Formatting and Editing dialog box—Only comments can be added to region

CERTIFICATION READY? **1.2.1**

How do you apply restrictions and limit a document to comments only?

6. Click the Stop Protection button at the bottom of the Restrict Formatting and Editing pane. The Unprotect Document dialog box is displayed. Key **BYA$%HRDept** and click OK.

7. Click the Allow only this type of editing in the document box to remove the check mark.

8. **SAVE** the document with the same filename as *peerreview_1* in your USB flash drive in the lesson folder.

PAUSE. LEAVE the document open to use in the next exercise.

 **Ref**

In Lesson 9, you learned about inserting, editing, and deleting comments.

STEP BY STEP   **Limit Formatting Styles in a Document**

USE the document open from the previous exercise.

1. In the Formatting Restrictions section, click the check box at Limit formatting to a selection of styles. Selecting this option enables you to set formatting restrictions for this document.

2. Click the Settings link. The Formatting Restrictions dialog box, as shown in Figure 13-10. The check mark indicates that styles are allowed.

Figure 13-10

Formatting Restrictions
dialog box

By default, formatting is limited to a selection of styles.

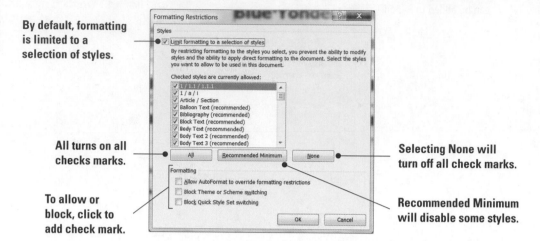

All turns on all checks marks.

To allow or block, click to add check mark.

Selecting None will turn off all check marks.

Recommended Minimum will disable some styles.

3. Under the Formatting section, click the check box at *Block Theme or Scheme switching* and then click OK. Selecting this option will block the user from making any changes to the structure, pattern, or theme of the document. A prompt will appear on your screen stating that *This document may contain formatting or styles that aren't allowed. Do you want to remove them?* Click Yes.

4. On the Page Layout tab, in the Themes group, notice all commands are shaded gray, making them unavailable.

5. Click Settings again and in the Formatting Restrictions dialog box, turn off the check mark by Block Theme or Scheme switching. Click OK.

6. Click Yes to the prompt to remove. Notice the Themes group is now available. You can now use the Themes commands in the group.

7. In the Formatting restrictions section, click the check box at Limit formatting to a selection of styles to remove the check mark. Close the Restrict Formatting and Editing pane.

8. SAVE the document with the same filename as *peerreview_1* in your USB flash drive in the lesson folder.

9. In the Styles group of the Home tab, click the Change Styles button, then click Style Set to change the style to Fancy.

10. Click the Page Layout tab, and in the Themes group, click to select Foundry.

11. Keep the document open for ten minutes—later in this lesson, you will learn about managing versions. Minimize the document to place it on the taskbar. You will be using this document later in this lesson.

PAUSE. LEAVE the program open for the next exercise.

<table>
<tr><td>CERTIFICATION READY?</td><td>1.2.1</td></tr>
</table>

How do you restrict formatting styles in a document?

Take Note

Restricting comments can be made to the whole document or you can select portions of the document where editing changes are allowed.

STEP BY STEP   **Mark a Document as Final**

OPEN the *reviewform* document from the lesson folder.

@ The *reviewform* document file for this lesson is available on the book companion website or in WileyPLUS.

1. Click the File tab, then Permissions. Click the drop-down arrow by the Protect Document button, then Mark as Final. A dialog box appears indicating this document will be marked as final and then saved. Click OK.

2. A Microsoft Word dialog box displays, as shown in Figure 13-11. The Mark as Final prevents recipients from making changes to the document—the document becomes read only and is displayed on the title bar. When a document is marked as final, the status property is set to "Final" and typing, editing commands, and proofing marks are turned off. Notice the Marks as Final icon displays in the status bar.

Figure 13-11

Microsoft Word Mark as Final

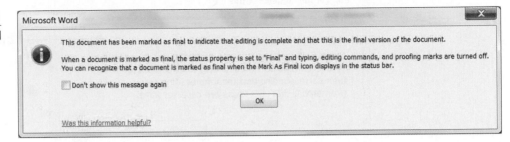

3. The *Don't show this message again* check box message is off by default. If you do not want to see this message again when marking a document as final, click the check box to add a check mark. Click **OK**. The document is Marked as Final and displays in the Permissions section highlighted in a light orange color to discourage editing.

4. Click the **Home** tab and notice the yellow bar below the Ribbon indicating that *An author has marked this document as final to discourage editing*. If you needed to edit the document, you would click the **Edit Anyway** button. Click the **tabs** on the Ribbon and the commands are not available. Continue to click the other tabs to view how the commands are not activated.

5. Select the **title of the document** and try to delete it. When a document is marked as final, typing, editing commands, and proofing marks are disabled or turned off, because it becomes a read-only document. The title bar also shows the document as a (Read-Only) document.

6. On the File tab, click the **Protect Document** button and then select **Mark as Final** to return the document to its original status. Click the **Home** tab to return to the document screen.

7. Select the **B** in Blue Yonder Airlines and press the **Delete** key. You can now make changes to the document.

8. Click the **Undo**  button on the Quick Access Toolbar.

9. **SAVE** the document as *reviewform_1* in your USB flash drive in the lesson folder.

PAUSE. LEAVE the document open to use in the next exercise.

Another Way
On the document screen, click Edit Anyway to return document to its original status.

CERTIFICATION READY? **1.2.1**

How do you mark a document as final?

Take Note

Documents that have been marked as final in a 2010 Microsoft Office program will not be read only if they are opened in earlier versions of Microsoft Office programs. The Mark as Final command is not a security feature—anyone who receives an electronic copy of a document that has been marked as final can edit that document by removing the Mark as Final status from the document.

Applying Protection Using the Ribbon

Encryption protects a document and cannot be opened without a password.

USE the document open from the previous exercise.

1. On the File tab, click the **Protect Document** button in the Permissions section, then select **Encrypt with Password**. Encrypting protects the document by making it unreadable.

2. The Encrypt Document dialog box opens, as shown in Figure 13-12. In the *Encrypt the contents of this file* box, key **HRDept&%3**.

Enter password.

Encrypt Document

Encrypt the contents of this file

Password:

Caution: If you lose or forget the password, it cannot be recovered. It is advisable to keep a list of passwords and their corresponding document names in a safe place. (Remember that passwords are case-sensitive.)

OK   Cancel

3. Retype the password and click **OK**. Notice that Permissions is highlighted and indicates that a password is required to open this document.

4. Close the document and when prompted with *Do you want to save the changes you made to reviewform_1?* click **Save**. Reopen the document and key **HRDept&%3** to open the document.

5. Click the **File** tab, then click the **Protect Document** button in the Permissions section, and select **Encrypt with Password**. In the Encrypt Document dialog box select the password and delete it to remove the password. Click **OK**. The password is removed, allowing you to open the document without entering a password.

6. **SAVE** the document as with the same filename as ***reviewform_1*** in your USB flash drive in the lesson folder and **CLOSE** the file.

PAUSE. LEAVE Word open to use in the next exercise.

CERTIFICATION READY?   **1.2.2**

How do you protect a document through encryption?

Opening Documents in Protected View

Protecting your document from an unsafe location is necessary to avoid viruses, worms, or other kinds of malware that may harm your computer. Documents received by email as an attachment could possibly harm your computer; therefore, it is very important to know if the source is reliable. Files that open in Protected View could have been opened from the Internet, you may have received it in your Outlook 2010 email as an attachment and the sender was marked as unsafe, the document was opened from the Temporary Internet Files on your computer, the Information Technology Department may have blocked certain file types, or the Office program may have detected a problem with the file. In this exercise, you will open a document in Protected View and enable editing.

STEP BY STEP   **Open a Document in Protected View**

@ The *proposal* document file for this lesson is available on the book companion website or in WileyPLUS.

OPEN the ***proposal*** document from the lesson folder.

1. The document opens in Protected View. The yellow prompt states *This file originated from an Internet location and might be unsafe* as shown in Figure 13-13.

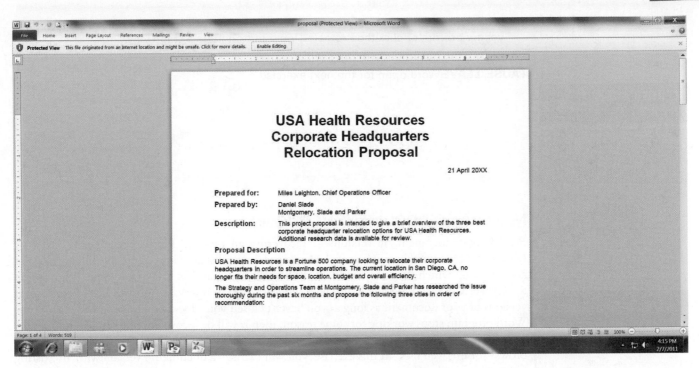

Figure 13-13

Document in Protected View

Another Way
On the yellow bar,
click Enable Editing.

2. Click the **File** tab; notice that the Enable Editing button by the Protected View category is highlighted in a light orange color informing you that *This file originated from an Internet location and might be unsafe* as shown in Figure 13-14.

Protected View Settings allows you
to enable or disable Protected View.

Learn more about Protected View
takes you directly to the Help feature.

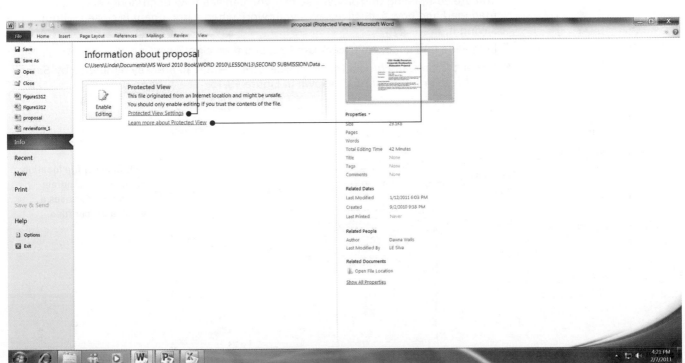

Figure 13-14

Backstage view—Protected View

3. When you are ready to edit the document, click the Enable Editing button on the yellow prompt or click the Protected View button in Backstage view.

4. **CLOSE** the document without saving.

PAUSE. LEAVE Word open for the next exercise.

MANAGING DOCUMENT VERSIONS

Retrieving a document by versions or recovering an unsaved file has been made easier by Microsoft. Document versions can be managed in Backstage view using the Info command and selecting which version to save. In the Recent command in Backstage, there is an option to Recover Unsaved Document and your work is saved in intervals. You will be able to recover versions of your document as long as you haven't closed your document or program. Also, if the Word program stops working for some reason, then it will be recovered, but you will not be able to see your previous versions until the document is saved. Under Manage Versions, you can also browse for unsaved files. In this exercise, you will manage a document's version with an existing file and a new file, and recover an unsaved version.

STEP BY STEP   **Manage Document Versions**

1. On the taskbar, click the *peerreview_1* document and click the File tab, then Exit without saving. Keep Word open and keep a document open before exiting. Closing the Word program will lose your versions of the *peerreview_1* document.

2. Open the *peerreview_1* document from your USB flash drive in the lesson folder.

3. Before beginning, you will be changing the default for the Save AutoRecover minutes. You are completing this process so that you can see how document versions are managed and how Autosave saves your work when a document is closed without saving it.

4. In the File tab, under Help, click Options, and then click Save.

5. Under the *Save documents* section, select the default 10 and key **3** minutes by *Save AutoRecover information* as shown in Figure 13-15.

Figure 13-15

Word Options dialog box

Checked by default

AutoRecover file location is where the program automatically saves a version of your files.

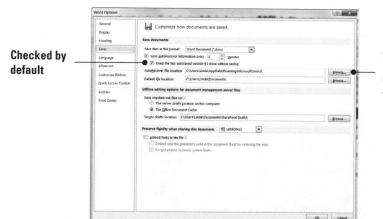

6. Create a new blank document and key Working with unsaved documents can be found in Backstage view in the Recent command. Keep this document open, until you are instructed to work on the next step.

7. Click the *peerreview_1* document from the taskbar to display on the document screen.

8. Click the File tab and under Versions, you should see at least one or two versions of the document saved, as shown in Figure 13-16. Note your screen on your computer will not resemble Figure 13-16. As shown in Figure 13-16, one version of the document was saved while the other version was closed without saving.

9. **SAVE** the document with the same filename *peerreview_1* in your USB flash drive in the lesson folder.

Figure 13-16

Manage Versions displays Autosave

Version automatically saved. A yellow prompt will appear on your document screen, "Autosaved Version A newer version is available."

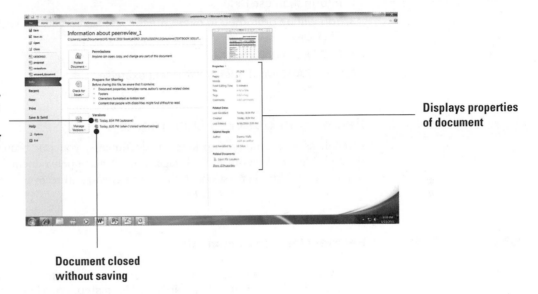

Displays properties of document

Document closed without saving

PAUSE. LEAVE the document open for the next exercise.

Take Note   Clicking the down arrow key in Manage Versions will allow you to Recover Unsaved Documents; the Open dialog box will open files specifically from the target location where unsaved files are saved.

Restoring an Earlier Version of Your Document

The Save AutoRecover saves documents automatically by time and it will indicate Today for the current day. In the previous exercise, you changed the Save setting from the default of 10 minutes to 3 minutes. As you modify your document, AutoRecover will autosave changes. These updates to different versions can be located in Backstage view under Manage Versions. In this exercise, you will restore an earlier version of your document.

STEP BY STEP   **Restore an Earlier Version of Your Document**

USE the document open from the earlier exercise—the peerreview_1 document.

1. Click the File tab and under Versions, click the version where it indicates autosave. A new window opens showing a yellow bar below the Ribbon displaying Autosave Version—a new version is available with two options available. One is Compare and the other is Restore. If your document only contains one autosave version, you should

be able to see the two available options, Compare and Restore, but you will not be able to complete step 2 (see Figure 13-17).

Figure 13-17

Autosave Version

⚠ **Autosaved Version**   A newer version is available. | Compare | | Restore |

2. When you click on Compare a summary that compares the original document and the revised document on one screen displays. The Restore button will prompt you to overwrite your previous document. Click Restore to overwrite your previous document. Compare versions is one of Word's advanced features; for more information use Help.

3. You will be prompted to overwrite the last saved version with the selected version. Click OK.

4. **CLOSE** the document.

PAUSE. LEAVE Word open for the next exercise.

Recovering Unsaved Documents

Overall, as you continue working on documents, you can browse or recover unsaved files through Manage Versions in Backstage. You can also open a document based on the time or the last version within that session. In this exercise, you will recover an unsaved document.

STEP BY STEP   **Recover Unsaved Documents**

1. Earlier you keyed, *Working with unsaved documents can be found in Backstage view in the Recent command.* And in a previous step, you changed the Save AutoRecover information from the default to 3 minutes.

2. Click the File tab, then Exit. A prompt appears on your screen to save changes. The prompt states, *If you click "Don't Save," a recent copy of this file will be temporarily available.* It will also indicate that a temporary file will be saved. If you do not see this, see the information in the Troubleshooting sidebar next (see Figure 13-18). Click Don't Save.

Figure 13-18

"A recent copy of this file will be temporarily available"

Microsoft Word   ✕
⚠ Do you want to save changes you made to Document186?
If you click "Don't Save", a recent copy of this file will be temporarily available.
Learn more
[Save]   [Don't Save]   [Cancel]

Troubleshooting   If a prompt did not appear on your screen to save your document, you can change the AutoRecovery preferences from the default. The default for AutoRecovery is to save every ten minutes; it can be found in Backstage, Options command, in the Save settings category. For instructional purposes, you may need to change the settings to 3 or 5 minutes. Close the document without saving, and the prompt will indicate that the file will be temporarily saved.

3. Click the **File** tab, then **Recent**. On the bottom-right side of the screen, click **Recover Unsaved Documents** as shown in Figure 13-19.

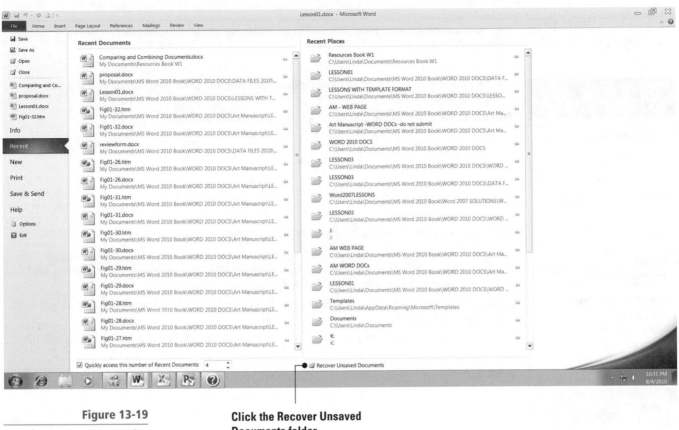

Figure 13-19

Backstage view—Recovering
Unsaved Document

**Click the Recover Unsaved
Documents folder.**

4. At the Open dialog box, locate your file based on the date and time you closed the document or program (see Figure 13-20). The document was closed without saving it with a filename; therefore, the Name will show the text that you keyed. Unsaved documents are in a temporary location on your hard drive and identified by the ASD extension. Select the unsaved document and click **Open**.

Figure 13-20

Open dialog box for
Unsaved files

Indicates the location for unsaved files

**Type file
extension
(*.asd).**

**Unsaved files available.
Select and click Open.**

5. The document opens with the Recovered Unsaved File yellow prompt appearing above the document stating, *This is a recovered file that is temporarily stored on your computer.* Click Save As (see Figure 13-21).

Figure 13-21

Recovered Unsaved File

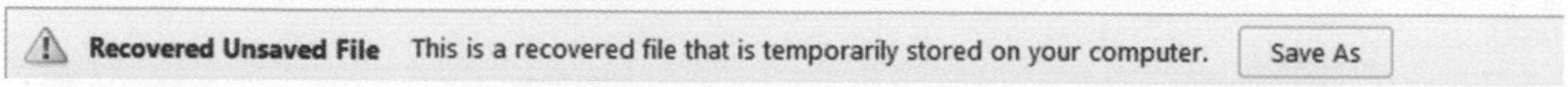

⚠ **Recovered Unsaved File**   This is a recovered file that is temporarily stored on your computer. | Save As |

6. **SAVE** the document as *unsaved_document* in your USB flash drive in the lesson folder.

PAUSE. LEAVE the document open to use in the next exercise.

CERTIFICATION READY?   **1.3.1**

How do you recover an unsaved document?

STEP BY STEP   **Delete All Draft Versions**

USE the document open from the previous exercise.

Another Way
At the Open dialog box for Unsaved Files, click the Organize button, then Delete. At the prompt Are you sure you want to move this file to the Recycle Bin? click Yes.

1. Click the File tab, then click the Manage Versions button, then Recover Unsaved Documents. The Open dialog box for Unsaved Files opens. You should see the first few words of the document in the Open dialog box.

2. Click the *Working with unsaved documents can be . . .* then right-click and select Delete This Version.

3. Click Yes to the prompt *Are you sure you want to move this file to the Recycle Bin?*

4. **CLOSE** *unsaved_document*.

PAUSE. LEAVE Word open to use in the next exercise.

CERTIFICATION READY?   **1.3.2**

How do you delete draft versions for unsaved documents?

Take Note   Recovering Unsaved Documents are found in a specific target location on your hard drive. A file extension of .asd has been assigned to unsaved documents. The files located in the Recovering Unsaved Files are temporary files until saved.

SHARING DOCUMENTS

Word contains a feature that will remove unwanted information from your document. The Document Inspector is used to find and remove hidden data and personal information in Word 2010 documents as well as earlier versions. It is a good idea to practice inspecting the document before sharing an electronic copy such as an email attachment. In this exercise, you will inspect the document and remove personal information.

Using the Document Inspector

OPEN the *emploffer* document from your lesson folder.

@ The *emploffer* document file for this lesson is available on the book companion website or in WileyPLUS.

1. Click the File tab and by Prepare for Sharing click the Check for Issues button, then click Inspect Document.

2. The Document Inspector dialog box appears. Click the Inspect button (see Figure 13-22).

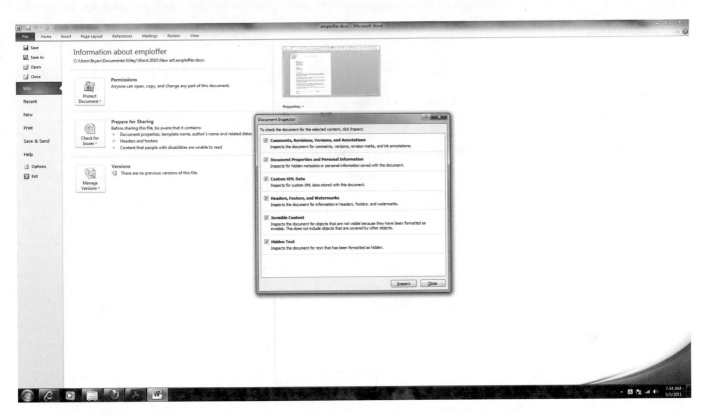

Figure 13-22

Document Inspector dialog box

3. In the *Document Properties and Personal Information* section, click Remove All. Personal information from the properties is removed and the document is ready to be shared. The items are removed and the dialog box is updated.

4. Leave the Headers, Footers, and Watermarks as is. Click Close.

5. In the Prepare for Sharing section, click the link to Allow this information to be saved in your file.

6. Click the Save As button to open the Save As dialog box. Save the document as *emploffer_1* in your USB flash drive in your lesson folder.

PAUSE. LEAVE the document open to use in the next exercise.

Checking Accessibility

The Accessibility Checker determines if there are potential errors in your document and will alert you that the content may be difficult for an individual with a disability to read. Accessibility is defined as being accessible to those with disabilities. Before sharing your document, it is important to inspect your document in case someone with a disability will be opening the document. In this exercise, you learn to check if there are errors in your document.

STEP BY STEP | **Check Accessibility**

USE the document that is open from the previous exercise.

1. Click the File tab and click the Check for Issues button, then click Check Accessibility.

2. The Accessibility Checker appears on the right pane, as shown in Figure 13-23. If there are errors in your document, the Accessibility Check will show errors, warnings, or tips.

Figure 13-23

Accessibility Checker Inspection Results

Errors

Warnings

Read more about making documents accessible link.

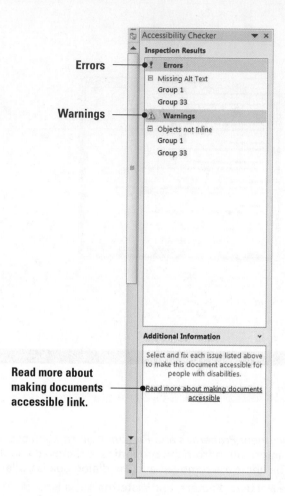

3. Click the **File** tab and notice that below Prepare for Sharing indicates that "Content that people with disabilities are unable to read." Word flags the document letting you know that there are problems in the document and not everyone will be able to read it.

4. **SAVE** the document with the same filename in your USB flash drive and **CLOSE** the file.

PAUSE. LEAVE Word open to use in the next exercise.

Checking Compatibility

Before sharing documents, it is good practice to check whether the document is error free and the formatting appears professional. Word's built-in Compatibility Check will ensure that a document's features are compatible with other versions of Word. The Compatibility Checker searches a document for features that are not supported by earlier versions of Word and lists a summary of these features. When documents are opened in an earlier version, they will open in Compatibility Mode and display in the Title bar. It is recommended that you run the Compatibility Checker to identify features that are supported. In this exercise, you learn to check for issues in a document.

STEP BY STEP   **Use the Compatibility Checker**

1. **OPEN** the *employment_offer* document from the lesson folder. When documents are created in an earlier version of Word and opened in newer versions of Word, they will open in Compatibility Mode and it will display in the Title bar. It is recommended that you run the Compatibility Checker to identify features that are supported.

2. Click the File tab, then Save As. When the Save As dialog box opens, save the document as *employment_offer_2011* and make sure the file type displays as Word Document. A prompt will appear stating you are about to save your document to one of the new file formats. Compatibility Mode will allow you to edit your document, and the enhanced features used in Word 2010 will not affect your document—your document in the earlier version will be preserved. Click OK.

3. Click the File tab, click Check for Issues, and click Check Compatibility. The Microsoft Word Compatibility Checker dialog box is displayed as shown in Figure 13-24. When sharing Word 2010 or Word 2007 documents with individuals using earlier versions of Word, your document will need to be saved in the Word 97-2003 format. It is good practice to use the Compatibility Checker to ensure the features you have included in your document will not be removed or changed when you save it in the Word 97-2003 format. This document contains features that are not supported by earlier versions.

Figure 13-24

Microsoft Word Compatibility Checker dialog box

Click drop-down arrow to select versions to show.

Summary and number of occurrences

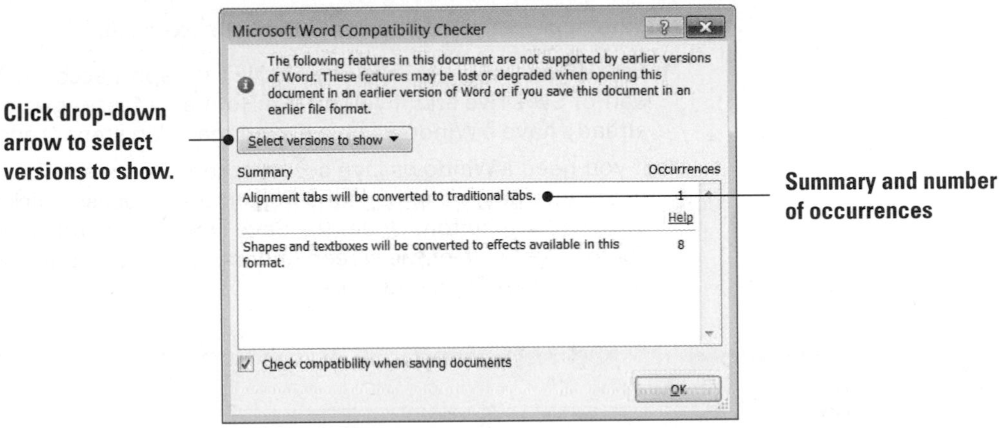

4. Click OK.
5. **SAVE** the document with the same filename in your USB flash drive.

PAUSE. LEAVE the document open to use in the next exercise.

Sending Documents

Electronic documents are sent via email, web, and Internet fax. In Backstage view, you can save the document in a PDF and XPS format and attach it to email. You can also change and create a document in different file formats. In this exercise, you will send a document by email, SkyDrive, discuss how installation of drivers is used for the Internet fax, change files type, create PDF/XPS documents, and register and publish a blog.

STEP BY STEP   **Send Documents via Email Using Outlook**

USE the document open from the previous exercise.

1. For this exercise, you must be using Microsoft Outlook. Check with your instructor to determine whether you have access to Outlook on your computer.

2. Click the File tab, then click Save & Send. Send using email is automatically selected.

CERTIFICATION
READY? **1.4.1**

How do you send a document
as an attachment by email?

3. Under Send Using E-mail, click Send as attachment. The open document is automatically attached to the email message and is ready to be sent.

4. Key the email address of a friend, classmate, or coworker in the *To* box and click the Send button.

PAUSE. LEAVE the document open to use in the next exercise.

STEP BY STEP   **Send Documents via SkyDrive**

Windows Live **SkyDrive** is an online service provided by Microsoft. SkyDrive is an online file storage location where you can store documents and pictures. Microsoft has provided 25GB of free online storage space, and SkyDrive is password protected—so you control who has access to your files.

You can share your documents in Word, Excel, PowerPoint, and OneNote; create your personal album; and share pictures with your contacts or on your social networking site; create and send emails, and manage your contacts; add events to your calendar and share; access Messenger with real-time chat; and stay updated and connected to your social networking sites, such as Facebook, MySpace, and LinkedIn.

USE the document open from the previous exercise.

1. For this exercise, you will need a .NET Passport account. The Windows Live Office is part of SkyDrive and if you have a Hotmail, Messenger, or Xbox Live account, you already have a Windows Live ID and may skip steps 2 and 3.

2. If you need a Windows Live account, complete steps 2 and 3. You must be connected to the Internet to complete the registration process. Click the File tab, then click the Save & Send button. Under the Save & Send section click the Save to Web button. On the right side of the screen under Sign In, click the link, Sign up for Windows Live SkyDrive (see Figure 13-25).

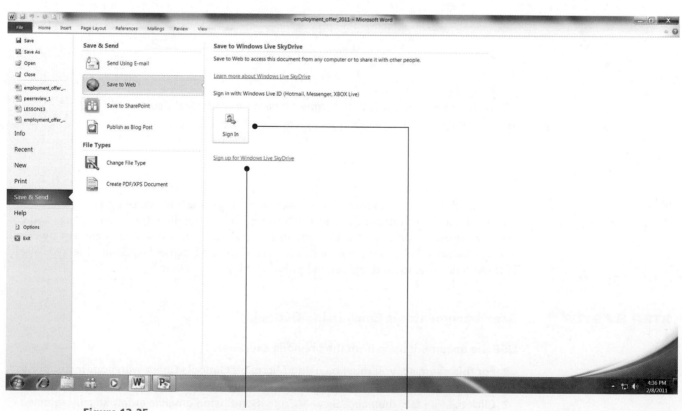

Figure 13-25

Backstage—Save & Send

**Sign up for Windows
Live SkyDrive.**

**Sign into Windows Live SkyDrive
after you create an account.**

Another Way
Launch the Internet, and key signup.live.com in the address bar.

3. The Internet opens at the Windows Live website, as shown in Figure 13-26. Click the **Sign up** button and follow the prompts on your screen to complete the registration for a Windows Live account. Once you complete the process, exit the Internet. You will be signing in to your account in the Word's Save and Send section of Backstage.

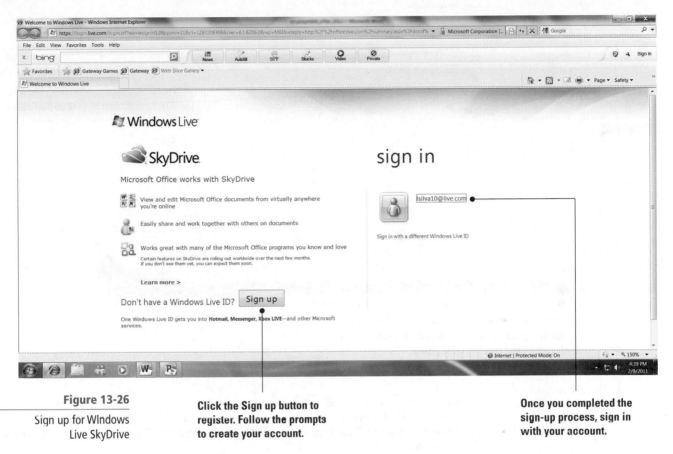

Figure 13-26

Sign up for Windows Live SkyDrive

Click the Sign up button to register. Follow the prompts to create your account.

Once you completed the sign-up process, sign in with your account.

4. In the **File** tab, click the **Save & Send** button.
5. Click **Save to Web** and click the **Sign In** button to display the *Connecting to docs.live.net* dialog box (see Figure 13-27).

Figure 13-27

Connecting to docs.live.net

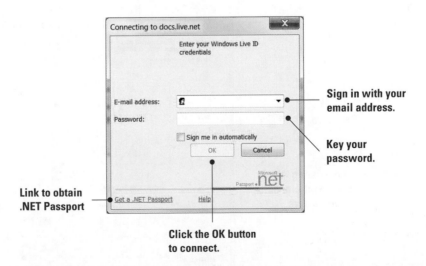

Sign in with your email address.

Key your password.

Link to obtain .NET Passport

Click the OK button to connect.

6. Enter your Windows Live ID, email account, and password. Click **OK** to connect. Once you are connected, the screen changes and your Personal Folders > My Documents folders will appear. You will be able to upload, create, edit, and share documents in a web browser (see Figure 13-28).

Opens the Windows Live SkyDrive Web
page to sign in or create an account.

Create New Folder   Refresh Button

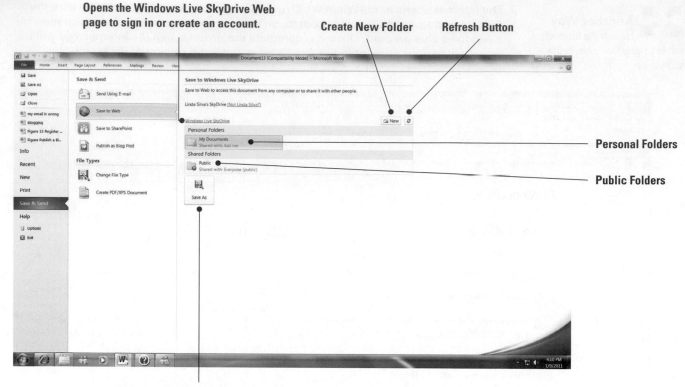

Personal Folders

Public Folders

When you click the Save As button, the
Save As dialog box opens with a target
location to save your document.

Figure 13-28

Backstage–Save to Windows
Live SkyDrive

7. Select **My Documents** under Personal Folders. You have an option to share
information in the Public folder and you can grant individuals permission to view and
edit the contents in your folder. You can also create a new folder in which to place your
documents.

8. Click the **Save As** button. The Save As dialog box appears and the address bar displays
the location of your folder as well as the filename (see Figure 13-29). Click **Save**.

Figure 13-29

Save As dialog box

SkyDrive file location

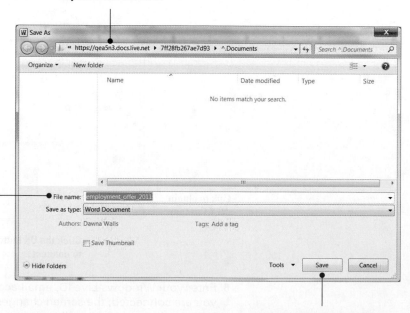

The existing Word
document filename
appears here.

Click the Save button to save
in the docs.live.net account.

9. Launch the Internet and sign in to your Windows Live account to view your document.

10. At the top screen in your Windows Live Account, click the Office link, then Your Documents. Double-click the My Documents folder. You have an option to edit your document in the browser, open it in Word, or Share it (with an option to add permissions), and under More you can view the versions history, move, copy, rename, download, and view properties.

11. In step 9, you signed in to your email account. Keep your Windows Live email account open.

PAUSE. LEAVE the document open for the next exercise.

| CERTIFICATION READY? | 1.4.2 |

How do you send a document using SkyDrive?

STEP BY STEP   **Send Documents via Internet Fax**

Word provides the Internet Fax feature without the use of a fax machine. You can send Office documents online as Internet faxes. To set up your computer to send Internet faxes, you would need to install the Windows Fax Printer Driver or rely on a Fax Service provider.

USE the document open from the previous exercise.

1. By default the Windows Fax feature is disabled and it must be installed before sending documents via Internet fax. A utility is built into Windows Vista and Windows 7 to use the Windows Fax and Scan utility. For Windows XP, you will need to add Microsoft Fax in the Add/Remove Programs in the Control Panel.

2. The Internet fax command is available in Backstage view. This feature has the capability to send Internet faxes without a fax machine.

3. On the File tab select Save & Send and then click Send as Internet Fax. A prompt will appear stating *To use Fax Services to send your fax, you must sign up with a fax service provider.* If you click OK, your web browser opens and you choose a provider. Your screen would resemble Figure 13-30. Each fax service provider charges a fee for their services. Check with your instructor to see if the services are available.

Figure 13-30

Available Fax Services

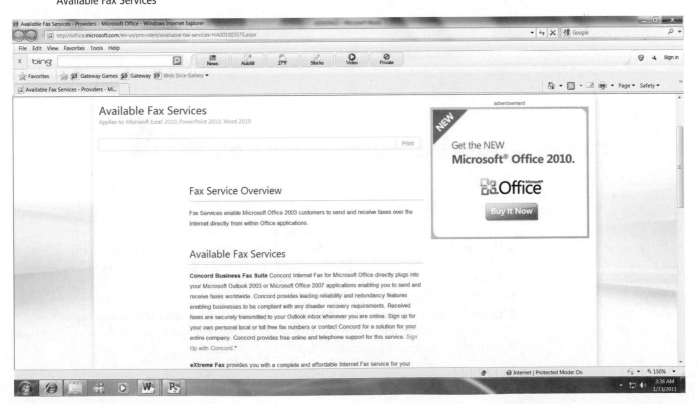

CERTIFICATION
READY?   1.4.3

How do you prepare to send
a document by Internet Fax?

4. After a fax service provider is selected and an account is set up, a New Fax window opens with the current document attached. Complete the fax form, then click **Send**.

5. Exit the Internet.

PAUSE. LEAVE the document open for the next exercise.

STEP BY STEP   **Change and Create File Types**

USE the document open from the previous exercise.

1. On the File tab, select **Save & Send**.

2. Under File Types, click **Change File Type**. You will be saving a Word document as another file type. The right side of the screen displays Document File Types and Other File Types. When you select one of the file types, it will automatically add the appropriate file extension to the document.

Take Note   In Lesson 1, you learned to save a document and change file types.

3. Under Other File Types, select **Single File Web Page** as shown in Figure 13-31. A web page will be created for this Word document as a single file web page. The extension associated with the single file web page is .MHT. The file extension .MHT is reserved for web pages, and .MHT is commonly used for HTML (HyperText Markup Language).

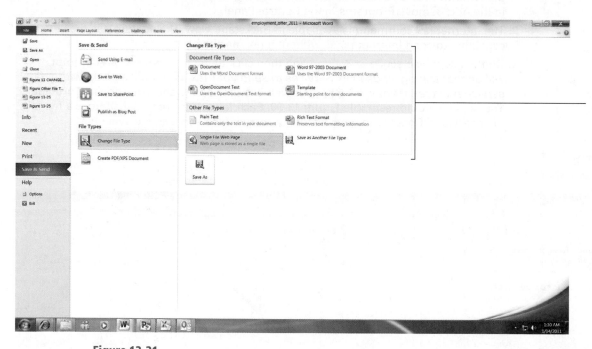

Figure 13-31

Backstage view—Change File Type

4. Click the **Save As** button. After saving the document as a single file web page, it will open in Word. Notice that the elements applied in the document are gone. You can also view the document in a web browser.

5. **CLOSE** the single file web page.

6. **OPEN** the *employment_offer_2011* document from the lesson folder. You are opening the same document as a Word document with the extension .DOCX.

7. Click the **File** tab and select **Save & Send**.

8. Under File Types click the **Create PDF/XPS Document**. As you learned in Lesson 1, .PDF and .XPS are file formats that preserve document formatting. The PDF file will open in the Adobe Reader Viewer while the XPS file will open in the XPS Viewer. The right side of the Save & Send screen changes as shown in Figure 13-32.

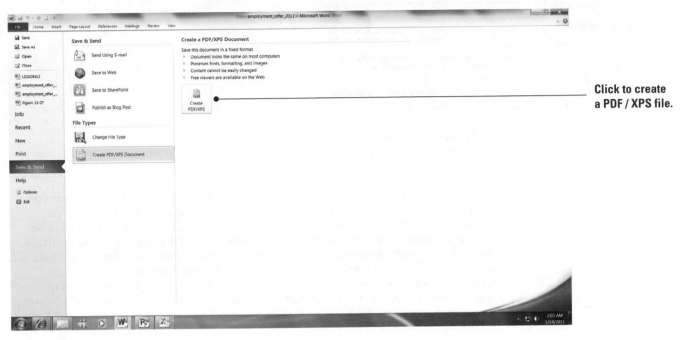

Click to create a PDF / XPS file.

Figure 13-32

Backstage view—Create a PDF/XPS Document

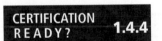

CERTIFICATION READY? 1.4.4

How do you change the document file type?

CERTIFICATION READY? 1.4.5

How do you create a PDF document?

CERTIFICATION READY? 1.4.6

How do you create an XPS document?

9. Click the **Create PDF/XPS** button. The *Publish as PDF or XPS* dialog box appears. You have the option to change the default file type from PDF to XPS Document. Click **Save**.

10. The document opens in Adobe Reader as a read-only document. If your computer does not have Adobe Reader installed, you will need to install it on your computer. It is free to download from get.adobe.com/reader. Close the PDF file and keep the *employment_offer_2011* Word document open and minimized to the taskbar.

PAUSE. LEAVE the document open for the next exercise.

Register and Publish a Blog Post

A **blog** is an online interactive location where anyone can leave comments. Blogs are maintained by companies, instructors, and individuals who post information, events, news, and more. Word provides a feature where you can register your blog's URL, add a post, and publish it.

STEP BY STEP **Register and Publish a Blog Post**

OPEN a blank document screen.

1. A Word document can be published as a blog post or you can create a new blog.

2. On the **File** tab select **New**.

3. Under the Available Templates section, select **Blog post** and then double-click or click the **Create** button.

4. The Register a Blog Account dialog box opens, as shown in Figure 13-33. Click the **Register Now** button, then click the **drop-down arrow** and select **WordPress**. Click the **Next** button. WordPress services are free.

Figure 13-33

Register a Blog Account
dialog box

Register Now button links
to an external website.

5. At the WordPress website, you will be required to enter a Wordpress address or you can get your own URL with a custom domain name, for example, wordwise2010. As you enter a domain name, the screen will display whether the name is available. Enter any name you would like for your URL and, once it displays as being available, complete the registration process by entering your username and password. (It should be a strong password—the screen will indicate if it is weak or strong.) Enter your password again, then enter your email address. If you would like to subscribe to their blog and learn about new themes, features, and other news, click to add a check mark in the check box. Click the **Sign Up** button and check your email to activate your blog by clicking on the link in the email.

6. Click the link sent to your email account by WordPress.com. Your screen should resemble Figure 13-34 stating that *Your account is now active*. In the first paragraph, **click your URL link** to open your blog site. Your site should resemble Figure 13-35. You can customize the site by changing the theme and features.

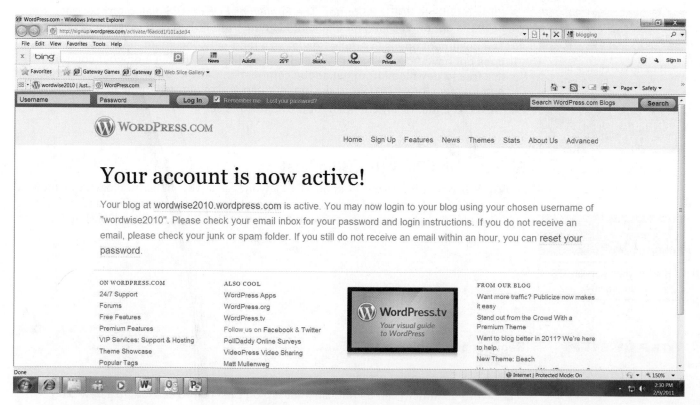

Figure 13-34

Your personalized URL—Your
account is now active

Figure 13-35

Your personalized blog site

7. The Word screen displays **[Enter Post Title Here]**. Key, **What do you think about the NEW features in Word 2010?** In the Blog Post tab, in the Blog group, the Publish button contains two options, **Publish** and **Publish as Draft** (see Figure 13-36).

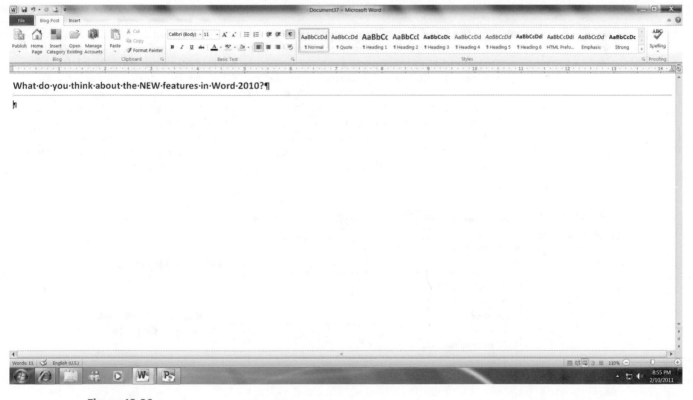

Figure 13-36

New post entered

8. After you complete a few more steps, you will post and publish your first blog. On the next step, you will be adding your blog URL to your account.

9. On the Blog group, click the **Manage Accounts** button to display the Blog Accounts dialog box, as shown in Figure 13-37.

Figure 13-37

Blog Accounts

10. Click the **New** button. When the New Blog Account dialog box opens, click the drop-down arrow to display the menu. Select **WordPress**, and click **Next**. The New WordPress Account dialog box opens as shown in Figure 13-38. Enter your Blog Post URL, *<Enter your blog URL here>* for example, wordwise2010.wordpress.com, then enter your username and password. If you would like Word to remember your password, click the Remember Password box to add a check mark. Another option is Picture Options. When you publish your blog post, your picture needs to be uploaded to a picture provider on their storage location. Options to consider if you decide to upload a picture: you can upload to your my blog provider, My own server, and None—Don't upload pictures. For this exercise, do not use the Picture Options.

Figure 13-38

New WordPress Account dialog box

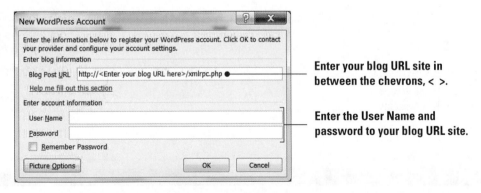

11. After entering your Blog Post URL, username, and password, a prompt will appear stating *When Word sends information to the blog service provider, it may be possible for other people to see that information. This includes your user name and password. Do you want to continue?* Click **Yes**.

12. Click the **Manage Accounts** button again in the Blog group to see your account, as shown in Figure 13-39. Click **Close**.

Figure 13-39

Blog Accounts Entry

Blog URL site added to Manage Accounts dialog box

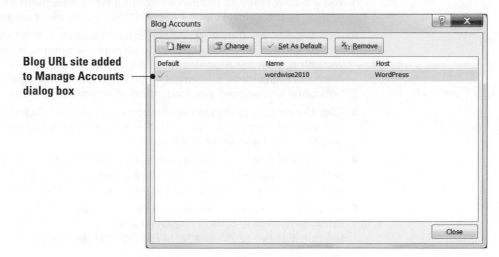

13. Click the **Publish** button on Blog group to display the *Connect to [your Blog URL]* dialog box. Figure 13-40 displays *Connect to wordwise2010*. Key your username and password to post and publish.

Figure 13-40

Connect to wordwise2010

14. A yellow prompt will appear in your Word blog document screen stating, *This post was published to <your blog URL site> followed by the time and date.* For example, *This post was published to wordwise2010 at 10:41:40 AM 2/9/2011.*

15. Close the blog post. A prompt may appear stating *Do you want to save changes made to the document? If you click "Don't Save," a recent copy of this file will be temporarily available.* Click **Don't Save**. Earlier in this lesson, you learned about managing document versions.

CERTIFICATION READY? 1.4.8

How do you register a blog?

16. When you click the **Home Page**  button on the Blog group, it will automatically

Home Page

launch the Internet directly to your Blog URL website after you have logged in.

Take Note   You can blog and publish from your blog URL site.

CERTIFICATION READY? 1.4.7

How do you publish a blog post?

17. The Insert Category button allows you to categorize postings on your blog. When you click this button, a drop-down menu appears below the blue horizontal line. When you categorize your blog post, you can select from the drop-down menu. In the meantime, you do not see any category. If you clicked the **Insert Category** button, click the **Undo** button on the Quick Access Toolbar to remove. The Open Existing button opens a published blog.

PAUSE. LEAVE Word open for the next exercise.

STEP BY STEP   Publish a Word Document as a Blog

1. You are now ready to publish an existing Word document as a blog. Click the taskbar to display the *employment_offer_2011* Word document on your screen.

2. Click the File tab, then click Save & Send. The Save & Send command appears on your screen. Click Publish as Blog Post to display the options for different sites to publish your blog. Click the Blog Post button on the right side of the screen. The *employment_offer_2011* document is inserted in the Word Blog layout and appears below the horizontal line without any formatting or any of the Word elements applied.

3. Click the Publish button in the *Blog* group to display *Connect to <your Blog URL site>*. The example shown in Figure 13-40 displays *Connect to wordwise2010*. Enter your username and password, then click OK.

4. A prompt will appear stating, *When Word sends information to the blog service provider, it may be possible for other people to see that information. This includes your username and password. Do you want to continue?* Click Yes.

5. A yellow prompt will appear on the screen stating *This post was published to your <Blog URL site> at time is displayed and date.* For example, *This post was published to your wordwise2010 at 4:12:14 PM 2/9/2011* (see Figure 13-41).

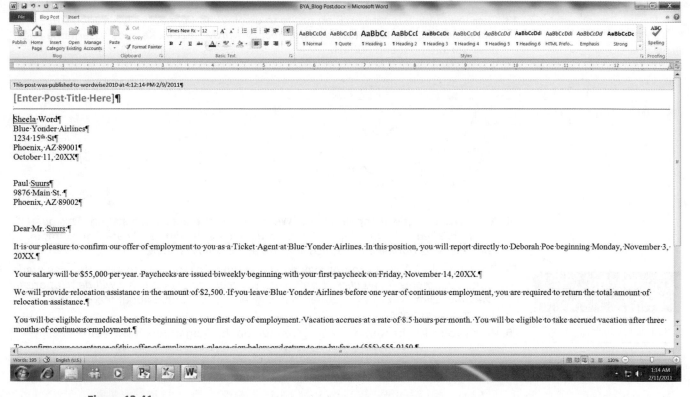

Figure 13-41

Post published

6. Close the blog post. A prompt may appear stating *Do you want to save changes made to the document? If you click "Don't Save," a recent copy of this file will be temporarily available.* Click Save.

7. Save the document as **BYA_Blog Post** in your USB flash drive in the lesson folder.

8. Close the *employment_offer_2011* Word document.

PAUSE. CLOSE Word.

CERTIFICATION READY?   **1.4.7**

How do you publish a blog post?

  Ref

Earlier in this lesson, you learned about restoring and recovering unsaved documents under "Managing Document Versions."

STEP BY STEP **Remove a Blog on Your Blog Site**

1. **LAUNCH** the Internet and log in to your blog URL site. On the left side of the screen, click Post, and all posts will appear.

2. Add a check mark in the check box and hover your mouse pointer over the post to delete, then select Trash. Click Apply.

3. Log out of your blog URL site. Have fun blogging!

CLOSE the Internet.

SKILL SUMMARY

In This Lesson You Learned How To:	Exam Objective	Objective Number
Apply protection to a document	Apply protection by using the Microsoft Office Backstage view commands.	1.2.1
	Apply protection by using the Ribbon commands.	1.2.2
	Use Protected Mode.	1.5.2
Manage document versions	Recover draft versions.	1.3.1
	Delete all draft versions.	1.3.2
Share documents	Create a shared document.	1.4.6
	Send documents via email.	1.4.1
	Send documents via SkyDrive.	1.4.2
	Send documents via Internet fax.	1.4.3
	Change file types.	1.4.4
	Register a blog account.	1.4.8
	Publish a blog post.	1.4.7
	Create PDF documents.	1.4.5

Knowledge Assessment

True/False

Circle T if the statement is true or F if the statement is false.

T   F   1. You can specify two different passwords, one to open a document and one to modify it.

T   F   2. You should run the Compatibility Checker on all document files.

T   F   3. The Compatibility Check will ensure that the document's features are compatible with other versions of Word.

T   F   4. The AutoSave Version will appear on your document with a prompt stating that a newer version is available. As a user, you have the option to compare and restore.

T   F   5. The Compatibility Checker will list a summary of features not supported by earlier versions.

T   F   6. SkyDrive is another way of sharing documents.

T   F   7. Restrict Formatting will allow users to limit the formatting styles in a document.

T   F   8. Read-only prevents changes to a document.

T   F   **9.** Inspect Document does not provide options on removing features that may have been used in the document.

T   F   **10.** The Restrict Formatting and Editing pane cannot be accessed on the Ribbon.

Multiple Choice

Select the best response for the following statements.

1. *Requires a password to open a document* is accomplished by using
   a. Encrypt with Password
   b. Restrict Editing
   c. Restrict Formatting
   d. Word does not support this feature

2. A document protected with comments was created using which feature?
   a. Restrict Formatting
   b. Protected from using comments
   c. Comments features was turned off
   d. Restrict Editing

3. Unsaved documents can be recovered using
   a. Multiple users
   b. Manage Versions
   c. SkyDrive
   d. Save As

4. Internet faxing is available to users
   a. At no charge
   b. For a fee by service providers
   c. Only if you have access to a fax machine
   d. It is not available

5. Word provides blogging as an option, but as a user you must
   a. Register a blog URL
   b. Post and publish
   c. Maintain your blog URL site
   d. All of the above

6. You must register a space name before
   a. Blogging
   b. Posting a blog
   c. Sharing
   d. Publishing

7. If your document contains potential problems where the content is difficult to read by an individual with a disability, you would be alerted under which command?
   a. Check Accessibility
   b. Check Compatibility
   c. Inspect Document
   d. All of the above

8. Before sharing a document, it is good practice to remove personal information using which command?
   a. Check Accessibility
   b. Check Compatibility
   c. Inspect Document
   d. No command is available

9. Draft versions of documents can be deleted by
   a. Right-clicking then selecting Delete
   b. Using Manage Versions
   c. Pressing the Delete key
   d. a and b

10. Recovering unsaved documents is located under which command?
   a. Info
   b. Recent
   c. Open
   d. Save & Send

Competency Assessment

Project 13-1: Prepare the Coho Winery Document for Review

You are ready to send an article titled "How to Reap the Health Benefits of Wine" to a classmate for review. Inspect the document and mark it as final.

GET READY. LAUNCH Word if not already running.

The *benefitsofwine* document file for this lesson is available on the book companion website or in WileyPLUS.

1. **OPEN** *benefitsofwine* from your USB flash drive for this lesson.
2. Click the File tab, point to Info, and select Check for Issues, then Inspect Document. The Document Inspector appears.
3. Click Inspect.
4. In the Document Properties and Personal Information section, click Remove All.
5. Leave the Custom XML Data as is.
6. Click Close.
7. Under Prepare to Share, click Allow this information to be saved in your file.
8. **SAVE** the document as *benefits_of_wine* in your USB flash drive and **CLOSE** the file.

LEAVE Word open for the next project.

Project 13-2: Prepare Stock Agreement for Distribution

Your task is to remove all document properties in the stock agreement document before sharing with eligible employees.

GET READY. LAUNCH Word if not already running.

The *stockagreement2* document file for this lesson is available on the book companion website or in WileyPLUS.

1. **OPEN** *stockagreement2* from the lesson folder.
2. Inspect the document. Click Remove All on the Document Properties and Personal Information setting and on the Headers, Footers, and Watermarks setting.
3. Click Close.
4. Select the second paragraph that begins with *Agreement made...* and click the Restrict Editing button.
5. Click Allow only this type of editing in the document box for Comments only.
6. Click Yes, Start Enforcing Protection and enter the password BYA%$#agree in the dialog box. Close the Restrict Formatting and Editing pane.
7. **SAVE** the document as *stock_agreement_2* in your USB flash drive in the lesson folder.

LEAVE the document open for the next project.

Proficiency Assessment

Project 13-3: Computer Use Policy

Your manager has asked you to format the computer use policy document appropriately and have it ready for a meeting in an hour.

GET READY. LAUNCH Word if not already running.

@ The *computeruse2* document file for this lesson is available on the book companion website or in WileyPLUS.

1. **OPEN** *computeruse2* from the lesson folder.
2. Change the default settings for the Save AutoRecover minutes. In the File tab, under Help, click Options, and then Save.
3. Under the Save document section, click the down arrow by Save AutoRecover information until it changes to 5 minutes.
4. On page 1, select the content within the border beginning with *Disclaimer . . . All rights reserved*. Add the Olive Green, Accent 3, Lighter 40% shading color. Add a page border with a shadow style with the border color of Olive Green, Accent 3, Darker 50%, 2¼" wide.
5. Select COMPUTER USE POLICY, bold, 18 pts.
6. Select Section One through Section Ten, and change the style to Intense Reference.
7. **CLOSE** the document without saving. A prompt should appear on your screen. *If you don't save, a recent copy of the document will be temporarily available.* If the prompt did not appear, check step 2. Click Don't Save. In the next exercise, you will be recovering your unsaved document.

LEAVE Word open for the next project.

Project 13-4: Computer Use Policy Contents

You are continuing with the previous project and realized that you inadvertently didn't save the document. Your task is to retrieve the unsaved document.

GET READY. LAUNCH Word if not already running.

1. Click the File tab, then click the Manage Versions button.
2. Select Recover Unsaved Documents.
3. Locate the file and click Open.
4. **SAVE** the document as *computer_final* in your USB flash drive in the lesson folder and **CLOSE** the file.

LEAVE Word open for the next project.

Mastery Assessment

Project 13-5: Stock Agreement Finalized

You have finalized the stock agreement document and are ready to share it with employees. Your task is to save the document as a PDF file before sending it to eligible employees.

GET READY. LAUNCH Word if not already running.

1. **USE** the *stock_agreement_2* document from the previous project.
2. **SAVE** and **Publish** the document as *stock_agreement* in your USB flash drive in the lesson folder.

LEAVE Word open for the next project.

Project 13-6: Create a Document with a Password

Create a document that only you can access.

GET READY. LAUNCH Word if not already running.

1. Key the following:

   Name: Giovanni

   Email address: someone@live.com

   The importance of using a password:

   Unauthorized access to your document

   Password added to prevent changes in the document

   The document can only be opened by those who know the password

2. Apply the default numbering format to the three items above.

3. Protect the document by securing it with the password **dap&27#%**.

4. **SAVE** the document as *password* in your USB flash drive and **CLOSE** the file.

CLOSE Word.

INTERNET READY

For more information about job strategies used, use the Help feature and select the link on Office Casual: How to Get your Resume Noticed & Story Time (a double bill)—blog.

Workplace *Ready*

WORD'S SECURITY OPTION

In today's electronic world, sending a document to a co-worker as an email attachment is quickly replacing the use of interoffice mail. Along with the many advantages of sending a file in electronic format rather than as a hard copy, a concern remains over who may be able to access the file once it leaves your computer. Securing sensitive business information has always been a top priority for even the smallest companies. Word provides many security options that can help you in achieving this goal.

You work as a research analyst for A Datum Corporation, an investment consulting firm. You regularly prepare confidential research reports on investment opportunities for clients. Each report is prepared exclusively for a specific client, and you need to ensure that the information contained in the report cannot be accessed by unauthorized individuals.

You find that assigning a password to each file is the perfect way to ensure that a report is viewed only by the intended client. You choose to set a password for each individual client in regards to their investment report. Only users with access to a file's password will be able to open the file. If needed, you could also set a separate password for modifying a document. Once set, a document can only be modified if the user has provided the appropriate password.

With the security options offered in Word, you can feel confident knowing you will retain control over your documents long after they leave your desk.

14 Using Advanced Options

LESSON SKILL MATRIX

Skill	Exam Objective	Objective Number
Customizing Word		
Changing Research Options		

You are employed as a researcher at A Datum Corporation, a company that provides custom consulting services to information technology companies. Many of the default options for Word are suitable, but there are times you need to make changes to settings for features such as compatibility, editing, printing, and saving. In this lesson, you will learn how to access options that enable you to customize Word to best fit the tasks that you perform such as changing display options, setting save options, using advanced options, customizing the Quick Access Toolbar, and changing research options.

SOFTWARE ORIENTATION

Word Options

The Word Options dialog box provides a wide variety of methods to customize how Word is used. Ten different option groups are provided. To access these options, click the File tab and then click Options, as shown in Figure 14-1.

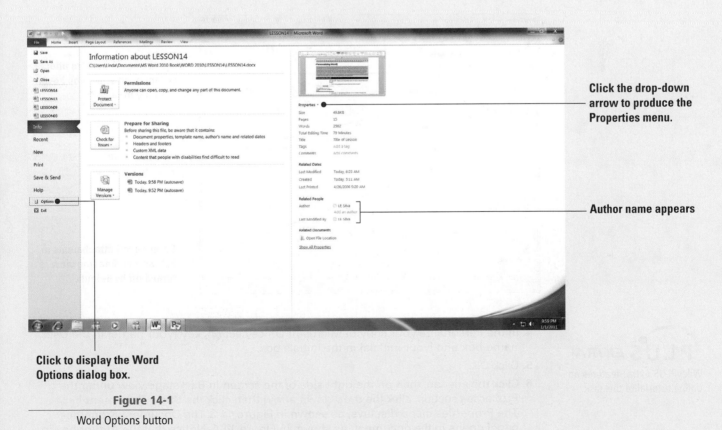

Click the drop-down arrow to produce the Properties menu.

Author name appears

Click to display the Word Options dialog box.

Figure 14-1

Word Options button

Use this figure as a reference throughout this lesson.

CUSTOMIZING WORD

The Bottom Line

Word can be customized through the different options available in the Word Options dialog box.

Personalizing Word

NEW to Office 2010

The Word Options dialog box is located in Backstage and as you learned in Lesson 1 this is new in Word 2010. The General screen of the Word Options dialog box contains some of the most popular options that can be customized in Word, including changing your name and initials. The general options are some of the most frequently used when customizing Word. Take time to explore the contents of each screen of the Word Options dialog box because there are too many choices to cover in this lesson. The more familiar you become with the options available, the better able you will be to customize Word to suit your needs. In this exercise, you learn to personalize Word.

STEP BY STEP | **Personalize Word**

GET READY. Before you begin these steps, be sure to launch Microsoft Word.

 The *a_datum* document file for this lesson is available on the book companion website or in WileyPLUS.

1. **OPEN** the *a_datum* document from the lesson folder.

2. Click the **File** tab and then click the **Options** button to display the Word Options dialog box.

3. The General options on the left is already selected and displays the personalize options, shown in Figure 14-2.

Figure 14-2

General options screen

Provides quick access to formatting tools when you select text

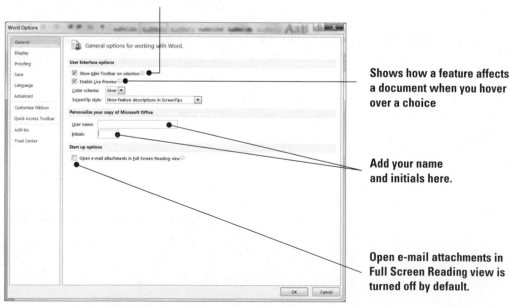

Shows how a feature affects a document when you hover over a choice

Add your name and initials here.

Open e-mail attachments in Full Screen Reading view is turned off by default.

4. In the Personalize your copy of Microsoft Office section, key [your name] in the User name box and [your initials] in the Initials box.

5. Click **OK**.

6. Click the **File** tab, then on the right side of the screen in Backstage view under the Properties section, click the **drop-down arrow** then click the **Show Document Panel**. The Properties menu displays, as shown in Figure 14-3. The Document Properties panel opens in the document, as shown in Figure 14-4. Notice that the Author box in the Document Properties Panel has your name.

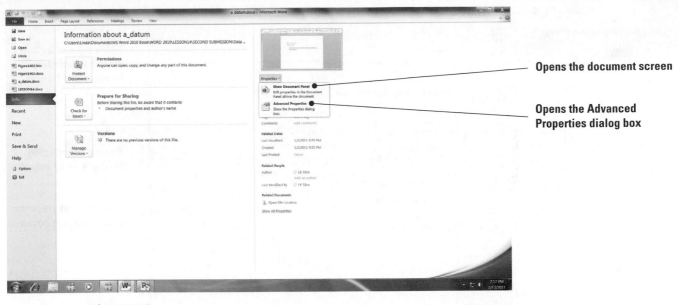

Figure 14-3

Properties menu

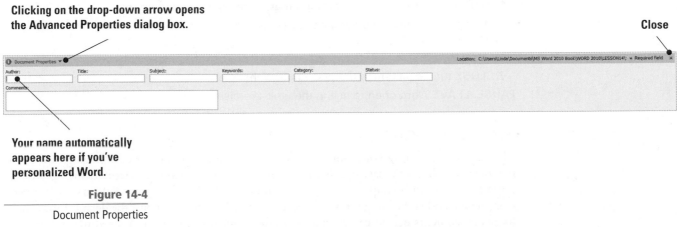

Figure 14-4

Document Properties

7. Click the Close button to close the Document Information Panel.

PAUSE. LEAVE the document open to use in the next exercise.

Changing Display Options

The Display screen of the Word Options dialog box contains options for changing how document content is displayed both on the screen and when printed. Changing options on the Display screen affects how content is displayed both on your computer screen and for all printed documents, not just the document that is currently open. Select or deselect the check box for any option you want to turn on or off. In this exercise, you learn to change the display options.

STEP BY STEP   **Change Display Options**

USE the document that is open from the previous exercise.

1. Click the File tab and then click the Options button to display the Word Options dialog box.

2. Click Display on the left pane to view the display options, shown in Figure 14-5.

Figure 14-5

Display options screen

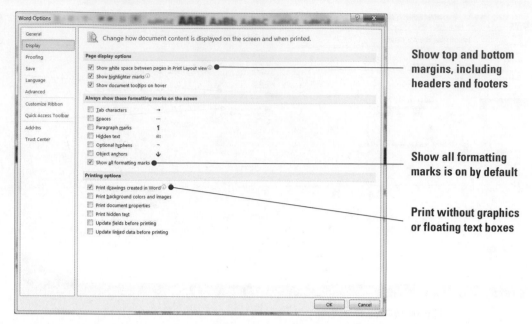

Show top and bottom margins, including headers and footers

Show all formatting marks is on by default

Print without graphics or floating text boxes

3. In the *Always show these formatting marks on the screen* section, notice that the **Show all formatting marks** check box is checked. Click to turn it off.

4. Click **OK**. Notice that the Paragraph marks are off in the document.

5. Open the Options dialog box and select the **Show all formatting Marks** to turn back on. By default they are on.

6. Click **OK**.

7. **CLOSE** the document without saving the changes.

PAUSE. LEAVE Word open to use in the next exercise.

Setting Save Options

The Save screen of the Word Options dialog box contains options for customizing how documents are saved. Use the save options to determine how documents are saved, including preserving information in backup files for your documents, sharing files using a document management server, and embedding fonts in a file. For example, you can change the default format used to save documents or you can change how often your documents are backed up by using the AutoRecover feature. The Documents folder, located on drive C, is the default working folder for all the documents created in Microsoft Office programs. If the operating system on your computer is Windows XP, the default is My Documents, and in Windows 7, the default folder is the Documents Library. On the Save screen, you can choose a different default working folder (for example, your USB flash drive). In this exercise, you learn to change and set save options.

STEP BY STEP   **Set Save Options**

1. Click the **File** tab, and then click **Options**. Click **Save** in the left pane to display the save options shown in Figure 14-6.

2. In the Save documents section, click the **drop-down arrow** in the Save files in this format box. The menu displays the options available for changing the default file format used when saving backup files. The default setting to save your work is set to every 10 minutes.

3. Before changing, check with your instructor regarding this next step. In the *Save AutoRecover information every* box, click the **down arrow** to change the number of minutes to **3**.

4. Leave the Word Options dialog box open for the next exercise.

PAUSE. LEAVE Word open to use in the next exercise.

Figure 14-6

Save options screen

On by default

Document will be saved in
this format-default settings.

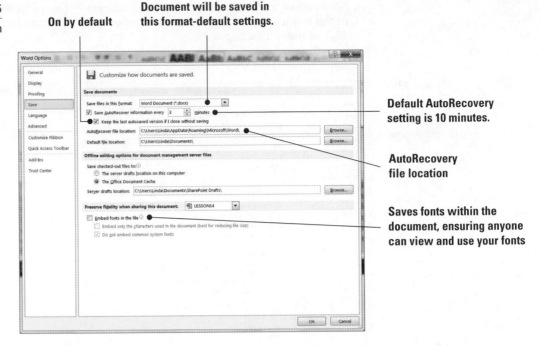

Default AutoRecovery
setting is 10 minutes.

AutoRecovery
file location

Saves fonts within the
document, ensuring anyone
can view and use your fonts

Take Note   Any change made to the default working folder applies only to the program that you are currently using. For example, if a different default working folder is selected for Word, the default
working folder for Excel will remain Documents if you are using Windows 7.

Using Advanced Options

The Advanced screen of the Word Options dialog box contains advanced options for working with
Word. The Advanced screen contains many advanced choices for working with Word documents,
including options for editing, displaying, printing, and saving. Some are selected by default and
some are not. Browse through them and see how you might use some of the options to work more
efficiently in Word. In addition to the multitude of options found on this screen, several dialog boxes
can be accessed for additional customization. In this exercise, you learn to use the advanced options.

STEP BY STEP   **Use Advanced Options**

1. From the Word Options dialog box, click **Advanced** on the left pane to display the
   advanced options. There are several advanced options, many of which are shown in
   Figures 14-7 through 14-10.

Figure 14-7

Advanced options screen;
Cut, copy, and paste;
Image Size and Quality;
and Show document content

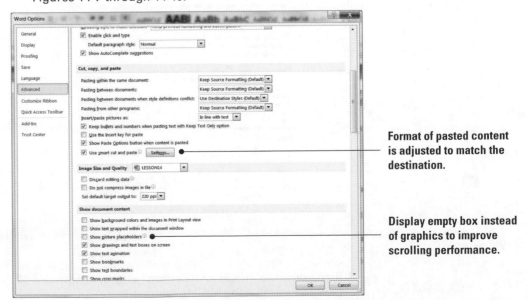

Format of pasted content
is adjusted to match the
destination.

Display empty box instead
of graphics to improve
scrolling performance.

2. Scroll down and in the Display section (shown in Figure 14-8), click the **up arrow** next to the number in the Show this number of Recent Documents list box to change it to **15**. The default setting is 25.

Figure 14-8

Advanced options screen: Display options and Print options

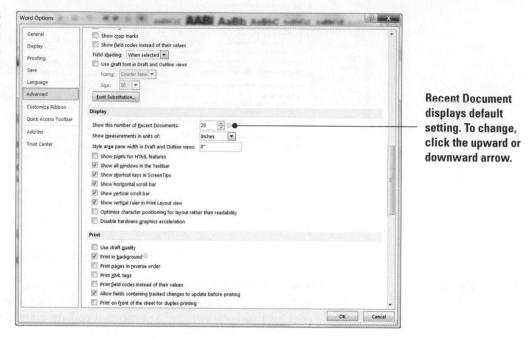

Recent Document displays default setting. To change, click the upward or downward arrow.

3. Click **OK**.

4. Click the **File** tab, then click **Recent**. Backstage view displays 15 documents. Return settings back to default.

5. Click the **Options** button to display the Word Options dialog box.

6. Click **Advanced** and scroll down to the Save section (shown in Figure 14-9) and click to select the **Prompt before saving Normal template** check box. Now if you change the default template, Word will ask if you want to save the changes to that template.

Figure 14-9

Advanced options screen: Print and Save options

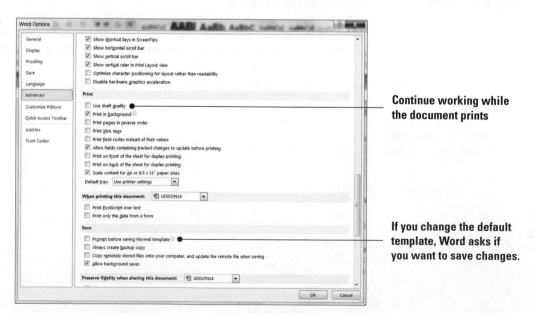

Continue working while the document prints

If you change the default template, Word asks if you want to save changes.

7. Scroll down to the General section (shown in Figure 14-10) and key [your name] and [your address] in the Mailing address box.

Figure 14-10

Advanced options screen:
General and Compatibility
options

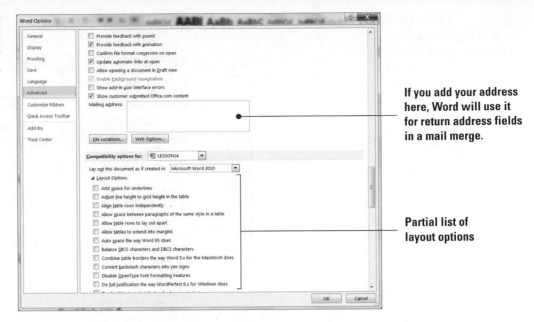

Figure 14-10

Advanced options screen:
General and Compatibility
options

If you add your address
here, Word will use it
for return address fields
in a mail merge.

Partial list of
layout options

Another Way
The keyboard
shortcut Ctrl+N will open a
new blank document.

8. Click **OK**.

9. Click the **File** tab, click **New**, and then click **Blank Document**. Then click the **Create** button to create a blank Word document if necessary.

10. On the Mailings tab, in the Create group, click the **Labels** button.

11. In the Envelopes and Labels dialog box, click to select the **Use return address** check box. Notice that your name and address is displayed in the Address box.

12. Click **Cancel**.

PAUSE. LEAVE Word open to use in the next exercise.

Customizing the Quick Access Toolbar and Ribbon

The Customize screen of the Word Options dialog box enables you to customize the Quick Access Toolbar and keyboard shortcuts. Adding frequently used commands to the Quick Access Toolbar ensures that those commands are always just a single click away. Only commands can be added to the Quick Access Toolbar. The contents of most lists, such as indent and spacing values and individual styles, which also appear on the Ribbon, cannot be added to the Quick Access Toolbar. In this exercise, you will add a command to the Quick Access Toolbar.

STEP BY STEP   **Customize the Quick Access Toolbar**

1. Click the **File** tab, and then click **Options**. When the Word Options dialog box opens, click **Quick Access Toolbar** on the left pane to display the customization options, shown in Figure 14-11.

 Ref   You first learned about the Quick Access Toolbar in Lesson 1.

2. In the Choose commands from list, Popular Commands is already selected.

3. Scroll down the list of commands, and select **Page Setup**.

4. Click the **Add** button or double-click.

5. Click **OK**. Notice the New command button is now on the Quick Access Toolbar. The Page Setup dialog box will open when you click on the command on the Quick Access Toolbar.

PAUSE. LEAVE Word open to use in the next exercise.

Figure 14-11

Word Options dialog box:
Customize the Quick Access
Toolbar

Scroll bar

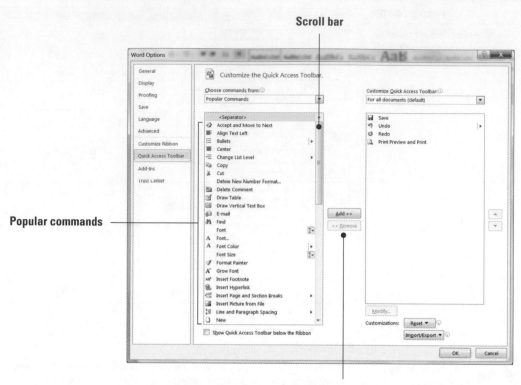

Popular commands

Add / Remove buttons

Take Note

To remove a command from the Quick Access Toolbar, place the insertion point on the command in the Quick Access Toolbar, right-click the command, then click Remove from Quick Access Toolbar.

STEP BY STEP   **Customize the Ribbon**

USE the document open from the previous exercise.

1. Click the **File** tab, then **Options** to open the Word Options dialog box. Click **Customize Ribbon** on the left pane and the Customization screen (see Figure 14-12) appears.

2. On the bottom left, click the **Customize** button next to Keyboard shortcuts. The Customize Keyboard dialog box appears, as shown in Figure 14-13.

3. In the Categories box, click **Home Tab**.

4. In the Commands box, click **Bold**. Two shortcut key commands appear in the Current keys box. These two keyboard shortcuts have been assigned to bold text quickly using the keyboard in your document while editing.

5. In the Current keys box, select **Ctrl+Shift+B** as shown in Figure 14-14.

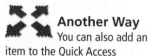

Another Way
You can also add an item to the Quick Access Toolbar in the Ribbon by clicking the Customize Quick Access Toolbar button or by right-clicking anywhere on the bar.

6. Click the **Remove** button to remove the shortcut key for the *Bold* command. Removing the **Ctrl+Shift+B** now makes it available to be used for another shortcut keyboard command.

7. Click **Close** to close the Customize Keyboard dialog box.

8. Leave the Word Options dialog box open for the next exercise.

PAUSE. LEAVE Word open to use in the next exercise.

Figure 14-12

Word Option dialog box:
Customize the Ribbon and
keyboard shortcuts

Customize the Ribbon

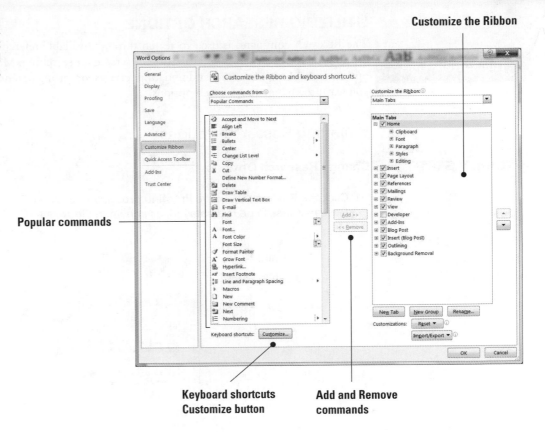

Popular commands

Keyboard shortcuts
Customize button

Add and Remove
commands

Figure 14-13

Customize Keyboard
dialog box

Category listing

Commands

Existing keyboard
shortcut (if any exists)

New keyboard
shortcut

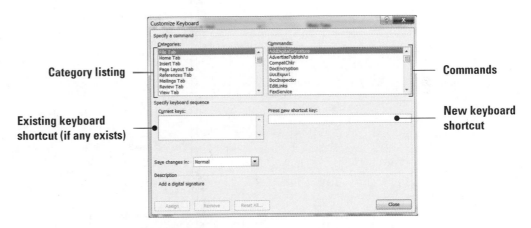

Figure 14-14

Customize Keyboard
dialog box with command
highlighted

Category listing
by tabs and more

Current keys assigned
to the Bold command

Click to assign new
keyboard shortcut.

Click to remove
keyboard shortcut.

Select the command
to assign a keyboard
shortcut.

When you press keys to add a
new keyboard shortcut, Word
will display if assigned or
unassigned in this dialog box.

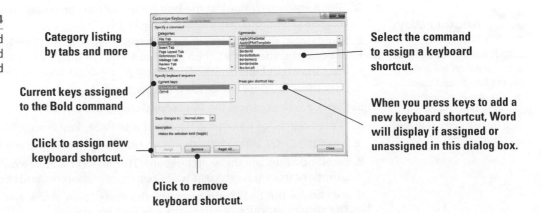

UTILIZING RESEARCH OPTIONS

The Research command is used to search through available reference materials. The Research Options dialog box enables you to activate a service for searching. Manage the available research options by adding, removing, and updating services, or setting parental controls. In this exercise, you learn to change the research options.

Changing Research Options

STEP BY STEP | **Change Research Options**

1. Click the Review tab, in the Proofing group, and click the Research button. The Research Task Pane is displayed, as shown in Figure 14-15.

WileyPLUS Extra! features an online tutorial of this task.

Figure 14-15

Research Task Pane

Another Way
To open the Research Task Pane, place your insertion point on the text, press the Alt key, and then click once. Note the text will automatically be placed in the Search for box of the task pane.

2. Click Research Options at the bottom of the Research Task Pane to display the Research Options dialog box, shown in Figure 14-16.

3. Scroll down to the Research Sites section, click the text Factiva iWorks™ to select (do not click the check box), then click Properties to display the *Service Properties* dialog box, shown in Figure 14-17. This displays the details about the service.

4. Click Close to close the Service Properties dialog box.

5. Click Cancel to cancel the Research Options dialog box.

6. In the Search for box in the Research Task Pane, key immigration.

7. Press the Enter key or click the Start searching green arrow beside the box.

8. Scroll down to see the search results. The search results reveal definitions and short summary from government websites, immigration organization, Wikipedia, and more.

9. Just below the Search for box, click the drop-down arrow and select Factiva iWorks™. The results produce publications and Web News.

Figure 14-16

Research Options dialog box

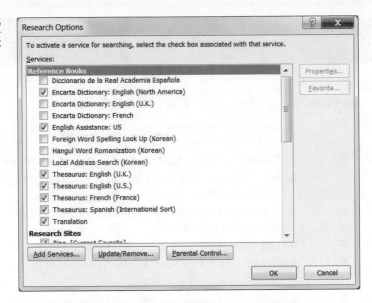

Figure 14-17

Service Properties

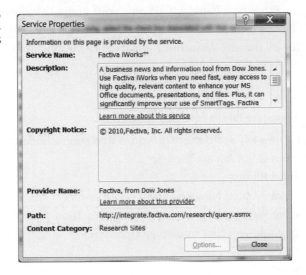

10. Scroll down to see the search results.

11. Just below the Search for box, click the **drop-down arrow** and select **All Business and Financial Sites**.

12. The Thomson Gale Company Profiles displays the available information. Two company profiles on immigration appear. To read more about each company, click on the individual link where it reads, *Click to read full profile*.

13. Click the **Close** button to close the Research Task Pane.

STOP. CLOSE Word.

SKILL SUMMARY

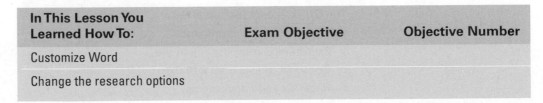

In This Lesson You Learned How To:	Exam Objective	Objective Number
Customize Word		
Change the research options		

Knowledge Assessment

True/False

Circle T if the statement is true or F if the statement is false.

T   F   **1.** The Advanced screen contains the largest number of options available in the Word Options dialog box.

T   F   **2.** The Quick Access Toolbar and keyboard shortcuts cannot be customized.

T   F   **3.** The Research command is used to search through available reference materials and services.

T   F   **4.** In the Word Options dialog box, you can add your name and initials under the Personalize section.

T   F   **5.** The default settings in the Word options cannot be changed.

T   F   **6.** The Research Task Pane button is found in Backstage.

T   F   **7.** Changing the display will affect how content appears on your computer.

T   F   **8.** When you personalize Word by adding your name, the Document Properties Panel will display your name in the author's box.

T   F   **9.** The formatting marks can be turned off in the Display options screen.

T   F   **10.** By default, Windows 7 will display My Documents as the default folder to save documents.

Multiple Choice

Select the best response for the following statements.

1. To assign a new keyboard shortcut, you would access Backstage, Word Options, and then
   a. Customize Quick Access Toolbar
   b. Customize Ribbon
   c. Customize Ribbon, New Keyboard commands
   d. Customize Ribbon, Keyboard shortcuts, and then Customize button

2. Which tab would you click to display Options?
   a. Insert
   b. Advanced
   c. File
   d. Display

3. The Research tab allows you to see results from
   a. Websites
   b. Publications
   c. Company profiles
   d. All of the above

4. The Display category will display which hidden formatting mark?
   a. Spaces
   b. Tab characters
   c. Paragraph marks
   d. All of the above

5. The Quick Access Toolbar is for
   a. Frequently used commands
   b. Commands from the File menu
   c. Contents of lists on the Ribbon
   d. Recently used documents

6. Which reference materials or services are available using the Research Task Pane?
   a. Dictionaries
   b. Encyclopedias
   c. Translation services
   d. All of the above

7. As a user of Word, you can change the AutoRecover minutes to set how Word protects you from losing your work in which screen?
   a. Save
   b. Options, Save
   c. Save As
   d. None of the above

8. The Research pane under all Research Sites does not complete which action?
   a. Add a website address
   b. Run through the Speller
   c. Provide additional articles
   d. All of the above

9. You open the Research pane from which tab?
   a. References
   b. Review
   c. View
   d. File

10. If your computer is running on Windows 7, the default working folder for all documents created in Microsoft Office 2010 programs is
    a. My Documents
    b. Documents Library
    c. Word 2010
    d. b and c

Competency Assessment

Project 14-1: Lost Art Photos Return Address

In your position as a marketing assistant at Lost Art Photos, you frequently mail promotional letters. You prepare envelopes for these mailings in Word, and making the company's return address your default option would save time. Change your Word options to set this up.

GET READY. LAUNCH Word if it is not already running.

1. Click the **File** tab, and then click **New**. Blank document is already selected; click **Create**.
2. Click the **File** tab and then select the **Options** button to display the Word Options dialog box.
3. Click **Advanced** on the left to display the advanced options.
4. Scroll down to the General section and in the Mailing address box, key:

   LostArtPhotos

   5500 Bissell Street

   Grand Junction, CO 98445
5. Press the **Print Scrn** button on the keyboard. Click **OK** to close the Word Options dialog box.
6. Right-click in the document screen, then click **Paste**.
7. Save the document as ***mailing_address*** in your USB flash drive in the lesson folder.

LEAVE Word open for the next project.

Project 14-2: Setting Research Options

A Datum Corporation has an overseas branch in the United Kingdom. In your position as a researcher, you sometimes need to take this into account when using Word to look up information. Set the research options accordingly.

GET READY. LAUNCH Word if it is not already running.

1. Click the File tab, and then click New. Blank document is already selected; click Create.
2. On the Review tab, in the Proofing group, click the Research button to display the Research Task Pane.
3. Click Research Options to display the Research Options dialog box.
4. In the Reference Books section, click the check box to select Encarta Dictionary: English (U.K.).
5. Press the Print Scrn button on the keyboard. Click OK to close the Research Options dialog box.
6. Right-click, then click Paste.
7. Repeat step 3.
8. In the Research Sites section, click the check box to select Bing (United Kingdom).
9. Repeat steps 5 and 6.
10. Save your document as *setting_research* in your USB flash drive in the lesson folder. Your research options are now set to include those specific to the United Kingdom.

LEAVE Word open for the next project.

Proficiency Assessment

Project 14-3: Customizing the Quick Access Toolbar

As a paralegal in a busy legal practice, you are always looking for ways to streamline your work. As you learn more about Word, you want to use the available options to help customize the program for your daily tasks.

GET READY. LAUNCH Word if it is not already running.

1. Press Ctrl+N to open a new blank document.
2. Click the File tab, then Options to open the Word Options dialog box.
3. Display the customization screen for the Quick Access Toolbar.
4. Choose five commands that you use frequently, but that are not currently located on the Quick Access Toolbar. Add the commands to the Quick Access Toolbar. Click OK to close the Word Options dialog box.
5. Press the Print Scrn button on the keyboard. Click OK to close the Research Options dialog box.
6. Right-click, then click Paste.
7. Save the document as *customizing_QAT* in your USB flash drive in the lesson folder.

LEAVE Word open for the next project.

Project 14-4: Removing Commands from the Quick Access Toolbar

You are continuing to work with Project 14-4. Now that you have added five additional commands to your Quick Access Toolbar, you realize that you added a command that you do not use as frequently. You remember seeing the Remove button below the Add button.

GET READY. LAUNCH Word if it is not already running.

1. **OPEN** the Word Options dialog box.

2. Display the customization screen for the Quick Access Toolbar.

3. Select all the commands that you added and remove them from the Quick Access Toolbar. Click OK to close the Word Options dialog box.

4. Press the Print Scrn button on the keyboard.

5. Right-click, then click Paste.

6. Save the document as *removing_commands* in your USB flash drive in the lesson folder.

LEAVE Word open for the next project.

Mastery Assessment

Project 14-5: Save Settings

Your instructor has asked you to change the Save settings in Backstage view to five minutes.

GET READY. LAUNCH Word if it is not already running.

1. Create a new, blank Word document.

2. **OPEN** the Word Options dialog box.

3. Change the Save settings options to five minutes.

4. Press the Print Scrn button on the keyboard.

5. Right-click, then click Paste.

4. **SAVE** the document as *save_settings* in your USB flash drive in the lesson folder and **CLOSE** the file.

LEAVE Word open for the next project.

Project 14-6: Word Options

Your task is to remove the Lost Art Photos Return Address that you added in Backstage for Project 14-1. To show your instructor that you completed this project, you will be using the print screen button located on the keyboard, then pasting it in a Word document.

GET READY. LAUNCH Word if it is not already running.

1. Create a new, blank Word document.

2. **OPEN** the Word Options dialog box and click Advanced.

3. Remove the Mailing address that you keyed in Project 14-1.

4. Press the Print Scrn button on the keyboard.

5. Right-click, then click Paste.

6. Key your answers into the Word document.

7. **SAVE** the document as *address_removed* in your USB flash drive in the lesson folder and **CLOSE** the file.

CLOSE Word.

 INTERNET READY

To ensure that your computer is up to date, click the Trust Center in the Word Options dialog box, then click the Trust Center Settings. Select the Privacy Options button and click the link, *Read Privacy Statement*. Prepare a document for your instructor explaining the features that are turned on and their benefits.

Project 1: Inspected Speaker Letter

Now that you have incorporated the changes suggested, prepare the document for distribution.

GET READY. LAUNCH Word if it is not already running.

@ The
speakerthankyou2 file
for this Circling Back is
available on the book
companion website or in
WileyPLUS.

1. **Open** *speakerthankyou2* from the data files for this lesson.
2. On the File tab, click Check for Issues, and select Inspect Document from the menu.
3. Run the Document Inspector and choose Remove All Document Properties and Personal Information. Leave Headers, Footers, and Watermarks as is and close the window.
4. **SAVE** the document as *thank_you_inspected* in your USB flash drive in the lesson folder.
5. Click the File tab, click Check for Issues, and select the Check Compatibility from the menu. No compatibility issues were found.
6. Click OK and **CLOSE** the file.

PAUSE. LEAVE Word open for the next project.

Project 2: Master and Subdocument for Research Paper

You are taking a computer class this semester and have been assigned a group project. The research project needs to be divided into sections so that you and your group members can work separately on the document.

GET READY. LAUNCH Word if it is not already running.

@ The *research* file
for this Circling Back is
available on the book
companion website or in
WileyPLUS.

1. **OPEN** the *research* document from the lesson folder.
2. Create a new folder named Master Research in your USB flash drive in the lesson folder.
3. **SAVE** the document as *master_research* in the Master Research folder in your USB flash drive.
4. Select the Introduction heading.
5. On the Home tab, in the Styles group, click the More button to display the Quick Styles gallery.
6. Click the Heading 1 option.
7. Apply the Heading 1 style to the remaining headings in the document: Community in the Classroom, Technology within Literature Circles, Computer-Mediated Discussion Groups, and Conclusion.
8. On the View tab in the Document View group, click the Outline button.
9. In the Outline Tools, click the drop-down arrow at Show Level and select Level 1.
10. On the Master Document group, click Show Document.
11. Select the plus (+) symbol by Introduction to select.
12. On the Master Document group, click the Create button. Introduction is surrounded by a border.
13. Repeat your steps for the remaining headings in the document, Community in the Classroom, Technology within Literature Circles, Computer-Mediated Discussion Groups, and Conclusion.
14. **SAVE** the document and close.
15. **OPEN** the *master_research* document. The subdocuments are hyperlinks.
16. Press the Ctrl key and click to open the Computer subdocument.
17. In the first paragraph, locate and select Students that are physically handicapped and even speech impeded students are afforded a safer place.
18. In the Styles group of the Home tab, select Intense Emphasis.
19. **SAVE** the subdocument and **CLOSE**.

20. Click the Show Documents button to display the controls.

21. Select the plus (+) symbol for Computer-Mediated Discussion Groups.

22. Click the Move Up button until it is positioned below the continuous section break below Community in the Classroom.

23. Click the Show Document button.

24. Click the Create button to create a subdocument.

25. Click the Collapse Subdocuments button.

26. **SAVE** and close.

PAUSE. LEAVE Word open for the next project.

Project 3: Sharing Documents

You have prepared the *master_research* document and created and saved the subdocuments. You are now ready to share sections of the document with your group and send to your NET Passport account.

GET READY. LAUNCH Word if it is not already running.

1. **OPEN** the *Introduction* document from the *Master Research* folder.

2. In the File tab, click Save & Send.

3. Click Save to Web and select Sign In.

4. Enter your Windows Live ID and password. Click OK.

5. Select My Documents under Personal folders.

6. Click the Save As button. The Save As dialog box appears and the address bar displays the location of your folder. Click Save.

7. On the File tab, select Save & Send.

8. Under File Types click the Create PDF/XPS Document.

9. Click the Create PDF/XPS button and save in your NET Passport account.

CLOSE Word.

Matrix Skill	Objective Number	Lesson Number
Sharing and Maintaining Documents	1	
Apply different views to a document.	1.1	
Select zoom options.	1.1.1	2
Split windows.	1.1.2	2
Arrange windows.	1.1.3	2
Arrange document views.	1.1.4	2, 12
Switch between windows.	1.1.5	2
Open a document in a new window.	1.1.6	2
Apply protection to a document.	1.2	
Apply protection by using the Microsoft Office Backstage view commands.	1.2.1	13
Apply protection by using Ribbon commands.	1.2.2	13
Manage document versions.	1.3	
Recover draft versions.	1.3.1	13
Delete all draft versions.	1.3.2	13
Share documents.	1.4	
Send documents via email.	1.4.1	13
Send documents via SkyDrive.	1.4.2	13
Send documents via Internet fax.	1.4.3	13
Change file types.	1.4.4	13
Create PDF documents.	1.4.5	13
Create a shared document.	1.4.6	13
Publish a blog post.	1.4.7	13
Register a blog account.	1.4.8	13
Save a document.	1.5	
Use Compatibility Mode.	1.5.1	1
Use Protected Mode.	1.5.2	13
Use Save As options.	1.5.3	1

Matrix Skill	Objective Number	Lesson Number
Apply a template to a document.	1.6	
Find templates.	1.6.1	12
Formatting Content	2	
Apply font and paragraph attributes.	2.1	
Apply character attributes.	2.1.1	3
Apply styles.	2.1.2	3
Use Format Painter.	2.1.3	3
Navigate and search through a document.	2.2	
Use the Navigation Pane.	2.2.1	2
Use the Go To command.	2.2.2	2
Use Browse by button.	2.2.3	2
Use Highlight features.	2.2.4	2
Set Find and Replace options.	2.2.5	2
Apply indentation and tab settings to paragraphs.	2.3	
Apply indents.	2.3.1	4
Set tabs.	2.3.2	4
Use the Tabs dialog box.	2.3.3	4
Set tabs on the ruler.	2.3.4	4
Clear tabs.	2.3.5	4
Set tab stops.	2.3.6	4
Move tab stops.	2.3.7	4
Apply spacing settings to text and paragraphs.	2.4	
Set line spacing.	2.4.1	4
Set paragraph spacing.	2.4.2	4
Create tables.	2.5	
Use the Insert Table dialog box.	2.5.1	6
Use Draw Table.	2.5.2	6
Insert a Quick Table.	2.5.3	6
Convert text to table.	2.5.4	6
Use a table to control page layout.	2.5.5	6

Matrix Skill	Objective Number	Lesson Number
Manipulate tables in a document.	2.6	
Sort content.	2.6.1	6
Add a row to a table.	2.6.2	6
Add a column to a table.	2.6.3	6
Manipulate rows.	2.6.4	6
Manipulate columns.	2.6.5	6
Define the header row.	2.6.6	6
Convert tables to text.	2.6.7	6
View gridlines.	2.6.8	6
Apply bullets to a document.	2.7	
Apply bullets.	2.7.1	4
Select a symbol format.	2.7.2	4
Define a picture to be used as a bullet.	2.7.3	4
Use AutoFormat.	2.7.4	4
Promote and demote bullet levels.	2.7.5	4
Applying Page Layout and Reusable Content	3	
Apply and manipulate page setup settings.	3.1	
Set margins.	3.1.1	5
Insert non-breaking spaces.	3.1.2	5
Add hyphenation.	3.1.3	5
Add columns.	3.1.4	5
Remove a break.	3.1.5	5
Force a page break.	3.1.6	5
Insert a section break.	3.1.7	5
Insert a blank page into a document.	3.1.8	5
Apply themes.	3.2	
Use a theme to apply formatting.	3.2.1	7
Customize a theme.	3.2.2	7
Construct content in a document by using the Quick Parts tool.	3.3	
Add built-in building blocks.	3.3.1	7
Create and manipulate page backgrounds.	3.4	
Format a document's background.	3.4.1	7

Matrix Skill	Objective Number	Lesson Number
Set a colored background.	3.4.2	7
Add a watermark.	3.4.3	7
Set page borders.	3.4.4	7
Create and modify headers and footers.	3.5	
Insert page numbers.	3.5.1	7
Format page numbers.	3.5.2	7
Insert the current date and time.	3.5.3	7
Insert a built-in header or footer.	3.5.4	7
Add content to a header or footer.	3.5.5	7
Delete a header or footer.	3.5.6	7
Change margins.	3.5.7	7
Apply a different first page attribute.	3.5.8	7
Including Illustrations and Graphics in a Document	4	
Insert and format pictures in a document.	4.1	
Add captions.	4.1.1	8
Apply artistic effects.	4.1.2	8
Apply picture styles.	4.1.3	8
Compress pictures.	4.1.4	8
Modify a shape.	4.1.5	8
Adjust position and size.	4.1.6	8
Insert screenshots.	4.1.7	8
Insert and format shapes, WordArt, and SmartArt.	4.2	8
Add text to a shape.	4.2.1	8
Modify text on a shape.	4.2.2	8
Add captions.	4.2.3	8
Set shape styles.	4.2.4	8
Adjust position and size of shapes.	4.2.5	8
Insert and format clip art.	4.3	
Organize clip art.	4.3.1	8
Add captions.	4.3.2	8
Apply artistic effects.	4.3.3	8
Compress clip art pictures.	4.3.4	8
Adjust position and size of clip art.	4.3.5	8

Matrix Skill	Objective Number	Lesson Number
Apply and manipulate text boxes.	4.4	
Format text boxes.	4.4.1	8
Save a selection to the text box gallery.	4.4.2	8
Apply text box styles.	4.4.3	8
Change text direction.	4.4.4	8
Apply shadow effects.	4.4.5	8
Apply 3-D effects.	4.4.6	8
Proofreading Documents	5	
Validate content by using spelling and grammar checking options.	5.1	
Set grammar.	5.1.1	9
Set style options.	5.1.2	9
Configure AutoCorrect settings.	5.2	
Add or remove exceptions.	5.2.1	9
Turn AutoCorrect on and off.	5.2.2	9
Insert and modify comments in a document.	5.3	
Insert a comment.	5.3.1	9
Edit a comment.	5.3.2	9
Delete a comment.	5.3.3	9
View comments.	5.3.4	9
Applying References and Hyperlinks	6	
Apply a hyperlink.	6.1	
Apply a hyperlink to text or graphic.	6.1.1	10
Use a hyperlink as a bookmark.	6.1.2	10
Link a hyperlink to an email address.	6.1.3	10
Create endnotes and footnotes in a document.	6.2	
Demonstrate difference between endnotes and footnotes.	6.2.1	10
Manage footnote and endnote locations.	6.2.2	10
Configure footnote and endnote format.	6.2.3	10
Presentation.	6.2.4	10
Change footnote and endnote numbering.	6.2.5	10

Matrix Skill	Objective Number	Lesson Number
Create a table of contents in a document.	6.3	
Use default formats.	6.3.1	10
Set levels.	6.3.2	10
Set alignment.	6.3.3	10
Set tab leaders.	6.3.4	10
Modify styles.	6.3.5	10
Update a table of contents.	6.3.6	10
Performing Mail Merge Operations	7	
Set up mail merge.	7.1	
Perform a mail merge using the Mail Merge Wizard.	7.1.1	11
Perform a mail merge manually.	7.1.2	11
Use Auto Check for errors.	7.1.3	11
Execute mail merge.	7.2	
Preview and print a mail merge operation.	7.2.1	11

Component	Requirement
Computer and processor	500 MHz or faster processor
Memory	256 MB RAM; 512 MB recommended for graphics features, Outlook Instant Search, and certain advanced functionality.[1,2]
Hard disk	3.0 GB available disk space.
Display	1024 $\times$ 3576 or higher resolution monitor.
Operating system	Windows XP (must have SP3) (32-bit), Windows 7, Windows Vista with Service Pack (SP) 1, Windows Server 2003 R2 with MSXML 6.0 (32-bit Office only), Windows Server 2008, or later 32- or 64-bit OS.
Graphics	Graphics hardware acceleration requires a DirectX 9.0c graphics card with 64 MB or more video memory.
Additional requirements	Certain Microsoft® OneNote® features require Windows® Desktop Search 3.0, Windows Media® Player 9.0, Microsoft® ActiveSync® 4.1, microphone, audio output device, video recording device, TWAIN-compatible digital camera, or scanner; sharing notebooks requires users to be on the same network.
	Certain advanced functionality requires connectivity to Microsoft Exchange Server 2003, Microsoft SharePoint Server 2010, and/or Microsoft SharePoint Foundation 2010.
	Certain features require Windows Search 4.0.
	Send to OneNote Print Driver and Integration with Business Connectivity Services require Microsoft .NET Framework 3.5 and/or Windows XPS features.
	Internet Explorer (IE) 6 or later, 32-bit browser only. IE7 or later required to receive broadcast presentations. Internet functionality requires an Internet connection.
	Multi-Touch features require Windows 7 and a touch-enabled device.
	Certain inking features require Windows XP Tablet PC Edition or later.
	Speech recognition functionality requires a close-talk microphone and audio output device.
	Internet Fax not available on Windows Vista Starter, Windows Vista Home Basic, or Windows Vista Home Premium.
	Information Rights Management features require access to a Windows 2003 Server with SP1 or later running Windows Rights Management Services.
	Certain online functionality requires a Windows Live™ ID.
Other	Product functionality and graphics may vary based on your system configuration. Some features may require additional or advanced hardware or server connectivity; **www.office.com/products**.

[1] 512 MB RAM recommended for accessing Outlook data files larger than 1 GB.

[2] GHz processor or faster and 1 GB RAM or more recommended for OneNote Audio Search. Close-talking microphone required. Audio Search is not available in all languages.

Word 2010 Glossary

A

alignment   A setting that refers to how text is positioned between the margins.

ascending   An arrangement of text from the beginning to the end, such as from A to Z, 1 to 10, and January to December.

AutoComplete   A command that automatically completes the text of the current date, day of the week, and month.

AutoCorrect   A feature that replaces commonly misspelled words with the correct spelling or replaces symbols and abbreviations with specific text strings.

B

Backstage view   A tool that offers quick access to commands for performing many file management tasks all displayed in a single navigation pane that can be customized to meet users' needs.

badges   Small square labels.

balloons   Shaded blocks of text used for comments appearing on the right side of the document.

block style   A format style that aligns text along the left margin.

blog   An online interactive location maintained by companies, instructors, and individuals who post information, events, news, and more, where anyone can leave comments.

bookmark   A location or a selection of text that you name and identify for future reference.

building blocks   Built-in reusable content such as text, graphics, and objects that can be easily managed and inserted in a document for a quick format.

C

caption   A few descriptive words providing readers with information regarding a figure, table, or equation.

cells   The rectangles that are formed when rows and columns intersect.

character   Any single letter, number, symbol, or punctuation mark.

character styles   A style that is applied to individual characters or words that users have selected.

chevrons   In a mail merge, the symbols (<< and >>) that surround the field name in the merged document.

clip art   A collection of media files available to insert in Microsoft Office documents that can include illustrations, photographs, video, or audio content.

Clip Organizer   A tool supplied within Microsoft Office that collects and stores clip art, photos animations, videos, and other types of media to use in your documents.

columns   Vertical blocks of text in which text flows from the bottom of one column to the top of the next.

command   An instruction users give Word by clicking a button or entering information into a command box.

compress   Reduces the size of an object.

Connection Status menu   A menu that lets users determine whether the Help screen displays content available at Office Online, or only those help topics currently installed on the computer.

content controls   Individual programs within Word that allow you to add information in a document, such as a header or footer.

copy   A command in Word that places a duplicate copy of selected text in the Clipboard.

crop   The process of trimming the horizontal or vertical edges of a picture to get rid of unwanted areas.

cut   A command in Word that removes selected text from the original location and places the deleted text in the Clipboard collection.

D

database   A collection of information that is organized so that you can retrieve information quickly.

data source   A file that contains information to be merged in the main document during a mail merge.

descending   An arrangement of text from the end to the beginning, such as from Z to A, 10 to 1, and December to January.

dialog box   A box that displays additional options or information you can use to execute a command.

dialog box launcher   A small arrow in the lower-right corner of the group.

document theme   A set of predefined formatting options that includes theme colors, fonts, and effects.

drawing canvas   A frame-like boundary that keeps multiple drawing objects together.

drop cap   A large initial letter that drops down two or more lines at the beginning of a paragraph to indicate that a new block of information is beginning and to give interest to newsletters or magazine articles.

E

embedded object   A picture or other object inserted into a document that becomes part of the document. Compare to *linked object*.

endnote   A citation in a document placed at the end of the document in which the citation is located.

F

field names   In a mail merge, the description for the specific data, such as a person's first name, last name, address, city, state, and zip code, to be merged from the data source.

fields   A placeholder where Word inserts content in a document. Word automatically uses fields when specific commands are activated, such as those for inserting dates, page numbers, and a table of contents.

first-line indent   A setting that inserts a one-half inch of blank space between the left margin and the first line of the paragraph; one-half inch is the default setting for this indent.

floating object   An image or other object positioned precisely on the page, allowing the text to wrap around it in one of several available formats. Compare to *inline object*.

font   A set of characters that have the same design.

footer   Text that appears on the bottom of a page.

footnote   A citation in a document placed at the bottom of the page in the document on which the citation is located.

G

Go To   A command in the scroll box that enables users to browse by field, endnote, footnote, comment, section, page, edits, headings, graphics, or tables.

gridlines   A tool that provides a grid of vertical and horizontal lines that help you align graphics and other objects in a document.

groups   Collections of related Word commands.

H

hanging indent   A setting that begins the first full line of text in a paragraph at the left margin; all the remaining lines in the paragraph are indented one-half inch from the left margin.

header   Text that appears on the top of a page.

header row   The first row of the table that is formatted differently and should be repeated for tables that continue beyond one page.

horizontal alignment   A setting that refers to how text is positioned between the left and right margins.

hyperlink   A block of text or a graphic that when mouse-clicked takes the user to a new location to an internal or external page.

hyphenation   A dash that is used to join words and separate syllables of a single word; by default hyphenation is turned off in Word so that words appear on a single line.

I

I-beam   The large "I" created when users place the cursor near the insertion point.

indent   A blank space inserted between text and the left or right margin.

inline   Another way of displaying comments, instead of using balloons on the right, is to display them within the paragraphs of text itself.

inline object   An image or other object that moves along with the text that surrounds it. Compare to *floating object*.

insertion point   The blinking point at the upper-left side of the document where you will begin creating your text.

K

key tips   A tool that replaces some keyboard shortcuts from earlier versions of Microsoft.

L

landscape orientation   A format commonly used for brochures, graphics, tables, and so on that orients text across the longer dimension of the page.

leaders   A tool identified with symbols such as dotted, dashed, or solid lines that fill the space before tabs.

line spacing   The amount of space between lines of text in a paragraph.

linked object   A picture or other object inserted into a document by creating a connection between the document and picture file but not combining them in the same file. Compare to *embedded object*.

M

main document   In a mail merge, the document that contains the text and graphics that are the same for each version of the merged document.

margins   The blank borders that occupy the top, bottom, and sides of a document.

markup   A markup is a version of a document with comments and revision marks displayed for easy viewing.

master document   The main document from a Word file; it is organized into smaller sections.

menu   A list of options.

merge cells   To combine two or more cells into one.

Mini toolbar   A small toolbar with popular commands that appears when you point to selected text.

mixed punctuation   A style that requires a colon after the salutation and a comma after the closing.

monospace   A font in which all of its characters take up the same amount of horizontal space.

multi-selection   A Word feature that enables users to select multiple items of the text that are not adjacent.

N

Navigation Pane   A tool that appears in the left side of the window when you select its command in the Show command group.

negative indent   A setting that extends paragraph text into the left margin.

non-breaking spaces   A tool used to keep selected text on a single line.

non-printing characters   Symbols for certain formatting commands that can help users create and edit documents.

O

open punctuation   A style that requires no punctuation after the salutation or the closing.

orphan   The first line of a paragraph that appears alone at the bottom of a page.

P

page break   The location in a document where one page ends and a new page begins.

paragraph styles   A style in which the formats are applied instantly to all text in the paragraph where the insertion point is located, whether or not text is selected.

paste   A command that pastes text from the Clipboard to a new location in the original document or new document.

point size   A measurement that refers to the height of characters with one point equaling approximately $1/12$ of an inch.

portrait orientation   A format commonly used for business documents in which text extends across the shorter length of the document.

Preview   A tool that enables users to visually check your document for errors before printing.

print   To send a document to a printer.

proportional space   A font in which the horizontal spacing varies.

pull quote   A sentence or other text displayed within a box on the page for emphasis and for ease of movement; often used along with drop caps in newsletters, advertisements, and magazines.

Q

Quick Access Toolbar   A toolbar that contains commands that users use most often, such as Save, Undo, and Redo.

Quick Tables   Built-in preformatted tables.

R

redo   A command that repeats a user's last action.

replace   A command that enables users to replace one word or phrase with another.

resetting   Discards all formatting changes you made to a picture, including changes to contrast, color, brightness, and style.

Ribbon   A tool that is divided into eight tabs that contain groups.

rulers   Measuring tools to align text, graphics, and other elements used within a document.

S

sans serif   A font that does not have the small line extensions on its characters.

Save   A button in the Quick Access Toolbar that saves an existing document.

Save As   A dialog box that will save a document in a specific format.

scale   The process of increasing or decreasing an original picture's height and width by the same percentage.

Screen Clippings   An image capture of only a part of your computer screen that you have selected.

screenshot   An image capture of the entire current display on your computer screen.

ScreenTip   A tool that provides more information about commands.

scroll bar   A tool that allows the user to move up or down within the document.

scroll box   A tool that allows users to move horizontally and vertically through a document more quickly than the scroll buttons, or to see a ScreenTip displaying a user's position in the document.

scroll buttons   A tool that allows users to move up or down one line at a time, or more quickly if users click and hold the button.

section break   A tool used to create layout or formatting changes in a portion of a document.

serif   A font that has small lines at the beginning and end of characters and that is usually used with large amounts of text.

settings   An option that enables users to set document properties.

shapes   Figures such as lines, rectangles, block arrows, equation shapes, flowcharts, stars and banners, and callouts that you can add to your document or drawing campus.

shortcut menu   A menu that contains a list of useful commands.

SkyDrive   An online file storage service provided by Microsoft where you can store up to 25GB of documents and pictures for free.

SmartArt graphics   Graphical illustrations available within Word from a list of various categories, including List diagrams, Process diagrams, Cycle diagrams, Hierarchy diagrams, Relationship diagrams, Matrix diagrams, and Pyramid diagrams

sort   To arrange data alphabetically, numerically, or chronologically.

split cells   To divide one cell into two or more cells.

subdocument   The sections within the master document that have been separated into smaller sections.

T

tab leader   The symbols that appear in a table of contents between a topic and the corresponding page number.

table of contents   An ordered list of the topics in a document, along with the page numbers on which they are found. Usually located at the beginning of a long document.

tables   An arrangement of data made up of horizontal rows and vertical columns.

tabs   Eight areas of activity on the Ribbon that contain groups or collections of related Word commands.

template   A master document with predefined page layout, fonts, margins, and styles that is used to create new documents that will share the same basic formatting.

text box   An invisible, formatted box in which you can insert and position text and/or graphic objects.

Text Effects   A new font command group that adds a distinctive appearance, such as outlines, shadows, glows, or reflections, to selected text.

thumbnails   Tiny images of your document pages.

U

undo   A command that allows users to cancel or undo their last command or action.

V

vertical alignment   A setting that refers to how text is positioned between the top and bottom margins of the page.

W

watermarks   Built-in text that display lightly behind the document's main text conveying the sensitivity of the document, such as, *confidential*, *draft*, or *urgent*.

wildcards   Characters that find words or phrases that contain specific letters, or combinations of letters.

widow   The last line of a paragraph that appears at the top of a page.

WordArt   A feature within Microsoft Word that creates decorative effects with a string of text.

Word Wrap   A tool that automatically wraps text to the next line as it reaches the right margin.

Credits

Troubleshooting icon © Matthias Haas/iStockphoto
Another Way icon © Anatolii Tsekhmister/iStockphoto
Internet Ready Icon © Orlando Rosu/iStockphoto
Beach photo © Steven Allan/iStockphoto
Palm trees and stop light photo © jim kruger/iStockphoto
House photo © Linda Johnsonbaugh/iStockphoto
Lesson 1 © Rouzes/iStockphoto
Lesson 2 © Adriana Spurio/iStockphoto
Lesson 3 © kzenon/iStockphoto
Lesson 4 © Don Bayley/iStockphoto
Lesson 5 © Steve Debenport/iStockphoto
Lesson 6 © Rubén Hidalgo/iStockphoto
Lesson 7 MOURIER NINA /Getty Images, Inc.
Lesson 8 © Robert Rushton/iStockphoto; © Alessandro de Leo/iStockphoto
Lesson 9 © Stephen Strathdee/iStockphoto
Lesson 10 © Chris Schmidt/iStockphoto
Lesson 11 © ivanastar/iStockphoto
Lesson 12 © George Doyle /Getty Images, Inc.
Lesson 13 © Thinkstock Images /Getty Images, Inc.
Lesson 14 © Diane Diederich/iStockphoto

Index

Windows 7, 4
Window views, changing, 39–41
Word 2010
  advanced options, 357–359
  closing, 25
  customizing, 354–361
  display options, changing, 355–356
  Help system, 11–13
  opening screen, 2
  personalizing, 354–355
  research options, changing, 362–363
  save options, setting, 356–357
  shortcut keys, 9, 44, 64, 65

  starting, 3–4
  tools, onscreen, 4–9
WordArt. *See also* Clip art; Images; Pictures; Shapes; SmartArt graphics
  definition of, 202
  inserting, 207–209
Word Options dialog box, 353
Word Wrap, 14

Z

Zoom, using, 37–38
Zoom slider, 37, 38